D1465684

C334444459

INSIDE TRUMP'S WHITE HOUSE

THE AUTHORIZED STORY

INSIDE
TRUMP'S
WHITE HOUSE

DOUG WEAD

Biteback Publishing

First published in Great Britain in 2019 by
Biteback Publishing Ltd
Westminster Tower
3 Albert Embankment
London SE1 7SP
Copyright © Doug Wead 2019

ISBN 978-1-78590-556-8

10 9 8 7 6 5 4 3 2 1

A CIP catalogue record for this book is available from the British Library.

Printed and bound in Great Britain by
CPI Group (UK) Ltd, Croydon CR0 4YY

To Amelia and Elisa

CONTENTS

INTRODUCTION

TRUMP TRIUMPHANT

"How can you recover from some of these books?
They are filled with false stories."
—President Trump to the author, in an Oval Office meeting[1]

It was December 23, 2018. Many on the White House staff had scattered for Christmas vacation. The mansion was almost empty, at least compared with most nights. Outside, spotlights illuminated the building and the grounds. Inside, many of the sparkling Christmas decorations had gone dark. Only security and some service personnel remained on the job, and some of them were shifting their schedules to be home with their families as soon as possible.

President Donald Trump was spotted moving among the Christmas trees on the State Floor of the White House mansion. He was alone. In the shadows, hovering nearby, were staff, some using high-density penlights to guide their footsteps, trying to remain invisible. As he passed, the president smiled and bantered good-naturedly, asking about their families. Then he stepped into the Blue Room, where the mansion's most important Christmas tree was dark, and from the blackness he looked outside at the glittering night. Just to the left, floodlights illuminated the Washington Monument, which towered above the city.[2]

Straight ahead, outside, was the massively lit national Christmas tree, and beyond that one could barely see the glowing marble dome of the Jefferson Memorial.

Donald Trump was now at the halfway mark of his first term as president of the United States, but that night he was one lone man, standing in the darkened Blue Room of the White House, with the images of distant marble monuments to other great men reflecting off the windows.

DEFYING THE GRAVITY

It had been a spectacular ascent. In 2016 Trump had defied the unanimous opinion of political experts by winning the Republican nomination for president. Months later he had defied the experts again by winning the presidency. On the very morning of the election, the *New York Times* had given him only a 9 percent chance of winning.[3] He had been opposed by Hollywood, academia, Wall Street, and the national media. Every living president, Republican and Democratic, had voted against him. Two hundred and forty newspapers had endorsed his opponent, Hillary Clinton. Nineteen had supported him.[4] Billionaires had voted against him twenty to one.[5] But he had won in an electoral landslide.

As a candidate he had promised to be "the greatest jobs president God ever created." But the world's economists universally scorned him and derided his economic predictions. They were denounced as mathematical impossibilities.[6]

Just before the election, the *Washington Post* declared that if he won he would "destroy the world economy."[7]

The day after his election, Paul Krugman of the *New York Times* predicted "a global recession, with no end in sight."[8]

Larry Summers, a former secretary of treasury and top economic adviser to both Clinton and Obama, dismissed Trump's budget as "ludicrous." Summers, who had also once been the president of Harvard University, said it would work if you believed in "tooth fairies."[9]

"No, pigs do not fly," said Robert Brusca, senior economist at FAO Economics. "Donald Trump is dreaming."[10]

But by the end of the year Donald Trump's dreams had become America's reality. His economy had effortlessly defied gravity. By the second quarter of 2018 the gross domestic product had topped 4.1 percent.[11] Wages were up. Unemployment was down.

CNN had promised "A Trump win would sink stocks."[12] Instead, the New York Stock Exchange broke record highs ninety-six times in his first two years in office. They were even now saying that a recession was imminent and the spectacular growth of the previous two years was finally at an end. But they would be wrong yet again. The boom would continue well into 2019. A market correction would come, of course, at some point, but while the world's economic growth was stagnant, Trump's America was still vibrant. By the end of Donald Trump's first year as president he had dramatically delivered on the two biggest issues of the 2016 presidential election campaign, creating jobs and destroying the terrorist caliphate of the Islamic State of Iraq and Syria (ISIS).[13]

By the end of his second year in office the growing list of accomplishments had been vastly expanded. It was chronicled by Paul Bedard in a *Washington Examiner* article entitled, "Trump's List: 289 Accomplishments in Just 20 months, 'Relentless' Promise-Keeping."[14]

The critics had not anticipated Donald Trump's upset election as president. They had not believed in his promises of an early economic recovery. They were in denial about the fall of ISIS, which had lost its 35,000 square miles of territory. Now they were saying that it had not been completely eliminated and therefore the war had not been won. It was like saying that the allies had not really won World War II because there were still Nazis in the world.

Even before he had run for president, still as a businessman, Donald Trump had favored a quote from the German philosopher Arthur Schopenhauer. In 2014 Trump had tweeted, "Talent hits a target no one else can hit. Genius hits a target no one else can see."[15]

Both Barack Obama and Hillary Clinton had mocked Trump on the campaign trail. "Where's he gonna get these jobs?" Obama asked. "Does he have a magic wand?"[16] Clinton had ridiculed his "secret" plan to destroy ISIS. "The secret is that he has no plan."[17]

What economic and foreign policy experts could not see, what Obama and Clinton could not see, what the media could not see, Donald Trump had seen clearly and openly proclaimed. Like Schopenhauer's genius, Donald Trump had found a different way to make the government work, and the results were undeniable.

When Donald Trump was first elected president, Robert F. Kennedy Jr. declared that the colorful businessman had a chance to be a great president because he "thought outside the box."[18] It was Trump's iconoclastic, sometimes outrageous, methods that allowed him to jump-start an economic recovery. In the process, the forgotten American middle class was able to once again find its footing and renew its dreams. And it was Trump's ability to think outside the box that had finally brought the elusive ISIS to heel.

Ironically, the more hysterical and desperate the attacks on President Trump and his family, the more outrageous the move toward impeachment, the more deeply the Trumps would be etched into the marble of history. Future writers would not be moved by fabricated stories dubbing him a Russian spy. Or by the national publication that promoted false and vulgar stories about the first lady. Or by popular late-night comedians who asked their television audiences to promote pornographic images about the Trump family.[19]

In time, the gleeful, obscene, personal attacks on the Trump family, egged on by corporate media executives and promoted by their chosen public figures, would make most reasonable observers recoil. History would be built with facts, not by the crude emotion that was used to drive television ratings. Yet that very passion, intended to diminish Donald Trump, ultimately strip him of power, and reverse the will of the people who had elected him president, only ensured that his hours and days in the White House would be more memorable.

The accusations added to the drama and helped ensure that the real achievements would not be forgotten. Eventually, the stories that were false would be ground to powder by history. Meanwhile, their very whispered existence would be an irresistible lure for writers, artists, and playwrights. They would add to the fascination and mystery of this rich and powerful family.

WRITING AN OFFICIAL HISTORY

In January 2019, I would begin writing the authorized history of the Trump presidency. It would be the beginning of months of discussion with the president, his family, and senior members of his administration. At the time, I fully expected that this would be an unprecedented and fascinating journey into the most colorful presidency in American history. But nothing quite prepared me for what was to come.

It would turn out that the third year, the year that I would be working, would unfold as one of the most eventful years in our nation's history. The presidency itself, and our democracy, would be put to the test. And I would be there, on the inside, capturing it all. My job would be to take the readers with me on this journey, inside the White House and inside the Trump family, and let them see and hear what I was witnessing. This was a chance to capture these important events of history from a different angle, from inside the eye of the storm, looking back out at the ferocious winds swirling around them.

It is quite conceivable that in a hundred years, when all of us are gone and most of our grandchildren are gone, they will still be writing books and creating theatrical productions about the Trumps. Whether they will be portrayed cruelly as the Borgias and Medicis, or celebrated grandly as the Rockefellers and Kennedys, will depend on what is written now and on the primary sources that tell their stories. My intention was to write something accurate and something fair.

As the weeks passed, I devoured many of the insightful and controversial books that had already been written. Most depended on secondhand testimony, which usually was anonymous. In a court of law it would be considered hearsay. Even those few books that included first-person encounters with Trump himself were often flatly contradicted by the president and the other actors involved. Over and over again I would hear the following refrain from the named sources and witnesses of such stories: "That never happened."

The president was clearly frustrated by the process. "Somebody gets a ride on *Air Force One*," he told me, "and they write a book about it. A reporter was calling this week to ask about my 'close aide' who had left the White House to write a book. They said, 'You know? Your close aide?' When they told me the name I honestly didn't know who they were talking about. If he was my close aide you would think I would have remembered his name."

In contrast, there was a sense of relief from the president, his staff, and his family that someone was going to take on the tedious work of reconstructing the record accurately, brick by brick. They were ready for someone to capture the words that they themselves were willing to say, on the record, and not later deny.

"I'm so glad you are doing this," the president's son Eric Trump said, interrupting his own narrative in the middle of one of our interviews. "There are so many books out there that have it wrong."[20]

"I have two thousand stories," the president's daughter Ivanka Trump told me.[21]

"I will take them all," I answered.

"Want to hear the real story of how dad picked Mike Pence?" Eric Trump teased during one of our conversations. "There's a book out there, but the facts are all wrong."

"I'm ready!" I laughed.

Day by day, White House staffers sent me names and phone numbers of people to contact. Many times they were names that I had never heard before. "You've got to talk to Dan Scavino; he has been with the president every day. And you've got to talk to Keith Schiller, his security guard and friend of many years."[22]

Ivanka was especially concerned about people who had done so much work and gotten so little credit. Early on she arranged a call for me with Brad Parscale, one of the key players in Trump's upset victory in 2016, and now head of the Trump's 2020 campaign.

THE ENIGMATIC ROLE OF JARED KUSHNER

During the first days of my research, Jared Kushner, Ivanka's husband and the president's brilliant son-in-law, was an unseen presence behind many of the stories I was pursuing. Most of the big things that happened in Trump's first two years had his fingerprints all over them.

At first they were impossible projects that Jared himself was pursuing quietly at the president's behest. Early in the administration some staffers were irritated, fearing that Kushner was stepping into their hotly contested territory, but no one formally objected. Why should they? Jared's projects weren't going anywhere. To complain would only give Kushner more credibility.

With time, when those impossible projects bore unexpected fruit, Jared Kushner's White House reputation grew to legendary proportions. He became the president's fireman, called on to save projects that were burning out of control. My own young team of researchers began to see him in almost heroic terms, often concluding, "This sounds like something Jared Kushner has done."

Eventually it became clear that the secret to both Jared and Ivanka Kushner was the president himself. He was the power at work behind his son-in-law and his daughter, not the other way around. This was Donald Trump at work, bypassing his own bureaucracy and short-circuiting the lines of authority to get his business done on his own hurried timetable.

For several months, there was a very real question of whether or not my access would extend to Kushner. He was a prominent behind-the-scenes figure in all the other books, and yet none of them had tapped him as a source. All the stories were told second or thirdhand. Would he ever be available for me?

Eventually, cautiously, that door was finally opened, and as I expected, it revealed a rich vein of insider treasure. At first, Jared Kushner wouldn't let me record our interviews, forcing me to rely on scribbled notes. But his stories were the biggest of all, told from a couch in his Georgetown home, with a crackling log in the fireplace nearby, or told from his office squeezed between the Oval Office and the chief of staff's suite in the rarified south hallway of the West Wing. Every story was worth patiently waiting out. My young team was impressed. "You are now actually interviewing Spiderman?"

As it turned out, Jared's biggest fan was his eight-year-old daughter, Arabella. She apparently followed the news on her own computer and had developed her own metrics for measuring results. When he came home late from the White House one night, after seeing a criminal justice reform bill signed into law, Arabella greeted him at the door and then ostentatiously spoke to her computer, "Siri, how many innocent persons has Jared Kushner helped get out of prison?"

The artificial intelligence hadn't yet caught up with the facts and couldn't give her an answer, so Arabella announced it herself. "Until yesterday, my daddy had spent his whole life and had only helped two persons get out of prison. Today, he helped ten thousand go free. Hmmm. Not a bad day, daddy."[23]

Bill Shine, the White House deputy chief of staff, and Sarah Huckabee Sanders, the White House press secretary, were at the heart of everything I did. There was no way I would have been able to write this book without their leadership. Getting the right facts was crucial, and Bill and Sarah were key to that work. When Bill left, it was Sarah alone. And when Sarah finally left, it was Stephanie Grisham, the new White House communications director and press secretary, and her excellent team.

Finally, during the last frantic months of finishing this book, it was the authority of the White House chief of staff, Mick Mulvaney, who made everyone accessible and everything possible.

The great irony for me was that the real stories, told the way they really happened, with the right persons in the room, saying the things that everyone else remembered, were usually far more interesting than the pop creations of booksellers and public relations promoters. The stories that were unknown, that had never been told, were often spellbinding.

AN IMPACTFUL PRESIDENT

When I finally sat down with President Donald Trump himself and turned on my voice recorder, he would become the sixth American president I have interviewed. And as the months progressed, he would become the fifth American president that I would get to know. It would be my humble privilege to serve as an adviser to two of them, to co-author a book with another, and to be one of the few living authors to have written about all of the forty-four presidents.

Donald J. Trump may be the most impactful president in modern American history.

That was my conclusion after reviewing his first two years in office.

Other presidents, such as Gerald Ford, Jimmy Carter, and Ronald Reagan, desperately sought energy independence. Donald Trump found it.

Some presidents saw young, nonviolent drug offenders as threats to society and changed laws to put them behind bars. Donald Trump got them jobs.

In 1964, President Lyndon Baines Johnson had declared "all-out war on poverty and unemployment in these United States."[24] Johnson gave the poor subsidized housing, food stamps, and welfare based on the number of children in a family. Under Donald Trump, unemployment would fall to the lowest levels ever recorded in American history, and 6 million Americans would be able to get off food stamps.

Other presidents, both Democratic and Republican, stood by as crony capitalism corrupted the nation. It was seemingly the poor and senior citizens on fixed incomes who financed the process. Retirement funds suffered. But in the first two years of Donald Trump's administration, free enterprise erupted. Many senior citizens saw a greater return in retirement accounts in Donald Trump's first two years than the sixteen years of the two previous presidents, Bush and Obama.[25]

The middle class, who had seen the value of their homes wiped out by the years of Bush and Obama, now saw that value coming back.[26]

Other presidents avoided tax reform. Even Ronald Reagan took five years to get it done. Donald Trump did it his first year in office.

Other presidents stumbled over Supreme Court nominations. Liberals had come to expect their own judges from Democratic presidents and an occasional liberal judge, as a gift, from a Republican president. The liberal social and cultural agenda, abetted by the national media, saw itself ahead of the voters in attitude and thus dependent on the judiciary to do what the voters would not.

Donald J. Trump was different. Elected with the help of conservatives, libertarians, and labor Democrats, he kept his promise and nominated a conservative, Neil Gorsuch, as his first Supreme Court justice and Brett Kavanaugh, another conservative, when he had a second chance. The American Left was outraged. Protestors, some paid by the leftist billionaire George Soros, shouted obscenities in the halls of Congress and interrupted Senate Hearings.[27] The process became fierce and contentious. There was every expectation that Trump would back down and withdraw the nomination as past Republican presidents might have done.

Trump never wavered. Brett Kavanaugh was duly confirmed. At the end of his first year in office, Donald Trump would appoint four times as many federal appeals judges as Barack Obama and more than any other president in American history.[28]

"MAYBE I'LL BE KNOWN AS A FOREIGN POLICY PRESIDENT"[29]

No matter where our conversations began, Donald Trump would soon find himself sliding into a discussion of some critical foreign policy issue. He hated the waste of American lives and money in unnecessary nation building. Once he caught himself doing this in a discussion of history and suddenly said, thinking aloud, "Maybe I'll be known as a foreign policy president."

On August 20, 2012, President Barack Obama drew a red line in the sand and dared his enemies to cross it.[30] The Syrian dictator Bashar al-Assad was told that he could not use sarin gas on his own people without consequences. When the Syrian dictator did exactly that only a few months later, killing and paralyzing hundreds of children, Obama fell silent.

When newly elected President Donald J. Trump was confronted with the same enemy, violating that same, exact, red line, he rained down fifty-nine missiles on Syria.[31]

The world was on notice.

Many presidential candidates, including George H. W. Bush, Bill Clinton, George W. Bush, and Barack Obama, promised to recognize Jerusalem as the capital of Israel. Their promises vaporized when they won office. Donald Trump got it done.

When Trump warned that America's bad trade deals were crippling our economy and costing American jobs, he faced immediate outrage and opposition. Media personalities and spokespeople for academic think tanks warned that by breaking the North American Free Trade Agreement (NAFTA), he had forever ruined our relationship with Canada and Mexico, our closest neighbors and most critical trading partners. Once broken, the critics warned, the relationship could never be put back together again.

Trump ignored the hysteria and sent his son-in-law, Jared Kushner, to craft a new and better trade deal. It was like rebreaking and resetting a broken bone that had healed incorrectly. It was a painful process to experience and see, but it had to be done. And it is not likely that any other president in modern history would have had the nerve to do it. Mexico's foreign minister declared it a better deal for all three countries.[32]

Likewise, when Trump asked NATO members to honor their commitments and pay their small, token share of providing for their own defense, he was accused of destroying one of our oldest alliances and putting the free world at risk.

"Imagine," he told me in one of our interviews, his voice taking on an incredulous tone, "we spend billions of dollars on missiles and just give them to these rich countries? We just give them away. And to some of the richest countries in the world."

With Trump as president, NATO nations that were the most flagrant abusers of their own agreement started coming into line. Trump's action raised more than $40 billion for the United States—money that would have never come in without him. NATO nations added $100 billion toward their own defense. According to NATO's secretary general, Jena Stoltenberg, the alliance was now stronger than ever.[33]

Past presidents had kept America's negotiations for the release of hostages a secret process. It was embarrassing for America to appear so weak in the face of international terrorists or belligerent nations. In some cases, even our own allies, such as Turkey, were holding Americans hostage. Just during the months that I had access to the Trump administration, Donald Trump brought home twenty-one American hostages from countries all over the world.[34] For the most part, the national media ignored these stories. I was able to interview some of the rescued hostages for this book.

Arguably, eleven American presidents had failed to make peace with North Korea or stop its ongoing, imposing development of nuclear weapons. Donald Trump met with North Korean dictator Kim Jong-un in Singapore on June 12, 2018, and signed an agreement to denuclearize the Korean peninsula. And for the first time since the end of the Korean War in 1953, remains of American soldiers were finally brought home to the United States.

Before Donald Trump, four American presidents, presiding over twenty-eight years of history, had witnessed and abetted what was, arguably, one of the largest transfers of wealth in world history. It had been the wealth of Americans, primarily from the middle class, transferred year by year, dollar by dollar, to what some were saying would soon surpass the United States as the greatest economic power on earth, the People's Republic of China.

By 2017, Donald Trump's first full year in the White House, the United States was importing $505 billion of Chinese goods a year.[35] By one estimate, China had stolen $600 billion worth of American intellectual property. The massive flow of money out of the United States had been ongoing for years. The American presidents George H. W. Bush, Bill Clinton, George W. Bush, and Barack Obama, backed by a powerful, greedy corporate lobby, had presided over this staggering transfer of wealth and intellectual theft. Diplomats and politicians, some with good intentions perhaps, but others with deep financial obligations to corporate interests, had forced America into a deadly embrace with the Chinese.

Ironically, it would take a New York businessman, thinking outside the box, unencumbered by his own deals with China, to see the danger and to develop the painful strategies to begin the slow walk back from what many saw as an ongoing economic trap.

NO TIME FOR MAR-A-LAGO

On December 23, 2018, Donald Trump was one lone man, standing in the darkness in the Blue Room of the White House, with the glow of distant marble monuments reflecting off the glass windows. More challenges and more bitter attacks were coming his way. He had lived a long and eventful life, creating an immortal brand name and reaching the pinnacle of world power. Yet, ironically, he knew that the greatest challenges of his life were coming in the days just ahead of him. That Christmas the findings of the special counsel Robert Mueller, who was investigating the president, hung over his White House like a dark cloud.

Just after noon on Christmas Eve, Donald Trump had tweeted, teasingly, "I am home alone (Poor me) in the White House waiting for the Democrats to come back and make a deal on desperately needed Border Security."[36]

The president had been looking forward to the balmy breezes and moonlit nights of his Florida estate. The plan was to take his family to the midnight Christmas Eve services at the Episcopal church of Bethesda-by-the-Sea. It was becoming a new Trump family tradition. He and Melania were married in that church. After the presidential election, in 2016, when the president-elect and the new first lady had gone there for Christmas services, they had received a standing ovation. They had come back the next year, this time with their son Barron.

So Florida and Mar-a-Lago represented a much-needed time for family and friends, an escape from the cruel political winter of Washington, DC—but then, Trump was a fighter. If there was a chance for "his wall" and thus delivering on one more campaign promise, he would take it.

Jared Kushner, the president's son-in-law, had left for Mar-a-Lago the Saturday before Christmas and would come back the next Wednesday. Before leaving the city, he had told the president, "I can stay with you." He didn't like the idea of Donald Trump spending the holidays without family. "You don't have to be alone."[37]

"No, no, you go to Florida with your family," the president had insisted, then added wistfully, "You know, I own Mar-a-Lago. I have all these other houses I own. I can stay in them anytime I want. This one is a rental. So I'll just stay here and enjoy it."

Jared smiled when he related the story. "He knew perfectly well that the White House didn't belong to him, that it belonged to the country and that his stay would be brief."

Eric Trump, the president's third child, remembers checking in with his father that December as well. Eric often spent Christmas at the home of his wife, Lara, in North Carolina. This year they too had opted for Mar-a-Lago. Lara, who competed in triathlons, loved the sun and could get in her training, swimming, biking, and running. This was a chance, in the middle of winter, to walk the dogs on the beach. She knew how much her father-in-law loved Florida. "I thought, how sad that he wasn't going to be there."

Eric and Lara had an earnest discussion about it. "I think we should go to DC to be with my dad," Eric said.[38]

"Let's call him," Lara suggested. "If he wants us to come, let's go. My parents will understand."

But when they called the president, he would have none of it. "No, no, you kids have fun. Don't worry about me. I will be here working for the country." He was playfully teasing them, acting the martyr.

MELANIA COMES BACK FOR CHRISTMAS

The next afternoon, on Christmas Eve, December 24, 2018, First Lady Melania Trump flew back to Washington, DC, to be with her husband. She and the president took calls to Santa Claus. It was becoming a new presidential tradition. Back in 1955, a child had called the North American Aerospace Defense Command (NORAD) to ask to speak to Santa. Now NORAD took calls every year and the first lady, at least, loved it. The media was allowed in to record a few moments and picked up a comical exchange between the president and a seven-year-old boy named Coleman.

"Are you still a believer in Santa?" the president asked. "Because at seven, it's marginal, right?" They talked and the president listened for a while and then laughed, "Well, you just enjoy yourself."[39]

Melania had clearly been able to shake her husband out of his lethargy. Near midnight, they attended the Eve of the Nativity of our Lord Jesus Christ Festival Holy Eucharist at the National Cathedral.[40] They were escorted to the front row.

The president and the first lady appeared happy to be with each other and to enjoy the familiar Christmas Eve service. The massive organ shook the cathedral, and the young voices of the choir echoed into the highest rafters of the church, the boy sopranos reaching the impossible octave above the others. "Hark the Herald Angels Sing."

Some of the recent mysterious movements by the president and first lady and some of their coy conversations with family over the holiday had been for security reasons. They were planning a secret trip to Iraq together to visit the troops. It would be his first presidential visit into a combat zone and one of the few times ever for an American first lady. The Secret Service had not wanted it at all, but she had insisted. She would not let him go alone. They would fly out together on Christmas night.[41]

When the congregation at the National Cathedral turned softly to "Silent Night," there was a hush and the president gripped Melania's hand. It would be the last silent night for the Trump family for many months to come.

★ 1 ★

NO NUCLEAR WAR
ON MY WATCH

*"These are the personal letters exchanged between me
and Kim Jong-un. You can't keep them, but I'm going to
let you read them. These are amazing. This is history."*
—PRESIDENT DONALD TRUMP[1]

There was a stark contrast between the atmosphere in the White
House and the dark political storm that was blowing outside.

It was January 24, 2019. The nation was in turmoil. The
government was experiencing the longest shutdown in American history. Only the day before, Nancy Pelosi, the Democratic Speaker of the
House of Representatives, had canceled the president's State of the Union
address to the nation, refusing to allow the president to use the House
chamber. No one had seen such bitter partisanship since the days of
the Civil War. The national media, still stung by its failure to have their
anointed candidate elected president, was seriously promoting the idea
that the current president of the United States was a Russian spy. It would
soon be proved, they insisted, by the special counsel Robert Mueller.

As president of the United States, Donald Trump had seemingly
accomplished the impossible. While being pounded daily by a hostile,
contrarian media, he had helped rebuild the American economy, quietly

brought home twenty-one hostages, all but abandoned by past administrations, and delivered on his promise to be "the greatest jobs president God ever created." During the campaign, in the face of universal scorn, Trump had promised an economic rate of growth at 3 percent. The last quarter it had already broken 4.5 percent. Unemployment was at record lows in almost all categories.[2]

During the 2016 election campaign, Trump had promised to crush the terrorist group ISIS. They had built a 35,000-square-mile caliphate across a large swath of the Middle East. Now they were all but vanquished, holding on to their last few square miles of territory.

That very morning, during a television appearance, I had been shown a clip of President Lyndon Johnson's famous State of the Union address of 1965. He had declared a war "on poverty and unemployment."

It was stunning. For sixty years, everything that Republican and Democratic presidents had ever wanted for the poor, the disenfranchised, African Americans, Hispanics, and women was now happening under the leadership of a businessman with no prior political experience. "LBJ gave them food stamps and welfare," I pointed out in my television interview. "Donald Trump is giving them jobs."[3]

GETTING THE ASSIGNMENT

The president was in a good mood. His expansive personality filled the Oval Office and had everyone else in the room smiling and laughing. They were all waiting for what he would say next. Bill Shine, the deputy chief of staff, was there, along with Sarah Huckabee Sanders, the White House press secretary. All three were smiling broadly at me when I walked in. This meeting had been delayed far too long

I had been in the Oval Office many times over the years. I had met other presidents in this room. But this would be more than a sit-down interview. This time, I was being given the nod to write an official history of a presidency. And significantly, just that morning, I had been given permission to record my interviews. Considering all the investigations and controversies surrounding this president and how badly he had been burned by outside writers, this was a practice that was becoming less common for this White House.

I had the impression that my project represented some sort of internal staff breakthrough. Bill and Sarah were both beaming with pride. And while I was, apparently, the direct beneficiary of this project, I got the impression that this team and the many assistants who had been helping me, emailing me, and setting up interviews had won something too. Whatever victory it might have been would have involved the arcane and unfathomable world of White House politics, and was, therefore, beyond my own understanding. Still, I was humbled and grateful. If the door to the Oval Office was open, I would step inside.

"Did you see my tweet?" the president asked. He had commented on my television appearance.

"Thank you, Mr. President." I laughed. "Yes, I saw that." It is pretty hard to miss a Trump tweet when you are the target. He has millions of Twitter followers. Every person I knew and many I didn't had been texting me all morning.

The president waved a small handful of papers above his head, as if he were teasing a child with candy. "So, we've agreed to show you everything."

He waved the papers. "Nobody's seen this. My people don't want me to give these to you. But I want you to read them. If you are going to do this book, you need to read this.

"These are private. These are the personal letters exchanged between me and Kim Jong-un. You can't keep them, but I'm going to let you read them. These are amazing. This is history. I want to know what you think."

Donald Trump had obviously signed on to the idea of this book, because without any prompting from me, or without a single question, he was now waving these letters—the crown jewels—before me.

"Right there, right over there," he said, pointing to the two chairs in front of the fireplace, "is where Barack Obama told me that my greatest problem, when I became president, was the possibility of war with North Korea. In fact, privately, he said, 'You will have a war with North Korea on your watch.'"

The president dramatically lowered his voice, continuing his story, "And I said to Obama, 'Well, Mr. President, have you called him?'

"And Obama said, 'No, he's a dictator.'" As if that, in itself, explained everything.

Then the president paused, letting those words sink in. "No, he hadn't called him because he's a dictator?"

Now, two years later, Donald Trump was still amazed by that conversation. And then he concluded, out loud, to all of us in the room: "Stupid."

I was riveted.

"So, they don't want me to let you see these letters, but I think you should," he said. "I think you should. This is my personal correspondence with Kim Jong-un. I want you to read it."

I didn't know who he meant by "they," the people who had told him not to show me the documents, but I assumed it wasn't Bill or Sarah, the only others in the room. It was more likely NSA advisers, or State Department folks or intelligence experts. And they would all have good reasons to tell him not to let a writer see them. But that, of course, meant that my project was known to them, as well, and that it had been discussed.

"You can't photograph these or copy them in anyway," the president said. I imagined he was passing on protocols to which he had agreed.

And then he added, "Nobody will ever know how close we came to war."

This was the president outlining his own history book. He was starting with North Korea, which even during the campaign he had realized was the single greatest strategic problem facing the United States. He wanted me to see that. His predecessor, President Obama, had agreed and had come to the same conclusion. Indeed, so had most of the nation's top policy thinkers.

Beyond the great economic numbers he had achieved, beyond the defeat of ISIS, the single most important thing that had happened, in the president's mind, had been that a nuclear threat had been averted and tensions with North Korea had been reduced. Later on, when we had lunch together, the president drove home this point. It wasn't just the nuclear weapons themselves; many nations now had nuclear weapons. Russia was obviously far more powerful than North Korea. The danger came from the likelihood that such weapons would be used by one nation more than another. Or that they would be passed into the hands of others who would use them.

Of course, most writers and pundits and journalists understood that. They also understood how horrific a nuclear war would be. And yet, in the president's mind, they didn't fully understand. It took more than a two-hour seminar or ten good books to get it to sink in. You had to live with it, day by day, with modern, relevant models of what would actually happen. You had to understand it, step by step, nation by nation, city by city. It took days to fully comprehend. It would be clear in our conversations that Donald Trump had been living with it. North Korea was a problem that had been put off far too long by too many presidents, and that neglect had allowed a crisis to reach a very dangerous temperature.

THE VICE PRESIDENT'S EMERGENCY INTERRUPTION

The Oval Office has two main doors. If you sit at the president's desk, the Resolute desk, a priceless gift from Queen Victoria to President Rutherford B. Hayes in 1880, you face the fireplace on the east wall. The portrait of Washington is just above it, and flanking both sides are the two chairs that Trump had just pointed out. To the left of the fireplace is the main door, the traditional entrance to the Oval Office. To the right of the fireplace is a door that leads to the president's secretaries and personal assistants.

Most heads of state and officials come through the main door. There is a Secret Service agent sitting just outside. If you leave the Oval Office through this door you enter a hallway with a thick, deep carpet. The hallway splits to the left and the right. To the left it passes doors opening into the Roosevelt Room, where the senior staff meets and where many of the group meetings with the president take place. It passes Jared Kushner's office, finally ending at the chief of staff's corner of the West Wing.

If you leave the Oval Office through the main door, and head out to the right instead, the hallway passes the Cabinet Room and eventually leads into the maze of White House press offices and the James S. Brady Press Briefing Room.

Meanwhile, to the right of the fireplace in the Oval Office is the second door. The door that leads to the president's secretaries' offices, and a niche for the president's personal assistant. This is the young man who carries the nuclear codes (in a briefcase known as "the football") and who keeps the president functioning day to day. This office has a direct door into the Cabinet Room and backs out into the same hallway that fronts the main door.

Most guests enter the Oval Office through this secretaries' office. That's how I'd come in only minutes earlier. The secretaries and the president's personal assistant had stood and smiled and greeted me kindly. They would have seen me on the official schedule for lunch with the president that day. When I had served on senior staff at the White House and was the action officer for an Oval Office event, I knew everything about that person down to his shoelaces. And I usually knew all of it weeks before the visit. My staff and I would see the name on the calendar and watch it grow closer. We would even create the dialogue, what the visitor was likely to say and how the president should respond. I shuddered to think about what they had learned about me.

It was though this door, the secretaries' door, that suddenly, unexpectedly, the vice president of the United States, Mike Pence, came bounding into the Oval Office, interrupting our meeting.

The president was on the other side of the room, talking to us about Kim Jong-un and North Korea, his booming voice and colorful personality dominating the room. Now we were suddenly distracted by a softer, younger, female voice, struggling bravely to find the volume to be heard from her doorway across the Oval Office. It was like two competing televisions in the same room. But her announcement was too faint and the vice president was moving so fast that he was already in the middle of the room before she could finish announcing him.

"Excuse me, Mr. President." Mike Pence was huffing and puffing. "This can't wait. I've got to speak with you, sir," he said urgently. "And I'm sorry, sir, but I'm afraid that I need to speak to you alone."

I was ready to leave, but the president, hardly flinching, only joked good-naturedly, saying something to the effect that well, after all, he was just showing Doug Wead his secret communications with Kim Jong-un so, whatever it was, it couldn't be any more secret than that. "Well, Doug here is writing a history of this White House," the president said. "He can hear anything."

The vice president laughed, came over and shook my hand, "Hi, Doug, good to see you, sir." He smiled broadly.

"Hi, Mr. Vice President." And then I added softly, "I promise I won't tell, at least until the book is published, which is probably much more than a year away."

There was more laughter.

Pence turned back to the president, face-to-face, speaking quietly, affording a bit more privacy, "Well, sir, the senators just want you to know that they are behind you."

That explained the interruption. And it explained why the vice president was huffing and puffing. He had just come from Capitol Hill, where he presides over the Senate, and he wanted the president to know that the Republican senators would support him if he wanted to give his State of the Union speech at another location, such as the Senate chamber. They would be there, wherever it might be, and they would lend dignity to this event that was mandated by the US Constitution. The State of the Union speech was scheduled for the following Tuesday,

January 29, 2019, so the country was waiting for news. Would it still happen? And, if so, where?

The president turned to me, the outsider, to offer a little explanation, "You see, Doug, to do this right we need for the Senate to be unanimous, and the Democrats aren't going help us with that, it just ain't gonna happen."

Then he turned back to Pence, "No, no, tell them thanks so much."

"They support you, sir."

"I know that."

"And they want you to know that they are behind you, sir."

"Yes, and I want you to thank them," the president said. "But I've already decided, we will do it later. So, we are going to postpone it. I've just decided."

And that was that. The vice president would take the news back to the Senate, and it would be announced to the public that very day.

Two days later, on January 26, 2019, the Republicans and Democrats would agree on a spending bill, and the longest government shutdown in American history would come to an end. Meanwhile, President Donald Trump would deliver his State of the Union address, in the House chamber, on February 5, 2019. And as Speaker of the House, Nancy Pelosi would give her famous, sarcastic applause.

LUNCH WITH THE PRESIDENT

There are other doors in the Oval Office that I didn't mention. To the president's right as he sits at his desk is a whole wall of French doors that open out onto a small portico. The manicured grass stretches out to the South Lawn. To the immediate right, just outside those French doors, is a little trail that leads to the president's private garden. It is a secluded spot where he can take a Diet Coke and read newspapers and memos when the weather is nice. And then there is a branch off that trail that leads, almost unseen, down to the White House swimming pool. The tennis courts, surrounded by towering trees, are deeper into the South Lawn and hidden from view until you are upon them.

The secretaries' offices also have a wall of French doors, along the east side of their room. These doors open out onto a portico that overlooks the Rose Garden.

Finally, there is one more door that I haven't mentioned.

As the president sits at the Resolute desk, to his extreme left, curving along the wall that stretches behind him, in the closest place you can find that might qualify as a corner in an oval room, is one more door. It is this door that leads to an inner sanctum of privacy. This door opens into the narrow "Monica Lewinsky hallway." Of course, that is not what the White House Historical Association calls it, but it is a name that, nonetheless, comes to mind for most visitors. It was in this narrow hallway that President Bill Clinton and his twenty-two-year-old intern Monica Lewinsky were able to achieve some degree of private, sexual intimacy. It was in this hallway that Kathleen Willey, a White House volunteer and longtime Clinton fundraiser, says she had been pinned against the wall and sexually abused.

To the right of this narrow hallway is the presidential toilet. To the left is the "real office" of the president, where he works. It is how he keeps the Oval Office so tidy. It is how he keeps the Resolute desk so empty. That famous desk, by the way, was built from the English oak timbers of the HMS *Resolute*, and it has served FDR, JFK, Ronald Reagan, Barack Obama, and many other presidents.

Straight ahead, down to the end of this short hallway, is the private presidential dining room. At this small table President Ronald Reagan had a weekly lunch with his vice president, George H. W. Bush. And this is where President Donald Trump invited me to begin interviewing him for this book.

"Where do you want me to sit, Mr. President?"

He took a seat at the head of the table. There was a white, starched tablecloth, heavy silverware, and White House bone china.

"Sit right here." He motioned to the seat to his right. Bill Shine and Sarah Sanders took seats on the other side of the table.

The president had a Diet Coke. Some joked that, for a man who didn't drink alcohol or smoke cigarettes, it was his only sin. I took a water. And then they served us a salad. In fact, it was just a lettuce salad, its pieces cut to bite size. There were no tomatoes, or olives, or onions, but the dressing reminded me of the tasty house dressing at Carrabba's Italian Grill.

We all waited for the president to take the first bite. And when he did we began eating our lunch.

"We were talking about Kim Jong-un, Mr. President."

"So Kim and I started off very rough," the president said, picking up where he had left the story. "Because this country was ready to go to war with North Korea. Under President Obama, I really believe we would have had a war had he stayed longer. And I also think that thirty to one hundred million people could have been killed. When I saw predictions by experts on television that said one hundred thousand people, two hundred thousand people would die." He shook his head at the absurdity.

"That's almost the population of a small town or a village in Korea. Imagine that? Some experts on television were saying that a nuclear war would wipe out the equivalent of a village. At first, this was what some television networks were telling their audiences.

"Well, as you know, Seoul, the capital city, is right by the so-called border. And that is a tough border by the way. An impenetrable border. And Seoul has a population of thirty million people. Kim has ten thousand guns, artillery, they call them cannons. He doesn't even need a nuclear weapon to create one of the greatest calamities in history.

"But a nuclear war? I see these people on television talking about it so casually. They have no idea. They give it a few days' thought and talk like experts. Or they say that some other country has more nuclear weapons than North Korea and is therefore more dangerous. But it doesn't take a hundred nuclear missiles to really hurt a country, even destroy a country. One nuclear device can do that. Which city in America would you be willing to give up? As far as I'm concerned? Not one. Not one.

"So when I came into office the rhetoric with Kim became extremely tough, extremely tough. And if it weren't so tough, we would have gotten something going immediately. Because this was the biggest problem I faced."

THE WORD THAT KIM HATES

The president was interrupted by a phone call. "Excuse me just a second." He took the call from a phone that was on a small table behind him. As you look toward that table, just beyond are two windows behind it, opening up on the president's private garden.

I used the moment to finish my salad and study the letters from Kim Jong-un. Somehow they had finally been passed over to me, although, even now, thinking back on this experience, I can't remember exactly when that had happened. I suspect it was while we were still in the Oval Office, which meant that I had actually carried them into the president's private dining room. In any case, I was conscious that I now had this stack of papers. The letters on top were in the Korean language and were on the official, embossed stationary of the Democratic People's Republic of Korea, with fancy ink signatures at the bottom. There were English translations right underneath, probably prepared by our own intelligence services.

While the president took his phone call I had a moment to look and quickly read some of them. It was clear that the two men had grown close and were quite friendly, that there was something almost paternal about Trump's relationship with Kim.

When the president finished his call, I moved the stack of letters farther away from my plate. I didn't want to get any food stains on these precious papers. In my own personal collection I have letters from presidents Millard Fillmore, Rutherford B. Hayes, and William Howard Taft, and notebooks full of many others. A spot could cost a collector $10,000. And I suspected that in a hundred years these letters might end up under glass in some collector's display.

The White House waiters took our salad dishes and replaced them with dinner plates with a filet mignon, french fries, and broccoli. How can I describe the steak? They hadn't asked how I wanted it cooked, but it was so fresh, almost like it had been cooked on a stone and had only just been transferred to the plate. It certainly hadn't been sitting under a heat lamp. This was what you would expect from a White House steak. Having served years before on senior staff, I knew it had been delivered by an elevator from the kitchen downstairs.

"Mr. President," I asked, "why do you think Kim responded to you and not to your predecessors? Is it because you finally tried something more direct, and they wouldn't take that chance?"

"No, that's not it. They tried. If you read the internal history, the signals were sent, an effort was made. Other American presidents tried. Maybe not enough, maybe not the right way, but North Korea wouldn't even talk to them. They didn't even respond."

"Was it a celebrity thing?" I asked. That brought up a discussion of Kim's fascination with American culture, including its celebrities. There was the basketball star.

"Dennis Rodman," Sarah Sanders said.

"Maybe Kim wanted to meet you as a celebrity president?"

"I don't know about that," Trump said. "I don't know about that. You can read those letters and see what you think. But I can tell you the exact moment when everything changed.

"Our language started to get really violent, the toughest. Violent. Nobody had even seen anything like this. But something had to be done. And what Americans missed was how he was threatening the whole region."

The president was talking about the wider implications of the North Korean nuclear threat, which was something that the myopic American news media had not fully covered. Anything beyond our own shores often went unreported. In the United States we had watched the progression of the North Korean missile program as steps to reaching the American mainland. "Now he can reach Guam." "Now Hawaii." "Now

San Francisco." But the fact was that Kim Jong-un's threats had not been directed solely at the United States. Early in the summer of 2017, Kim announced that his nuclear missiles could now reach Brisbane, Australia. In America, the news did not even merit a mention, as we were preoccupied by fires in California, but it was on the front pages in Australia. Likewise, Kim's bullying of Japan, whose defense was totally reliant on the United States, was ominous and dominated the daily national discussion in that country.

Kim's threats had become so angry that Trump had finally responded in kind. During a briefing on the opioid epidemic, held at his clubhouse at his Bedminster, New Jersey, country club, Trump invited in reporters and gave them an earful. "North Korea best not make any more threats to the United States," he said. "They will be met with fire and fury like the world has never seen."[4]

That summer, using back channels, the Trump administration succeeded in gaining the release of Otto Warmbier, a University of Virginia student who had been arrested during a tour of North Korea. He had allegedly tried to take home a propaganda poster as a souvenir. A North Korean court sentenced him to fifteen years of hard labor.[5] But Warmbier's return to the United States was bittersweet. The young man was in a coma and died within a week.

In September 2017, President Donald Trump announced he would be meeting the parents of Megumi Yokota on an upcoming visit to Japan.[6] Megumi was a teenager who had been snatched from her Japanese homeland and taken to North Korean forty years before. She was heading home after school badminton practice when North Korean agents had landed by boat, abducted her, and taken her away. Her parents learned the details of the abduction only long after, in 1997, when a former North Korean spy defected to the South and told the story. The North Koreans claimed that the teenager had committed suicide, but when they sent her remains back to Japan in 2004, DNA analysis showed it was another body.

Against advice, Trump outed the whole story in a public speech before the United Nations. "We know it kidnapped a sweet thirteen-year-old Japanese girl from a beach in her own country to enslave her as a language tutor for North Korea's spies."[7] By some estimates, North Korea was holding up to one hundred hostages from around the world. The Kim government was humiliated by Trump's speech. But the family of the girl and the Japanese government thanked the president for speaking up.

While past American presidents kept stories of hostages quiet, saying that more could be done if the offending nations were not publicly embarrassed, Trump's style was the opposite, and it soon bore fruit.[8]

We were reviewing some of this history when President Trump suddenly looked up from his lunch, with a mischievous smile on his face. "Kim especially doesn't like it when I talk about hostages. He hates that word. 'Hostages.'"

"Really?"

"Yes. He said to me, 'Please, do not say that. Please do not use that word.'"

Trump had found a nerve.

"You want to know why?"

"Why?" I asked.

"Because it makes him look bad. And because Obama paid the Iranians $1.8 billion dollars for hostages. I paid nothing. And I got ours back from Kim for nothing.

"But I will tell you all about that. It's not over. There is still a long way to go, but I will tell you how it all turned around, the turning point. This will be good for the book."

★ 2 ★

LUNCH WITH PRESIDENT TRUMP

"He better watch his ass!"

—President Donald Trump, talking to the author about Kim Jong Un

I t all turned around that week at the United Nations," President Trump said. "That's when it happened. I told everybody, 'The Little Rocket Man is going to cause the total annihilation of his country.'"

On November 30, 2017, President Trump tweeted the message publicly: "The Chinese Envoy, who just returned from North Korea, seems to have had no impact on Little Rocket Man. Hard to believe his people, and the military, put up with living in such horrible conditions. Russia and China condemned the launch."[1]

At the time, President Trump's critics, which consisted primarily of the American media, were on all sides of the issue. They complained when the Trump White House sent out feelers to talk to North Korea. He was consorting with an evil dictator, they said. Or he was giving away too much by his apparent willingness to talk. But they were hysterical when Trump began talking tough to Kim Jong-un. "He's going to start a war." And yet, at the same time, everyone agreed that it was the status quo that had brought America to the brink. Eleven American presidents had failed to make peace with North Korea. Even some of the most unadventurous State Department bureaucrats were wondering if Donald Trump's hyperactive motions might force the issue.

"Understand what I am saying to you, Doug," the president said, "I was saying stuff that you would never say no matter how close you are to the edge. No matter how much dislike there is. You only say this if you are ready to act on it. It was unbelievably close."

The critics were complaining that Trump should watch his language. That he should only talk like that as a last warning, a last effort to shock the enemy into realizing that war was imminent. Otherwise, you may unintentionally provoke the very war you fear. As early as April 2017, *New York Times* columnist Nicholas Kristof had written an op-ed speculating on a possible nuclear war with North Korea.[2] Was President Trump now telling me that the United States had actually been there? Had we, indeed, been on the verge of going to war? He would know, because he would have had to make that decision.

"It was unbelievably close."

Others were actually discerning this at the time, but their voices were often obscured. Uri Friedman, writing for *The Atlantic*, claimed that the Trump confidant Lindsey Graham, the Republican senator from South Carolina, "was telling me there was a 70 percent chance of the president launching an all-out war against the Kim regime if North Korea tested another nuclear device."[3]

Trump's tough talk to Kim was not a bluff. That was what he was making clear to me during our lunch interview. He was not going to let America be hit by a nuclear missile on his watch. And yet the national media was furious with him, blaming him for the growing escalation. Calling for a more reasonable approach.

When it came to Communist dictators, history tends to favor Trump's hard line. When John F. Kennedy met with Nikita Khrushchev in Vienna in 1961 he had tried to extend an olive branch, and the Soviet dictator had seen it only as a sign of weakness.[4] Khrushchev ordered nuclear missiles to Cuba, and it brought the world to the brink of a nuclear war.

At the Yalta Conference in 1945, the American president Franklin Roosevelt had tried to be generous to the Soviet dictator Joseph Stalin. The two men carved up post–World War II Europe, as Churchill looked on. It resulted in sending tens of thousands of Eastern Europeans to their deaths in the Gulags.[5] Historians note that Roosevelt had been sick and weakly. He would be dead within two months of the Yalta Conference.

By contrast, critics had been upset by Ronald Reagan's tough, American cowboy approach. He had called the Soviet Union "the evil empire." They said he was only provoking them. They were afraid. But most historians now accept that Reagan's strength helped bring an end to the Cold War and saved the world from nuclear annihilation in his day.

Although a young man, Kim Jong-un had been born into a line of old Communist dictators, in the tradition of Nikita Khrushchev, Pol Pot, and Mao Zedong. He ran concentration camps. He tortured prisoners. A sensational story in a Hong Kong newspaper claimed that he had executed his uncle by feeding him alive to 120 starving dogs.[6] North Korea said he was shot. In February, 2017 Kim Jong-un was believed by many to have orchestrated the murder of Kim Jong Nam, his own half brother and a possible political rival. It had been an audacious, public assassination at the Kuala Lumpur International Airport.[7]

One of the most troubling issues had been the ongoing famines in North Korea. I am a founding board member of Mercy Corps, the relief organization that had taken the lead in distributing food during the 2008 North Korean famine.[8] Our people had been some of the few outsiders allowed into the country. They saw firsthand, on the ground, the devastation. In 2017, even while developing its nuclear arsenal, North Korea was apparently facing famine yet again.[9] The very real concern was that if Kim Jong-un was willing to allow hundreds of thousands of his own people to starve in a famine, why would he have qualms about risking the annihilation of an American city within reach of his missiles? San Francisco, Los Angeles, or Seattle?

Kim Jong-un, who had learned from his father and grandfather, and who came from the old Communist dictator tradition, was apparently a man who respected strength. Communist dictators are predators. And like predators in the wild, they target the weak, not the powerful. Donald Trump's rhetoric, which rattled the American media, apparently had its impact in Pyongyang.

"Kim said, 'I have a button on my desk, a red button,'" Trump said, telling the story, "I mean, you can't misunderstand this. I mean foreign policy people study the tea leaves, but you don't have to study these words very long to know what they mean.

"And I said, 'That's right and I have a much bigger button than you do and my button works.' By the way, he knew what that meant. He knew what that meant. We both knew what North Korea could and couldn't do."

From this exchange, I got the impression that the North Korean missile program had some limitations and the United States knew what they were. Trump wanted Kim to know that we were aware of what was real and what was only bluster.

"And everybody said, 'Oh, it is so vicious.'" Trump began to act the part of his panicked critics. "They were all saying this. And for some reason, when I made that speech at the United Nations. Remember? Where I call him 'Rocket Man'? Where I say, 'He better watch his ass!' Well, after that, everything changed. It got so incredible. And then they wanted to talk! It is really an amazing thing."

If the American media was frightened by Trump's rhetoric, the United Nations got the point. The Security Council voted 15–0 to adopt hard-hitting resolutions against North Korea. Trump was able to bring China and Russia into the effort. Kim was isolated and soon reached out to America to solve the problem.

Incidentally, this whole conversation with President Trump was at times surreal because there was actually a long, narrow, wooden block on the luncheon table, connected to a cable, and there was a big, fat red button in the middle of it. At one point the president actually pushed the button. It did not launch missiles on North Korea, but it did magically produce a steward with another Diet Coke.

TRUMP'S DESCRIPTION OF THE SINGAPORE SUMMIT

On June 12, 2018, American president Donald Trump and North Korean chairman Kim Jong-un met at the Capella hotel on the resort island of Sentosa in Singapore. It was the first time in history that the leaders of these two nations had met.

Trump, ever the television artist and stage manager, was enthusiastic as he described the setting. "We got a great location. In between South Korea, Russia, and China. How good is that? And I can tell you that it was quite a nice piece of real estate."

"What surprised you?"

"Well, first I can tell you that Kim and I had great chemistry. That I can tell you. As you may know, that is important to me. All through my life, whether in business or politics, I know when I have it with someone and I know when I don't. And very often, it's not there. By the way, Doug, I think you and I have good chemistry. That's going to be a good thing for this book."

We all laughed.

"Thanks, Mr. President. But you and Chairman Kim had such harsh words leading up to that moment. So I'm wondering, after all of the hurtful things that you and Chairman Kim said about each other, how could you suddenly have good chemistry? Some of the attacks were very detailed and personal."

"Well, at a certain point," Trump continued, "as we met and talked, you could begin to feel that we both wanted this to work."

"Did that surprise you?'

"Some. It surprised me some. Look, we both wanted it to work. For the sake of our people. For the sake of the world. I went into the meeting with a positive attitude. Sure, I went in there with Otto Warmbier on my mind too, that his life would not be in vain. But a lot depended on us finding answers. War was a real threat. Nuclear war. Who wants that? But yes, I was surprised by the immediate desire to get things resolved."

"What else surprised you?"

"I'll tell you a moment that neither one of us fully expected. How could anyone prepare for this moment? And that was when Kim and I were introduced to the international media.

"Now, I have some experience onstage before cameras. I had been to conventions and awards ceremonies. Melania and I first went to the Academy Awards back in 2001.[10] There were a lot of cameras. But this? This was something I did not fully expect. And I am sure, Chairman Kim, living in North Korea, did not expect it either. When we walked out onstage and shook hands and then turned to face the international press, each photographer there had to get their photo for their organization, from countries all over the world, well it was amazing."

"The noise?"

The president nodded. "The noise."

He was referring to the repetitive sound of digital single-lens reflex (DSLR) technology.[11] It turns a camera from a picture-taking sniper rifle into a machine gun, capturing hundreds of pictures that can be viewed and edited later. While the president is known for his enthusiastic hyperbole, on this occasion he was probably exactly right. This was the first time when this technology had intersected with a historic world summit. It was a unique moment. Instead of hearing a flutter of shutters that can sound like a flock of birds stirring, Trump and Kim heard a sound more like the roar of a thousand helicopters lifting off.

"That moment was unexpected. I can tell you. Though we both kept a straight face. And I can tell you that it took us both by surprise. There were thousands and thousands of cameras. And the flashes. Nobody had ever seen anything like it.

"It was a great summit. It was a tremendously successful summit. Again, think of this: No more missiles. No more launches. No nuclear. We are now talking about economic development. And I think that is what he really wants."

The president was hopeful at this luncheon back in January 2019. The next summit would bring him back down to earth.

MELANIA TRUMP WAS WATCHING CNN

"Melania called me and said that she was watching CNN," the president said. "And they were stunned by what had happened. The idea of a summit had just been announced. They were talking about what a breakthrough this was. How previous administration had tried to set up a meeting and failed.

"'They are saying this is a great achievement,' Melania said, 'They cannot believe it because, you know, it is the hermit kingdom.'"

It had been a long time since the first lady had seen such objective reporting about her husband, such straight news.

"The media didn't know how to react," the president continued. "They hadn't got their marching orders yet so they were just frozen and had to act like real journalists for a change, reporting on a story. And so for twenty-four hours I got the best press since I had been elected president. Everyone. The haters. They were all saying, 'This is the most incredible thing that we have seen.'"

For more than a year, right up to the moment of the announcement of a Trump-Kim summit, pundits had been daily attacking the president, suggesting that the United States was locked into a one-way pneumatic tube toward war.

The former CIA director James Clapper had declared on CNN that Trump's words were to blame. "They can easily construe what he has been saying as a declaration, or at least a threat, of war."[12]

Mike Mullen, who had served as the chairman of the Joint Chiefs of Staff under George W. Bush and Barack Obama, had appeared on the

ABC show *This Week* with George Stephanopoulos to say that "we are actually closer, in my view, to a nuclear war with North Korea, and in that region, than we've ever been, and I just don't see the opportunities to solve this diplomatically at this particular point."[13]

As a guest pundit on MSNBC, Dan Rather had joined the queue. "We're probably closer to an outright war with North Korea," said Rather, "than we have been in a very, very long time."[14]

Joe Scarborough of MSNBC had said, "You have reason to be scared of a war that can wipe out five hundred thousand people."[15]

His sidekick, Mika Brzezinski, had attributed the worst intentions of all to the president, "No," she said, "I just think he wants to use nukes."[16]

After a year of such expert commentary, the news that North Korea was actually ready to meet and to talk with Donald Trump came to the monolithic, single-minded American national media like a head-on collision.

"In fact, in some cases, they didn't believe it," President Trump said. "They would accept any bogus, false story that they thought would hurt me or the people who supported me, but here was real news, a real story, and they were just stunned. 'Could this be true?' Then when it was being reported around the world and the people from North Korea were issuing statements, our own media followed after them, saying, 'Well, I guess it's true. I guess it's true. It's on German television, it's on French television, so now we can tell the American people.'

"You can go back and look," the president chuckled. "For twenty-four hours, held in time on the internet, you will find positive press for one day about Donald Trump and the coming summit with Kim Jong-un. You would have thought that I was the greatest genius of all time. At least for one day. And then the media got their bearings and the bosses called in and said to the anchors, 'What are you doing?' And so the whole message shifted the next day to 'What is the big deal?'

"And it went downhill from there. They actually started telling the American people that we had lost by having the summit; that the very act of meeting was a net loss because we had given up too much. Have you heard that one?"

"Yes," I agreed. "I had heard it."

"And in fact, nothing we did was irreversible. Canceling the war games saved us millions of dollars and we can start them up anytime we want.

"So what had we given up, what? We put vicious sanctions on them. The sanctions are still on, and they involve nations that had never joined in before. Now that they see we are talking with North Korea, that we are getting somewhere, the other nations are more committed than ever to keep it going. These are tough sanctions. North Korea is paying a price for what it is doing. We got the hostages free. We got the remains back of our soldiers from the Korean War. We had to wait for many presidents to get that."

"Eleven," I said.

The president was easily making his case. "Look at what has happened since: There are no nuclear tests. No missiles firing over Japan, No bellicose statements about attacking the United States. No more hostage taking."

"No Nobel Peace Prize," I shot back.

The president laughed.

THE NOBEL PEACE PRIZE

After the Singapore summit there were many who argued that in a fair world, Donald Trump should have won the Nobel Peace Prize. James S. Robbins, a USA Today columnist and a senior fellow in national security affairs at the American Foreign Policy Council, called the summit "a critical element in shifting the ground toward peace, something that was unprecedented in U.S./North Korean relations." Robbins wrote that "what President Trump achieved—and which few thought was even possible—more than merits the Nobel Peace Prize."[17]

Trump's supporters were arguing that he had achieved in months what had eluded other American presidents for more than a quarter of a century. President Barack Obama had pursued a policy of "strategic patience" with North Korea. It hadn't worked. Foreign policy experts were openly ridiculing the policy as "strategic passivity."[18]

Dan Rather, who had only weeks before insisted that we were headed to war, now argued in a headline that Trump should not get the Nobel Peace Prize. "Hold Trump's Nobel Prize, for Now: Kim Jong-un Won Big.[19]

Trump was amused by the rapid change in language. "So the big criticism was that I had 'met.' That was what they said was wrong. 'He met.' In other words I lost because I met Kim Jong Un. 'I met.' What does that mean? 'I met.' That was the best thing they could come up with? That's all they could think of?

"And what is funny," President Trump said—although he was not laughing—"is that finally, afterward, the media found a way to make the whole summit disappear, like it never happened. So there will be no nuclear war, after all. So what? That doesn't count as news. That is not important."

The president was making a good point that was frustrating to media critics and to a previous generation of journalists. Monday we avert a nuclear war, but Tuesday the news shifts to a rainstorm in Denver, Colorado.

"I have never been given so little credit for something that was actually so important," the president said. It's interesting. As I read those words now on the page, they sound harsh, or pouty, but if you could hear them on the voice recorder, you could tell that there was not the slightest trace of bitterness in his voice. Rather, he seemed genuinely fascinated.

"We would be in a war right now. It would probably be a nuclear war, to be honest with you. Right now. And if a normal guy had been president, it would have happened. Nothing would have stopped it. It would have been a rough one.

"You know, they've got several million soldiers, by the way? North Korea? That is a lot of bullets even if you look at it that way.

"And my administration gets no credit for it. But we get no credit for anything. You know the economy, you said it this morning, the economy is really good and the world is collapsing. The economy is really good, great numbers came out today on Wall Street. They do not even talk about it. They never talk about it."

I had appeared on *Fox and Friends* that morning and had talked about the good unemployment numbers. One report claimed that the media devoted 0.7 percent of its coverage to the booming Trump economy.[20]

"Doug, they don't talk about it, because they are such good stories."

"Well, Mr. President"—I laughed—"you won the election and it wasn't expected. And the economy is flourishing in spite of the prediction of the world's greatest economists. ISIS is on the run; you've got to give your enemies a win somewhere."

"But the big one, Doug, was North Korea. Remember, it's not how many nukes you have that make you dangerous. One nuke is dangerous. Now we have a great relationship. If you were to come here two years ago and you had asked, 'So what is your biggest problem?' I would have said North Korea.

"When I said to Obama, 'What is your biggest problem?' No hesitation! 'North Korea. I think you will go to war with North Korea.'

"So I said to Obama, 'What is that all about? Tell me why?' And then I realized it was really tough, really tough. My first few months. The level of anger at us was terrible."

"Do you mean from Kim?"

"Yes. Do not forget we have forty thousand soldiers in South Korea all year around. Do you know how much we spend defending South Korea? Four and half billion dollars a year. Figure that one out?"

"It's a lot of money."

"So now you understand."

"Yes. I understand."

"If Obama would have been able to pull off that summit he would have had five Nobel Peace Prizes," Trump concluded.

"That may be true," I ventured. "But he would say that he got one anyway, even without having a summit."

"He got one and said he didn't know *why* he got it." Trump chuckled. "They asked him why he got it and he said he didn't know. And that was the right answer too, by the way, because there was no reason.

"Look, at what happened in Idlib, in Syria?" the president said. "At the time all kinds of terrible motives were tossed at me. But as the world later learned, I got the Russians and Iran to suspend their attacks. What they were going to do could have killed three million people. Nobody writes about it. Everyone knows it. It was very real. Now nobody writes about it. Nobody cares. Three million lives saved."

When that crisis was imminent, the *Washington Post* published a big story about it. They mocked the president. "Can a Tweet Stop Another Bloodbath in Syria? Evidently Not."[21] When it was over, when Trump's private diplomacy had worked and the lives had been saved, the story quietly disappeared. Trump is right: it is almost never mentioned.

HISTORY KEEPS A RECORD

Donald Trump seemed resigned to a monolithic, corporate media opposition. His rank-and-file supporters would say that he was taking on the establishment, both the Democratic and the Republican. "The Swamp" they called Washington, DC. Trump didn't respond to the lobbyists. They had ways of getting money to congressmen and office holders. It was how politicians came to Washington broke and left as multimillionaires. Presidents, if they did what they were supposed to do for lobbyists, came out especially well, with corporate jets available for their use the rest of their lives. The author was, himself, sometimes involved in making those arrangements. Incidentally, the lobbyists often came from the same companies that financed the network news. It was an unbroken, insular cycle.

The presumption was that if Donald Trump played to the monopolies and gave into the big companies, as other presidents usually did, they would finally let up on him. If he made their corporate CEOs ambassadors, in his retirement their companies would give plush jobs to his children and nieces and nephews, or donate to his foundation.

The problem was that Donald Trump already had money. He already had his own jets. And his children had their own companies. So, was his money a curse as well as a blessing? It gave him independence and freedom, but he was using that freedom to take on entrenched powers. At least, that was how the young men and women in the red MAGA hats saw it.

The conversation returned to the Nobel Peace Prize and some Republican senators who were wanting to advance it. Trump would be meeting with Kim again in two months.

"Hey, that's okay," the president said about the snub. "I expect that." And since we were on the subject of unrequited love, he added this thought, "I should have had the Emmy three times for *The Apprentice* too." If we were going to take the trouble of reviving aspirations for the Nobel Peace Prize, why not add an Emmy to the list?

We all laughed.

I was reminded of President Theodore Roosevelt, who had risked his life charging up San Juan Hill in the Spanish-American War. So I told the president the story. Roosevelt had been recommended for the Congressional Medal of Honor. It was refused. Again and again. Three of his sons would be wounded in battle, trying to make up for it. Trying to win it for their wronged father. One of the sons, Theodore Roosevelt Jr., would finally be awarded the Medal of Honor posthumously, only months after his death, after the landing on D-day in World War II.

And then, 103 years after the Battle of San Juan Hill, President Theodore Roosevelt was finally awarded his Medal of Honor. It would come from President Bill Clinton, on January 16, 2001, four days before Clinton would leave office. Of course, Theodore Roosevelt and his family never lived to see any of it. But at least history kept a record.

"Nobody notices those things," Trump said.

"Well, somebody noticed," I answered. "After all, you were elected president of the United States."

Sarah Huckabee Sanders spoke up: "Sixty-three million people noticed."

"And we are a stronger country today," the president said. "It's all worth it."

DON'T FORGET THE LETTERS

There was no dessert. No two scoops of ice cream. No crème brûlée or miniature hot fudge sundae. It was my misfortune to have had lunch with the president after the first lady's big summit meeting with the White House kitchen personnel. At that meeting she had kindly explained that she wanted her husband to eat a healthier diet.[22]

Throughout the luncheon I had the impression that the president was keenly conscious of the Kim letters. He occasionally glanced at them stacked on the table next to me. No doubt he wanted to maintain discretion and protect his relationship with his partner on the world stage. And then there were protocols about state secrets.

Before we left the room, the president said, "Sarah, Doug hasn't had a chance to read these yet. Can you get him a little room where he can read them?"

And then he reiterated, "Sorry, Doug, you can't take them, and you can't take pictures of them. But I want you to read them. This will be good for the book."

I thanked the president and said goodbye to him and deputy chief of staff, Bill Shine, and followed Sarah Huckabee Sanders out of the Oval Office. We retreated into the labyrinth of back offices in the press secretary's lair. Sarah gave me a little cubicle and left me alone.

The letters were truly history making. Better than any dessert.

I would later have to submit to the White House anything I wanted to write or say about the exchange. Without recounting all of the details here I can offer this impression. Kim is fascinated by Donald Trump. He sees him as a unique figure on the stage of world history. And he wants to make history with him.

In one letter Kim wrote, "I firmly believe that the strong will, sincere efforts and unique approach of myself and your Excellency, Mr. President, aimed at opening up a new future between the DPRK and the US will surely come to fruition."

Included in the remarkable exchanges was the very clear goal of actually, formally, ending the Korean War. The armistice was signed in 1953, and when I had lunch with the president that January, it was still, just that, an armistice. Could these two men finally end that war?

A few days after my interview with the president I was able to visit alone with his son-in-law and close adviser, Jared Kushner. He was surprised when I told him that the president had allowed me to read the letters from Chairman Kim. After I quoted from them, he overcame his initial skepticism and actually seemed pleased to be able to talk to someone about them.

"It's a father thing," Jared observed. "You can see from these letters that Kim wants to be friends with Trump, but his father told him never to give up the weapons. That's his only security. Trump is like a new father figure. So, it is not an easy transition."[23]

THE SAIGON SUMMIT

The second Trump-Kim summit was set for March 2019 in Saigon, Vietnam. After my luncheon with the president I strongly suspected that at some point in the future, Trump and Kim were wanting to shock the world again. But it would not be in Saigon.

Trump's opponents, the American media and their Democratic Party allies, would prove to be every bit as formidable as the Communist dictator. In an extraordinary moment in American history, the national media and the Democratic Party offered the world's television audiences a split screen. In one corner would be the picture of an American president, trying to negotiate with a man who had threated to level American cities with nuclear bombs. On the other screen would be a witness testifying before a congressional hearing called by the

Democrats. Michael Cohen, the president's estranged former lawyer, ironically convicted of lying to Congress, would be telling the world that Trump was "a con man and a cheat." And the American media would make his accusations a coequal story with a summit held by the heads of state of two nations.

For some, the message that the media and their partners in the Democratic Party was sending to Saigon, Vietnam, was deeply troubling. Trump called it almost treasonous.[24] Chairman Kim should not give up, the message seemed to say. America was a divided nation. If Donald Trump wanted to find peace for the world, he would first have to find more of it at home. The American media seemed to be more committed to hurting Donald Trump than protecting their own children and the world from a nuclear war.

President Trump walked away from the Saigon summit rather than play a weak hand. In his book *The Art of the Deal* Donald Trump wrote, "Sometimes your best investments are the ones you don't make."[25]

There is an interesting postscript to this story.

Michael Cohen, the president's attorney turned accuser, was asked when and why he had changed his mind about his old friend Donald Trump. Cohen told Congress that it had happened after the president's words following events in Charlottesville, Virginia, and after the Helsinki summit with Trump and Russian president Vladimir Putin. In fact, after both of those events, Michael Cohen was still very positive about Donald Trump. He had actually presented a proposal to a number of publishers, including mine.[26] Cohen's book would have been called "Trump Revolution: From the Tower to the White House." It would have been an enthusiastic endorsement of his old client, which, many would say, makes Cohen's second testimony to Congress also patently false.

★ 3 ★

IVANKA'S WEST WING OFFICE

"He had the vision to cross over the bridge."
—IVANKA TRUMP[1]

On March 29, 2017, only weeks after the inauguration, the media broke the story that Ivanka Trump would be serving on the White House's senior staff.[2] She would be an unpaid assistant to the president. She would have her own office in the West Wing. Immediately, television pundits and bloggers bombarded the airwaves with wild commentary.[3] Critics of the new administration insisted that such a thing had ever happened before. This was outrageous.

In fact, when Donald Trump named Ivanka Trump to his White House staff, she became the nineteenth son or daughter of a president to serve his or her father. No less than George Washington had written his successor, urging him to appoint his own son to high office. "If my wishes be of any avail they should go to you in a strong hope that you will not withhold merited promotion from Mr. John Adams simply because he is your son."[4] America's second president duly appointed John Quincy Adams as minister to Prussia.

I had studied and written about presidential children for thirty years. I had met or interviewed twenty-four presidential sons and daughters and had written the book *All the Presidents' Children*. It wasn't long before I started getting calls from reporters, but what I said could hardly stem the tide. The journalists had mostly written their stories before they found me. When the *New York Times* called, I made an attempt to tap down the widespread fallacious analysis. Nevertheless, their article read, "While relying on family members for advice is hardly unusual for a president, giving them a formal role has few precedents."[5] Really?

Other journalists insisted that it was breaking precedent because Ivanka was a woman, which seemed an odd criticism for a modern, liberal-minded media to be making. In fact, Susan Ford, the daughter of President Ford, had been on staff, serving as a White House photographer. And Anna Roosevelt was practically running the White House in FDR's last year in office.

"No, it is not unusual," I patiently told the BBC. "This happens over and over throughout American history. Anna Roosevelt, the president's daughter, planned and ran the Yalta Conference. It just hasn't happened as much recently."

"But why?" the BBC wanted to know. "Why would Donald Trump want to appoint his own son or daughter?"

"Because very soon the president will learn that, in the White House, the most important quality in a staffer is loyalty. Nothing else even comes close. And because a son or a daughter will offer continuity for the sake of ongoing policy. The chiefs of staff will come and go, but a daughter will always be a daughter. And she will always have a seat at the dinner table on holidays."

Ivana Marie Trump, or "Ivanka," was born October 30, 1981. It was easy to understand why the president wanted her at his side. Since Ivanka joined him in business as an adult, Donald Trump had counted on her to get things done. They would walk into a room, and even before they were seated at a conference table she would have gotten an agreement. She was a legend within her own family. Her father loved to tell stories about her.

Donald Trump had asked Ivanka to introduce him when he ran for president. He had asked her to introduce him as the nominee at the Republican National Convention. In the White House, she got things done, quietly and efficiently. Obviously, she has known the president longer than anyone else in Washington, DC. She created continuity for him. She was low maintenance, with a positive attitude and a diplomatic ability to sidestep a personality conflict. Working in the corridors of power, she would find that latter quality to be no small thing.

Finally, since the White House and a family brand was at issue, it didn't hurt that Ivanka Trump made all the lists. She was named by *Forbes* as one of the one hundred most powerful women in the world.[6] *Time* had her pegged as one of the top one hundred most influential.[7] *Fortune* listed her, along with Jeff Bezos and Mark Zuckerberg, in their prestigious list of forty under forty.[8] Meanwhile, numerous sources routinely named her as one of the most beautiful women in the world.[9] Ivanka Trump was doing just fine without a White House job.

CREATING HER OWN SPACE
Ivanka Trump's office is on the second floor of the famous West Wing, just above the Oval Office and two stories above the White House mess, which is run by the US Navy and is where the senior staff can take their meals.

Tina Tchen, the director of public engagement under Barack Obama, once operated out of this same office. Tchen, who would serve as chief of staff to First Lady Michelle Obama, would become famous as the so-called fixer in the Jussie Smollett case in Chicago. Karl Zinsmeister, who was assistant to the president for domestic policy for George W. Bush, also once worked in this office. But in the coming years it will be Ivanka's name that will mark this territory. No future staffer will likely complain when they are assigned these quarters; they will simply be told that Ivanka Trump once operated from this corner of the White House, and that will be all the reassurance their troubled ego will need.

Ivanka has windows with views that are blocked by parts of the White House building just outside. One of them overlooks the South Lawn, where the president and first lady take off on *Marine One*, the helicopter that shuttles them to Andrews Air Force Base and beyond. But there is no way to see it from Ivanka's office. When there is a state visit, the prominent guests motorcade up the South Lawn's driveway and are welcomed under the awning that extends out from the Diplomatic Reception Room.

The South Lawn was where, in the mid-nineteenth century, Martha Johnson, the daughter of President Andrew Johnson, let cows graze. Andrew Johnson, the seventeenth president, was fiercely opposed by Congress, which was trying to impeach him. Martha, his daughter, had marched down to Capitol Hill and demanded appropriations. They may not like her father, she told them, but the White House belonged to the people and it was in disrepair; they needed funds to sustain it. To shame the stubborn congressmen, Martha maintained milk cows on the lawn, to provide milk for the first family. Congress was impressed with the presidential daughter, but it didn't help her father, who was impeached anyway.

The decor in Ivanka's office is clean and minimalist. There is an hourglass near her desk, which is a purposeful reminder that her time to do good things is limited. There are books and interesting pictures, including one of Ivanka and Kim Yo-jong, sister to the North Korean dictator. The two women were seen as diplomatic rivals by the international media, but they are all smiles in the photo.[10] On the walls there are copies of signed, bipartisan legislation she has worked on. One visitor noticed "a framed copy of Trump's typed 'Remarks Regarding the Capital of Israel'—signed 'To Ivanka, Love Dad.'" It was written "in the president's oversized Sharpie scribble—and lyrics to Journey's 'Don't Stop Believin.' Handwritten to her by the songwriter."[11]

I was struck by the creative use of such limited space. To the left, back behind a wall was Ivanka's working desk. No casual observer could see the papers on it. She herself could work with privacy and simulta-neously look to a big-screen TV, which was mounted in the opposite corner above a long beige chaise lounge that ran the entire length of the east wall. To the right of this was a small conference area, with a table and chairs on all sides (a luxury for most West Wing offices). The table and chairs were not of the White House traditional Kittinger dark mahogany veneer, but were light and modern.

The decor and the limited sunshine from the blocked windows gave Ivanka's office a mood that was quite distinct from other parts of the White House. Many of the other rooms are windowless, interior rooms, lit only by lamps and chandeliers, but even offices with win-dows—Jared's, for example—tend to have the sunlight obscured by heavy drapes. Ivanka's office felt open. When you closed the door you wouldn't know you were in the White House. You might just as well be in a sleek, downtown New York office, or someplace in Silicon Valley.

It was at her conference table, sitting opposite each other, that we began our interview. Members of the White House staff sat at both corners taking notes.

IT'S THE PRESIDENT'S STORY
"Where do you want to start?" she asked.[12]

"Well, there are no rules," I explained. "Some histories begin with the inauguration. Others are biographies that begin with the birth of the president or even his great-grandparents."

"Well, are you going to revisit some of the campaign?"

I could sense that she had some stories to tell, and if so, that was where I wanted to go. Throughout my interviews with the president and his family, I would constantly order myself to be still and let them tell as much of the story as they were willing to give. I was not going to force them into my outline. The treasure would most likely be found where I didn't expect it to be buried.

"Do you feel that what has been written about the campaign has been accurate?" I asked. "Is there more to tell?"

"There's a lot that hasn't been told," she answered. "There are people who have gotten no credit for what they have done. And there are many people who tell the story as if it is their own. I have found that the staffers who talk the most often do the least. It is really the president's story."

"Well, let's start with that," I suggested. "Tell me about the president, your father."

"What he has done is truly remarkable," she said. With all the negatives bombarding the White House, she seemed relieved to finally have room to say something positive. "Here is an individual who has achieved an extraordinary level of success in real estate. I mean there are people who have built one great building and they are famous forever for what they have achieved. And rightly so. But here is someone who built buildings, one after another, across New York City and later the world. And that is exceptional in itself. These were not just ordinary buildings. They were the tallest or the biggest or the most spectacular, again and again, setting a new bar, overcoming all of the many complicated obstacles. That alone is enough achievement for one person, in one lifetime.

"And then he replicated that success in an entirely different medium, in television entertainment. *The Apprentice* was the number one show in America. It was syndicated in countries across the globe. It went on for numerous seasons. The ratings that first year were in excess of the Super Bowl. It was a wild success.

"What is amazing is that there was this consensus against the whole idea of this show. Most of the experts said a business show would fail. They had numbers, they had focus groups that could tell you what was going to happen. That was the traditional feedback at NBC. But my father had a vision for what it would do, and as it turned out, he was right; it succeeded, beyond anyone's wildest dreams.

"So even before he ran for president, even before he got involved in politics, he had succeeded in two entirely different mediums. Each one had their own obscure rules for achievement, their own traps and lessons to be learned. It would take most people a lifetime to master either one of them. Let alone do both. And then, finally, he would run for president. And he would win."

Everything Ivanka was saying raised the question, how had he done it? Donald Trump's critics were still dismissing him as an aberration. His election was an accident of history that would soon be corrected. It was Hillary Clinton's loss, some said, not his win. The recovering economy was the work of Obama, delayed. The collapse of ISIS was just good timing. The generals had done it. Trump was lucky. Problem was, he was getting luckier by the minute. Energy independence had been the goal of seven presidents. How had that suddenly happened?

Ivanka understood the critics, their need to believe their own ideas. She too, supposedly, had different political views from her father on many issues. But she had seen too much. She had heard this chorus of attacks and doubters before. In good conscience she could not buy into the media consensus. How had he been so lucky in so many distinctly different mediums, as she put it? Something was at work here, and if the media didn't want to know it, if history didn't believe it or care, well, she wanted to know for herself. At least.

In our conversations it became clear that she had given this a lot of thought over the years. America was just now becoming intrigued, but Ivanka had been a student of Trump for much of her life. She knew that building buildings was not easy, because she herself had worked at it. She knew that having a hit television show was not easy, because she herself had been pitched on the idea. And while she had not contemplated a political career, she had seen enough to know what an endless Rubik's Cube it could be. Donald Trump had conquered all three separate disciplines, right before her eyes. The media was convinced that Donald Trump was lucky? Ivanka was not going to make a fuss about it, but privately, personally, she knew better.

Between 1999 and 2001, Ivanka Trump and other young wealthy teenagers had been talked into doing a movie documentary entitled *Born Rich*, in which she had come off as quite circumspect. In one scene she described a public event when a strange man walked up to her and asked, "What's it like to be wealthy?"

The teenage Ivanka Trump had been taken off guard. "Excuse me?"

And he persisted, "What does it feel like to have never felt any pain?"

"That really upset me," she said in the film, "Not because I was upset for myself but because I was upset for him. I was bothered by the fact that he could be so ignorant. . . . To think that with money comes happiness."[13]

At Christmas or birthdays, Ivanka had her own unique wishes as a child. "Rather than getting Barbie dolls, I used to get upset. I always wanted Legos or erector sets," she recalled, laughing.

"I love looking at the New York skyline," she said in the film, "and being able to figure out what I'm going to add to that. What patch of sky will one of my buildings be in?"[14]

This was a teenager, an ambitious, hungry Ivanka Trump, unashamed, wanting to build on her father's success. While some of the other teenagers in the film, all the sons and daughters of wealth, seemed tormented by their privilege, Ivanka came off as inspired.

She would go on to build some iconic projects, including what the family refers to as Trump Doral and Trump DC.

Years later, when Ivanka's father was running for president, Gayle King of CBS News would ask her about her role as a mother. How was she doing, raising a daughter of her own? "My parents taught me to be self-reliant," Ivanka said. "They were not people who overflattered. They encouraged us and pushed us to be the best that we could be, but they also recognized that you gain confidence from small successes. And then bigger successes."[15]

She told Oprah Winfrey, "I've never been interested in being a wild party girl, an 'It girl.' My dad is very strict. No drugs, no smoking. His brother died of alcoholism. It's a horrible, horrible thing."[16]

Eric Trump would bring up this same theme in my interviews with him. "Even when I was five years old, leaving to go to a friend's place to play for an hour, my father would come up to me to say good-bye and then he would look down at me and say very seriously, 'No drugs, no smoking, no alcohol!'"

Eric laughed as he remembered. "Imagine? I am a five-year-old kid! "'Okay, Pop.'"[17]

THE MAGIC OF THINKING BIG

In my conversations with other members of the Trump family and the Trump administration, this question kept lingering. What was behind Donald Trump's success? One could see his weaknesses. It seemed after any great success he would unnecessarily self-destruct. It was something that happens to all of us, but Donald Trump's moments were so visible. He was so transparent.

"Honest," as Ivanka put it.

So what were the positives that transcended the negatives? How had he won the presidency? How had the economy turned around? How had ISIS been so easily tamed? My researchers and I tore apart his book *The Art of the Deal*. We had notes and markings on every page without drawing any firm conclusions. And then finally, one day, one interview with Ivanka yielded some good answers.

"He learned a lot from his own father," she said. "They were builders. That's one thing that some people get wrong. Dad is not primarily a marketer. He is good at that. He understands the bells and the whistles. But his real skill is as a builder, which he learned from his great mentor, his father."

And yet Fred Trump, the father, had stayed in Queens, I pointed out. There he had built homes, apartments, and office buildings. He knew and understood every neighborhood and every block of that borough. He warned his son, Donald, to stick with what he knew, to stay in Queens, not to venture across the bridge into Manhattan, where the stakes were higher and the risks so much greater. But Donald Trump, who taught his children to think big, was not frightened by Manhattan.

"Donald Trump is a big thinker," she said. "A big dreamer. He had the vision to cross over the bridge. He came to Manhattan and then ultimately we took that vision and extended it around the globe based on the brand that became synonymous with luxury at the highest level.

"I have to say, as a young girl growing up, he had this incredible pop-culture connectivity even prior to *The Apprentice*. I remember as a little kid his name would be on the *Fresh Prince of Bel-Air* or in a rap song. He would hang out with Puff Daddy. When I was young I would ride around with him and they would go to movie premieres together. He and my mother were sort of this golden couple."

What does he expect from his team? I wanted to know. What's it like to work for Donald Trump?

"In the Trump organization he was always an incredible mentor. He gave a bold vision for the company. He would give people room, they would have the freedom to perform, but he would always be watching and encouraging and making sure that his vision was being followed. I think he is running the country the same way, although some people in his administration are just starting to figure that out."

But what was the secret? I persisted. What was the common denominator? What principle did he apply to all of these ventures? To building, to television entertainment, to politics?

"There is one principle," Ivanka said, "going back to my childhood, something that he would always tell us. And it has become a quote that he is quite famous for. It's no secret, really. He would say, 'If you're going to be thinking anyway, think big.'

"That," Ivanka insisted, "is very much his philosophy." It was his approach in business and entertainment and finally in politics. He would swing for the fences. He wouldn't try for a single. He would try for a home run.

"That principle has yielded incredible results. It applies to every one of his buildings. Each in its own way defined the skyline of a city, often breaking records like the ninety-two-story building in Chicago, which was the tallest building built in North America in decades. This applied to *The Apprentice*, which was not limited to a network or cable.

"When he entered politics, they told him that he had to run for governor first, or the Senate. He should at least run for Congress. He needed a constituency, a field army to be successful. A group of political workers who had experienced a campaign together and who knew how to get things done. No one had ever been elected president as a businessman. Yes, Ronald Reagan had been in show business, but he had served two terms as governor and run for president once and lost before he had finally won.

"So, once again, it was the same thing. Against the advice of many experts, he ran for president. Think big. Don't try to hit a single. Go for the home run."

Ivanka laughed. "He's not an elitist about it. He believes everybody should think that way."

A SCARY THOUGHT COMING DOWN THE ESCALATOR

Within the family, Trump's pursuit of power had not been totally unexpected. He had been asked about running for president for years. He was usually coy in such interviews. Often, when asked, he would say no, but then, before letting the question go entirely, he would yank it back suddenly, like a fisherman who had hooked a fish. And when he had kept the discussion alive, he would admit that he was occasionally tempted. There were so many things that the country needed to do, he would say. In the end, while sometimes coming close to making the announcement, he would never finally take the plunge.

"He asked me about two weeks before to introduce him when he announced his candidacy," Ivanka remembers. "But he was so casual about it. He said, 'I'm going to do this thing. Do you want to introduce me?'" She laughed when she remembered the moment.

"So I worked on it. I wanted to do it right. I wanted to give him a solid introduction. Something that would make him proud."[18]

Donald Trump's announcement for president was choreographed at Trump Tower on June 16, 2015, when the candidate and his wife,

Melania, rode down an escalator to a waiting crowd of supporters and journalists.

According to Ivanka, twenty minutes before the press conference, Donald Trump was still reworking the program. "Amanda, this is all wrong," he said to a staffer, Amanda Miller. "I want 'Phantom of the Opera.' And, Ivanka, you have to walk out to 'Memories.'"

"I thought, 'Memories?' Really?

"It was his whole playlist," Ivanka laughed, as she retold the moment. "These were his favorites. 'Rocket Man' is on there too!"[19]

But Ivanka had to come down the escalator first, and she was alone.

Her father had planned this and envisioned it. He was ready. Ivanka was not. She saw all the cameras and was shocked by the size of the crowd.

"My friends asked me a week or two later, 'How did you feel? Introducing your father? How do you feel about him running for president?'

"I told them that I always knew he had this civic urge, that there were things in the country that he felt were wrong and he wanted to fix them, but I never really knew for sure he would do it until he said it. So here I was announcing 'the next president of the United States,' in front of all those cameras, wondering if he would come down to the lobby and say, 'Oh, no, I'm not running, after all,' and I would be left standing there."

The point was that if Donald Trump had been thinking about this for years, many of his friends and family were nevertheless caught by surprise. "So I spent zero time thinking what it would be like when my father announced for president," said Ivanka. "None of us did. We were wildly unprepared for the chaos."[20]

A ROLE TO PLAY

The modern women's movement has been conflicted over the concept of beauty. On the one hand, they protested the Miss America contest but then viciously turned on their own champion, the celebrity Ashley

Judd, who they complained had gained weight.[21] Judd had been ill and had been treated with steroids. But what should her weight matter to women's activists?

Ivanka Trump was intolerable to some critics simply because she was a beautiful woman. Marin Cogan wrote that she "once seemed built in a lab to be covered by the high-gloss world of women's fashion media." Another writer described her as "perfectly crafted."[22]

When she appeared on the cover of *Town & Country* in 2008, with the headline "Smart, Successful and Sexy" it was intolerable.[23] The fashionistas would not allow it. In the progressive world of New York society, one cannot be both blonde and smart.

Ivanka had been a cover girl for decades. She had appeared on *Seventeen* in 1997. Ten years later she was crowned "the new Queen of Diamonds" in a cover story for *Harper's Bazaar*. *Forbes* magazine ran her on its cover in 2014. She was now a wife, a mom, and "the emerging power behind the family empire." In the two years leading up to the election of her father as president, she was the rage, appearing in a series of cover stories from *Good Housekeeping* and *Redbook* to *Shape*. A second *Town & Country* cover story was entitled "Vote Ivanka."

Then abruptly, as if all of the publishers had met in a room and taken a solemn vow, the curtain fell. Ivanka Trump had agreed to work in her father's White House. One last parting cover story appeared in the July 2016, in the Spanish-language version of *Marie Claire*. "*¿Hasta Cuando Defenderas a Tu Padre?*" it asked. "How long are you going to defend your father?"[24]

Ivanka was the same person. She had ideas about jobs, about families, about doubling the child credit as part of tax reform, about education and retraining, about ending the growing crisis in human trafficking. Her ideas were innovative and would soon become an important part of the economic recovery that was ahead. But Ivanka Trump had offended on two counts.

One, she had remained loyal to her father. Only betrayal was acceptable to the New York media, shamed by their miscalculation about the

American voters in 2016 and finding themselves increasingly shamed by the great, ongoing Trump economic recovery.

Two, she was proving to be competent. Even effective. A competent cover girl?

In Washington, DC, where Ivanka had decided to work, a woman could not be both beautiful and smart. This was not the exotic world of Cleopatra and ancient Egypt. This was not a glamorous court in the Middle Ages where Diane de Poitiers could have both beauty and power. This was the United States of America, where women who mattered were Janet Reno, Loretta Lynch, and Hillary Clinton. Glamor was seen as a negative. Ivanka was a target.

SHE JUST GETS THINGS DONE

"Ivanka's my secret weapon," Donald Trump would tell anyone who would listen. When he needed a diplomat to finesse relationships with foreign leaders, he dispatched Ivanka. It was reminiscent of Theodore Roosevelt, who had sent his daughter Alice on a secret mission to Japan, right under the noses of the press. But Trump used Ivanka for economic and legislative chores as well. When tax reform was deemed impossible, he sent her to the toughest congressional districts, to try to capture the most unlikely supporters.

On March 17, 2017, Ivanka sat next to Chancellor Angela Merkel in a meeting in the Cabinet Room of the White House. Staffers watched with curiosity and anticipation. They had seen Ivanka Trump in action. How people first reacted to her beauty and then were surprised by her humility and graciousness. It was an unexpected combination. Like fending off an opponent's right only to be suddenly hit by a left uppercut that came out of nowhere. This was what the president himself had often talked about, how Ivanka would close the deal before they even had a chance to sit down.

This time, the whole world was watching it happen in real time. They saw Chancellor Merkel and Ivanka in animated conversation. They saw the delight spread across the chancellor's face.

The president, looking on from the other side of the Cabinet Room table, smiled knowingly. He had seen it in boardrooms, law offices, and sales meetings. Now it was happening in the Cabinet Room of the White House.

Later, when my interviews with the president turned to foreign policy and I asked about Chancellor Merkel and the unique American relationship with Germany, that specific Ivanka moment came up. If Ivanka was impressed with her father, well, he was obviously impressed with her.

Ivanka's efforts to get the tax reform bill passed were critical. Local media did not always observe the rules dictated by network television producers in New York, meaning that Ivanka's trips across the country, ignored by national media, received wide coverage in local papers and on local television.

When tax reform miraculously passed, all House members in districts that Ivanka had visited voted yes. She had been sent into difficult districts in California and New Jersey. In the Senate, the work she did with Senator Collins and Senator Corker was crucial.[25]

Did the incessant media attacks get to Ivanka Trump? How did it feel to have people who had never met her now openly proclaim that they hated her? How did it feel to have public figures call for the death of her father and her own family? She was once the cover story on magazines around the world. Now that she was actually making a difference, creating effective job-training programs, for example, leading the remarkable efforts to fight the flood of human trafficking, taking on issues that defied partisanship, she was attacked or ignored.

"I think I was a little blindsided by some of the ferocity. At least on a personal level," Ivanka said. "But for me, I'm trying to keep my head down, not listen to the noise and just work really hard to make a positive impact in the lives of many people."[26]

"There's a story in Bob Woodward's book *Fear* about you meeting with Steve Bannon," I said. "You are in the office of the chief of staff, Reince Priebus. And Bannon is shouting at you. Angry at you. Saying,

'You are just a fucking staffer!' And you say, 'I'll never be a staffer. I'm the first daughter.'"[27]

"It never happened," Ivanka said calmly.

"There's no truth to it?" I persisted. This was a pretty famous story that the media prominently featured and constantly repeated.

"None whatsoever," she said.

And then she added, "My life is too important for me to waste in rivalries and in personal vendettas. I choose not to do that. I choose to think the best of people. Most of all, I choose to be happy and aim for impact. This is really important to me. I have no time for bitterness."

Ivanka had said something similar in her interview with Gayle King at CBS: "You can't be a confident, secure person if you are not happy."[28]

In her book, *The Trump Card*, Ivanka took Rudyard Kipling's view of criticism. "I get it from both sides, the good and the bad. And I've learned to ignore it. To rise above it. I refuse to let the opinions of others define how I see myself."[29]

"I value the opinions of those I love," Ivanka once told me. "And those I work with. Anyone else? It's all noise."

In a subsequent interview, as journalists and writers like to do, I repeated some of the same questions, just in case I might get a nuanced, more revealing answer. Once more I asked her, "How do you handle the criticism?" I was glad that I did.

"On a human level," she said. "On a very personal level, it can be very difficult, very challenging. Especially when it is wrong. Although, I'm pretty thick skinned."

Then she added this line: "For me, the most important thing is the truth that I know."

★ 4 ★

DONALD TRUMP JR. AND WHISPERS ON AN ELEVATOR

"He knew a storm was coming."
—Donald Trump Jr.[1]

Born December 31, 1977, Donald Trump Jr. is the eldest child of the president and one of the most complex members of the family. Like his siblings Ivanka and Eric, he has a winning personality. He thinks and speaks with a rapid-fire openness. When the president left his iconic business in New York behind, he appointed Donald Trump Jr. as the boss.

As an advocate of his father's policies and a cheerleader of his accomplishments as president, Don Jr. is one of the family's most effective surrogates. Toward the end of the 2016 election campaign he was sometimes outdrawing the Democratic nominee, Hillary Clinton, at rallies and events.

Late one night, in the middle of the campaign, Don Jr. got a call saying, "Congratulations, you are going to be on television in the morning." His father had apparently said something controversial about Muslims.

"What are the talking points?" Don Jr. asked. His early-morning appearance was only a few hours away. There would be no sleep that night.

"Talking points?" the voice on the other end of the call said, "*You* tell us what the talking points are. You handle this better than anybody."[2]

That was life on the campaign trail for Donald Trump Jr.

In many personal ways, the Trump children are alike. Especially Don Jr., Ivanka, and Eric, the three born to Donald and his first wife, Ivana. They could almost be triplets. While in most families there is a sloppy one, or an introvert, or an intellectual, or one who is good or bad with money, the Trump children are all bright and personable. On the surface, at least, they are sanguine. They are all positive. They are all confident and well groomed. It is only when they are together that one can begin to distinguish the differences. I would interview each one of them in a succession of repeated cycles, and that afforded me the opportunity to compare.

Ivanka Trump avoids hostility and creates her own positive atmosphere as a mechanism to get things done, Eric allows himself to become more engaged by the process and finds the need to fight back. Don Jr. is more complex. He may be the strongest personality of them all, but he can also be deferential. For example, he did not condemn a campaign staffer who was suspected of exploiting the process for personal gain; rather, he assumes that he did not have all the facts or fully know the other side of the story. He concluded, "I did things differently." Without any condemnation.

Don Jr. is also less insular. He allows that his father, the campaign, the administration and he himself are sometimes wrong and should have done things differently. For most of the family, the criticism is ignored or not addressed, or the unfairness is so overwhelming that it doesn't seem to require a discussion. Ivanka tends to compartmentalize it and not let it be a distraction from her work. It's there, but it's tucked away neatly in a Tupperware container placed somewhere in the freezer to be brought out, if it has to be, at some other time.

Donald Trump Jr., more than all the others, presses to find out what is behind the opposition to his father and the family. Why is it happening? And sometimes he feels the need to acknowledge that it is occasionally self-inflicted.

ADVICE FROM A FATHER

Ivanka was the first family member I would interview, Don Jr. was one of the last. His reluctance had a reason. He had just signed a contract to do his own book.

"Normally, they would frown on me working with another author when I am writing a book of my own," he said, "but since we have the same publisher and the same editor, I think they can make an exception, right?"

Lucky for me. I was on track to interview the whole family and the most important members of the White House staff. The loss of Don Jr. would have been a gaping hole in the story.

Ivanka had talked to me about her uncertainty over her father's planned presidential announcement. It turns out that her big brother was having the same doubts. "Even days before the announcement I was unsure," he told me. "I was wondering. 'Was this the real thing or not?'"

Just before Donald Trump announced for president, he and the family gathered in his office on the twenty-sixth floor on the commercial side of Trump Tower. There they were all given final instructions. When they left, they took an elevator down to the mezzanine floor, where the family separated. Ivanka would take to the stage to introduce "the next president of the United States"; Don and Eric would take the elevator down to the ground floor and join the crowd. Donald and Melania Trump would pause for a few moments and then descend the escalator to one of the most controversial press conferences in political history.

"The day of the announcement," Don said, "my father told me something that I would remember, again and again in the coming weeks and months. It would be one of the most accurate observations

I would hear since my own immersion into politics. We got on the elevator and he turned to look at me and he said, 'Now we find out who our real friends are.'

"My father is not very philosophical about things. He is very practical. A results-driven guy. But he knew that this was not going to be easy. This was his understanding of the real world. He knew a storm was coming. He knew that there would be controversy either manifested or created by the establishment, the media, and sometimes, certainly, because of our own actions. He recognized very quickly that this would separate the wheat from the chaff among the friends we had known our whole lives.

"I often think of that moment and the look in his eyes. I don't know that truer words have ever been spoken."

I asked Don Jr. if I could find that story somewhere online so I could flesh out more of the details to give a fuller description of the moment.

"Well, I don't think so," he said. "I've never read it or seen it. I will certainly use it in my own book.

"To me," he said, "that was one of the memorable things he has told us over his lifetime because it was so prescient. My father was always teaching us about life and business. This was one of the most fundamental Trumpian quotes I can remember. Direct, succinct, and to the point."

Life and reality. There is always the way we want things to be and then there is the reality.

"My father has always had a good understanding of the real world. How difficult. How rough it can be. How brutal it is.

"People are always saying, 'Did you know it was going to be this bad?'

"Well, we didn't go into this naive. We didn't get in thinking that it was going to be easy. People are not going to be nice.

"Sure, we didn't have a full appreciation of just how vicious and how brutal it would be. I don't think anybody had. Jimmy Carter spoke up about it. He said, 'Listen, I've taken my share of heat but nothing like this.' And that's the reality."

I was curious about another reality.

WHEN TRUMP MADE HIS DECISION

There was a mythological sequence of events, etched in stone, unassailable. The story, promoted by the *New York Times* and reinforced by almost everybody in the media, both left and right, held that Trump had been provoked to run for president by his humiliation at the April 30, 2011, White House Correspondents Dinner.[3] The authoritative Fox News anchor Bill O'Reilly had insisted that this narrative was the right one.[4] One could actually see the video footage online. There was Trump, shoulders hunched, taking the stinging mockery. How could the public deny what they, themselves, had witnessed?

According to Marcus Brauchli, who was nearby at that famous dinner, Donald Trump had been "incredibly gracious and engaged on the way in, but departed with maximum efficiency."[5]

I had spent the last forty years researching stories about presidents and knew how many of the "most certain" moments were often flawed. Consider George Washington's cherry tree episode, dreamed up by Parson Weems. Or Lincoln's tribute to his "angel mother," promoted by his law partner William Herndon and featured in the opening pages of a Pulitzer Prize–winning book. I personally knew how the Bush family enjoyed a chuckle over books and "authorities" who were convinced that Dick Cheney ran the White House during those years and it was he who had convinced George W. Bush to invade Iraq. Of course, Karl Rove, the media assured us, was Bush's brain.

There were some other theories about Trump's motivation for pursuing the White House; most of these theories were the inspiration of family critics, and all of them ascribed bits and pieces to the businessman's ego. The tongue-in-cheek theory of the director Michael Moore got the most attention. He insisted that Trump had been jealous of

Gwen Stefani's paycheck for her appearances on *The Voice* and wanted to run for president to prove to NBC that he was more popular.[6] Such was the parochial world of American entertainment. Everything, even world politics, was about them.

My own experience and research gave me little assurance that I could convince anybody else about the truth of Trump's decision, even if I could find it, but it did make me curious enough to press the Trump family. What was their own version of what had prompted this moment in history? Regardless of what the media thought, where did the Trump family itself believe it had all begun? And what did the president say?

The president told me it was born out of frustration, watching the country he loved falling into decline. "Stupid deals," he often said.

He had always brushed away the idea that he was reacting to the Obama attack at the correspondents' dinner. "I loved that dinner," Trump later told the *New York Times*. "I can handle criticism."[7] He told me that he had the thought years before that dinner.

I was eager to speak to Donald Trump Jr., the oldest Trump sibling of his generation, to get his take on how his father made those early steps toward a decision. When and where was the idea born? How had it evolved?

"I'd been hearing about it my whole life," Don Jr. said. "If you look at the feed on my Twitter account, he was talking about it in the mid-eighties. That was a full twenty years before the correspondents' dinner. Then, of course, I remember his appearance on *Oprah*.

"For years he had been watching the drain on the American economy and how the government was doing such a bad job on trade deals. Back then it was Japan that was screwing us. Now it's China and others. But not a lot has changed.

"I remember him getting so fired up. Frustrated. That America was leaving so much money on the table. Getting bad deals because the departments were being run by a bunch of incompetents. They shouldn't have been running anything, let alone what I call the largest company in the world, the United States government.

"So I saw him get upset about it. I saw him, over the last decade or two, become increasingly more vocal about it. He's the kind of guy, you can only throw stones for so long before you have to step up and act. He's more of a man of action than anything. So finally it was time."

I asked Don Jr. about the 2011 *Wall Street Journal*–NBC poll showing his father as a presidential contender, within 4 points of Mitt Romney.[8] "Do you remember the poll?" I asked. "Did you have any thoughts, maybe this could happen?"

"Yes," he said, "I remember the poll. I remember believing it."

In 2011, Donald Trump appeared on CNN with Piers Morgan.[9] "Well, I'm a Republican," Trump said. "I'm a very good Republican. But I thought Bush was a terrible president. I thought he was a terrible leader. The country had no spirit. And ultimately, he did so bad at the end that we have Obama. That's what we have. It was a gift from President Bush.

"I'm tempted to run."[10]

That was 2011.

Donald Trump talked about jobs going to China and India.

Piers Morgan asked about the unemployment rate, and both men agreed that the real figure was close to 10 percent. Probably more.

"Smart guys write regulations," Trump said. "But smarter persons figure out how to get around them."

THE BLUE-COLLAR BILLIONAIRE

How was 2015 different? If Don Jr. had been seeing his father running for president all his life, were there any signals that this time it would really happen? That this was more than a boost to the brand?

"Well, like I said, he had been toying with it for a while. I'm not sure I actually believed it was going to happen until it happened.

"Certainly we could see that he was immersing himself into the process. He was meeting with the people he needed to meet. He was asking the right questions. He was reading the right papers. He was weighing the risks required.

"Understand, there are great consequences for a businessman running for president. There is a great cost. Especially if you are going to run as a conservative or worse, as someone who wants to turn around the economy. People are making money the way things are now. They don't want it changed. There is a reason why people in middle America are growing poorer. So if you are taking on the big companies, and they finance the media, and they run Hollywood, it is not going to be easy. He knew that and he was preparing for that."

It turns out that Donald Trump Jr. had his father's instincts for branding and came up with one of the more enduring definitions of just who Donald Trump really is. Don Jr. would call him "the blue-collar billionaire."

"Again, I knew my father in a way that others didn't necessarily know him. I knew, for example, that *The Apprentice* was very good for him because it humanized him. He was not seen by the public as a Ken Lay–Enron type guy. He had a personality that related to regular people in America. I had seen that my whole life.

"I saw him interacting with construction workers on job sites. Union workers. People who were building our buildings. He was not some executive who sheltered himself behind a glass office on Fifth Avenue. He was always with the workers. He wanted their opinions. He listened to their ideas. He valued those ideas and put them to work.

"These were not token visits, these were real moments. I would see it again, years later on the campaign trail; he wanted to know what was wrong and how to fix it. This was one of his secrets as a builder and it later became one of his secrets for winning the presidency.

"There's something else. From the workers he learned how to be more efficient. How to get the same thing accomplished with less wasted money and time. And they appreciated it. Nobody likes to see waste and stupidity even if it isn't their responsibility or their company. They hate it. And they lose respect. Why should they care about efficiency if the company itself doesn't care?

"By the way, that is exactly how he started to turn around the

American economy so quickly. He listened to people. He brought them into the White House not to give them speeches but to listen to them.

"I fully understand the irony of the brash New York billionaire appealing to American workers, but this didn't happen just out of the blue. This was a lifetime in the making. He had actually spent a lot of time with workers throughout his life, and he recognized their plight when he met them on the campaign trail in Michigan and Pennsylvania, where they had lost their jobs.

"I got criticized years ago for an interview I gave where I called him 'a blue-collar billionaire.' That's how I saw him. The media scoffed at the idea. But there is a real truth in it. He cares about the workers and he is frustrated to see government cheat them.

"While there was this early, colorful image of the New York playboy, the truth was he didn't drink alcohol, he disdained the rubber-chicken-dinner black-tie social circuit. He much preferred a cheeseburger or pizza and watching a baseball game. He socialized more with his workers than with jet-set celebrities.

"During the general election campaign you could see a motorcade pulling into a McDonald's drive-through at eleven at night. That would be my father.

"You remember all of this talk about the forgotten man? Well, that's why he ran for president. He hadn't seen change in decades. He hadn't seen anyone step up and correct the obvious. Politicians would make promises and then not even try to deliver on them. It was so blatant.

"It is so interesting to see that my father is getting hell for actually doing what he promised the voters that he would do. They heard him. They agreed. They voted for him, and when he started to actually do what the people wanted, the media and the establishment went wild."

TRUMP WILL NEVER WIN THE NOMINATION

In the spring of 2015, there was universal agreement: Donald Trump could not win the Republican nomination for president. Ivanka and Don Jr. were not alone in questioning whether or not he would even run. Critics saw it as posturing, a publicity stunt, to keep his name, his brand, in the news.

Even beyond the disdain of political observers and journalists, there was a massive pool of resentment already beginning to manifest itself toward the billionaire. The English comedian John Oliver, reacting to the news that Donald Trump might run for president, looked bug-eyed into the camera lens toward his television audience and proclaimed sarcastically, "Do it. Do it." Oliver pointed his fingers to his eyes. "Look at me. I will personally write you a campaign check now, on behalf of this country that does not want you to become president but badly wants you to run." Oliver's audience howled with laughter.

What was the source of this hostility, this bite? Why was John Oliver's audience laughing with him? Most likely this was a moment to ruin things for the Republicans and allow Hillary Clinton, the presumed nominee of the Left, to win. This was to help pave the way for the first woman president. Trump was an early, conspicuous target.

It certainly wasn't about policies. Keep in mind, at the time, Donald Trump's public plan for health care called for universal coverage. Some Republicans were aghast. It was like the Canadian system.[11] Bernie Sanders wouldn't have had a problem with it, they said. As of then, there was not even a hint of the Russian collusion conspiracy theories. There had been no meeting about the Magnitsky Act at Trump Tower. Trump hadn't talked about a Muslim ban, or illegals coming across the border from Mexico. And yet, without any of these props, Hollywood and New York were already predisposed to bitterly hate him.

In April 2015, the syndicated columnist and former ABC News star George F. Will appeared on a Fox News panel hosted by Bret Baier. Each of the panel members was asked to put "play money" on which GOP candidate would win the nomination. Will put most of his money on Wisconsin's governor, Scott Walker, and the former Florida governor Jeb Bush, with a little left over for Senator Marco Rubio and the governors Chris Christie, John Kasich, and Bobby Jindal. And then Will added this little irritated aside, he said he would add "one dollar on Donald Trump in the hope that he will be tempted to run, be predictably shellacked, and we will be spared evermore this quadrennial charade of his."[12]

As it turns out, George Will would not be spared. At the time, he was only expressing what many of his colleagues felt. But what was the basis of this resentment?

For one thing, Donald Trump was considered to be a "birther"; that is, he had questioned the validity of President Obama's official birth certificate. Was Obama actually born in the United States or not? If so, why wouldn't he produce his official birth certificate? This whole discussion made Trump appear racist to some and a certified lunatic to others. Trump would eventually accept the fact that Obama was born in Hawaii when his official birth certificate was finally released, but he would declare victory for forcing it to be produced.[13]

There was more than conspiracy theories at work. Jealousy? How dare this upstart businessman Donald Trump even think he could be a president when so many of us, who are much more qualified, patiently stay in our place on the sidelines? Perhaps their anger was self-directed. Perhaps they felt that they should have tried to enter public life themselves, and now it was too late. They had been bluffed into thinking that they had to be a governor first, or at the very least a member of Congress. Was Donald Trump's arrogance an indictment, exposing their own timidity and lack of imagination?

If Trump were really so harmless and so inconsequential, as they maintained, why did his public musings about running for president provoke such a reaction? It was not so much that they thought he might actually win as it was that they were afraid that he himself hadn't yet figured that out. And that was infuriating. The gall.

It is important to understand that these feelings, this anti-Trump anger, already existed. It was there before the policies and words and conspiracies of the Left eventually emerged. In fact, it may have been the cause of some of them.

Finally, there was something more ominous. Trump had been outspoken on many issues. He had long opposed nation building, including the Iraq War, the Iran deal, our deficit with China, and most of our trade deals. The American elite, both Democratic and Republican, were making money off things the way they were. So yes, he was a comic book figure, as Chris Matthews declared to his television audience, and yes, he could mess things up for the Republicans, but the things he was advocating were gaining some modest traction, and that could eventually be costly to elites. Why not stop him now?[14] You've got the guy on the ropes, go ahead and knock him out. So, even this early, there was also a little bit of fear. In retrospect, these were the wise men of the American political-corporate establishment.

On June 15, 2015, Lawrence O'Donnell of MSNBC gave his own assessment of Trump's presidential ambitions. "He is obviously never going to be president. He is obviously never going to be the Republican nominee for president and he is obviously never going to be a candidate for president."[15] O'Donnell's tone was malevolent.

The next day, Donald Trump made it official. He was running.

Ron Reagan Jr. told Chris Matthews of MSNBC, "This is going to turn a three-ring circus into a freak show."[16]

Eventually there would be sixteen announced candidates. Donald Trump was the only one without any political experience. He had never served in office in any capacity, anywhere. He had never run for office either. And yet, by late summer 2015, he was leading in polls among Republican voters.

Media pundits, politicians, and historians all dismissed the numbers as a mirage that would soon evaporate. "If Trump is nominated, then everything we think we know about presidential nominations is wrong," said Larry Sabato, head of the Center for Politics at the University of Virginia.[17]

The highly respected FiveThirtyEight podcast had its three experts rate Trump's chances to win the nomination. They came in with probabilities of 2 percent, 0 percent, and –10 percent.[18] Their interactive endorsement tracker had Jeb Bush in the lead with Trump "not even on the list."[19] By September 2015, the *New York Times* had Marco Rubio as the likely front-runner.[20]

Trump's Republican rivals disagreed about many things but were all united in the belief that his popularity bubble was going to burst. "Donald Trump is not going to be the Republican nominee," said the former Florida governor Jeb Bush.[21] He was both the son and the brother of previous American presidents. Headed into the election cycle, he had already raised more money than any other contender.

Florida senator Marco Rubio, who won the early share of political endorsements, was asked by CNN if he would support the eventual nominee, even if it were Donald Trump. "Well, I'm going to support the Republican nominee, and I'm comfortable that it's not going to be Donald Trump."[22]

On WABC radio, Texas senator Ted Cruz was asked if he would support Trump if he were the nominee. Cruz, who would later emerge as the best challenger to Trump, said, "In time, I don't think that Donald is going to be the nominee."[23]

Governor John Kasich of Ohio made it clear, saying, "He is not going to be the nominee."[24] When Trump won the nomination anyway, Kasich refused to attend the Republican National Convention, even though it was held in Cleveland. Historically, it should have been his moment in the sun. He was the governor of the home state, he was host to the Republican National Convention. But for Kasich it didn't matter, Trump may have won the nomination, but he was going nowhere afterward. He would never be president of the United States. And when Donald Trump did become president and when his success as president swept the Republican Party almost unanimously into his camp, Kasich could still not bring himself to accept it.

The 2012 Republican candidate for president, Mitt Romney, told Jake Tapper of CNN, "Well, I don't think it's likely that Donald Trump will be the nominee."[25]

On NBC's *Meet the Press*, the political veteran Charlie Black, who had worked on every Republican presidential campaign since 1972, said flatly, "He is not going to be the nominee."[26]

When a Fox News anchor asked the political analyst Karl Rove, the man who had advised George W. Bush, how Republicans should treat Donald Trump, Rove said simply, "Ignore him."[27]

BEHIND THE SCENES AT THE GOP DEBATES

In 1988, the Democratic candidates for president were derisively referred to as "the seven dwarfs."[28] The same couldn't be said for the sixteen Republicans who were running for president in the 2016 election cycle. They were governors and senators with intellectual and financial heft. Jeb Bush, a former governor of Florida, was heir to what was arguably the nation's greatest political dynasty. He would have two former presidents raising money for him. Senator Marco Rubio was a demographic contortionist. He was a Hispanic and a Catholic who attended an evangelical church and represented the key state of Florida, which was critical to winning a national election and was an early primary state. Senator Rand Paul was touted on the cover of *Time* as "the most interesting man in politics" and with good reason.[29] His conservative-libertarian following had the best ground game in Iowa and New Hampshire. In 2012, his father been in a virtual tie for first in the Iowa caucuses and had come in second place in New Hampshire.

In the early Republican debates, taking place in 2015, with sixteen candidates on the stage, the key was to distinguish oneself from the pack. Almost anything would do it. But doing something different involved risk. Both were points that politicians would thereafter take to heart.

Donald Trump Jr. laughed as he remembered the early GOP debates. "He was himself," he recalled, referring to his father. "He didn't spout the typical dogma. Everyone was a sheep on this. He distinguished himself from the pack. Obviously you saw his wit.

"To me one of the most telling moments was the very first question in the very first debate. 'Will you automatically support whoever gets the Republican nomination? Is there any one here who cannot guarantee that they will do that?'

"Well, he was honest. He didn't know who the nominee would be or what they were going to advocate. He was not a blind partisan. He had seen how the establishment had ruined the country. So he was the only person who raised his hand. He was alone. You ask how he distinguishes himself from the pack? Well, there you go."

It was his targeted rapier wit that had his opponents cringing.

I had served as a shill in the elaborate debate preparation for George H. W. Bush in 1987 and 1988. The whole process had been choreographed by Roger Ailes, later the president of Fox News. It involved hours of privately videotaped practice debates. To prepare the shills, the candidate's son, George W. Bush, played the role of his father. So I had actually spent hours debating both Bush presidents. In 2015, I was advising Senator Rand Paul. After the first debate, the whole discussion turned to the question of what to do about Donald Trump. He was seen as a political suicide bomber. It was believed that his comments were irresponsible and disqualifying to himself but were also utterly destructive to his target. The question among the Republican debate teams was what to do. Ignore him and hope he attacks someone else? Or stand up to him?

"He has this uncanny ability to brand someone immediately," Donald Trump Jr. said. "He's always had that. His whole business was branding and creating the brand. But it was more than that. It worked because he actually built a better product. His skill was in building but, yes, he could find the perfect brand to make it be seen for what it is.

"He is able to see other people's flaws and weaknesses and exploit them quickly. It's just devastating to them. His 'low energy' comment to Jeb Bush was just devastating. And worse, it was funny because it was seen as right on.

"You could see that his comments got to Jeb Bush. The next day he put up ads with him running down the street with people following him. But it was too late. Everybody heard it and everybody, even Bush supporters, chuckled, and said, 'Nailed it. That's it.'

"So there you go. He summed up Jeb Bush in two words in two seconds in a way that none of the other fifteen guys would have even thought about. *Bam*. There goes your front-runner with his millions of dollars of establishment, insider-donor money. Gone."

WAR WITH THE RNC

The Republican National Convention, held at the Quicken Loans Arena in Cleveland, Ohio, from July 18 to 21, 2016, had all of the masterful Trump technique going for it. There was the staging, the lighting, the colors, the timing, the camera angles. Trump, the showman, knew how to work a brand and how to make it fit into a television screen. He knew how to make his brands visible and remembered. He knew how to use words and color and fonts.

Each night had a successive theme. Make America Safe Again. Make America Work Again. Make America First Again. Make America One Again. And, of course, all of it under the ubiquitous brand umbrella of MAGA, Make America Great Again.

Melania, Don Jr., Ivanka, Eric, and Tiffany would all give speeches. Ivanka would introduce her father. The Trump family, in all its beauty and intellect, was on full display.

"We had national exposure from *The Apprentice*," Don Trump Jr. says. "But from that I had the best of both worlds. I could put on a suit and take advantage of being recognized, being the celebrity, then I could put on a pair of jeans and run around unnoticed.

"After the speech, there was a lot of attention. Rudy Giuliani got on *Meet the Press* and said, 'That guy's gotta run for office. He should run for governor or mayor of New York.' Rachel Maddow said something to the effect, 'I have no words.' Which is about as good as I'm going to get from her.

"All of this helped me as a surrogate leading up to the election. After the speech, I had a newfound strength to help in a more profound way. That's when I started getting crowds."

The convention was one thing; the Republican Party was something altogether different. Donald Trump had won the nomination. He had been given his convention, to run as he pleased as the nominee but the Grand Old Party, the GOP, the elected officials and their staff, and the party infrastructure had their own interests to protect. State chairmen and county chairmen were threatened by new participants who were flooding their precinct meetings and their state conventions. New people sometimes translated into new party chairmen. They had not been able to stop the Trump juggernaut, but they were fully prepared to protect their turf, to survive his political tsunami and come back to power when this wave had passed over them and was gone.

"The convention was one thing," Don Trump Jr. remembers. "The relationship with the Republican National Committee was a different one. That relationship now is incredibly good. But at the time of the convention and really up through the election itself there was a feeling within the RNC that, 'Okay we lost this one. We will do better in four years. Let's just chalk this up as a loss.'"

They were utterly convinced that Donald Trump would lose the election.

"I experienced this firsthand in fundraising," Don says. "I asked them to give me their top five hundred donors.

"They said, 'Seriously? Now why would we do that?'

"I said, 'Why do you think? I'm going to call them all and raise money for the campaign.'

"'No, no, no,' they said. 'Susie Smith from the RNC is going to call them.'

"'Well, I don't know who Susie Smith is, but my guess is that I can do better. I can tell you one thing. When their assistant says—"Donald Trump Jr. is on the line for you"—they are going to take the call. They're probably not going to take the call from Susie Smith.'

"There was a real reluctance on their part working with us. They had relationships for years with people who they were cultivating to be the next leaders of the Republican Party, and we had interrupted that process and those plans. Here was this brash guy from New York without the best conservative track record in history. He comes in and runs against the most powerful political families in history, the Bushes and then the Clintons. This was so unexpected.

"As it turns out, as we would learn with time, these political experts in Washington were all delusional. The most incompetent of all were in fear of being found out. So there was no rush to admit any of that. Bottom line? There was a real reluctance to help us.

"So I brought in a couple of my friends and we just accepted that they were not going to share with us the RNC database and we put together our own lists and started making our own phone calls. These were some of my old hunting buddies, oil and gas businessmen. They weren't all that political. But we started raising money for the campaign on our own. Just from friends.

"It wasn't long before we were raising some real dollars, rivaling what they were doing at the RNC and topping some records from prior elections.

"So suddenly there was this reckoning. We started getting calls from the RNC wanting our list. They were wanting to tap into the new Trump donors to get money for their Senate and congressional races.

"I wouldn't say that they were all thrilled with us winning the nomination. There were people there that were happy with us and plenty that were not. Now we have a new team in there. Ronna Romney McDaniel is the RNC chairperson and she is doing a good job. And the Republican Party is beginning to learn how to fight back.

"They used to hear the media and the Democrats call them racist for no reason at all and they would just sit back and not respond and say well, we just have to take a loss on that. Trump fights back and answers his critics. The RNC is beginning to get that. They are beginning to understand that they are a voice for millions of Americans, but not if they don't speak up.

"When you have a track record like we have and yet you get 93 percent bad press, it's an uphill battle every day.

"On paper, 2020 should be over now. But it's not because it's not a fair fight. Media is against you. Pop culture and Hollywood are against you, academia is against you, the moneymaking elites in the establishment are against you. So it's not a level playing field. We are fighting an uphill battle.

"For decades the Left has used aggressive tactics against the conservatives, and now you have someone pushing back on the Left and they can't handle it. Republicans were a bit surprised by the truthfulness of Donald Trump and they were startled. And some said, 'Wait a minute, you mean you can actually win with this? Just answer back and tell the truth?'"

★ 5 ★

ERIC TRUMP AND THE JOURNEY TO TRUMP TOWER

"Somebody's got to tell the truth about all of this.
It is really a very special story."
—ERIC TRUMP[1]

O n March 5, 2019, I took the Amtrak Acela Express from Union Station in Washington, DC, to Penn Station in New York City. I had been interviewing Eric Trump by phone, and he had invited me up to Trump Tower to meet other members of the family and to get a tour at the center of the family business enterprise. If I was going to reconstruct some of the more studied moments of the campaign, including the drama of Election Night, it would be helpful to get the lay of the land.

"It's so interesting," Eric told me over the phone. "You have every joker in the world coming out with stories that are boosting the author's own self-importance or are simply inaccurate. It literally makes me laugh. Some of these people weren't even there. Some were, but they did not play the roles they said they were playing. Some didn't give the advice they claimed, and some of them spent time doing more harm than good. Then, all of a sudden, here is a book with them taking credit for winning the election! It's actually flabbergasting."

Eric Trump was obviously frustrated. "If you are willing to do this and get this right, this is a story that is unmatched in political history. There has never been an account from my father, or members of the family; you have the opportunity to get this right and do something that is very special."

Trump Tower is a New York skyscraper that houses private residences, offices, restaurants, and retail shops. It also has numerous floors sealed off from the public. This includes the president's private residence as well as the Trump Organization's offices.

As instructed by phone, I walked across the famous gold and brass lobby to a stand by the elevator, where a kindly, trim attendant was waiting. He immediately recognized my name, which actually surprised me. I suppose I was expecting an argumentative, hostile security person, who would scowl at my driver's license, like the Secret Service at the White House. A high school band was playing in the foyer, just across from the famous golden escalator where Donald and Melania Trump had coasted down to his presidential announcement ceremony. Almost immediately, a cheerful young lady appeared. It was Kim Benza, Eric's assistant, and she accompanied me on the fast ride up to the twenty-fifth floor.

When the elevator doors opened we faced a counter in front of a black wall with the golden words THE TRUMP ORGANIZATION dramatically spread out across its length.

I was ushered into a waiting room, no doubt one designed for clients and visitors, to soften them up for the business deal that was coming. A Secret Service agent lingered there, and we got into a conversation while I waited. He was obviously assigned to the Trump children, and I had written the book on the subject of presidential children, so we knew many of the same people and were soon exchanging stories.

The walls in this waiting room showcased dramatic pictures of Trump properties around the world, including some of the buildings that Ivanka had described in her conversations with me. But the gaze of any visitor was inevitably drawn to a north wall of windows looking out onto a spectacular view of New York City. One could look down on the canyons of other skyscrapers and then beyond them to the lush green of Central Park. It was a cold but sunny day.

From this vantage point one could easily understand why Donald Trump eventually had to buy the Plaza Hotel. That famous property sat like a toy model on display just below. It must have been a persistent temptation for years to the billionaire businessman before he finally pulled the trigger and bought it in 1988, announcing to the *New York Times* that "I haven't purchased a building, I have purchased a masterpiece—the *Mona Lisa*."[2]

Trump would tell me in a subsequent interview that it was best to buy a poorly managed business because then you could improve on it and sell it at a profit. Conversely, he explained, one should never buy an expertly run enterprise, because if you can't improve on it you may end up selling it at a loss. This, he insisted, was why he had become president of the United States at the perfect time in history. In Trump's assessment George W. Bush and Barack Obama had driven the country into economic ruin. Fortunately, for him, it made his economic recovery all the more spectacular. But in the case of the Plaza Hotel, now sitting like a dollhouse below me, most believed that Donald Trump had overpaid for the place, spending $850 million in today's money.

Ironically, Trump must have gazed down on the Plaza Hotel every day, tormented by its fame, telling his children and visitors that the Mills Brothers performed there throughout the 1930s. Truman Capote once threw a party there. Liza Minnelli lived there. Miles Davis performed on its ballroom stage. This was where the Beatles stayed when they visited America. This was the hotel they used for the movie *Home Alone 2*. As the proud new buyer, Donald Trump would have embraced its illustrious history, never knowing at the time that in fact he himself would now become its most famous connection. Long after the names of its many celebrated residents had passed from memory, buyers and sellers would forever say, "Donald Trump, the forty-fifth president of the United States, once owned this hotel."

"Much of what you see in the hotel today," Eric would tell me, "from the chandeliers that still hang in all the spaces, to the lobby, were all put in by my father and mother. Their fingerprints are all over the fabric of this iconic building."

By the mid-1990s, his lust for the property sufficiently sated, Donald Trump sold his "*Mona Lisa*" to an assortment of outside investors. Now it still sits below the windows of his tower, no longer a temptation, more like a trophy from an earlier chapter in his life.

ERIC TRUMP ON WHY HIS FATHER RAN FOR PRESIDENT

Eric Trump was born January 6, 1984. At thirty-five years of age, he is the third child, after Don Jr. and Ivanka. He is already one of America's savviest young businessmen, serving as a trustee and vice president of the Trump Organization, running all its hotels, golf properties, commercial and residential buildings, retail spaces, and private estates and the Trump Winery.

Eric has amassed a $300 million net worth on his way to becoming one of New York's most famous and generous philanthropists, a favorite charity being the Saint Jude Children's Hospital in Memphis, Tennessee. There he built the ICU and surgery unit that houses the sickest children on the planet, and it bears the name of the Eric Trump Foundation.

Eric is one of the most personable members of the family, dynamic and a bundle of energy. He is also the tallest Trump, at least for now, standing in at six feet, five inches. His younger brother, Barron, a son from the marriage of Donald and Melania, is only thirteen years of age and is already pushing the numbers skyward. By the time I finish this book, Barron may stand taller than any of them.

My conversations with Eric had begun the month before I made the trip to Trump Tower. I had asked him why he thought his father had finally decided to run for president.

"For years, I could see that my father was very frustrated with politicians in the United States," he said. "He would read a story in the newspaper and he would just roll his eyes. And I don't mean to put all of this on Barack Obama; he was just as frustrated with some of the policies and mistakes made by George W. Bush.

"This frustration was especially evident when Obama gave $150 billion to Iran, including $1.7 billion in cash. I can still see him sitting there reading a newspaper. He was shaking his head and saying, 'What the hell are our politicians doing? What are these stupid people doing? This country doesn't like America, they do not care about our people, they hate our way of life. What do you think is going to happen to the money?'

"Remember, my dad is a builder. He would often look at the problems in America from that perspective. We have bridges that are collapsing. Our highways are falling apart. Our airports were once the best in the world and now they are terrible. Our politicians are squandering away our country's money and doing nothing to fix our own nation.

"La Guardia Airport, for example, is a joke. They have garbage cans under collapsed ceiling tiles that have been there for five years, all because they are not willing to fix the roof. It would drive my father, and all of us, to be honest, crazy.

"We have major drug problems.

"We have these endless wars that we weren't winning, because our politicians handcuffed our great troops.

"The economy wasn't growing. We had stagnation of wages for sixteen years, and under Obama we had the slowest recovery since the Great Depression.

"I remember my father shaking his head, knowing that our educational system was ranked thirtieth in the world. He took it personally. What were these people doing? What was going on?

"I remember him watching CBS *Sixty Minutes* one night, and they did a segment on how our nuclear program had deteriorated. They were talking about unusable missiles and our depleted nuclear arsenal. He was just amazed that the US government was allowing journalists from *Sixty Minutes* to go into the nation's silos to show the world how vulnerable we were.

"Sometimes he would read stories in the newspaper and would literally shake his head in frustration.

"Doug, this is what made my father run for president of the United States. He didn't run for president just because he wanted to be president. He did not do it because he wanted to give up an amazing life. He knew no one had the backbone to do what was needed to fix the nonsense that he was reading about every single day. He also knew he was going to shake up the swamp. He was going to make certain politicians very angry, many of the same people who benefit from all of the problems created in Washington, DC. He was using his own money. He did not need lobbyists and the politically connected. He made them all powerless."

"Well," I said, "he surely didn't have to run. And if he had talked about it for such a long time, as you say, then he had to have been told and he had to have known how traumatic, how devastating, it would be. The criticism. The hostility. Even under normal circumstances, let alone with the idea that he was going to change things in a big way."

"I've said it a million times," Eric answered. "This is a guy that didn't need to run for president. He had every politician seeking his favor. He could do any deal he wanted to do around the world. He had freedom. He wasn't getting hit from investigations, political harassment, fake news like he is now. He was the last guy that needed to do this."

I wondered why he hadn't run for president before, and Eric thought it had a lot to do with the maturation of the second generation of the Trump Organization.

"It is obvious that he was frustrated. For a very long time, but he was primarily a businessman, and the company was his primary responsibility. I think he hoped some political figure would step forward who would actually have common sense and backbone. At that point, Don, Ivanka, and I were not ready to take on the responsibility of the Trump Organization. In 2016, we were, and all the stars aligned. That was part of it."

It became apparent that the run for president would not only be a journey for Donald Trump, it would also a moment that involved the whole family.

"I want to put this thing in context," Eric Trump said. "It wasn't an easy decision. I remember being in the office when NBC was offering hundreds of millions of dollars to do seasons fifteen and sixteen of *The Apprentice*. They wanted to sign him and all of us for another two or three years. We were all part of the show at that point, and it was a tremendous success. I remember him looking at the executives who were in the meeting saying, 'You know what, I am not willing to do this right now.' By the look on their faces, it was clear that it was the first time they had ever been rejected when that kind of money was on the table.

"Very soon after the meeting with NBC, we had the famous family meeting in Trump Tower. I will never forget him saying, 'Kids, let's give this a go, I am going to do this!'" Obviously that started the whole thing. 'He could say, 'I've made billions of dollars in my life. I've succeeded at everything I have ever done and I am going to jump into it.'"

SO WHAT'S A CAUCUS?
"When we started out we had no one, Doug; we had no one that believed in him. We had no one that believed in the family. When he gave that speech, day one, at Trump Tower, we were there, standing right next to him, as he announced for the presidency. And soon we would be out there fighting in every state.

"We spoke at all the caucuses. And this is funny—no one knew what caucuses were. I remember driving to our first caucus location in our first state of Iowa. I asked the political team, 'Guys what the hell is a caucus?' This is not something we did as a family. We built hotels, residential buildings. We know operations, management and business. The political world was brand new to all of us.

"They said, 'Well, you are going to be speaking at a large high school in Sioux City.' It is the biggest series of gyms I have ever seen in my life, with overflow cafeterias and other assembly rooms, all filled with people.

"They continued, 'It is going to be you, and candidates or representatives from every campaign: Jeb Bush's campaign manager, Ted Cruz's comms director, candidates themselves. You are going to have exactly five minutes, not a second more, because they will cut you off. You are going to pitch your candidate and they will be pitching theirs.'

"As it turns out, I ran from gym to gym, room to room, talking about why I thought my father would do an incredible job and why he was in the fight and why the country needed him. We knew nothing about politics at that point, but we were humans. We represented family and love. America could read through the others. Paid campaign operatives. Paid politicians.

"We were just getting started. We had not won anything yet. But the movement was beginning. It was incredible. The whole thing was incredible.

"The passion we were seeing in the states was amazing. Ted Cruz, who spent many years of his life preparing for that moment, went on to beat us in Iowa, but the engines were ignited and the momentum at our backs was indescribable. People were fed up with politics. They wanted results. And that core base would grow into a national movement.

"As it turned out, just before the Iowa caucuses reporters accused the Ted Cruz campaign of calling caucus goers and telling them that Ben Carson was dropping out. Carson was splitting the Cruz vote, so that little political play helped him win. But we were off and running." In the following weeks, candidate Trump would go on to secure the Republican nomination in New Hampshire, South Carolina, and Nevada. From that point on, the campaign proceeded full steam ahead, never looking back.

"I had a similar experience in Nevada. I went to speak at one of the caucuses and wasn't even able to make it into the assembly room. There was a line, maybe five hundred yards long, four to five people wide, and as I was walking in, I was immediately noticed. I took a picture with every single person in that line, half of which were wearing Make America Great Again hats. And virtually all of them were saying that they were honored to be voting for my father. I took pictures for almost three hours that night the entire time, thinking that this movement was unstoppable.

"I remember my father calling me as I was on my way home, to meet him at Trump International Hotel and Tower Las Vegas. He asked how it felt. And I said 'Pop, I don't know how we don't win this by a large margin.' I told him the story and that I didn't even have the chance to address the masses. He said, 'What do you mean you didn't talk?'

"I said, 'I got cornered by the crowd. I ended up taking selfies with every single person on the way into the place. The enthusiasm was incredible, and honestly I was more effective at just taking selfies and talking to people and saying hi to the kids. People were giving me hugs.'

"Over and over people were saying, 'I'm praying for you. Praying for the family. We need him.' The enthusiasm was just different. It was at a different level.

"As the Trump movement emerged, I quickly realized how desperate America was for somebody who wasn't a politician, who was somebody unconventional, maybe somebody who was a little bit non-PC." Eric laughed, correcting himself, "No, *very* non-PC. They saw him as a fighter, and that whole kind of enthusiasm continued through to winning the Republican nomination and eventually culminating on Election Day."

CHOOSING MIKE PENCE: THE REAL STORY

In July 2019, new books and online reports promoted insider stories about how Donald Trump had picked Mike Pence as his running mate. At the time, I was editing parts of this book with Eric Trump. He asked about the Mike Pence story. Eric had been frustrated by so many false accounts. He had been there. He knew what had happened, but somehow, with all the hours of interviews and editing, his remarkable story had ended up on the cutting room floor.

With the rash of new books and false theories, there were urgent reasons to write about it. One story declared that "Trump was manipulated by staffers into picking Mike Pence as his running mate."[3] It was Karl Rove, the theory insisted. It recounted conversations between Trump and Rove, saying that the political pundit had been the catalyst.[4] I knew Donald Trump and I knew Karl Rove and I knew the story was false. Another theory, from the same book, claimed that White House staffer Kellyanne Conway allegedly told Pence, 'I'm going to make sure you get it.'"[5]

Still another article claimed that Trump's campaign manager Paul Manafort had tricked Trump into thinking that his airplane had mechanical problems. It had all been a setup, to keep Trump stranded in Indianapolis, where Pence could seal the deal.[6]

So in between exhausting edits, I prevailed on Eric Trump to tell me, one more time, how in 2016, Donald Trump had actually selected Mike Pence as his running mate. What had really happened? His story didn't disappoint.

"My father and I were at a campaign event near Westfield, Indiana," Eric Trump said. "Governor Mike Pence and his wife, Karen, were with us. Governor Pence was introducing my father at the rally. We got word that one of the tires on the Trump plane had been damaged when we had landed. It had been apparently cut by a piece of metal on the runway. It would have to be changed and we would have to stay for the night.

"After the rally, the campaign booked us into the Conrad Hotel in Indianapolis. Mike and Karen invited us to dinner. That night, the four of us, Mike and Karen Pence and my father and I, went to a back room of the Capital Grille, right in the hotel. There was nothing we could do. So it was an unexpected break, a brief moment to relax in the middle of a marathon campaign. I can tell you that there was great conversation that night. I know my father, and I could tell that he and Pence were on the same page. When we got back to the hotel corridor, outside our rooms, my father pulled me aside and told me to call Don, Jared, and Ivanka and get them out to Indiana right away."

The next morning the media was all over the story. The Trump family had breakfast at the governor's mansion. Later, media reports would say that Melania weighed in when they got back to New York City. She thought that Pence offered good balance to the ticket. Another member of the family suggested that days later the candidate and Pence had bonded on the golf course at Bedminster. But the first indication that lightning had struck came that night at the steak house in Indianapolis. There, at a dinner with Mike and Karen Pence and his son Eric Trump, the candidate had checked off all the boxes. It was an intimate discussion.

"I knew that it was going to happen," Eric Trump said, "when my father whispered in the hallway of the hotel, 'Get Don and Jared and Ivanka on the next plane out here.'

"If there had not been that piece of metal on the runway, Mike Pence may not have been his running mate or vice president of the United States. Sometimes, things happen for a reason."

NO ONE ELSE FIGHTING ALONGSIDE US

Heading into the general election with Hillary Clinton, the Trump family was hearing the conventional wisdom that they were going to lose. They had to brace themselves, steady themselves emotionally. And yet they had to project optimism if they were going to have any chance of winning. I asked Eric how he juggled those feelings.

"It wasn't so much personal emotion about losing or not losing," Eric said. "It was more confusion between what I was seeing with my own eyes out on the campaign trail and what I was seeing on television when I got home. And as far as the emotion? It was easier and happier to be in those swing states fighting and seeing the love and support than it was to come back to New York City and turn on the television.

"Don, Lara, and I literally crisscrossed every town in Iowa, Ohio, New Hampshire, Nevada, Florida, Maine, and Pennsylvania. We spent eighteen months in thirteen swing states talking to every factory worker and concerned citizen. And the reception that we were getting at these places was incredible. We would be in the middle of a very quaint part of rural Iowa and we would have one thousand people show up to see us. It was pretty remarkable, but we had no one else fighting alongside us. The media called the campaign a joke, and the political elites dismissed us, but the movement was very real, as they would soon come to find out."

It was interesting to hear Eric talk about the loneliness of the political process, his sense that the family was on their own. After Trump won the nomination, there were other major Republican figures who traveled with the candidate and were part of his entourage. New Jersey governor Chris Christie, Alabama senator Jeff Sessions, the Republican National Committee chairman Reince Priebus, General Mike Flynn, and former New York City mayor Rudolph Giuliani come to mind. Governor Mike Pence was demonstratively loyal and was out on the campaign trail himself. Of course, there were layers of iconic and diverse Trump friends that went back for years, from Keith Schiller to the televangelist Paula White. But much of the hired staff, from Steve Bannon to Kellyanne Conway, Bill Stepien, David Bossie, and, earlier, Corey Lewandowski, were not there when everything was in doubt. Almost all of them came later, after Trump had won the big primary states. They came after Trump had essentially won the nomination. Until that time, most of them were still hedging their bets. Eric Trump was surely revealing how it must have felt to be inside the Trump family bubble running for president in early 2016.

It is likely that the sense of loneliness the Trump family was experiencing in the campaign was something that all political families have felt in their quest for power. It was probably shared by the Kennedys and the Bushes and the Clintons. And yet, I had been on the trail with George W. Bush, during his father's campaign. We had flown in commercial aircraft and private jets, ridden in car caravans, coaches, and Winnebagos. We had stayed in nice hotels and fleabag motels. We went days with little or no food, from one radio interview to the next. There was never a sense of abandonment. The Republican Party—indeed, half of the nation—was behind us. What Eric Trump was talking about was different.

"There are five living US presidents," the Clinton campaign bragged. "None of them support Donald Trump."[7] I could see how it must have felt lonely.

Yet when I traveled for Bush, there was none of the enthusiasm that Eric Trump described. There were never convention centers, spontaneously full of thousands of people waiting to see the candidate—with thousands more standing in line outside. There weren't barns across the Midwest with BUSH painted on the side. I had traveled on campaign trips with Ronald Reagan and had not seen that. The Trump family was leading a revolution. They were trying to make America great again. It meant making powerful people less powerful and poor people less poor. Did such a process provoke enemies? Certainly. Did it seem lonely from the inside? Sure. I could see that. But if they succeeded, some of the people who were now outside would be in, and some of the people who were now inside would be out. It was a struggle.

WIN OR LOSE? WHICH NARRATIVE DID YOU BELIEVE?

In the last days of the 2016 presidential campaign, there were two very distinct narratives inside the Trump family. Brad Parscale, the campaign's digital director, had numbers showing them winning the election. But almost all of the national polls continued to show them losing, and losing decisively.

"We certainly heard both narratives," Eric Trump said. "There is no denying that.

"One thing that needs to be in the book is that the morning of the election the *New York Times* had a graph showing my father's likelihood of winning at fifteen percent.[8]

"I remember that we saw polls of him losing Pennsylvania by a wide margin. Now, you have to understand, we had practically lived in Pennsylvania for eighteen months. I think I visited every single town in the state.

"Driving across the state was like immersing yourself into Trump country. You would see a barn and you would see the entire side painted TRUMP. I can't tell you how many times I pulled off the side of the road and I went into one of those houses, and I would just say that I was driving by and saw the barn and wanted to say thank you. Just to tell them that what they had done meant the world to our family. By the way, you never saw that reciprocal on the other side. There were no barns painted HILLARY.

"There were sides of delis or hardware stores in the small little towns. Sometimes brick walls were painted TRUMP MAKE AMERICA GREAT AGAIN. This wouldn't be a three-by-three sign. This would be an entire side of the building. Maybe sixty feet long and thirty feet high. Somebody was up there with a ladder and probably put in a week's worth of work because they loved my father and because they loved his message. It was the very thing all other candidates lacked.

"I was in a little town in Ohio. We had heard that the owner of an eyeglass store happened to be our biggest fan and I had to stop by and say hi.

"Well, he called his neighbor and all of a sudden we had twenty people in the store and then thirty. I went out into the street and everyone was calling their friends. As we walked the five blocks that encompassed the entire town, I will never forget arriving at a hardware store, situated exactly across from the fire station. By that point, I had over a thousand people, the entire town showed up. The streets were blocked. People were cheering. I would not have guessed that that many people lived in that area. The support was unbelievable. How do you explain that to a pollster?

"It would never make sense to us, Doug. I would be in Iowa or Pennsylvania, driving down the road and I would see one hundred Trump signs to every Hillary sign."

"So, what was your personal life like during this time? Where did you eat? Where did you sleep?" I asked.

"My wife and I were on the road every single day," Eric recalled. "We would come home, spend half a day together on Sunday, and then grab a bag and repack and go back out to our assigned swing states until we saw each other again the next Sunday.

"I was kind of quasi-depressed, and I use the word 'depressed' loosely, but I would be looking up at the TV and see the stories on CNN saying that Trump is down in Pennsylvania. I'm thinking, 'I just spent six days in Pennsylvania, and everywhere I went I would have one thousand people turn out for me, and I wasn't even the candidate.'

"They would say, 'Trump is losing in Ohio.' I'd be sitting there thinking, 'There is just no way we are going to lose Ohio. There's just no way. They're wrong.'

"They would say, 'Michigan is safe for Hillary. Trump is going nowhere in Michigan. Michigan is done.'

"But we would see wild enthusiasm. We had members from the United Auto Workers come up to us, and they would say, 'Eric, I have voted Democratic all my life. Every election. And I always, always vote. I voted twice for Obama. But we are voting for your father. All of us. Everybody you see here is voting Trump. But don't tell our leaders.

"I'd go to another plant and the workers would say the same thing. 'You realize that we are one hundred percent behind your father. Everybody here. One hundred percent.'

"Others would say, 'We have seen all of these plants close and go overseas. We are sick of it. We are with you.'

"I would say, 'Well, look, I know you are union leaders and you have obligations.'

"And they would say, 'No, no, the rank and file are completely behind you. Everyone you see here is voting Trump. These are tough guys. No one tells them what to do.'

"Others told us, 'Our guys at the top don't even try to get us to do what they want anymore. We would throw the bums out. They tell their Democratic bosses what they have to say to keep them happy but we all do what we want.'

"It didn't surprise me to hear on Election Day that the media was getting bad exit polling data. Some people were telling the exit poll surveys that they were voting for Hillary but they had pulled the lever for my father.

"There would be stories saying that Trump cannot carry Florida. And I remember watching Senator Tim Kaine, Hillary Clinton's vice presidential running mate, having an event in West Palm Beach. I had my own event nearby. I jumped in a car and quietly drive past his event so I could see it for myself. It looked like there were fifty or sixty people, including his staffers and others. Yet the nation was being told Hillary was winning. It did not fit the narrative being spewed on CNN or in the *Washington Post*. It was totally dishonest.

"It just did not make sense. I was going to these small towns with shut-down factories, and there would be hundreds of people turning up, yet the Democratic vice presidential candidate goes to an event in a heavily populated Palm Beach County and no one shows up. They had no enthusiasm."

A POLLING CONSPIRACY?

Eric Trump grew frustrated with the talking heads, the television pundits who were commenting on the political campaign. NBC and MSNBC operated out of Rockefeller Center. CNN studios were up on Columbus Circle.

"You listen to the pundits, preaching from Rockefeller Center, preaching from Lincoln Center or Columbus Circle. They were telling audiences that the American people didn't really understand Donald

Trump and he didn't understand them. And I'm thinking, 'This is kind of odd, because I just had one thousand people show up for me in Michigan and I'm not even the candidate. I'm actually a guy that wants nothing to do with politics. My only role is that of a son and a surrogate doing everything humanly possible to make sure this guy wins.' So, for me, it was a strange disconnect.

"Let me give you one other story that I think is meaningful. Go back and you will find an ABC–*Washington Post* poll, only a couple of weeks before the election.[9] And it said we were down twelve percent. It ended up becoming one of the most famous polls of the whole campaign. Everybody hopped on it and said, 'Look, Trump is down, there is zero chance he is winning.' Well, I am a numbers guy, that's what I do in life. I work numbers. So I would always read the backup explanations in a poll. I would study the sample sets.

"So after this poll, Kellyanne and I went over to ABC we met with James Goldston, president of ABC News. George Stephanopoulos and John Karl were there, as well as John Santucci and some others. And our message was basically, 'Your poll is b— s—.' Pardon the language. We said, 'It is absolutely garbage.'"

George Stephanopoulos had worked on the Bill Clinton presidential campaign of 1992, serving as communications director and later on senior staff in the White House. He was a star of the 1993 Clinton movie documentary, *The War Room*. And Trump was now pitted against Bill Clinton's wife, Hillary, in a national campaign for the presidency. Eric Trump was making the point that George Stephanopoulos was hardly an objective authority to be commenting on the election.

"They are all looking back at us like we are crazy. What are we even doing there? They were all looking at us like we were out of our minds. There's no chance you can win.

"Kellyanne and I said to the group, 'Your poll is b— s—. First of all, you're oversampling Democrats by eleven percent. D plus eleven. Go look at the backup. Your poll sampling is D plus eleven. If you move to D plus two or D plus three, we win the election. But you are sampling

D plus eleven. And you've got twice as many African American voters voting for Hillary as voted for Barack Obama in 2008. You have twice as many college-educated women voting in your poll than actually exist in the United States. That would be the result if you were to extrapolate out the numbers.'

"So, Kellyanne and I went through the poll, point by point. In their on air-discussions they weren't disclosing this subset information to the American people; they weren't telling their viewers that they had oversampled Democrats by almost eleven percent, that they had two times the amount of African Americans voting for Hillary than voted for Obama."

In the end, when the final numbers came in, the Republican candidate, Donald Trump, would win a higher percentage of votes among African Americans and Hispanics in 2016 than the Republican candidate, Mitt Romney, won in his 2012 presidential election. The network polls were off.

"You have to wonder," Eric continued. "Were they trying to rig the election? Were they trying to push it in the direction they wanted? Encourage Clinton voters to turn out? Suppress Trump voters by convincing them that it was a lost cause, that their vote wouldn't make a difference?

"So James Goldston says to me, 'What do you think is going to happen?'

"And I tell him, 'I think we are going to win.'

"He says, 'And why do you think that?'

"And I tell him what I told you. What I am seeing all across the Midwest and the South. You could drive an hour west of New York City and see Trump signs all over the farms and little towns across Pennsylvania. I told him what Lara was seeing, what Don was seeing, what Jared and Ivanka were seeing.

"'I'll tell you what,' I offered. 'If we lose, I will take you out to a steak dinner anywhere you want to go. Just a gentlemen's agreement. And if we win, you take us out.'

"By the way, they still owe me a steak dinner. I remind John Karl and Santucci about this any chance I get. It has become a friendly joke.

"All you needed to do is take a dive into the damn numbers in the background, which any human being could do.

"So Sunday, George Stephanopoulos has me on his television show. You can probably find it on YouTube. And now in retrospect, with what we know eventually happened, it's really an embarrassment for ABC and the *Washington Post*. I was so passionate that day. His very first question was about the poll.

"'Well, we have you down by twelve percent,' he said.[10]

"I told them it was a nonsense poll and that they were going to get it wrong. And they did, because they lacked objectivity and refused to understand the true sentiment of this country. What we were hearing was a very different message from what they reported on their shows every night. The facts did not matter to the media. Their narrative was everything. Most of our nation's media sits in an ivory tower on one coast or the other. We were living in the cities and towns all across the country, and the picture was very different."

WHEN THE VOTERS LIE

The television networks and the commentators claimed that they miscalled the 2016 election because voters had lied to them in surveys and exit polls. I asked Eric if there was any truth to this theory. He told me a story about an early primary poll, taken in Florida, when Donald Trump was in a showdown with Texas senator Ted Cruz and Florida senator Marco Rubio.

"We saw that the numbers didn't seem to be adding up in Florida, so we polled ten thousand people on our own. We polled some of them by email, some by using a human phone operator, and some using an automated phone system. It was set up so you could press one if you wanted to vote for Trump, press two if you wanted to vote for Cruz, three if you wanted to vote for Rubio. Obviously all of those would be alternated in the next phone call so they would press one if they wanted Cruz. So the poll would be truly objective.

"Anyway, what we found was really interesting. We found a thirteen-percent discrepancy between a human being calling up and saying, 'Who are you voting for, Trump, Rubio, or Cruz?' versus when we used an automated machine to call up people on our list. Think of that? There was a thirteen percent difference.

"Then we finally got the results of our email poll and it showed the exact same thing. Once again, there was exactly a thirteen percent difference between our email poll and the poll conducted by phone with a human operator. Not twelve, not fourteen percent, exactly the same number. Thirteen percent.

"Looking back on that experience, I suspect that as we approached the general election, the national media was missing this dynamic. On the one hand, they were openly shaming Trump supporters, and then on the other hand, they were asking people to tell them who they were going to vote for. And the people were answering back politely, like schoolchildren wanting to get a good grade, telling the teacher what she wanted to hear.

"So, first, I do not believe they were actually calling a fair representation of Republicans. Second, a lot of people weren't picking up their phones. Third, there were a hell of a lot of people that were hanging up on them. And finally, there were a lot of people that were just being polite to the pollsters, telling them what they thought they wanted.

"It was this latter category that made the exit polls even harder to measure. People were coming out of their polling booths and lying about what they had done. And the networks made a big deal out of that. Once again, it was all the voters' fault. They are 'deplorables' and some of them are also liars. But to be fair, that alone does not explain why the big newspapers and the television news networks got it so wrong. That's their business. That's why they exist. Reporting the national election is their Super Bowl.

"If their polls had given the Democrats a plus four or a plus three, I don't think anyone would have had an issue. But when they were running plus eleven, and not telling their television audiences what they were doing? When they were showing wacky numbers in states that we would later win by huge margins, well, they are smarter than that. They knew very well what they were doing."

THE PRESIDENT DOESN'T KNOW

At this point in our conversation, I pressed Eric Trump about what he thought was going on with the national media. Why did they march in lockstep? Why did almost every newspaper, every television network, every pollster, mindlessly insist on repeating the same thing, in tandem, at the same time? It seemed so intellectually suffocating. Such a narrow confine. How could such bright people be reduced to such servility?

Was it truly ideological? Was it related to tax percentages? Did they truly believe that one number was more moral than another? Surely not!

Was it the magnetic pull of a powerful, mutually prescribed cultural loyalty?

Was it just business survival? The bosses wanted it, so the anchors and pundits played along to curry favor? Paying the mortgage or keeping the yacht? Helped along by masters at the top, boards of directors, who made real money by steering the ship slightly this way or that, using regulations to build monopolies, smothering small-business competitors below? And did these owners-stockholders, television news advertisers, send signals to management, signals that were picked up and amplified by the more savvy corporate cogs and passed along unspoken? Was this a creature that was partly organic and partly strategic?

Eric Trump said, "I'm not a conspiracy theorist, but it is crystal clear that the media was in the pocket of Hillary's campaign. Stephanopoulos, for one, had worked for Bill and Hillary for years, and no one person watching the show on any given day could possibly say that he was not fully in their camp.

"I do think that there are people at the networks and newspapers who are smart enough to know that a poll oversampling Democrats by eleven percent is unfair and false.

"Are they smart enough to extrapolate out the numbers and realize that their samples are clearly skewed? Yes."

Conspiracies, of course, exist. Children conspire on the playground in the third grade. Ask Julius Caesar if conspiracies exist. There was that terrible moment when Nazi leaders met at Lake Wannsee in 1942 to decide the fate of the Jews of Europe, including some of the ancestors of Jared Kushner, the president's son-in-law. American prisons are full of persons who conspired to break laws.

In the closing months of the 2016 campaign, WikiLeaks released private emails that exposed the close relationship between the Clinton campaign and the American national media. Debate questions had been passed to Hillary Clinton in advance. And she had gratefully received them without public mention or protest. Reporters had submitted proposed articles to Clinton staffers for approval. Glenn Thrush of *Politico* emailed Clinton's campaign chairman, John Podesta. "Because I have become a hack," he wrote, "I will send u the whole section that pertains to u. Please don't share or tell anyone I did this. . . . Tell me if I fucked up anything."[11]

Others volunteered their services if the Clinton team wanted to make a point. "Please let me know if I can be of any service to you," wrote a *Huffington Post* contributor, Frank Islam, to John Podesta.[12]

Understandably, the media itself was embarrassed and alarmed by this unfolding story and quickly advanced the narrative that the leaked emails were, themselves, the real danger. It was a threat to a free press, they said. They needed to protect sources, and WikiLeaks had exposed some of them. Others insisted that the story amounted to an invasion of privacy. And then there was the idea that held that WikiLeaks had obtained its information from Russian government hackers. This amounted to Russian interference in an American election.[13]

Lost by the media's sleight of hand was what the emails themselves revealed and the degree of media collusion that had occurred with the Clinton campaign. In 2015, only days before Hillary Clinton had announced her candidacy for president, her campaign chairman, John Podesta, and her chief strategist, Joel Benenson, had hosted secret dinners and cocktail parties for media elites. ABC luminaries Diane Sawyer, David Muir, George Stephanopoulos, and Cecilia Vega had all agreed to attend. So had Norah O'Donnell of CBS News, Gloria Borger and John Berman of CNN, Rachel Maddow of MSNBC, and Savannah Guthrie of NBC. Of course, Maggie Haberman of the *New York Times* and Phil Griffin, the president of MSNBC, had replied yes.[14] As had many others.

Are "journalists too easily charmed by power, access, and creamy risotto?" asked the *Columbia Journalism Review*.[15]

When I raised the subject of a media conspiracy with Jared Kushner, the president's son-in-law, his eyebrows shot up and a grin slowly spread across his face. As I suspected, he was much too sensible to respond to such an idea. But he did offer a comment. "Have you ever noticed," he said, "not one single person ever got fired or lost their job for wrongly predicting the 2016 election? Not a single person. Not a pollster, not a programmer, not an editor, not a publisher or a producer, not an on-air anchor or contributor. No one. And that's what they do for a living. That's their job. They get paid to do that.

"And can you imagine how valuable such information would have been?

"Likewise, among the few who predicted it, nobody at the networks or anywhere else got any credit. They were despised for being right, just as Trump was despised for winning."

He said nothing more. He just smiled. They were all wrong, and none of them got fired.

President Trump himself wondered about all of this. I had led him into a discussion about the media and why there was such coordination, such as common talking points, among the networks in their ongoing attacks against him. Sometimes, multiple anchors on multiple platforms used the exact same words and sentences.

"I don't fully know why they are doing it," the president admitted to me. He looked genuinely curious but not bewildered, as though he had heard some theories postulated and was getting closer to a satisfactory explanation, at least for himself. So I just froze. I didn't say a word, hoping he would say more. And then finally, after an awkward silence, he just repeated, "I don't know why."

LARA TRUMP: "I CRIED ALL THE WAY"

"I think all of us hold out hope that the right thing will happen in the end. Maybe we will all be long gone but, eventually, we will be vindicated and validated."

—Lara Trump[1]

There was one recurring question that kept coming to me. It was never asked by the hostile media and never brought up by the sometimes Trump-friendly interviews during the evening on Fox News. You couldn't find the answer in any of the Bannon-fed books of Michael Wolf and Bob Woodward, nor in any of the books written by the hired help who had left Trump world to secure contracts to tell their stories. And that question was "How did it feel inside the Trump family?" Only the president and Trump's family members themselves could answer that question.

How did it feel when the polls said they were losing and they won anyway? How did it feel to enter the White House for the first time? Keep in mind that many in the Trump family had never even visited the White House as tourists. Some had seen it from the street only recently for the first time. How did it feel to see pundits on television insist that they were going to be indicted and sent to prison? That their father was a Russian spy? How did it feel to read things about themselves and their family that they knew to be false?

These were the questions I brought to Lara Lea Yunaska Trump, the beautiful, thirty-six-year-old wife of Eric Trump, as we sat in her office on the southwest corner on the fifteenth floor of Trump Tower. Through the windows there was a spectacular view of the city, with Fifth Avenue stretching out like a straight, slender arrow before finally disappearing into a steaming blur of skyscrapers in the distance.

"Well, it is very frustrating," she said. Lara was seated behind her desk. My iPhone was recording the conversation.

"I mean, first, foremost, I grew up in North Carolina. I come from a middle-class family. I was always taught that if you're a good person and you do the right thing then good things will happen to you. That has always been my mantra for life. It is something I still follow. I grew up going to Sunday school and church. I am a religious person in the sense that I want to go to heaven one day. I want to do good things for people.

"When my father-in-law decided to run for president, certainly he knew more than any of us that this was going to be challenging. He knew that they would write false stories or take things out of context and put things forward as their own narrative, but I don't think any of us knew fully what to expect. Certainly, for me, as an outsider, as someone who did not grow up in New York City, it was a shock. I didn't grow up in a family with a famous last name."

Lara Trump's baptism by fire came during an interview on the digital news network Bold TV in January 2019. The country was in the middle of the US government shutdown. She had been working with Angel Families, an organization that helps parents and children who have lost "loved ones at the hands of illegal alien criminals."[2] She was thinking of these families when the issue of the government shutdown was in the news.

"It's a little bit of pain," Lara had said, "but it's going to be for the future of our country and their children and their grandchildren and generations after them will thank them for their sacrifice."[3] Her comments were perfectly appropriate, but that one sentence, taken out of context, was a provocation. Trump's critics pounced. Joy Behar and Meghan McCain, stars of *The View*, compared her to Marie Antoinette. She was portrayed as a rich lady, with pearls, who had lunch with other high-society matrons, and who was out of touch with the masses.

"In reality," Lara said, "I grew up as a waitress having jobs where I worked for tips. Most of my family still lives paycheck to paycheck like the average American. So, for them to misconstrue that and make me out to be a person, clearly, that I'm not, is incredibly frustrating.

"Still, I think all of us hold out hope that the right thing will happen in the end. Maybe we will all be long gone but, eventually, we will be vindicated and validated.

"We can take some comfort in remembering what it felt like leading up to the election in 2016. People thought we were crazy and laughed at us for standing behind Donald Trump. We said that we believed he could be a great president. We were ridiculed nonstop. And then, wow, what a validation on November 8, 2016, when he shocked the world.

"So, when I go to bed at night, I know that I'm a good person. I know that I'm doing the right thing, fighting on the right side of history and doing what I truly, deep down in my heart, know is the right thing for the future of our country. I know it is the right thing for my son's future and for generations to come. So, while it is so frustrating and hurtful, and it's just not right what they do to all of us, I think we all know that we are doing the right thing. We all feel strongly that, one day, people who don't fully understand now or have been misinformed will get the truth, one day."

This was a recurring theme. I had picked it up from my interviews with the president, who was feeling embattled by a hostile news media. They seemed to wish him to fail, even when he was seeking to negotiate peace with a North Korean tyrant, on behalf of their own children and families. I had experienced the same sense, in a much different way, from Jared and Ivanka. Jared was sensitive to the idea of his voice being recorded. How could I be trusted? This was what Eric was saying, how they felt during the campaign, that they, the family, were all alone.

Ironically, the Trumps were surrounded by people. It had been that way for years. First there were those who wanted their money. Then their fame. Being in the Trump inner circle offered one an experience akin to what the Hindus call *darshan*. It allowed some of the magic to rub off. And now it had all vastly accelerated. Now it was all about power too. And yet, the bigger the crowds, the greater the needs of the people to be near the Trumps, the lonelier and more embattled it must have felt inside the family itself.

On the campaign trail, Donald Trump Jr. learned how to play on this celebrity. "I didn't just show up wherever my father was for the photo op. I decided pretty early on that the only place it didn't make sense for me to be was where my father was. He created such a vacuum. When he was there you really knew it. You didn't need anybody else. Anyone else was just extra.

"Unfortunately, that's what you usually find in a political campaign. People show up just to be in the photo op. I made sure I was out on the road, hitting the key states, all over the Rust Belt, hitting the smaller venues and smaller towns that my father couldn't get to. But also places that it didn't make sense for him to be, like college campuses."[4]

I said to Lara, "It must be very important, as a family, that you have each other."

"I'll say." She laughed. It was obvious. "I think the greatest thing we all have had throughout this entire process is one another. It has surprised many people that our family has not fractured in any way. We got into this as a family. We went through the whole campaign in 2016 as a family. And we are still today a very solid unit.

"It is because we all know the reality. Donald Trump didn't have to do this. He didn't need to be maligned and pushed around and accosted every single day. He did this because he really felt like he was the last hope for this country. And I think a lot of people would agree with that.

"So sure, having family, having one another when you get upset with things or something happens, to have a group text, to get a text from somebody saying, 'Don't worry about it, everybody knows the truth,' it's very helpful. Any family, I think, feels that way. You have one another. Sometimes, that's all that matters."

THE WAITRESS FROM WILMINGTON

Lara Lea Yunaska was born on October 12, 1982, in Wilmington, North Carolina. She grew up in a town nearby called Wrightsville Beach. Her parents still have the same home. The family attended the local United Methodist church. It was just Lara and a younger brother.

"My dad started a boat-building company in the eighties. He actually built Walter Cronkite's sailboat. That was his claim to fame. Then he started a car wash in Wilmington. He also developed commercial and residential properties. And my mom was an operating room nurse until my brother and I were probably five or six. Then she came home and took over the payroll and helped my dad run their business."

So, when did she work as a waitress?

"Oh, gosh. There were so many restaurants in Wilmington. I waited tables at my uncle Leon's restaurant. He had a Greek-southern fusion restaurant, if you can imagine that. So I know all about Greek food and, of course, southern food. Then, there is a restaurant called Brasserie du Soleil that I helped open in Wilmington. It's still quite popular and right by the beach. When I first moved to New York City, I was a waitress here right down in Rockefeller Center. I was also a bartender at several places. So I've had many jobs.

"It's interesting. I just tweeted something supporting my sister-in-law, which is another thing we do for each other. Ivanka was recently attacked by Alexandria Ocasio-Cortez, first saying that she would have no idea what it's like to have an hourly-wage job, which isn't true, and then attacking Ivanka's comment that people who aren't willing to work don't deserve a paycheck.

"I think it is terrible to try and make someone feel badly about their background. You don't get to choose the family you are born into. Now, you can choose what you do with your life. As a person who has worked for an hourly wage, I can tell you that most people want to work in this country. They don't want a handout. They want to feel pride for being able to take care of their family and take care of themselves."

So, how did she become a Trump?

"Eric and I met eleven years ago this month.

"I had followed the rules. I did what I was supposed to do. Went to college. Got good grades. But when I graduated there was just no job market. Nothing. It was a very hard time. I was a waitress in a restaurant, working, like so many, for tip money. I also worked part time as a personal trainer. I thought, 'Hey, I went through all of this, doing everything they told me to do to be successful, and after all of those many years and all of that disciplined work, this is it?'

"There had to be something more than this.

"Well, I was very interested in cooking and I thought, 'I have to see what's out there past North Carolina,' so I applied to the French Culinary Institute, which was in New York City, down in SoHo. Understand, I didn't know a single person in New York. Nobody. My parents thought I was crazy.

"I cried the whole drive from North Carolina to New York City. It was so scary. What had I done? What was going to happen to me now? Was I leaving behind dreams that would never happen? Was it all a waste? Was I supposed to get married and have a good life in North Carolina? Now I was just driving into the darkness, utterly alone, with nothing to show for all my work.

"Eventually, I got settled in the city. One night, my roommate had a friend in town and wanted to go out. I was in pajama sweatpants and was going to stay in and watch movies, but she begged me to go with her. So, reluctantly, I agreed."

And she met Eric?

"I ultimately met Eric.

"I actually had no idea who he was. I just saw the tallest guy in the room. Remember, I'm five eleven and with heels probably like six three. So I thought, 'This guy is tall, this could work.' So we started talking.

"Someone came up to me afterward and said, 'Do you know who you were talking to all night?'

"I said, 'You mean Eric?'

"They said, 'Yes. Eric Trump. He's Donald Trump's son.'

"I thought, 'I didn't even know Donald Trump had a son.'

"We got married in 2014 down at Mar-a-Lago and then, of course, June 2015 my father-in-law announced he was running for president, so it's been an interesting ride for sure."

HOW TO WIN NORTH CAROLINA?

Lara Trump would end up in a crucial role in the 2016 presidential campaign. She would be running the Trump campaign in North Carolina. It would be one of the most important swing states in the whole contest, one that Hillary Clinton would openly target and media experts were certain she would win, taking it out of its traditional place in the Republican column.

It would require a pretty quick learning curve. Lara was the first to admit that she knew nothing about politics. Not on the national level. Not on the state level. This was a typical Trumpian move. He was impressed by competence, but sometimes he was even more impressed by desire. He had learned that if someone wanted to do something and enjoyed what he or she was doing, he or she could be successful. It was a pattern that had worked for him over and over in business and later in entertainment. Would it work in politics?

"My involvement in the campaign, honestly, came as a surprise," Lara said. "I had been working for five years as a booker and producer for *Inside Edition*, a nationally syndicated television show. But it became very hard to continue to work there after my father-in-law decided he was running for president. He was in the news almost every single day.

We always reported on him, and not everybody that I worked with was particularly a fan.

"Oddly enough, before he decided to run for president, they often wanted to stop by Trump Tower and get a sound bite from him. They liked him then. They would want a comment about almost anything. They would say, 'Get a Donald Trump comment.' And we would send a crew over. But when he started running for president, and they saw him as a Republican, well, a lot of people decided they didn't like him.

"In August 2016, my father-in-law was going to go down to Wilmington, North Carolina, my hometown, for a rally. I decided I wanted to go with him. Nobody else from the family was able to go. Donnie, Ivanka, and Eric all had something going on. So I said, 'I will just go with him.'"

"You went down on the big Trump campaign jet?" I asked.

"Yes, we flew down on the Trump plane. And my whole family came to the rally. Everybody was very excited. Then we all flew from Wilmington to Fayetteville for another rally, which is only a twenty-minute flight. Fayetteville is the home of Fort Bragg, the big army base. And on the way there my father-in-law was complaining about something that was upsetting him, something he didn't like about the way the last rally had been done, and so I started opining on what people think about in North Carolina and how they feel.

"Well, you know how he likes to get opinions from people. He is a great listener. It is one of his gifts, and before I know it, he is looking at me and he goes, 'You know what? I want you to be in charge of—'

"And I say, 'Wait a minute. I have no idea about anything related to politics. I work in a newsroom. This is far outside of anything I have any knowledge of.

"But when Donald Trump tells you he wants you to win your own home state, I was like, 'Absolutely. Of course. I will do it.'

"So as soon as we landed, I called Eric and said, 'I don't know what happened, but your dad just tasked me with winning North Carolina.'

"Everything changed. I went to work the next day and told my boss that I needed a three-month leave of absence. I said, 'My father-in-law wants me to help him with the campaign. I would like to do it. If you guys will allow me, I will take three months off.'

"So, they granted me a three-month leave of absence, and that next day I was here in the offices of Trump Tower. I was actually in this office."

I knew from Eric's tour that the two floors below us had both been used for the campaign. In fact, entire parts of Trump Tower had been turned into a campaign machine for six months.

THE WOMEN ON THE BUS

"Lynne Patton, who was Eric's oldest assistant, was one of my best friends. I was chatting with her over lunch, and we were talking about how Donald Trump hired so many women and had them in leadership roles in his business but there weren't many women out on the campaign trail. She and I sat down and came up with this idea of a bus tour with women that know and love and have worked with Donald Trump.

"At first it was Lynne, Diamond, and Silk, the video bloggers who gained fame for their support of Donald Trump, and Katrina Pierson, who later became national spokesperson for the campaign. We also brought on Omarosa Manigault Newman, who at the time acted as though she was our friend and was very supportive.

"So, we literally set out on a campaign bus tour, and the first place we went to was North Carolina. We traveled the country for three months on a bus. Anytime we had any downtime, I would be back in North Carolina, where I worked very closely with our state director.

"It was probably the craziest three months of my life. I never saw Eric. We were always in different places.

"Once by accident we ended up in Columbus, Ohio. We didn't know we were going to be there at the same time. We ran into each other in the lobby of the same hotel, if you can believe that. It was a, you know, 'What are you doing here?'

"So I said to the other ladies, 'I don't need a room. I am with this guy for the night.'

"We had no idea that we would both be in town on the same day, because it was so crazy and hectic. Anyone that's worked on a campaign knows the pace. Our dogs didn't see us for three months. Thank God for two of our friends who constantly stayed with our dogs at our apartment. They were lifesavers.

"You have to understand, Eric and I didn't have kids then. So, there was really no excuse for us not to be out there working full time. I didn't want to wake up on November 9 and say I could have done one more thing, so I mean, we did our best."

The rallies and the personal appearances were energy packed, but in between there were long hours of boring travel on interstate highways. In the end, the bus tour would cover five states, dozens of cities, and thousands of miles.

"We had a television, which worked fifty percent of the time, depending on where we were in the country. And when it worked we were glued to the news networks."

When the news wasn't available, they didn't sleep or take long dinners in restaurants along the road. They stopped only for radio interviews. Back on the bus, they spent hours comparing notes about what they were seeing and feeling. One recurring theme was the persistent feeling that people were going to be surprised by the election.

"I am not even a blood relative of Donald Trump," explains Lara. "But the places we visited would draw hundreds of people. They would show up at event after event. People would say, 'I'm a lifelong Democrat and have always voted Democrat but I'm voting for Donald Trump. A ninety-four-year-old veteran came up to me at one stop saying that he had never voted in his entire life. He said he was a World War Two veteran. He said, 'I'm voting for Donald Trump. I can barely walk but I am getting to the polls on November 8.'

"On one of our visits to North Carolina, I was in the hotel gym, working out very early in the morning. I was watching the early news, and they were reporting locally that Hillary Clinton was in the state and I was in the state at the same time. And they were giving just as much time to my visit as hers. I thought, 'What is going on here?' But they just couldn't ignore the crowds of people that were involved. The local news outlets were still reporting actual news."

While the ladies on the bus were seeing their thousands, Donald Trump, the candidate, was drawing tens of thousands. Occasionally, the ladies would cross paths and experience a full-blown Trump event.

"It is unlike anything you've ever experienced in your life. The campaign put out all those RSVPs and they would get double the capacity. And the people actually showed. People would start lining up the night before. They would wait overnight. I mean, it's incredible. Political people told us that this was unprecedented and it had never happened before, and it definitely meant something. So we knew that something was going on. And the media was there. They could count the crowds at a Hillary Clinton rally and a Donald Trump rally. They knew. They just didn't report it."

THE OCTOBER SURPRISE

Presidential campaigns are fluid events with only a few crucial dates that are sacrosanct. Among them are the date of the candidate's announcement to run; the dates of the various state primaries, conventions, and caucuses; the filings for the Federal Election Commission; and finally the actual presidential election. But there is another date that in recent years has emerged as one of the most important of all. And that is the so-called October surprise. The latter, of course, is not a formal event, but in the last few decades it has become increasingly dependable. It refers to the last-minute surprise that a campaign will launch, just before the election, to tilt the results its way.

Timing is everything. If a story is released too early, it may be overcome and negated by Election Day. If it is released too late, it may be rejected by suspicious voters or even unknown by many it never reached.

An October surprise can be positive or negative. In 1972, with the

Vietnam War raging, the national security adviser, Henry Kissinger, held a press conference at the White House on October 26, announcing that "peace is at hand."[5] It was only days before a huge landslide victory for the presidential incumbent, Richard Nixon.

On the other hand, in 2000, the campaign for Democratic presidential nominee, Al Gore, released a story that many years before a youthful George W. Bush had been found guilty of drunk driving in Maine. The Democrats had been sitting on the information since the previous May. It came too little, too late.

In 2008, only days before the election, the campaign of the Republican nominee, John McCain, released a story about the aunt of the Democratic nominee, Barack Obama, which asserted that she was living illegally in the United States. It had no impact. The surprise has to have time to soak down into the layers of voter strata.

In 2016, one of Donald Trump's old partners from the entertainment industry, NBC, was emerging as one of his biggest and most earnest political enemies. The media giant had the right weapon and the right political experience for timing an October surprise. That summer, NBC had covered the Olympics in Brazil. One of its on-air anchors, Billy Bush, had been talking off-camera into a corporate microphone, with the sound picked up by engineers in New York City. Bush was overheard talking about a "tape of Trump being a real dog."[6]

NBC's employees went on the hunt, and after days of researching ultimately found the videotape of Donald Trump appearing on *Access Hollywood*. The candidate was using lewd, sexually explicit language.

Of course, this was not the first time that a presidential candidate's private life had become an open scandal, but in earlier years public servants were spared such humiliation. Early in my research on presidential children, for example, I would speak on the phone with Warren G. Harding's daughter, who had been born out of wedlock. Over the years the national media had railed at her when she dared to speak up publicly. Media was protective of presidents, who they needed as sources. Such stories were never raised when Harding was a candidate, and long afterward, the Harding family would fiercely defend their family torchbearer. In the case of the Harding love child, DNA evidence eventually confirmed her remarkable claims, but only after she had died.[7]

FDR was declared by history books to be impotent from polio. Journalists respected this idea and never raised the issue of his infidelities during his political campaigns. We know today that FDR likely had many sex partners and actually died while he was with a favorite mistress in Warm Springs, Georgia.[8]

According to his biographer, LBJ was serviced by young ladies on his White House staff.[9] There is John F. Kennedy, whose philandering was legend—but never mentioned when he campaigned for office.

And of course, there is the long saga of Bill Clinton. There is the story of numerous events with numerous partners, including his own intern and his own devoted supporter and fundraiser who claimed sexual assault, and the dubious role that his wife, Senator Hillary Clinton, played in dealing with these stories and events.

While Donald Trump's *Access Hollywood* scandal did not involve any physical activity, it certainly involved graphic language that was hard on the ears.

NBC's lawyers apparently reviewed the tape for days. Meanwhile, producers readied and polished their stories and waited for the right political timing. When it was learned that WikiLeaks was planning its own anti–Hillary Clinton October surprise, that they would be releasing voice recordings of the candidate's secret speeches at major banks, contradicting her public positions, the network decided to act. On the same day of the WikiLeaks dump, the *Access Hollywood* video was leaked to the *Washington Post*, which dutifully broke the story. A day later, NBC ran with its long-planned production. The story promised to knock Donald Trump out of the presidential race.

Ivanka Trump, the candidate's daughter, defended her father. Privately, she urged him to fight back. "It's eleven years old, you have to fight back. You have to say you're sorry, but you have to fight back."[10]

Trump answered immediately. "Everyone who knows me knows these words don't reflect who I am," he said. "I've never said I'm a perfect person, nor pretended to be someone I'm not. I've said and done things I regret, and the words released today on this more-than-a-decade-old video is one of them. I said it was wrong. And I apologized.

"I've traveled the country talking about change for America. But my travels have also changed me. I pledge to be a better man tomorrow, and will never, ever, let you down."[11]

A statement from his wife, Melania, followed. "The words my husband used are unacceptable and offensive to me. This does not represent the man that I know. He has the heart and mind of a leader. I hope people will accept his apology, as I have, and focus on the important issues facing our nation and the world."[12]

Hillary Clinton, who apparently knew the story was coming, posted on Twitter, "This is horrific. We cannot allow this man to become president."[13]

The following Monday, October 10, 2016, an NBC–*Wall Street Journal* poll showed Donald Trump's national numbers dropping precipitously. In the head-to-head contest, Clinton was winning 52 to 38 percent.

Republican public figures were openly abandoning Trump. House Speaker Paul Ryan told fellow congressmen to "do what's best for you in your district."[14] South Dakota senator John Thune, a Republican, called on Donald Trump to withdraw from the race and let Mike Pence be "our nominee effective immediately."[15]

As I wrote later, "Trump adviser Steve Bannon urged the candidate to bring Bill Clinton's victims to the next presidential debate. They should just be there to shake Hillary's confidence."[16] It would be an outrageous, nakedly desperate move.

JARED KUSHNER REMEMBERS

What happened next was crucial to the campaign and has been the subject of many books and news articles. One of the most critical players in the drama has never spoken up about it until now. In the winter of

2019, I sat down with Donald Trump's son-in-law, Jared Kushner, and talked to him about this dramatic time, when decisions were made that would change the course of American history.

"I remember talking to Paul Ryan earlier in the campaign," Jared said, "and I remember reporting to him about the enthusiasm at the Trump rallies and the feeling out across the country. He compared it to his last days of campaigning with Mitt Romney.

"And he said, 'Well, you know, we believed in the end too. We had big rallies too. We thought *we* were going to win.' So they were jaded by their own experience, and they just didn't believe that our experience was any different. But we had a lot more confidence, because our database was really strong."[17]

Paul Ryan had been the vice presidential running mate for former governor Mitt Romney, the Republican nominee in the 2012 election against the incumbent, President Obama.

"The Billy Bush thing was kind of critical," Jared said. He was referring to the *Access Hollywood* video, the October surprise. "Our online donations went from about $1.4 million a day to $2.6 million a day."

Wait a minute. Could this have been true? Had the Trump donations actually *increased* even while the scandal caused a collapse in national support for Trump's candidacy?

"What happened is that our people started rallying around us," Jared Kushner told me. "As the Republican establishment started to abandon us and started condemning Trump, the rank-and-file Republicans rose to support us. The RNC quickly learned that the base of their party was actually with Trump."

It would be a rude awakening.

"We had this joint funding account at the RNC. And we were supposed to get $45 million sent to us on Friday. But when the Billy Bush video hit, all the RNC folks jumped on the trains and left Washington. Basically, we didn't get any money.

"So, we had a meeting called at my father-in-law's apartment in New York on Saturday. Reince Priebus was supposed to be there."

In his book *Let Me Finish*, the New Jersey governor and Trump adviser Chris Christie writes that he spoke with the RNC chairman, Reince Priebus, that Saturday morning. According to Christie, Priebus was calling from the train as it approached Philadelphia. He wanted to make sure that Christie was going to be at the meeting too. It was getting politically dangerous even being seen with Donald Trump. Christie assured him that he would be there.

"Don't lie to me," Priebus said. He obviously didn't want to risk it otherwise. It was that bad.

And then Priebus added, "Oh, I hate this. I hate this. This is awful. It's terrible. I can't believe we're in this position."[18]

Jared gave me the story from inside the family. "Ivanka and I did a run in the morning and then went to the meeting at Trump Tower. Bannon was there. Don Jr. was there. Hope Hicks was there, wearing workout clothes. Hope goes, 'He's up there answering phone calls from journalists.'

"Somebody said, 'We better get up there fast.' And everybody laughed."

Hope Hicks was the press secretary and communications director for the Trump presidential campaign. She would later serve as communications director in the Trump White House.

"So, my father-in-law was telling journalists, one after the other, that he was never going to drop out. Which was the right thing to say. We went up and started talking. Chris Christie confronted my father-in-law and emphasized that he should apologize. Rudy Giuliani showed up and he was solid."

Rudolph Giuliani was the former mayor of New York City and a longtime friend of the Trump family. All of them admired him. He had been an adviser to the campaign for the past year.

"Reince showed up and told my father-in-law, 'You basically have two options. You can either drop out or you can have the worst defeat in the history of presidential politics.'

"And Trump answered back, 'Nice, I don't want either.'"

Jared Kushner was nagged by another problem. What if the Republican National Committee pulled its support? There was talk that they would shift all their resources to the Senate and House races. If so, the presidential race was over.

Shortly after the dramatic confrontation between Donald Trump and Reince Priebus, Jared Kushner pulled the RNC chairman aside, away from the group. "Look," he said to Priebus, "if we don't get our money I can't promise you what he will do. He may decide to run against the Republicans in all of these different places. The base is with him. It is not with the Republican Party. So you better know that."

Then, Jared cut to the chase: "Look, we had an agreement. Don't try to disqualify him and nullify the agreement. You better honor the documentation. Don't try to mess around."

And then Jared added a deadline: "Look, we'll know on Monday. We'll know if our money shows up."

On Monday the money was there.

Meanwhile, for whatever it was worth, Donald Trump counterpunched with a fiery Tweet: "Bill Clinton has actually abused women and Hillary has bullied, attacked, shamed and intimidated his victims. We will discuss this more in the coming days. See you at the debate on Sunday."[19]

Donald Trump Jr. was not happy with the way his father had been treated during the debates. "The networks and the tech people employed to run the events had been very happy to have my father destroy the other Republican contenders during the GOP debates," he said. "They had expected to be running against Jeb Bush or Ted Cruz or Marco Rubio. As far as they were concerned, our win made things easier for Hillary.

"All of that changed when we got into the debates with Hillary Clinton. In the very first debate there was a lot of screwing around with his microphone. So it didn't interfere with what went out on television, that would make the networks look bad, but it did mean that the studio audience couldn't hear him and they wouldn't be able to react to his comments. That would make him sound unsupported by the audience and would throw him off his game. It was really quite brazen."

At the next presidential debate, in St. Louis, Missouri, the Trump team had its own surprise for the television networks. Steve Bannon's ploy was uncorked. The ladies abused by Bill Clinton and, arguably, victimized again by Hillary Clinton's efforts to keep them quiet showed up to proclaim that while Trump's sins were verbal, Bill's and Hillary's were physical. It was a bizarre moment. Thus, what most expected to be the ill-fated flight of the Trump presidential campaign was held together by baling wire, Scotch tape, rubber bands, and spit. But could it actually get off the ground again and fly?

MOMENTUM ON THE BUS

Lara Trump had her own method for handling the emotions of winning or losing, and her own style of bracing for defeat, if that was what was coming.

"I think we were all cautiously optimistic. It's the same thing I do here in the winter." She looked out on the cold city from her skyscraper window. "I know we have another month of cold weather and, guess what? If it gets warm in two weeks, then I win." She keeps her expectations low, and anything better is a victory.

"We knew from the numbers we had internally, we knew from the feeling on the ground, that something was missing in the news. But then it is so hard to ignore when you turn on the TV and they say Donald Trump has a one percent chance of winning. How do you rationalize that?

"The one moment I specifically remember that gave us all hope was three days before the election when Hillary got rid of those fireworks on a barge in the Hudson. I remember all of us being together. I don't even remember what state we were in. But I remember we heard that news. And we thought, 'They know, they know what we know. They know that something is off. They don't want those fireworks out there because they are going to look so stupid when they are not going off."

The last week before the election, the ladies on the bus were living on adrenaline. Someone on the team had discovered DJ Khaled's popular rap song, "All I Do Is Win." They played it over and over, day and night, as they cruised down the interstate, zooming past another glowing Wendy's or McDonald's or IHOP, on their way to the next reception at a Hampton Inn or in a Marriott ballroom.

"All I do is win, win, win, no matter what . . ."

Lara was almost giddy remembering the feeling. "Oh my God, we played that song over and over, all day and night, leading right up to the election. 'All I do is win, win, win, no matter what.'

And then the bus tour ran out of gas. November 8 was upon them.

The Trump women bus tour never got wide media coverage for one simple reason: It contradicted the narrative that Donald Trump was a racist. Of the six ladies on the bus—Lynne Patton, Katrina Pierson, Diamond and Silk, Omarosa Manigault Newman, and Lara Trump—all were African American except for Lara.

The tour ended in North Carolina, where the ladies all hugged each other and Glenn, their dedicated driver, before catching flights back home across the country. Lara, meanwhile, spent the rest of the day with her father-in-law, traveling to rallies in Pennsylvania and New Hampshire before heading back to New York City to be together as a family.

"It was a very hard juxtaposition between what we felt," Lara told me, "what we just really knew, deep down, and what we were being told by the media. If you ever wondered if the media was giving you the facts or not, well, that was the defining moment for me. These people knew all along how strong we were in the polls, and how the American people were feeling, but it didn't fit their narrative. They hid the story of what was happening from all of those earnest people out across the country. They kept it hidden."

★ 7 ★

ELECTION NIGHT FOG

"Melania, Jared just told me that we lost!"
—DONALD TRUMP[1]

I t can be confusing, trying to understand how things transpired on Election Night in Trump Tower. For one thing, the witnesses have different and conflicting memories, including the president himself. And Trump Tower was surprisingly empty of credentialed journalists. There were no historians. On Election Night, almost all the journalists had been embedded with the Clinton campaign, simply because they believed she would win. Even some of those correspondents assigned to cover Trump stayed camped at the Hilton Hotel, the scene of the postelection party. No one wanted to venture near the tower and be associated with the loser.

The historians were busy doing television shows. Some of them could actually be seen on the streets of Manhattan, having abandoned their limousines, which were stuck in traffic. They were accompanied by their public relations escorts, walking at a fast pace up to Columbus Circle to do CNN or walking down to West Fifty-Seventh Street to do CBS. Some would venture onto Fifth Avenue—it was the only way to reach the NBC studios at Rockefeller Center—but they carefully avoided passing too close to Trump Tower, lest anyone get the wrong impression.

One famous presidential historian and his entourage were seen in the lobby of the spectacular Peninsula Hotel. It was Hillary Clinton's headquarters. An observer said that he and his assistants looked like a gaggle of ducks, shuffling along behind Clinton staffers, angling for a conversation, waiting for some bread crumbs to drop. The power was clearly shifting to the first woman president in American history, and he wanted to be there ahead of the competition. He never even bothered to stop by Trump Tower, where he could have feasted unchallenged on riches. He could have put those brief moments in the bank, just in case. But then, there was no "just in case." Hillary was going to win.

Keeping track of locations within Trump Tower itself is a challenge. It was one of the reasons I later decided to make the trip to New York to walk around the Trump property myself. For example, the city has its own creative building codes, which makes numbering a floor almost impossible to score. A floor does not have to correspond to its actual position in a building. A floor can be named whatever you want. "The John F. Kennedy floor." Or "The Dwight Eisenhower floor." And since offices and apartments on higher floors were worth more money than those on lower floors, smart builders and real estate entrepreneurs simply named floors with higher numbers. That explains how the Trump Tower can be a fifty-eight-story skyscraper, while Donald and Melania Trump live on the sixty-fifth and sixty-sixth floors. No, they are not living in the clouds.

It also explains how the so-called Election Night war room could be on the fourteenth floor and staffers could walk down a back stairway, one floor down, to the "headquarters" on the fifth floor. When Ivanka Trump told me that she was in the "war room" but could hear the shouting and cheering from the headquarters, it now made sense. It was just one floor away; the noise was echoing up the stairwell.

It gets worse. It turns out that there was more than one "war room." There was the acknowledged war room on the so-called fourteenth floor, where senior campaign staff had offices, and which the Trump family would frequently visit on Election Night, but there were at least two other rooms that other, less senior staff members referred to as the "war room." It mattered, because sometimes a junior staffer had a bigger story to tell than a senior staffer. One had to know the building through the eyes and personal experiences of multiple persons.

THE GREAT WISCONSIN RAID

When Eric Trump gave me the tour of Trump Tower, he started on the fourteenth floor, where much of the action had taken place.

"This is the Turnberry Conference Room," he said, showing me an empty, clean, carpeted room with windows looking out over New York City. The Trumps loved the name Turnberry. They had a mansion and a golf course with the same name, as well as conference rooms at other locations around the world.

"Right on this wall," Eric said, "was an easel, and there was a two-by-four paper. I remember Brad and Jared were here with me. We were about three weeks out. That's when the critical decision was made about Wisconsin and Michigan."

Brad Parscale was the Trump 2016 campaign's digital media director. At six eight, he is a giant of a man, with a beard that makes him even more imposing. Brad is a maestro with numbers. He and his staff were the ones who found the Trump supporters on social media and who helped determine where the candidate should go to have a successful rally. Working directly with Jared Kushner and sometimes with Eric Trump, Brad helped identify the right people for the RNC voter turnout programs. If Hillary Clinton had Silicon Valley, including Eric Schmidt, the former chairman of Google, as her digital director, Trump had Jared Kushner and Brad Parscale. It was Brad's data modeling that first alerted the campaign to the possibilities in Wisconsin.

Eric was describing to me the background on what had been a daring political move, a raid behind enemy lines. Michigan had voted for the Democratic nominee in six straight presidential elections, and no Republican presidential candidate had taken Wisconsin since 1984, when Ronald Reagan carried every state in the union except Minnesota, his Democratic opponent's home state.

Jared Kushner's confrontational moment with Reince Priebus over RNC money would have a profound impact on the campaign. First, it would free up money that the campaign spenders in that fateful Turnberry Conference Room would be able to assign. And equally important, it would signal to the Republican field that the party and the nominee were finally wedded. It was okay for establishment Republicans to support the New York outsider Donald Trump. The RNC was finally on board.

"We had about ninety-three percent of the Republican voters," Jared remembers. "But the seven percent, more establishment Republicans could have cost us dearly. We needed them too. It could have been the difference in many of the most contested Midwestern states."

Jared Kushner had been working on Wisconsin for months. "After my father-in-law won the nomination, I went down to Washington to be with Paul Ryan's team." Ryan was the Republican Speaker of the House, and he was from Wisconsin.

"We were trying to figure out how to mend fences with the Republican leaders and the nominee," said Jared Kushner. "I'm always inclined to make peace and try to figure out how to build bridges. How do we move people forward?

"So I met with his team. Actually we met in a law firm and I said, 'Guys, so I know we weren't your first choice.'"

Laughter.

"I know we weren't your sixteenth choice!"

Even more laughter.

"But in the end you'll be very happy with us because, first of all, the nominee agrees with Paul on a lot of issues. Not every issue, but a lot of issues. But most of all, you will be happy when you see that he is probably the only person in the Republican field who can beat Hillary

Clinton. And if he does get elected, you will find that he has the ability to be one of the most transformational political leaders you could have in the White House.

"And they were all looking at me like I was crazy. You could see it on their faces. Basically, it was, 'Man, I can't believe we're stuck with these idiots.'

"But we kept going forward, and I think we kept proving people wrong."

Getting Paul Ryan to campaign in Wisconsin was critical to pulling off an upset in that state.

"We kept trying to make it work, but he wouldn't do it. Again, we were talking about a small percentage of Republican establishment voters, but if you are going to pull off an upset, you need everybody. The problem was the establishment didn't think we would win anywhere, so why worry about Wisconsin?

"All the big donors were calling Paul Ryan and driving him crazy. He really felt like we were going to get wiped out. Finally, he agreed to do a rally with us, but in the end we couldn't get there. So we set it up with Mike Pence. It was just a couple of days before the election, but it was actually quite helpful in bringing the party together and especially helping us in Wisconsin."

At the meeting in the Turnberry room, a few weeks before the election, there was a discussion about where their remaining resources would go, including the money from the RNC. Senior members of the Trump campaign were all there, including Steve Bannon, Kellyanne Conway, David Bossie, and Nick Ayers. Brad Parscale explained that there were now sixteen states that were the key to the election. "And we only have enough money to compete in five of them. We have to decide."[2]

No one would decide. "They kept saying we need to get Trump to write out another check for $100 million," Parscale remembered. "They kept saying we need to compete in them all."

"And I said, 'It ain't gonna happen.'

"And so we were stuck." Finally, they all left the room, leaving Brad Parscale and Nick Ayers alone. "Nick, I'm just going to pick 'em," Parscale said.

Ayers shot back, "I think you're the only one who knows about this anyway."[3]

Brad checked with Eric Trump and Jared Kushner and then made the decision. He took the campaign money allocated for other places, including Virginia, painful as it was, and put it in Wisconsin and Michigan. Everybody else on staff was focused on what they would say on their next segment on Fox, CNN, and MSNBC. "I had to make a decision," Parscale said. "Afterwards, I told Eric and Jared what I had done." Jared had been working on a Wisconsin surprise since the Republican National Convention. He took no persuading. It was one of the most decisive strategic decisions in the 2016 presidential election.

Donald Trump Jr., the hottest surrogate in the campaign, practically lived in Wisconsin the last two weeks of the campaign. That made a difference.

The Clinton campaign did not know about the last-minute transfer of resources, but they were aware of Donald Trump Jr.'s forays into the state. It was dismissed as a fool's errand and raised no alarm. "Professional politicians were chuckling, some openly mocking Trump. Amateur hour. One pundit called the Trump campaign guilty of political malpractice."[4] On October 31, 2016, the *New Yorker* ran a story titled "Why Is Donald Trump in Michigan and Wisconsin?" It was such a puzzle.[5]

WE CAN WIN THIS THING

The Thursday before the election, Brad Parscale was showing numbers that Donald Trump would win the election, and he had the data to prove it. Brad was using a model that had Trump supporters showing up at the polls in greater numbers than Republicans had in previous elections. More important, he was showing numbers of voters who had not voted before at all. Ever. These "ghost voters" were not picked up by traditional pollsters, they were on no one's lists, but Brad's surveys showed that they were beginning to represent significant numbers.

Deputy campaign manager David Bossie and campaign spokesman Jason Miller were sufficiently impressed that they took Brad on a little media tour. They encountered the same reaction that Eric Trump had experienced at ABC. This time, Parscale was trying to convince executives and producers at NBC, FOX, and CBS. He laid out his case, with explanations about why his early turnout numbers provided a better model. Parscale insisted that Trump was going to win 306 electoral votes. The executives and anchors at CBS broke into laughter.

Brad Parscale persisted right up to Election Day. That morning, he showed the numbers again to Eric Trump. "This is over," Parscale explained, showing color-coded Excel pages. "Look. See this data right here? Statistically, they can't catch up with us now. Even if we don't win Michigan and Wisconsin, look, it's no longer a question of if we are going to win or not, but rather by how much." But most, even inside the Trump campaign, did not believe him.

Katrina Pierson, the Trump campaign's national spokesperson, was one who did. But she was perplexed. "There were staffers who had this look on their faces, like what they were seeing on TV was true. Like, he wasn't going to win, and he's down ten points in the polls. I felt like I was the only one who knew he was going to win. I said to myself, 'Am I in a bubble? Because it doesn't seem like anybody is as confident as I am.'"[6]

The mood in the situation room at Trump Tower had been mixed. Some were excitedly exchanging theories based on early numbers, both positive and negative; others were too exhausted to care anymore. As long as people remained active, they maintained hope.

"You lose yourself in your work," Ivanka said.

But those whose work was winding down, and surrogates who no longer had radio and television segments to do, found themselves growing more somber.

PLANNING TRUMP'S CONCESSION CALL

Donald Trump Jr. appeared on ABC's *Good Morning America* early on Election Day. George Stephanopoulos said, "The polls show you behind right now, what are you looking for—for hope?"

Don was right on message. "So, I want everyone to turn out. People who have been let down by the system. . . I want them to vote. I want them to bring their friends. And we'll see what happens. . . . So many people come up to us and they are screaming, 'We love you, keep doing what you're doing.' And I've had just as many people come up to me and they say"—at this point, Don Jr. feigned a whisper—"'We love you, keep doing what you're doing.'

"They've been put in a box. Sometimes by the media. By a false narrative that's been created out there. They can't be as vocal supporting Trump. And it's going to be interesting to see how that turns out."[7] He was referring to the silent voters that their numbers showed and that the networks weren't buying.

Before noon on Election Day, Donald Trump and his wife, Melania, cast their votes at Public School 59 in Midtown Manhattan. Trump's daughter Ivanka; his son-in-law, Jared Kushner; and one of their children had been along. The scene was chaotic. Just before the Trump family arrived, police had escorted away two boisterous, bare-breasted female1 Clinton supporters. They had painted obscenities on their chests.[8]

Inside the school a spectator yelled out, "Who'd you vote for?"

Trump smiled. "Tough decision," he said.

While the Trump family voted inside, a new crowd of Clinton supporters had gathered to ambush them afterward. When the family emerged, the crowd booed and shouted profanities at Donald Trump and his grandchild. There were shouts of "New York hates you!"[9] But the Trump motorcade was gone.

In the afternoon, when he was once again safely ensconced back at Trump Tower, the candidate moved all over his namesake building. He went to his office on the twenty-sixth floor to finish some last-minute get-out-the vote messages for social media. He was later spotted with staff on the eleventh floor and then in a little impromptu meeting with the data team on the fourth floor. Eventually, he would settle in a chair in the middle of the so-called war room on the unfinished fifth floor.

In the months leading up to the election, the "war room" had been used as a campaign headquarters. Throughout the afternoon and evening, staffers were coming and going, running errands, and setting up arrangements for the Trump Election Night celebration at the nearby Hilton Hotel—although, admittedly, most believed it would be a wake for a spirited but failed presidential bid. Still, at this hour, the campaign work was grinding on toward its climactic, inevitable conclusion. The polls would soon be closing across the country. The results would be out of their hands.

A block away, former secretary of state Hillary Clinton and her team were operating out of the Peninsula Hotel. According to Clinton staff, it was "selected so she could personally see Trump Tower, home of the foe she was set to crush."[10]

They had made sure that the suites, reserved for the Clintons and key staff, had walls of windows to look on as Trump Tower come tumbling down. They made sure that they had rented the rooftop. When victory came, when Hillary Clinton took the concession call from Donald J. Trump, she would be looking out across a lighted Manhattan skyline toward Trump Tower. She and her husband, former president Bill Clinton, would then ride to the massive, glass-covered Jacob K. Javits Convention Center, where a crowd of thousands would celebrate a unique and magical moment.

Near sunset, on Election Day, Kellyanne Conway, Trump's campaign manager, called her Clinton counterpart, Robby Mook. The two had corresponded via email the day before. Mook had written, "It's been a real pleasure. I was happy to be campaign managers together."

He had then laid out a plan for Election Night beginning, diplomatically with the scenario of a Trump win. "Within 15 minutes of the AP [Associated Press] calling the race for Mr. Trump, Secretary

Clinton will call him to congratulate him." And then Mook had added the most likely outcome, "Within 15 minutes of the AP calling the race for Secretary Clinton, she will take to the stage and accept, so in other words, we hope to hear from Mr. Trump in that window." If Donald Trump didn't want to look like a sore loser, he had to pay attention to the election returns and call right on time. With or without his call, Secretary Clinton was taking that stage.

Kellyanne had read the email to Trump.

"Did you respond?" he had asked her.

"No," she had answered, "I'm not going to respond. This is a good system, I'll respond later or tomorrow. We have a lot going on."[11]

And so tomorrow had finally come, and the call to Robby Mook could not be put off any longer. Kellyanne reached him and his latest instructions were clear. "Your point of contact is Huma Abedin," he told her. It was Hillary Clinton's closest aide and friend. It was said that when the Clintons moved into the White House, Huma Abedin would have her own bedroom in the family quarters.[12] Mook gave Kellyanne Huma's number. And so the two campaigns were now connected. If Trump had to concede, he would call Huma, and she would hand the phone to Hillary.

At the tower, as Donald Trump and his family came out of an elevator, they encountered John Fredericks, a conservative radio host. Ivanka had appreciated his on-air support and had gotten him into the building that night. He was interviewing everybody he could find.

"Fredericks!" Trump shouted in surprise.

"Hey, Mr. Trump! You're going to win, you know that, right?"

Trump smiled back, "From your lips to God's ears, John."[13]

When Trump met with his diversity coalition and was asked about being nervous, he replied, "Look, what do I have to lose? I'm gambling with house money. You know what I mean? If I win, great, I want to win. If I lose, what's my default position? The CEO of Trump International."[14]

WHO TOLD TRUMP HE HAD LOST THE ELECTION?

At 5:01 p.m., Trump's deputy campaign manager, David Bossie, got a phone call from an old friend, Chris Vlasto of ABC News. Vlasto had information about the early exit poll data coming from the Associated Press. This was supposedly the real stuff. This would tell the tale.[15]

In earlier times, the television networks had their own competitive Election Night polling operations. It was prestigious for a network to call a state early, before a competitor. In more modern times, the networks had pooled their resources and relied on the same common data. Using the AP exit polls as a base number, they then employed their own in-house analysts to work on specific precincts to get a jump in reporting. The point was, the base numbers for all the networks were really the same.

Vlasto had bad news for the Trump campaign. The worst.

Clinton was going to win and win big. There was no doubt.

More information followed as the news spread across New York City, the communications capital of the world. There had been meetings at the various television networks, the Trump team would learn, where the on-air anchors and senior producers had been called in and told that Hillary Clinton would be the winner. They were to develop language and themes to capture the historic moment as it was reported later in the day. Producers began to choreograph their evening shows. Artists were told to begin deciding on the final images and fonts they would be using on air that evening. Calls were made to some key television network board members and even some prominent network television advertisers. The nation's elite was now being given the advance word. It was done. Hillary Clinton would win.

In my interviews with the president and the Trump family, one point of confusion had to be cleared up. On election night, who had told the candidate that it was over, that he had lost?

At a December 2016 victory rally in Wisconsin, the president-elect told bits and pieces of his Election Night experience. He told the audience that his own daughter, Ivanka, had passed on to him the bad news.

"So it began with phony exit polls," Donald Trump remembered, later, recounting the story himself. "And I got a call from my daughter at about five o'clock, and she was called by people in their business, and her husband, Jared—great guy—he was called. Then they called me and they said, 'I'm sorry, Dad. It looks really bad. Looks really, really bad.'

"So, I sort of thought I lost, and I was okay with that. I wouldn't say great. In fact, I called my vice president and I said, 'It's not looking good. Not looking good.'"[16]

Trump later told the Fox News anchor Chris Wallace that going into Election Night, after his people had read the exit polls, they too thought he was going to lose. "That was just the accepted wisdom."[17]

As Donald Trump told the story, "So now the polls just closed, and they start announcing numbers, and I say, 'Oh, this is going to be embarrassing.' I'm trying to figure out what am I going to do. And I have this ballroom that's not that big because I didn't know if I was going to win or lose."[18]

In the book *Let Trump Be Trump*, coauthored by Trump's former campaign manager Corey Lewandowski and his deputy campaign manager David Bossie, there is a slightly different story. Bossie says he had just received the "insider" information from the source at ABC when he ran into the campaign's CEO, Steve Bannon, in a hallway.[19] They huddled to talk about the numbers when they were joined by Trump's son-in-law, Jared Kushner and, later, the Republican National Committee chairman, Reince Priebus. According to Bossie's account, they had stepped out onto a balcony that overlooked Fifth Avenue. And there they had reviewed the numbers. According to Bossie, Jared then called Trump and broke the news.

I asked Bossie how his account could differ from Trump's own recollection, and he was adamant. "My story is accurate."[20]

A couple of years after Election Night, visiting with Jared and Ivanka at their house in Georgetown, I asked them to talk about that moment.

"We were around the war room," Jared said. This would have been on the fourteenth floor.

"Bossie, Bannon, and Stepien came over to me with the exit polls they had gotten from ABC." The "Stepien" that Jared was referring to was Bill Stepien, a former campaign manager for Chris Christie's gubernatorial campaigns and a critical player in the 2016 Trump presidential run. He would go on to become the White House political director in the Trump administration.

"We went through the numbers," Jared Kushner remembered. "They weren't great. I said, 'I guess I better call the boss.' I had promised I would call him when I got the exits. I always called him before something big happened."

I wanted to get this part of the story straight. Other people had characterized Jared's conversation with his father-in-law. Were the others listening in?

Jared smiled. "Nobody heard what I said to my father-in-law. I stepped away from the others for privacy. I moved down the hall. They couldn't have heard me.

"I called up to him and said, 'Look we just got these exits in from the networks. They are not looking great. But you know, they've always screwed us on every poll before, so who knows where these numbers really are? Our people vote late, so these could be inaccurate, and also Stepien thinks the methodology is a little off. He doesn't like the way they are doing their weighting. But I just wanted you to know this.'

"He said to me, 'You know, Jared, look, it will be what it will be. We left it all on the field. I don't think we could have worked any harder. I'm very proud of the job we did here. And I'm proud of you. I'm proud of the team. And tonight, regardless of how it turns out, let's go and have some fun.'

"Basically, he was pretty cool. I was just telling him that he had lost the election. And he couldn't have been more at ease, actually more gracious, about it.

"He told me afterward that right after he hung up he said, 'Melania, Jared just told me that we lost!'" Jared laughed at this moment. He was amused that Trump had figured out more than he had meant to tell him. "I guess he had heard it in my voice because I hadn't actually said that. Actually, I was trying to sugarcoat it with him a little bit. But it was going to be what it was going to be."

Ivanka jumped into the conversation. "And I think my father believed it was really bad news because Jared had always dismissed such numbers. He largely argued against the polls that were coming from the networks. He knew how flawed they were. And this time he was more accepting."

So, who had first told Trump that he had lost the election? He himself said that Ivanka had called him.

"Well, I did," she said, laughing, as she recalled that emotional day. "I called several times throughout the evening and, of course, I passed on the information that Jared was giving me."

It appears that both accounts are accurate, having happened at different times. And Bossie's story was accurate as well. All of the stories were told from different angles and from different perspectives.

WE DON'T STOP NOW

"I called a friend of mine," Jared said. "He was someone who would have some information. I asked, 'What are you hearing?' And he said, 'I'm not talking to anybody, but I can tell you that the networks have been screwing with you guys the whole time. What makes you think that tonight will be any different? In a general election nobody really knows. It's such a big sample going at one time. In the primaries they can get a feel for what will happen, but in a general election it is such a big sample that they cannot really know for sure. The models are too unpredictable.'

"So, after that I called Hope and Boris Epshteyn, a senior adviser, and said, 'Let's get everybody on the drive time radio.' So we got Ivanka,

Don, Eric, Rudy, and Ivanka's father calling into the radio shows. We were thinking, 'What more can we do?'

"Hope called Donald and said, 'Do you want to do these with us?' And he said, 'Yeah, why not?' And then he called back and said, 'Hope, can you call into these radio stations for me, when I call in they keep hanging up on me.' The producers at the stations thought they were prank calls—not really Donald Trump.'"

It turned out that Lara Trump had been on the phones even before anyone from Hope Hicks's team had called to ask for help. She was a working machine. If she could compete in triathlons, hey, what were a few more hours without food or sleep?

"So, I did a ton of interviews the day of the election," Lara said, "and on every single one of them I remember people saying, 'So what do you think the chances really are that Donald Trump is going to win?'

"And on all of them I was one hundred percent. 'Donald Trump is going to win. There's no doubt in my mind.' And, of course, I get off the show and I'm thinking, 'I'm going to sound like such an idiot if this doesn't happen.'

"Around three or four o'clock in the afternoon we got some polling information that the panhandle of Florida needed help. It was an hour behind us here on the East Coast. So they asked for Don and Eric and me to do radio. So we said, 'Absolutely, yes.'

"We worked the radio until the polls closed at eight p.m. that night.

"Meanwhile, as a woman, you've got some getting ready to do. So, I was home in our apartment with headphones on, doing radio and trying my best to change and do my hair and my makeup. It was crazy, but we were not leaving anything on the table. We were going to do everything we could to win."

Jared Kushner remembers that feeling. "That night, with everybody working right up to the end, well, it was very special moment. We were a scrappy campaign."

Don Trump Jr. remembers the pace: "Election Day I woke up at six a.m. and started doing MSNBC and CNN. From three p.m. until the polls closed I think I did forty-eight radio interviews. Moving from east to west, trying to find the key places where our numbers were telling us that we needed to go.

"By the afternoon, there was screaming all over the place. 'Hey, Florida is in jeopardy, we need votes from the panhandle of Florida!' Trying to get the message out. 'Hey, if you are in line when the polls close, it's not too late, you can still vote. Stay there, we need you.'"

"We were a three-man band," Donald Trump Jr. said. "It was me, Charlie Kirk, and Tommy Hicks, now cochairman of the RNC. We had been together throughout the campaign, so it was comforting to see them in the final moments. Tommy was never that big on politics, but he was my friend and he helped me, traveling with me, helping me with logistics. For many days it was just Tommy, Charlie Kirk, and myself out there trying to get votes.

"I remember only two weeks before the election, we were in a Best Western outside of Detroit. It was nine thirty at night. I still had to do a call in to Hannity, and I looked at them and I said, 'Man, am I hungry.'

"They say, 'Yeah, and that makes sense because we haven't had a meal since yesterday breakfast.'

"I lost twenty-five pounds. I had to bargain. I would say, 'Well I can eat or I can make three fundraising calls.' 'I can eat or I can do another radio.' The whole process was fueled by Red Bull and testosterone and an incredible desire to win.

Don Jr. had spoken at seventy-five rallies in Wisconsin and Michigan during the last two weeks of the campaign. They would win Wisconsin by 1 percent and Michigan by 0.3 percent. "So on Election Day," Don said, "I can tell you, we left nothing on the table. Nothing."

In those last hours of voting in the Florida Panhandle, while he was in the middle of a radio interview, Don Trump Jr. texted Sean Hannity at Fox News.

Get me on TV. At that moment, Don Trump Jr. could get on just about any show. They had to carry Florida.

I'm in the middle of a show, came back the text. It was either from Hannity or his producer.

Then get me on the next show, right after yours.

BRAD'S COUNTER DATA

Inside the family and the hyperactive inner circle surrounding Donald Trump, there was a positive power that drove them on. The adrenaline that comes from work sometimes produces a pleasant sedative. But when they stopped and paused, as Lara described, they could feel the oppressive certainty of loss that hung, like a cloud, over the rooms in Trump Tower.

The lifeline, if one were inclined to take it, came from Brad Parscale, the digital media director who worked closely with Eric Trump and Jared Kushner. Using his own contacts and numbers, Brad had built an independent "skunkworks" Election Night operation. His numbers were still surprisingly positive.

He continued to insist, even after the evening news reports were coming in, that Donald Trump would win 306 electoral votes. "I had the world's best prediction model. I saw the path. I was using probability scores to determine where we were. And it was based on the actions of the people who had donated and clicked the buttons. I was constructing probability based on turnout."[21] Brad's reports, the ones printed out on Excel pages, with color codes to demonstrate the numbers, were plastered around his office as defiant rebuttals to the naysayers.

On Election Night, while other Republican campaign workers were sullen, accepting the worst, Brad Parscale was celebrating, flying paper planes around the situation room and his nearby office on the fourteenth floor. As far as Brad was concerned, Donald Trump was going to win. He passed his positive numbers on to Trump himself and to anyone else who would listen. And some believed. But the numbers were irritating and confusing to others. It all added to the roller coaster of emotions that were roiling the tower.

According to Donald Trump, he had already met privately with his wife, Melania. "Baby, I'll tell you what. We're not going to win tonight, because the polls have come out, and it's looking bad.

"But, you know what, I'm okay with it. I couldn't have worked any harder. You can't do any worse than that. I mean, I just couldn't have done it. And if I lose, I lose. And you know what? If I lose, I'm going to have a nice, easy life. We can all relax, together, right?"[22]

But Melania, who had consistently told him from the beginning that he would win, would have none of it. Again, at this moment, when the experts all agreed it was over, and it was being proclaimed on television and he was giving her the bad news, she was still not convinced. She listened politely and then then answered back once again. "It's not over," she told him. "You are going to win."

Eric Trump had lived with Brad's numbers, and at this late hour, with time running out, he still believed. But he believed also partly because of his own experience during the campaign.

"So, there was this discrepancy between what I was seeing day to day across America and what I was seeing on television," Eric said. "What I was seeing with my own eyes and what the *New York Times* was saying. On Election Day they were giving him one-point-nine percent chance to win. Declaring that there was a zero road map to an Electoral College victory, because he was not going to win Ohio, he was not going to win Pennsylvania, he was not going to win Iowa, he was not going to win North Carolina, and Florida was out of the question."

Donald Trump may have been a little skeptical, but he did not totally reject Brad Parscale's numbers. He wanted to believe. Late in the day, he patiently listened and followed the reasoning. But it was hard to fathom that so many media experts would put their reputations on the line and be so publicly and utterly convinced that it was a lost cause.

"Their numbers are all based on the wrong turnout probabilities," Parscale insisted. "You are going to win, sir."

"Well, you may be right," Trump said to Brad, apparently not wanting to hurt his feelings, letting him down a little easier than they had at CBS, where only a few days ago they had laughed in his face, "but if you are wrong, it will still be okay."

During this conversation, someone asked the candidate what he would do if the networks were right—which it appeared was going to happen. What should they plan? Would he stop by the party at the Hilton to greet the people who were waiting? They needed to know how to handle it.

"You know what?" Trump said, "I'm just going to go downstairs and make a statement and the next day I'll get on my plane and go play golf in Ireland."[23] That was it. That was how the marathon presidential campaign would end. Right where it had begun. At the bottom of that escalator in Trump Tower. Or out on the streets of Fifth Avenue.

8

THE BIGGEST UPSET IN AMERICAN HISTORY

"Look at these crying Clinton supporters, imagine how they feel?"
—DONALD TRUMP[1]

Not long after Donald Trump had retreated to his apartment with Melania, he got a call from Ivanka. She asked him to come down and watch the returns with the team. He agreed and spent the next two hours watching the returns in the big conference room on the fourteenth floor. This was the floor where several senior staff, including David Bossie, Steve Bannon, and Kellyanne Conway, had their offices.

CNN had begun its television coverage at six p.m., even while the Trump family were still working the phones, calling into drive time radio shows. Everyone at the networks was still confident that Hillary Clinton would win, but the anchors and contributors were making an effort to create some excitement to hold the viewers for as long as possible.

Jake Tapper promised there "could be new surprises," although he wouldn't say where that might happen. The Democrats had filed a lawsuit in North Carolina to keep the polls open an hour longer. That was the big news. The CNN television cameras showed long lines at polling places in Raleigh and Durham, where it was already dark. Jeff

Zeleny of CNN tried to muster some excitement by saying that Clinton's team saw North Carolina as the closest contest of the night and there were "urgent concerns in both North Carolina and Ohio. But they are confident in Florida and Michigan."

CNN's Trump correspondent, reporting from Trump's headquarters at the Hilton Hotel, claimed that his campaign's own "key internal metrics do not show a win." The correspondent had obviously not spoken to Bill Stepien or Brad Parscale.

One of the more ominous early data reports showed a positive/negative ratio on the candidates. Fifty-four percent of voters viewed Hillary Clinton as unfavorable. But a whopping 61 percent of all voters saw Donald Trump as unfavorable. Yet somebody had to win.

The opening commentary on CBS included the veteran Bob Schieffer saying, "I think we have all . . . thought that this was going to go to Hillary Clinton. I think it's important though, that if she is going to win, she needs to get Virginia. I think it will be extremely difficult for Donald Trump to get the presidency without Virginia."[2]

Before the election coverage was over, Donald Trump would do exactly that. He would win the presidency without Virginia.

Nancy Cordes, covering the Clinton campaign for CBS, said, "They're not popping the champagne corks just yet, but they probably are thinking about how good it might taste. And that's because all of the data they're seeing . . . matches up with what they expected. Good news for the Clinton campaign, because they have so many paths to those two hundred and seventy electoral votes. They are especially heartened by that turnout in key Democratic counties in Florida," Cordes said. "They can win without winning Florida, but Donald Trump cannot."[3]

She then added a message that drove a stake into the heart of Brad Parscale and his theories. "Other things that are encouraging to the Clinton campaign tonight? They are not seeing that secret Trump voter that the Trump campaign had been insisting was out there, that [voter who] wasn't talking to pollsters but was going to mobilize on Election Day."[4]

Apparently the polling information that Don Trump Jr., Eric Trump, Brad Parscale, and others had passed along to the television networks, information that had provoked laughter, had been immediately passed on to the Hillary Clinton campaign.

At seven p.m., the first returns were coming in. These were real votes. Trump had carried Kentucky and then Indiana but that was to be expected. The big news had Clinton up in Florida. And then it started to tip to Donald Trump and then back to Hillary Clinton. "Too early," people said.

Brad Parscale's office became a refreshing oasis of hope for those less masochistic. Pastor Darrell Scott, the cofounder of the National Diversity Coalition for Trump, was one of those. "I just kept in Brad's office because everyone was happy. They knew they were going to win."[5]

"The campaign owed my company $4.5 million on Election Night," Brad remembers. "So I will confess to occasional moments of anxiety. I knew that if the Trump campaign lost the election it would be almost impossible for them to pay. In any other campaign I wouldn't see a penny of it. That's how politics worked."[6]

Jared and the senior staff were in the data room with Bill Stepien, getting immediate returns from their computers. Trump called down, "Why don't you come up here? They've got TVs up on the walls, all the channels. This is the show right here. It's beautiful. So you are staring at computer screens and you are only getting it five minutes earlier. This is better."

They agreed, and the staff soon gathered around Trump in the conference war room.

A commentator on CNN was pointing out that Clinton would likely win because of her edge in the Electoral College contest. She went into the night with a likely advantage of 268–204. John King pointed out that it would be incredibly hard for Trump to win without Florida, which he was losing once again.

At 7:35 p.m., Hillary Clinton was winning North Carolina by 100,000 votes. Lara Trump, tasked by her father-in-law to win that state, was still on the phones at her nearby apartment, doing radio shows.

By 8:00 p.m., Hillary Clinton was declared the likely winner in Illinois, Massachusetts, New Jersey, Maryland, Delaware, and Rhode Island, and she was leading in Florida and North Carolina. Trump had added some southern states. When a report showed her taking the lead in Ohio, with 12 percent of the vote tabulated, CNN's John King declared, "If this holds up, it's all over."

Thirty minutes later, CNN's Dana Bash reported news from Republican sources that claimed "models show Donald Trump will lose Florida." Now more than half of the vote was recorded in North Carolina, and Clinton was leading by 150,000 votes. It was 51.9 percent. CNN host Wolf Blitzer concluded, "That's significant."[7]

A PARTY IN THE TRUMP KITCHEN

And yet while Hillary Clinton's victory was at times tantalizingly close, the numbers in the most contested states were not final. Sometimes it swung back to Donald Trump. In Ohio, Virginia, Florida, North Carolina, and New Hampshire, there was no clear winner. While there were still only early returns in Michigan and Pennsylvania, votes from the rural areas had Trump gaining and then surpassing Clinton, although it was assumed that this would not last.

Nevertheless, commentators on all of the networks were admitting that Trump looked better than they had thought possible. He was winning an early game of expectations. He might not actually win the presidency but he was putting the fear of God into the national media. Jake Tapper turned out to have been more correct than he knew when he'd said "there could be new surprises." Clinton was not running away with this. On CNN, Wolf Blitzer said, "Trump is doing remarkably well."[8]

Just before nine p.m., Donald Trump went upstairs with his family and senior staffers. Brad Parscale went with the crowd. "I walked up to Governor Mike Pence and said, 'You're going to be the next vice president.' He seemed to be in shock.

"And then I walked up to Mr. Trump and I said, 'It's just a matter of time now. Nobody wants to be the first to call it. But it's over, sir. My raw data says, it's over. I have the results. The AP has just verified them. And you're going to be the president.'"

Trump was not so sure. Only a few hours before, the very same AP had confirmed he was going to lose.

Perhaps remembering Brad Parscale's earlier visit to CNN, Jake Tapper mused on air, "If this turns out to be the way that the Trump advisers expect, it will put the polling industry out of business. I don't know of one poll that had this happening." Tapper was wrong. As Ivanka Trump reminded me, the USC–*Los Angeles Times* poll had seen it happening, although the man behind the poll was so browbeaten by his colleagues that he had eventually denied his own work, announcing that he, too, thought Hillary would win.[9]

The Trump team, now gathered in the family quarters, continued to excitedly discuss the unfolding events, but their deliberations only provoked more questions. The need for more information drew the party down a spiral staircase, to the only available television in the Trump apartments. The group ended up in the kitchen galley, where all of them crowded around a very small television.

On the staircase, Trump yelled at Parscale, "Brad, you said, 'It's over,' but they haven't called it!"

"But they're going to, sir. It's just a matter of time."

Bannon raised his voice too and said, "Yeah, it's just a matter of time."

"You could tell that Mr. Trump was frustrated," Brad remembers. "I had been telling him for days now that he would win. He wanted to believe it. And now he was getting just enough information on television to see that maybe, just maybe, I had been right the whole time. I could see it. I could hear it in his voice. He wanted it to be right, but he was frustrated. I knew him."

The downstairs kitchen was not a large room. Donald Trump does not cook for himself. It's described as more of a galley for staff.

"He doesn't have a lot of television sets in his apartment," Brad explained. "So we were all crammed in there waiting for the mid-Atlantic states to come in. We were all watching on this tiny little television in the kitchen."

"Isn't it funny?" Lara said later, describing that night. "It doesn't matter where a party starts, it usually ends up in the kitchen."[10]

At 9:58 p.m., Trump tweeted a picture of the family, joined by his vice presidential running mate, Mike Pence, and his wife and children.[11]

Some said that Donald Trump, Jared Kushner, and Ivanka, the three who were following the numbers most closely, looked glum. "I don't remember that," Ivanka told me. "But then, we still didn't know." Earlier in the week she and other members of the family had been shown a possible Electoral College win for her father that included taking the state of Nevada. The early returns for Nevada showed that Clinton was likely to win there.

There were about twenty-five family and staff now gathered around the small television. All of them had phones, and many were talking with staffers in other parts of the tower, at the nearby Hilton Hotel ballroom, at bars and restaurants across Manhattan, and in field offices in Florida, Ohio, and North Carolina. In Trump Tower itself, young staffers were gathered at the headquarters room on the fifth floor, the data room on the fourth floor, and the "war room" on the fourteenth floor. When there was a positive announcement, their shouts and cheers echoed from the dozens of phones in the Trump kitchen galley, adding to the audience, all of them trying to make sense of the unfolding events.

In between family pictures and tweets, Donald Trump sat on a chair, glued to the television screen. He was struck by the Election Night party that had been prepared for Hillary Clinton at the Javits Center.

"Wow! I love the set," Trump said with wide-eyed appreciation. "I think it's the most beautiful set I've ever seen." He was impressed by how the Clinton campaign had transformed the venue for their purposes and how good it looked for television. There was the map of the United States on the floor, the elaborate preparations for media, the choreographing of celebrities who would be rationed out onstage throughout the night. And, of course, the glass ceiling. As the first woman president, Hillary Clinton would be breaking the proverbial glass ceiling that night, the ceiling that holds women back from the top positions. Trump appreciated the work and planning it had taken to make it happen, and he seemed to enjoy pointing out some of the flourishes and details to his family.

Florida was still swinging back and forth. One minute it tilted to Trump and the next minute it tilted back to Clinton. Both sides claimed that large precincts of their voters were still uncounted, the panhandle for Trump and Broward County, near Miami, for Clinton. The media believed this was true for Hillary Clinton but could not bring themselves to believe that Trump could actually take Florida. "I think the Trump campaign is inflating their unreported numbers in the panhandle," one on-air analyst explained.[12]

At 10:21 p.m., there were wild exclamations from the fifth-floor headquarters, and the noise reverberated in the staff's cell phones in the kitchen galley. Trump had taken Ohio. How had that happened? For Trump, the state was a must-win for the presidency. Historically, Ohio had voted forty-four times for the winning presidential candidate, including two times for Barack Obama. Trump's chances were still viable. "The path," as the anchors described it, was still open for him. Members of the family, including Trump's two oldest sons, finally felt some vindication. What were the executives at ABC thinking now?

But North Carolina was still too close to call.

WHEN TRUMP WON NORTH CAROLINA

Lara Trump was worried. "Given the fact that I was in charge of North Carolina, I was really nervous about any news from that state. When the results started coming in, oh my God, it was so close. It was one of the closest things. Television anchors were sure that Hillary Clinton was going to win it. They said it was going blue this time. And I felt 100 percent responsible for North Carolina. So my father-in-law was sitting in front of me to the left. State after state was coming in. Oh my gosh, I am texting, you know, our state director. 'What is going on? Do you have any info?'"

At 11:14 North Carolina was finally declared for Trump.

"We had it on CNN, because if CNN admits that Donald Trump has actually won a state, you know he did. They always called a state last." Lara laughed.

"So once CNN said it was official, 'Donald Trump wins North Carolina,' I was like, 'Oh my gosh. I can die happy now.'

"Seriously, it was probably the happiest moment of my life save for my wedding day and the birth of my son. My father-in-law literally turned around and looked at me and he goes, 'That was all you. We won because of you.'

"By the way, that is so Donald Trump. I mean he gives credit where credit is due. That was the longest night ever. None of us had slept for days and we were up until four o'clock in the morning."

Then at eleven thirty, suddenly, without any further fanfare, Trump was declared the winner in Florida. The finality of the decision was stunning. It was a critical win. Television anchors, almost all of them openly Democrats, looked shocked. Could this be right? Was this really final? This information was coming from the Associated Press and the various television network analysts. This was not Brad Parscale; this was coming from the people who only days before had openly laughed at Brad Parscale and his numbers.

Now came news from the Trump data room on the fourth floor. There Bill Stepien and his team sat in front of monitors and input votes the traditional way, cross-checking exit polls with their own analysis. Earlier in the night, Trump had visited the data room, where he could see all the probabilities on maps, which was easier than making sense of Brad's dizzying Excel sheets of numbers. Now Stepien was calling up to Trump with analysis that agreed with Parscale. "I think you've won, sir. I think this is over."

Meanwhile, Brad Parscale got a call from his team. He took in the information and then turned to Donald Trump. "Sir, you've just taken Pennsylvania. We got all the raw data. It's done."

"Then why haven't they called it!" Trump roared in frustrated disbelief.

"Sir, again, they don't want to be the one network to call you the winner and get it wrong."[13]

At eleven thirty p.m., Fox News called the state of Wisconsin for Trump. It wasn't official. CNN, which would withhold from its viewers the same Associated Press numbers that informed all the networks, wouldn't report this news until close to two thirty a.m. And it wouldn't be official until 3:04 a.m. Still, this early announcement was a shocker. No one had expected it. Wisconsin hadn't voted for a Republican presidential candidate in thirty-two years. Hillary Clinton had not even bothered to visit the state. In the last days of the campaign, when they had heard that Donald Trump was holding a rally there, they had openly laughed about it with reporters. "Good, keep visiting Wisconsin!" they had mocked.[14]

After the Wisconsin announcement, reality finally hit, and Brad Parscale, who had been "this goofy numbers guy," whose explanations about "models" and "low propensity" voters made the listeners' eyes glaze over, was now a genius. Before, they had said to themselves, "Oh sure, Brad. You're right, and all those people at the *New York Times* and the television networks, who have been doing this professionally since before you were born? They are all wrong. You're the only one who's figured this out. Sure."

Now, people in the campaign started coming up to Brad Parscale to shake his hand. "Congratulations," they said. As if he was the one who had done it.

"Donald Trump had done it," Brad said. "I had only reported numbers."

On television, the Trump crowd at the Hilton Hotel ballroom had broken into wild celebration. The television anchors were in disbelief.

TRUMP RIPS UP HIS SPEECH
Leading up to this moment of victory, Donald Trump had already, internally, experienced a hundred imaginary defeats. All along he had

followed what the pollsters had been saying. He knew what the experts had believed. He understood the arguments inside his own campaign. He had been emotionally prepared either way. "If I win, great, I want to win. If I lose. . . . Well, we will have a great life."[15]

And yet, Donald Trump had chosen to act as if he would win. He had worked hard. He kept doing all the necessary things, right up to the last minute. This, he told friends, was the great lesson to take away from the Mitt Romney experience. Romney had let up during the last days and hours of the 2012 presidential campaign, and the incumbent, President Obama, had pulled away. At least, that was the legend. This time, only minutes before the polls had closed, Trump was still making those phone calls to radio stations in key battleground states.

For a moment, still uncertain, waiting for television anchors to confirm what his own team was telling him, Donald Trump sat transfixed by what he was seeing on television. He was now watching the Clinton supporters at the Javits Center as they tracked the returns. There was a slight, delayed reaction to what he was learning from his own team and what was being reported to the public.

"Look at these crying Clinton supporters, imagine how they feel?" Trump said, studying the tear-streaked faces of young ladies at the Javits Center. "They never saw it coming. Just think how hard they have worked. It must be terrible. It must be terrible." For weeks, he had been bracing himself for those same feelings.

Ivanka was struck by the contrast between her father's mood and the jubilation echoing in the staff rooms in other parts of Trump Tower. She understood the joy of the team, even the gloating. They had every right to rejoice in a very hard-fought and bitter political victory. "New York hates you!" the crowd had screamed at the Trumps when they had voted earlier that day. But Ivanka knew her father was in no mood to rub it in.

"This was a part of Donald Trump that the public doesn't see," she told me in an interview about that night. "He defies typecasting.

I think it's an area in which he is misunderstood. He is really very compassionate."[16]

All her life, even in her teens, Ivanka would be called into his office, where he would tear off a piece of the morning newspaper and say, "Ivanka, find this person." It might be a person whose apartment had burned, destroying everything he had owned. Once it was a young woman whose father had been murdered in the Bronx, and prosecutors would not make the arrest. The young woman was left destitute. Ivanka had finally tracked her down. Donald Trump had offered her help and a job.

"I had seen that look in his eyes before," Ivanka said. "He was moved by the Clinton supporters he was seeing on Election Night."

"You were there? You saw that too?" I asked Jared Kushner. I didn't doubt the story that Ivanka was telling me, but it was such a revelation that I instinctively sought other sources to back her up.

"I was there," Jared confirmed. "And Kellyanne Conway and Stephen Miller and many others. We were all gathered around."

Miller, who would later be a senior policy adviser for President Trump, was the speechwriter on the team. He had prepared two early drafts. A concession speech and a victory speech. Now it was time to take a look.

"No one had really focused on the winning speech." Ivanka laughed, recalling the moment. "Not because we thought we would lose, but rather to avoid being overconfident or arrogant. And maybe we were just a little bit superstitious. So nobody wanted to write it."

Donald Trump took a look at the victory speech. "It took a lot of shots at the people who hadn't supported us," said Ivanka. "Mainly, the elites who had said it wasn't possible."

Trump dramatically ripped up the speech. "This is totally wrong," he said. "We have to reach out to those people we saw crying tonight and we have to tell them that it's going to be okay. And we are going to come together."

Trump's senior staffers reconvened around the dining room table in the private Trump apartments to work on the speech. Campaign manager Kellyanne Conway was there, helping to make revisions. "It was already in his own voice," she remembered, "but taking a good fresh look at it and realizing he was going to be the next president of the United States, he changed a lot of it."[17]

Trump wrote the words, "I'm going to be the president of all Americans, including those who do not support me." And then he added the self-deprecating, sarcastic line, "and there are a few of you."

Ivanka remembered the moment as almost magical. "His instinct was so immediate and so strong," she said, referring to her father's mood. "It was a beautiful thing. His first reaction was to feel deeply about what the Clinton supporters were experiencing. And partly because everyone had told them that this was an outcome that was not possible. He was supersensitive to that, and you saw it reflected in his words.

"It was close to midnight by then." Ivanka recalled. "And yet, in that brief moment, none of us felt tired. We felt good about the country, and I felt good about my father and his desire to bring the country together. I have so many photos of us just sitting together and rewriting that speech. The feeling in that room was really something beautiful."

At 12:32 a.m. the networks called Nevada for Hillary Clinton. Ivanka's fear was realized. Her sources had been accurate after all. But then her model for an Electoral College victory, the one that all the experts had laid out, had been bypassed by another, parallel, more historically impossible combination. Nevada had been replaced by other, more important states. Nevada had not been necessary.

So when was the exact moment that Donald Trump finally realized he had won?

"My feeling is that [it was] sometime between twelve a.m. and one a.m.," Ivanka said. "Even while working on a victory speech, just in case, Donald Trump was finally beginning to realize that he was going to be president of the United States."

Late into the night the networks continued to refuse to declare Pennsylvania.

"We had this friend," Eric Trump remembers, "Mark Geist. He was a marine who became a government contractor, and he was one of the guys that was left on the roof in Benghazi by Hillary Clinton. He had vowed when my father entered the race that he would do anything within his power to help my father win. 'What that person did to me was so unthinkable,' said Mark Geist, adding, 'Under no circumstance can she become commander in chief of the United States. She left us on a roof with no support.'

"You probably saw his story in the movie *13 Hours*. He was the co-author of the book. He is still recovering from traumatic injuries, but he was credited with saving the lives of twenty-five Americans that night.

"So, the networks were not calling Pennsylvania. Ninety-nine percent of the votes were recorded. My father was winning by 330,000 votes, and even if Clinton got every single remaining vote she still would not have gotten over the threshold. CNN had been sitting on this for about five hours. If you want to talk about dishonesty in the media? They would not call it, because it would have put him over the top. And they didn't want to depress voters in California, where they were apparently trying to drive up the Clinton popular vote.

"So Mark Geist says to his buddy, 'We may be standing in this room, waiting for CNN, longer than she left us on that roof in Benghazi.'"

"I'll never forget that statement as long as I live," Eric Trump told me.[18]

"SCREW IT, LET'S JUST GO!"

At two a.m., Clinton's campaign chairman, John Podesta, appeared at the Javits Center to address the dispirited, waiting Clinton supporters. It sounded to some like a hopeful speech. "Well, folks, I know you've been here a long time. And it's been a long night and it's been a long campaign but I can say, we can wait a little longer, can't we?"[19]

"No, no, no," Trump said, watching the moment, right after

witnessing the weeping children of the Clinton campaign. "This is not right. This is not good for the country. I'm not going to let them do this. I'm going to go out and accept this thing. I've won. I know I've won."[20]

"You have sir," Brad Parscale said. "You've won."

"Screw it, let's just go!"

Steve Bannon was there. So were Kellyanne Conway and Hope Hicks.

Trump looked again at Parscale and said, "Brad, we've won this?"

"Yes sir, you've won this."

Bannon chipped in, "Yes sir, you've won."

"Okay, let's go."

As the motorcade worked its way a few blocks over to the Hilton, word came in from their own people that they had, indeed, carried Wisconsin. They had feared that the Fox News report had been a bit premature, but now it was confirmed by the others. The message that came into the motorcade was that Hillary Clinton had now been told by her own staff that she had lost the election and that it had been decisive. There would be no recount.

Erik Prince remembers Dave Bossie coming into one of the rooms at Trump Tower, where everyone was celebrating. "Hey, if you want to see the next president give an acceptance speech, get over to the Hilton!" The crowd broke up quickly and moved like a mob out of the Trump Tower and down the streets of Manhattan to the Hilton Hotel. Sean Spicer, the future press spokesman of the Trump administration, was in the middle of the pack, huffing and puffing down the sidewalk.

Arlene "A. J." Delgado, a Harvard Law graduate and a senior adviser in the Trump campaign, was overcome with emotion. "I broke down just in the middle of this dark street, just on the way to the Hilton, just crying like a little girl just because of the amount of work and the amount of emotion that had gone into stumping for this candidate for a year, to realize that it did all pay off."[21]

There had not been enough room for the whole Trump family and senior staff to get into the elevators at Trump Tower, so the crowd got separated in the motorcade to the Hilton. It took some time for them to slowly reassemble backstage. The Secret Service had an area roped off for them and recognized most of them by sight and others by the special, color-coded buttons affixed to their suit jacket lapels and dresses.

Eric remembers being driven over in the motorcade and then being ushered into hallways, lined by Secret Service agents, into the backstage area of the Hilton.

"There were two landings backstage. At first, we were upstairs, and they walked us down this little staircase—in fact, I have a picture of it. This was about two or three in the morning, and, remember, most of the people had been there at the Hilton since five the previous evening."

"It was pitch dark backstage," Brad Parscale remembers. "And there were so many people."

While they were organizing in the darkness, word came from a staffer's cell phone that one of the networks announced that Trump had taken Pennsylvania, confirming what his team had told him hours before. A few seconds later, as the news was relayed to television anchors on the big screens at the Hilton, the crowd on the other side of the curtain roared with approval. It was a surreal, delayed reaction.

In the darkness somebody handed Mr. Trump a cell phone and said, "It's Hillary Clinton, she's calling to concede." She had barely made it. Time was running out. Robby Mook had made it clear to Kellyanne Conway that within fifteen minutes of being declared the winner, Hillary Clinton would take to the stage at the Javits Center to address the American people. If Donald Trump wanted to have the dignity of recognizing the new president, he had to call her personal aide, Huma Abedin, within that window. But now it was Hillary who was almost left behind.

Earlier, during the campaign, when Donald Trump had complained about voter fraud, there had been questions about whether he would accept the election results and Hillary Clinton as the new president. The popular historian Michael Beschloss had said, "Fifty years from now historians will remember this debate for exactly one thing and that is Trump refusing to say that he'll accept the results of the election." Beschloss added that it was "absolutely horrifying."[22] Now almost no one remembered it, and Hillary Clinton was the one rushing to make her concession call and appear reasonable.

While the nation looked on, some pleased, some stunned by what was unfolding on television, Hillary Clinton called Donald Trump. "I was a foot away from him," Eric told me. "It was Don, Ivanka, my wife, and Jared. We were all kind of around him. So he got that call. It was short. It probably lasted a minute or two. That is when we knew the whole thing was very real."

Hillary Clinton wrote about it in her book *What Happened*. "I congratulated Trump and offered to do anything I could to make sure the transition was smooth. It was all perfectly nice and weirdly ordinary, like calling a neighbor to say you can't make it to his barbecue. . . . I was numb. It was all so shocking."[23]

In the darkness, still backstage at the Hilton Hotel, Donald Trump turned to his family and staff and said simply, "I'm president."

As he walked through the crowd toward the stage, he passed Brad Parscale one last time and gave him a half hug. "You did a really good job, Brad. You did really good." And then he said, "By the way, don't stand next to me onstage."

When he got to the side, ready to walk out, he turned back to the crowd of senior staffers and shouted out again, "Brad, I mean it. Don't stand anywhere near me onstage!"

Brad Parscale is six feet, eight inches tall.

It was Trump's backhanded, jocular way of giving recognition to Parscale for a job well done, without coming off as too sentimental.

Two of Donald Trump's grandchildren had stayed up for the entire Election Night drama, nine-year-old Kai Madison and seven-year-old Donald Trump III, or "Donnie." They had been in the Trump Tower war room, upstairs in the apartment, and later in the kitchen, where their grandfather, the candidate, and his team had watched television on that tiny screen. Their father, Donald Trump Jr., had wanted his children to be a part of history. But now, the night had dragged into the next day. "We hadn't planned for that. They had never been up so late," Donald Trump Jr. says.

The two children were now backstage at the Hilton, taking it all in, surrounded by adults, drifting somewhere in between sleep and wakefulness, uncomprehending of the political jockeying of the grown-ups around them. They were lined up, watching their uncle Barron just ahead of them. When the whole group would shuffle out onto the stage, they would follow him.

President-elect Donald Trump was flooded with memories of his parents, especially his father and his brother, Freddy, who had died too young and had missed so much of life. What would his parents and his big brother think about this night? And he brought with him fresh images of the heartbroken Clinton supporters he had just seen on television.

The president-elect and his vice president, and their families, now walked onstage at the Hilton Hotel. A massive battery of cameras filled more than half of the Hilton ballroom. But it was not the great show that one might have expected from a Donald Trump victory. A new hotel in Dubai would get more fanfare. The RNC stage had displayed much more glamour. There were no fireworks in the Hudson, as Hillary Clinton had originally planned. There stood Donald and Melania Trump and their son, Barron; Don Jr. and Vanessa; Jared and Ivanka; Eric and Lara; Tiffany; and the vice president–elect, Mike Pence, his wife, Karen, and his family. There stood little Kai Madison and Donnie in a daze.

"Now it is time for America to bind the wounds of division," Donald Trump told the nation. "We have to get together. To all Republicans and Democrats and independents across this nation, I say it is time for us to come together as one united people.

"It is time. I pledge to every citizen of our land that I will be president for all Americans, and this is so important to me. For those who have chosen not to support me in the past, of which there were a few people, I'm reaching out to you for your guidance and your help so that we can work together and unify our great country."[24]

THE PENINSULA HOTEL GOES DARK

"We left the Hilton in a state of shock," remembers Brad Parscale. "We didn't look for the motorcade, we just walked home." He and his wife had rented a small apartment in Manhattan. They had a window that looked out at the Christmas tree at Rockefeller Center. During the night they could hear the nonstop holiday music from Saks Fifth Avenue. For three weeks Brad had worked all day, every day, at Trump Tower, sleeping only a few hours each night at the small apartment.

"It was really a peaceful night," Brad remembers. "Not cold out. Very calm. No wind. The moon was bright. And the streets were filled with Trump people. I think we finally got home at five a.m."

For Katrina Pierson, the Trump campaign's spokesperson, the whole experience was dreamlike. "That night was unbelievable," she remembers. She had been standing onstage with the new president-elect and his family, but her thoughts went to earlier, more humble, years. "I thought about just growing up as a child with a 15-year-old mother who became addicted to drugs."[25]

With the very late night, and the unexpected election results, the streets of Manhattan quickly emptied. Only moments before there had been an estimated 200,000 people watching big-screen television sets in Times Square and lining all the streets to and from the Clinton headquarters at the Peninsula Hotel.

Now there was a deathly silence. Hillary Clinton's supporters, who had outnumbered Trump's supporters nine to one in Manhattan, were exhausted and had retreated into their apartments and thousands of hotel rooms.

The small, enthusiastic mob of Trump supporters who had raced down the street to the Hilton to see the president-elect give his speech to the nation now walked back through the empty streets to Trump Tower, their shouts and footsteps echoing harmlessly up the walls of the skyscrapers in the vast, darkened city.

When they passed the Peninsula Hotel there were heavy trucks, filled with sand, standing guard against any terrorists who might want to attack Hillary Clinton. She had been the presumed winner, and the city had to be prepared. One could envision where the crowds of thousands would have gathered on the streets to await a royal wave from a hotel window from the first woman American president in history. Instead, the building was darkened. There were no lights coming from the rooms.

"It looked ghostly. A lot of it was empty, because they had rented out so much of it," remembers A. J. Delgado.[26] Another Trump supporter felt as if Dementors from a Harry Potter novel were lurking behind the darkened windows, sucking the life out of any passersby.

Delgado was reminded of the *Titanic*. "Your hubris got the best of you. And you forgot to actually campaign, and you forgot about the actual voters. And now look, the Peninsula is empty and I'm walking to Trump Tower. And we just had an election night victory party and you just conceded."[27]

Hillary Clinton had enjoyed the backing of Wall Street. America's billionaires had overwhelmingly supported her.[28] Almost every major company in America and the world had donated to the Clinton Foundation, including, what would later become a great irony, more than $145 million from Russian oligarchs.[29] Most of the American executives had maxed out donations to her campaign. She had the support of Silicon Valley and the emerging tech monopolies. She had the support of academia and almost all the major universities. Hollywood was solidly behind her.

Politically, she was unsurpassed. She had 960,000 poll workers, the largest "ground game" in American history. All the living former presidents, Republican and Democratic, had voted for her.

Most important, many in the national media, abandoning all pretense of objectivity, were now openly joined at the hip with the Democratic Party. They had invested heavily in the 2016 presidential election. Two hundred and forty-nine newspapers had endorsed Democratic candidate Hillary Clinton, while only nineteen had endorsed Republican Donald Trump.[30] One report showed that 96 percent of personal donations from those who worked in media went to the Democratic candidate.[31]

Still, the American people had sensed that something was wrong. The more the media and the American establishment insisted that they vote one way, the more suspicious the public had become and thus voted another. They didn't like being spoon-fed cherry-picked information and were unforgiving when they discovered it was wrong or slanted or, sometimes, annoyingly, missing altogether. Americans now had the internet and cable television. They developed their own sense of what the evening news should be and were unforgiving when the selectivity of a New York television producer was different from their own. Journalism had moved from reporting verifiable facts to promoting opinions and conspiracy theories. But the public already had their own opinions and their own conspiracy theories.

They resented politicians who promised one thing and did another, who talked to them as if they were children, who adhered to a tight, unforgiving uniformity of thought and word. They wanted something different. Like a modern-day Benjamin Disraeli, or a rough-and-tumble Andrew Jackson. For years they had longed for an outsider, which past presidents had pretended to be, but this time, against all odds, Donald Trump had risen up to fight the establishment and win the election. His outrageous behavior and rough edges, which astonished the media, were reassuring to masses of people who deeply resented the patronizing domination of American elites.

Donald Trump's father, Fred, had urged him to stay in Queens and Brooklyn, on his side of the East River, where they knew all the players and knew what to expect. "Don't go over there," his father warned him, pointing to Manhattan. "We don't know those people. They play by different rules."[32] But Donald Trump could not stay in Queens. He saw the towering, shiny buildings and the glittering lights of Manhattan, and ultimately he saw even beyond them, to a whole nation in trouble.

And so, as Ivanka Trump described to me in our first interview, he crossed over the bridge.

9

MOVING INTO THE WHITE HOUSE

"It had been a long, bitter, divisive campaign,
but now the nightmare was finally over."
—LARA TRUMP[1]

O ne of the questions I asked the president and each member of his family was at what time on Election Night they finally realized they had won. They each had different answers. One talked about a growing realization after the win in North Carolina. Others said it was the moment when the networks called the state of Pennsylvania. Most mentioned the phone call from Hillary Clinton conceding the election. This took place in the darkness, backstage at the Hilton Hotel. At that very moment the family was poised to walk out to face the cameras and claim the prize anyway and acknowledge their supporters in the ballroom.

I was completely unprepared for the answer that Donald Trump Jr. gave me. He had experienced the resistance his father had provoked. Resistance from some in the corporate establishment, from the media, from the international banking institutions. From the global

consortiums. Trying to understand the driving force behind that resistance gnawed at him.

"The ups and down were so emotionally draining," he said. "It was
happening all day long. One minute something sent you in one direction and the next minute something sent you in another. You almost
felt like a caged animal that had been beaten.

"Even on Election Night, even after watching Pennsylvania with
ninety-nine percent of the vote reporting, even when they called it, for
me, I can tell you, I really didn't enjoy the moment that much.

"Oddly enough, my moment of joy had come when John Podesta got on stage and said, 'We'll see what happens, let's talk in the
morning.'" Don Jr. laughed. "I was told afterward that it was because
she [Clinton] had too much to drink, that she couldn't get onstage.
Fair or not, that's what was being said. But I thought, 'I finally get it.
The establishment is going to play this game. They are going to try
to screw us.'

"I was happier about that moment, knowing that I was beginning
to understand how this worked than I was about the fact that we had
won. This wasn't personal. This was being driven by the power of the
elites and their control over the country. The picture I had been seeing
was coming into sharper focus. By the way, that's how cynical you
become in a race like this.

"There was a source of triumph at seeing the curtain pulled back on
these sanctimonious people. To see them exposed to the public for what
they really were. That night everybody could see it in the faces of many
of the television personalities. They had the power. Their bosses and
advertisers made the money. They didn't really care about the country.
They were panicked because their power and control were in jeopardy."

So I asked Don Jr., "When did you finally believe you had won?
That it was over, that your father was going to be president?"

"I didn't fully enjoy the moment until weeks after the election. It
was during our trip to Washington, DC, and the visit to Arlington

National Cemetery. This is a ceremony that every new president participates in. It takes place the day before the inauguration. Laying a wreath at the Tomb of the Unknown Soldier.

"For some reason I couldn't let down my guard during the coverage on Election Night or throughout the excitement of the transition. It was on that drive into Arlington that the realization finally hit me that my father had won. He was the president of the United States. This was real. They weren't going to take it away. It was truly over. My whole body just began to relax."

Donald Trump Jr. was talking about January 19, 2017, the day before the inauguration. The whole Trump family had been flown by government planes into Washington for the event. But this was two months after the election.

Everyone deals with adversity differently. Some try to be positive and are almost superstitious about negative thoughts. Others prepare for the worst and live delightfully surprised by victories occurring all around them. Don Jr. had almost physically braced himself for defeat. It was if his muscles had hurt from the effort. It had taken days for him to finally accept that his father and namesake, Donald J. Trump, had won the presidency.

"The magnitude of what we had accomplished finally hit me."[2]

Each member of the Trump family was experiencing the moment in their own way. "It's a beautiful building," Eric Trump said, "the tomb of the unknown soldier, with the stairs coming down. So there we were, walking out as a family and it was just eerily quiet. I'll never forget how quiet it was."

DISCOVERING BLAIR HOUSE

After the wreath-laying ceremony at the Tomb of the Unknown Soldier, the Trump family was taken to Blair House, the government building just across the street from the White House. Their luggage was already in their rooms. The president-elect and his family traditionally stay at Blair House the night before the inauguration. Heads of state visiting the United States often stay there as well. The ghosts of Charles de Gaulle, Margaret Thatcher, and Boris Yeltsin filled the rooms. President Harry Truman had lived there while the crumbling White House was gutted and rebuilt. Queen Elizabeth lived there when she visited the United States.

Blair House looked like a simple street-front colonial apartment, adjacent to others on the same block. Next door was the Renwick Gallery, a branch of the Smithsonian American Art Museum. In fact, Blair House was only the entrance to a labyrinth of rooms and offices, every bit as complicated as the White House itself. Like the innocuous entrance to Number 10 Downing Street, the entrance to Blair House was just the doorway to other connected buildings that seemed to never end. One could reach the ten-story New Executive Office Building from here. And there were reportedly underground tunnel connections to the Eisenhower Office Building, the White House, and the Treasury Department.

Lara Trump was taken by surprise. "I had no idea. Yeah, I had heard of the Blair House, but I got my best explanation while we were in the motorcade on our way over there. We were told that we would be staying in this place where so many important leaders had stayed. And, of course, I am the crazy one who found a small gym with one treadmill. I couldn't sleep, so I just went to the gym at four o'clock in morning and worked out.

"That whole inauguration experience from start to finish was just unbelievable. You know something? They can try to take that away from us but they will never, ever, completely succeed. We have those memories forever. And we are not going to give them up. It was just really amazing. It was really incredible."[3]

News stories abounded about Donald Trump's hair and what should happen if it rained on Inauguration Day. The media scrambled to cover the new fashion model, First Lady Melania Trump. She could speak six languages and she was stunning. America had not seen such a glamorous first lady since Jacqueline Kennedy. Journalists rushed to file stories. "Her makeup artist—and close confidante of 17 years—Nicole Bryl" was quoted in *Stylish*.[4] Meanwhile *Us Weekly* reported on her hair: "First Lady Melania Trump chose a deep side-parted updo that she helped style with her longtime hairstylist, Mordechai Alvow."[5]

Nor did the media ignore all the other Trump women. The *New York Post* ran a story with the headline "Why Ivanka Will Be the Most Stylish First Daughter Ever."[6]

Was there competition among the Trump women? Jealousy? Each one was so striking.

"There was no jealousy," Lara insists. "I think we all had kind of texted beforehand about the colors. We were 100 percent sure what everyone else was wearing. I will tell you when we first got to Washington, DC, I didn't have the outfit I was planning to change into for the concert at the Lincoln Memorial. I was so upset. Nobody would even know, but all the women had changed into their beautiful dresses and matching jackets, and I was there in a pair of pants. I had a plan, I had an outfit to wear, but it didn't work out."

In fact, Inauguration Day itself was nearly a disaster for the Trump ladies.

"We had this company approach us in New York," Lara remembers. "They came to your place of work or to your event or wedding and did your hair and makeup. Well, they were opening a new business in Washington, DC, and offered to help us on Inauguration Day. So we checked to make sure that was okay and we agreed. That would take a lot of the burden off of us. But there was one big problem that we hadn't thought about. Security.

"Now that my father-in-law was president, the Secret Service was taking over. So when the team showed up early in the morning of the inauguration they couldn't get near us. They said, 'We're here to do the makeup and hair styling for the Trump ladies,' and the Secret Service said, 'Why, sure you are. Of course you are. Glad to hear it.' They wouldn't let them in.

"So it is getting pretty late and we are beginning to panic. You know, these things take time. We are on a schedule. We have to appear at a church service at a little church nearby and we can't skip it. Every president since James Madison has gone there for a service on Inauguration Day, so we are going to say, 'Well, sorry, the Trumps couldn't make it because we had a bad hair day!'

"So now we are calling all over the place. 'Where are the folks who were going to help us? Where are you guys?'

"They say, 'We are just outside on the streets held back by security. They don't believe us. They won't let us in.'

"So we finally get that resolved and the race was on to get ready."

Saint John's Episcopal Church is right across Lafayette Park, less than four hundred yards from Blair House. Some of the family said, "We can walk it." It would have been an easy trek, but the Trump family was in what the Secret Service calls "full motorcade." The president, the first lady, and their children and grandchildren were all trundled into limousines and driven around the block to the front door of the church.

The Reverend Robert Jeffress, the pastor of the First Baptist Church in Dallas, Texas, delivered the sermon. Jeffress remembered eating Wendy's cheeseburgers on the campaign trail with Donald Trump during a stop in Iowa. "I said that I believed you would be the next president of the United States. And if that happened, it would be because God had placed you there. As the prophet Daniel said, it is God who removes and establishes leaders."[7]

"Pastor Paula White was there," Lara Trump remembers. "Joel Osteen was there. And James Robison, who is really a great guy. They each gave short, meaningful remarks."

Two hours later, Donald Trump, Melania, and the Trump family would stand on the inaugural stage. Donald J. Trump would be sworn in as the forty-fifth president of the United States. After his inaugural address and a Capitol luncheon, at which Trump would ask the audience to give Hillary Clinton a standing ovation, the Trump family would parade down Pennsylvania Avenue to the White House.

FIRST TIME IN THE WHITE HOUSE

I was astonished to learn that most of the Trump children had never visited the White House before Inauguration Day. Not ever. Not for a seminar, a photo op, an East Room briefing, or a Rose Garden ceremony. Not even as a tourist waiting in line to walk through the State Floor. They had never heard the guide say, "And this is the East Room, where First Lady Abigail Adams actually hung up her laundry to dry when it was raining outside."

Donald Trump Jr. had visited Washington, DC, as a teenager. "I came down as part of some school event," he said. "I was just a kid. We toured Washington, all the monuments, and we actually passed by the White House. Everybody took a lot of pictures. But I never set foot on the White House grounds."

"Really?" I said. "In all of these years you never even had the tourist visit of the State Floor?"

"Never," he said. "Not until the day of the inauguration. It's truly incredible, to just pop into the Lincoln Bedroom. Just the history of everything that's there. It's truly incredible."

It was a new experience for Tiffany Trump, the president's fourth child, as well. When I asked her about previous visits to Washington, I got this surprise answer. "I had only been to Washington, DC, for a few hours for a college tour in high school," she said. "Actually, the first time I saw the White House was the same night that we moved in, the night of the inauguration."[8]

I asked Lara Trump what it was like, actually moving into the White House and spending the night.

"Oh my God." She laughed about it. "Well, it was first of all completely surreal. To have been told continuously by everyone that there was no chance that Donald Trump would ever end up in the White House. To have never dreamed in your entire life that you would ever set foot in the White House. I mean, I never thought I would ever be in there under any circumstances at all. And then to be there on Inauguration Day? And as a family having fought so hard and weathered such a storm. Think of what we had to deal with through that whole campaign and then to be there. It was just so incredibly surreal."

"You had never visited, even as a tourist? A seminar, a briefing, a reception?" I asked.

"No, and really, it's a process to get into a White House tour. You have to apply online, and sometimes it works out and sometimes it doesn't."

"But surely, as a tourist, at some point in your life you had walked by the White House. You had stopped and taken pictures."

"Actually, Eric and I were in Washington, DC, the year before the election. If you can believe this, we went for the White House Correspondents' Dinner in 2015. So yeah, on that trip we walked by the White House for the first time and took a picture in front. We started to take a selfie and I remember some guy saying, 'Do you want me to take a picture for you?'

"So I gave him my phone. He suddenly realized who Eric was and he said, 'Your dad is going to be in there next year.' Friendly people sometimes say that sort of thing to make you feel good. This was so early, before the primaries or anything. But never did I imagine we would be there and we would be there as a family."

Eric had lived in Washington, DC. "It's funny, I went to school at Georgetown. So I knew every square inch of Washington, and yet I'd never been to the White House. Truthfully, when you're in college, you probably don't care that much about it, you know?

"I had a lot of mutual friends with Jenna Bush. She lived two blocks away from me, and this was at a time when it was early in her father's presidency. It's not that I probably couldn't have visited the White House for a tour or gotten into a briefing or something. I just didn't really think twice about it. I mean, who knew what was going to happen?"

Jared and Ivanka had been there before. On official business.

"Ivanka and I came in 2009," Jared said. "We were invited in with a group of young entrepreneurs. This was the Obama White House, and we were supposed to present ideas."[9]

Jared and Ivanka were on a guest list that included Ben Kaufman of Kluster; Tony Hsieh, the founder of Zappos; Blake Mycoskie, the founder of Toms Shoes; and Evan Williams, a cofounder of Twitter. The eclectic group had been gathered to "discuss the future of the ravaged U.S. economy."[10]

Hsieh tweeted that they had been tapped to discuss "ways to help the economy that administration may not have thought of yet."[11]

"We ended up just meeting in the Eisenhower Executive Office Building," Jared remembers. "We thought we'd meet some real administration people. But it ended up just being somebody from OPL."

The more Jared described his visit, the more it sounded like the White House I understood and knew well. Invite in some high-profile people and listen to them and then do what you wanted to do in the first place. Only this time, they apparently, didn't even listen to them. They had twenty-year-old children read carefully written White House talking points.

Jared was philosophical about it and said he would use the experience to help improve on White House meetings when the Trumps took over.

"It was a great group," he said. "I met Jack Dorsey that day and Tony Hsieh, from Zappos. I met Jack Spero. He was with us. It was a very, very great group."

"Did you actually tour the White House? Or were you stuck over in the Executive Office Building?" I asked.

"That day we would actually go through another contact, to get a tour of the State Floor and even to figure out how to get in and see the real West Wing.

"You know, I remember the feeling of what it was like to be invited into the White House. It was a very exciting day to be able to go down and share with the administration. And I also remember being very unsatisfied. They just had us in there to lecture us. They didn't really ask our ideas on anything. They were just trying to get us to be talking heads for them.

"Now I think back on that. It makes me realize that everyone who comes to the White House to meet with us, for them, it's a very important day. Sometimes we have the ability to deliver for them the things they need. Sometimes we can deliver quicker and better than anywhere else they can go. This is a meeting they prepare for. It is a meeting they tell people about. It's an experience to come through here. We have to make sure that we give them one hundred and ten percent focus and that we follow through. We have to treat every meeting with that kind of respect.

"So yes, it was a big deal to come down here.

"Then I came down with my father-in-law during the transition. The president-elect had this meeting set up with President Obama. Trump asked me if I wanted to come along, so I joined him. So we were able to walk around and see the offices. That was a very, very neat experience."

A CHEESEBURGER FOR ERIC

As soon as the Trumps left the Blair House for the service at Saint John's, the famous White House staff set into motion. The Trump family's clothes and special items were packed and prepared for the move across the street. As soon as President and First Lady Obama left with the Trumps for the drive down Pennsylvania Avenue to the Capitol, accompanied by their children, the White House staff began to perform their famous magic trick. They would move the Obamas out and the Trumps in. All in a matter of a three hours. It was a performance worthy of David Copperfield.

"So when we left the Blair House that morning," Lara explained, "they told us, 'You won't be coming back here after the inauguration. You will be moving into the White House. But don't worry about your things, it will all be taken care of.'"

So who was telling you this?

"I don't know," she said, perplexed. "Whoever was in charge."

At this we both started laughing. The people had elected Donald Trump as president, but there always needed to be help to think through the details. I remembered being on White House staff and placing the footprints on the stage so the various dignitaries would know where to stand. Later I would look at videos of the biggest summits in world history, the leaders would walk out onstage and then look to the floor and rearrange themselves. "No, no, Prime Minister, you're over there, I'm here." They were matching up to the footprints that staffers had thought through. And they would soon be reading comments that staffers and aides had vetted. Donald Trump may be president, but someone else had to get his and the first lady's clothes from Blair House over to the White House. And fast.

The actual swearing-in ceremony, when Donald Trump took the oath of office, was a blur for most of the Trump family. Some remembered George W. Bush making wisecracks, or Dick Cheney admonishing one of the dignitaries who was taking pictures with a cell phone: "No, no, you can't do that."

To Donald Trump Jr. the whole moment was like a dream. In one of our interviews he described being stunned. As to his father's speech, which was criticized by some as being "unpresidential," Don Jr. was proud of him. "It was a very Trumpian speech," he said. "He made it clear that he was going to be a promises-made, promises-kept kind of president. His words were very straightforward. He didn't send the signal that, 'Well, now I'm here, I'm going to be just like all the other presidents.' He was sending a message back to the so-called forgotten man. 'I'm still with you. We did it and we are going to get this country the help it needs.'"

After the swearing-in ceremony, the Trump family motorcade joined the parade down Pennsylvania Avenue.

"We left the Capitol," Eric Trump said, "and we were going down the parade route when they suddenly stopped. It was all pre-arranged. They had snipers all over the rooftops and they had this, you know, 500-yard area, incredibly locked down. The family hopped out of the five or six limos we were in. You had all the press vehicles and you had everybody else, including bystanders." They walked 500 yards of the parade route before returning to the motorcade and being driven the last mile to the White House, up the curved drive of the South Lawn, where they were brought to the front doors of the Diplomatic Reception Room.

At the White House there was a formal signing ceremony in the Oval Office, and the whole First Family trooped in, including the eight grandchildren. "That was amazing," Eric Trump told me. "Going into the Oval Office for the first time. It is for anybody a time you will never forget. You look down at that carpet and you see the eagle holding the arrows and holding the olive branch."

Ten-year-old Barron, standing next to his mother, the first lady, played peak-a-boo with Theodore Trump, still a baby in the arms of his mother, Ivanka Trump.

"We got to the White House," Lara said, "and then had to turn around and go right back out to the first family reviewing stand in front to watch the rest of the parade, with all the marching bands from high schools across the country."

"The White House staff was probably stalling for more time," I suggested, "to get you all moved in."

"Probably."

The Trump family was walked out of the front door of the West Wing Lobby. The whole North Lawn had been reconfigured. "They had a big tent that allowed us to walk all the way down to Pennsylvania Avenue," Eric remembered. "They had a cut in the fence. And this grandstand was right on the street. So literally all of the soldiers and school bands were marching right by our reviewing stand down Pennsylvania Avenue.

"It was pretty amazing to see that my father had become the commander in chief. That's hard to describe. Now he was standing there with five generals, literally, it was the whole Joint Chiefs of Staff, and as we walked to the reviewing stand they were going by him and they were all saluting. The whole family was following him, and we could see the different cadets and soldiers standing at the doors, and they were all saluting and he was saluting back. It was an amazing moment. There had been a transformation. Our father, a citizen, a businessman that we had worked with all or our lives, had become the commander in chief of the most powerful nation on earth."

The reviewing stand was heated, but it was still somewhat exposed to the elements, and they were all freezing. Everyone in the Trump family was exhausted. Still, they beamed with gratitude. Sixty-three million Americans had voted for them. The inaugural balls would begin at seven p.m., which gave them little time to get ready.

In the next few hours of their lives, it was very possible that more pictures would be taken of Melania Trump and the other Trump sons and daughters than would be taken in all the rest of their lives put together.

The Trumps were now moved into the private quarters of the White House. This is one story above the State Floor, where tourists visit the East Room, the Red Room, the Blue Room, and the others, including the State Dining Room. The private quarters of the White House are depicted quite accurately in the American television series *House of Cards*, right down to the exact paint colors. The Lincoln Bedroom and the Queen's Bedroom are there, as is the private family dining room. The president and first lady have rooms. The president also has an office there, where I had occasionally met with presidents in earlier years.

There is yet another floor above this, with an atrium. But it was all constantly being reconfigured and changed to fit the newest first family.

"We stayed upstairs on the top floor," Don Jr. said. "I had my five children with me, running around, and we were all together in rooms nearby, so it was just insane. One of my kids went to lunch in the State Dining Room wearing his orange-and-green Ninja Turtle pajamas; another was dressed like Spider-Man."

"Eric and I stayed in what was arguably the smallest bed upstairs," Lara said. "I believe it was where Michelle Obama's mom used to stay and, of course, we were the tallest two members of the family.

"We really had to rush to get ready to go to the balls. All the women were trying to get their hair and makeup fixed. We were running so late.

My gosh, it was quite a fiasco. You know, everything runs behind anyway.

"I remember the White House butler coming up and saying, 'Does anyone want something to eat?'

"We were all starving, so we were like, 'Yeah!'

"I think I ordered sweet potato fries, and they brought us some food while we were changing clothes and trying to get ready. They brought it right to the room. They were amazing. So kind. The staff there is just incredible. I mean, just such nice people."

"So what did you have, Eric?"

"Cheeseburger. What else?"

I asked Tiffany where she spent the night. "I stayed in the room next door to Don and near Eric and Lara. I remember ordering an iced sweet tea." Tiffany, who now often spends the weekends at the White House, says, "Only at the White House can I get a sweet tea as good as it is when I'm home in Georgia!"[12]

Before sundown, Jared and Ivanka retreated to their bedroom for a special ceremony. "Ivanka and I had the Lincoln Bedroom," Jared said, "so that night we lit the Shabbat candles at the White House." This was a Jewish duty, to welcome the onset of Sabbath. "We were told that it was the first time that it had been done, that the Friday-night candles had been lit in the White House."

STUCK IN THEIR HIGH HEELS

The inaugural balls, including the big one held at the Walter E. Washington Convention Center, were held in honor of the president and first lady and, really, the whole Trump family. Such events are not as glamorous as they may sound. Having once attended, even if you are a close friend of the president, they are not something you make a habit of attending again. They are packed wall-to-wall with people. The dance floors cannot be seen, unless, in this case, the dance floor was in fact, the stage, where the president and first lady danced and the crowd watched.

Moving through the lobby of the center was like moving through Main Street at Disneyland on Christmas. You could time your progress by a few yards per hour. "Let's see, can I get to that door over there by eight p.m.?" Body odor, almost wiped out by American deodorant, makes a strong comeback. The restrooms turned into something you might find at a bus station. Even so, they were packed, with lines stretching out the doors with people in tuxedos and evening gowns waiting their turns for the toilet.

The president, the first lady, and the rest of the Trump family were escorted in through back doors and hustled down messy corridors. There was the stink of garbage. There were food trays and tall utility kitchen carts with dirty dishes stacked up. A Secret Service cordon cleared every aisle and led around every corner and then *bam*, though doors into the darkened backstage of the ballroom. Even this area was roped off into cordoned sections, with tents reserved for various officials and a presidential tent with couches and chairs and televisions and trays full of food covering tables.

"Don't eat the food," the Trump family was warned.

"Don't worry," they mumbled back. They were all in the hotel business.

"We went to two of the balls," Lara remembers. "My parents and some friends of ours were at one of them. I forget which one. There were so many people. Forget it. You weren't able to see anybody. Eric and I, and I think maybe Don and Vanessa, went to the hotel. We had no idea it would be like that. I mean, it was like a mob scene. People were so excited when we walked in.

"I didn't have Secret Service [protection] at the time," Lara explained. "Eric did. I didn't. So, for me, it kind of felt like I was being thrown to the wolves. Remember, I was a pregnant woman, but nobody knew that, so all of these people were bum-rushing us. It was great because they were excited for us. But I was so tired. So I told Eric, like, at one o'clock in the morning, 'I gotta get out of here.'

"Then my parents came in. I saw them and took a picture with them. It was quite an evening, to say the least. And that was the end of a very, very special day."

Lara Trump had been on a treadmill at four o'clock that very morning. It was now after two a.m. the next day. In a few hours it would be daylight, and the whole Trump family would have another special inaugural service awaiting them at the National Cathedral.

"I woke up to the most astonishing situation. I couldn't get my shoes on. My feet were swollen, they wouldn't fit. We had been walking around all day in high heels. What did we expect? I wondered if any of the other ladies were having that problem. I literally went down the hall of the White House calling out, 'Can anybody put your shoes on?'

"And all the Trump women screamed back the same thing. You could hear their reactions. None of us could get our shoes on. Our feet were so swollen."

Inauguration Day was an entirely different story depending on whether you were one of the men in the Trump family or one of the women. The ladies, including the president's wife, and his daughters, Ivanka and Tiffany, as well as the daughters-in-law, Lara and Vanessa, were all statuesque beauties. At least part of that was owing to their propensity for wearing high heels.

On January 19, the day before the inauguration, the Trump women had marched up and down the marble stairs of the Lincoln Memorial, making their appearance at a ceremonial concert of the voices of the people.

The next day, the day of the inauguration itself, they had climbed the slippery, elongated steps of the nation's capital and then down the other side onto the platform for the swearing-in ceremony, repeating the process afterward, back to their limousines.

Worse. The presidential motorcade had stopped, as was the tradition, midway through the parade down Pennsylvania Avenue. The Trump women, in all of their glory, had been force-marched down the street, with their husbands, smiling and waving to the cheering crowds. That night, they had glided across ballroom stages in their high heels at the inaugural balls.

Early in the morning of January 21, 2017, with little sleep to draw on, the Trump women, Melania, Ivanka, Tiffany, Vanessa, and Lara, were all in their White House rooms, racing to get ready for one more glorious day of celebration. Some of them were soaking their feet in cold water, hoping to reduce the swelling. "We had to somehow get back into our shoes."

"I didn't soak my feet in cold water," Tiffany told me. "But that would have been a good idea! I opted to carry as many Band-Aids as I could fit in my purse!"[13]

THE NIGHTMARE IS OVER

They were thirty minutes late for the service at the National Cathedral.[14] But all the Trumps agreed that this, the last event of the three-day-long inaugural festivities, was well worth it. What appeared to be a young, blind child wearing sunglasses was guided gently to a position in front of the high altar just at the crossing. But this was not a child, though quite small in stature. This was Marlana VanHoose. Born with a congenital disease that left her blind, she was not expected to live a year. At the age of two she was diagnosed with cerebral palsy. At the age of twenty-one, she now sang before the president of the United States and his family at the National Cathedral.

Some members of the Trump family had heard her sing the national anthem at the Republican National Convention. Others had missed the moment but had been told what they were about to experience. Marlana's mannerisms were timid and humble, accentuated by the involuntary movements provoked by her palsy. Her voice was confident and sure. Marlana VanHoose had this. She was holding back, and the audience could feel it.

"She was unbelievable," Don Jr. remembers. "She sang with such poise and power."

Marlana sang an old gospel hymn, "How Great Thou Art." Beginning slowly, understated, with a clear voice.

"Everyone was moved," Lara Trump says. "By the time she was finished there wasn't anybody in there who wasn't totally in tears."

At the end, First Lady Melania Trump rose to her feet, and the audience immediately followed her lead, giving Marlana VanHoose a thunderous standing ovation.

"There was this wonderful mood from the National Cathedral," Lara said. "The feeling that God was bigger than all the hatred and bitterness. There was the feeling that we were going to be okay."

Back from the National Cathedral, the Trump family was finally given a tour of the White House, with all the grandkids in tow. "That was the first real tour for Lara and me," Eric Trump says. It was a first for Don Jr. and his children.

"We walked all around the place," Eric said. "I wandered into the Lincoln bedroom. The first thing I noticed was how long the bed was. Remember, I'm 6' 5". Lincoln was really a tall guy. What was his nickname?"

"Rail-splitter." I said.

"Yeah, that's right. He was a big guy, a tall, strong guy. There was a very tall mirror in a wooden frame that could tilt. I had never seen one like that. I'm taking in all of the furniture that is so period specific to him. The chandelier and the lamps were gas lit and are now converted over to electric.

"On the far side of the room, between the two windows, was the famous Gettysburg Address. Later, when I made trips down to the White House and stayed overnight in that room, they would take down the Gettysburg Address and they would put it on the nightstand so as you go to turn off the lamp, there it is. It's not locked in 12 inches of glass with special lighting. It's very, very close.

"On the nightstand there is a little oil portrait of Lincoln's son, Willie, who died in that bed. He was eleven years old. Lincoln kept the picture on his office desk in the next room. Now they keep it in the bedroom.

"The first time I saw that portrait next to the bed with the Gettysburg Address sitting there, within eyesight, something that you could reach out and touch, trying to fall asleep in the bed where Willie Lincoln had died and broken the hearts of Abraham and Mary Todd Lincoln, well, it brought home the gravity of all the great, new responsibility we had as a family. I began to understand how our patterns were going to change, how life was going to change.

That night, January 21, 2017, the last night of the inaugural celebration, the night of the service at the National Cathedral, the Trump
family was exhausted. They gathered in the State Dining Room, a
bittersweet moment. They had won. The family was together. But soon
they would be scattered, with many of them headed back to New York
City. The first lady wanted her son, Barron, to finish school there before
moving down to Washington, DC. There was no decision yet on where
Jared and Ivanka would be.

I told Eric that in my study of presidential children, I'd found that
they almost all loved their White House years, because they'd been able
to spend so much time together with their family. They had usually
been separated while the father pursued power, but once they won the
presidency, that journey was over. He could stay home.

I had once pressed Jack Ford, the son of President Ford, on this very
subject. "But didn't you live in Wyoming?" I asked.

He said, "Yes, but every weekend the White House would send out
a jet to pick me up. We spent more time together than ever."[15]

Eric Trump looked wistful. "I would say that we are the opposite,"
he said to me, during an interview over lunch in New York City. "We
used to see our father every day. Not anymore. Not anymore."

Donald Trump's grandchildren now filled the White House. Don
Jr. and Vanessa had five children. Jared and Ivanka had three.

"That last night of the inauguration celebration we were all together," Don Jr. remembers. "The White House staff created a table
full of kids' food in the State Dining Room, and, as you know, the kids
always get the good stuff. Everybody likes kids' food. Soon the adults
were in there chowing down on hamburgers and chicken fingers."

The children didn't stay in the dining room long. They were soon
scattered throughout the State Floor in a rousing game of White House
hide-and-go-seek with Uncle Barron as the supervisor.

"The kids all love Barron," Don Jr. explains. "He rules the grandkids."

Within minutes there were shrieks of laughter and screams of delight as Trump children were rousted out from behind drapes in the Blue Room and from underneath chairs in the Red Room.

With the sounds of giggling grandchildren echoing in the halls of the White House, the adult members of the Trump family sat down together around the table in the State Dining Room. Carved into the stone fireplace were the famous words of John Adams, the first president to live there: "I pray heaven to bestow the best of blessings on this House and on all who shall hereafter inhabit it. May none but honest and wise Men ever rule under this roof."

Eric and Lara Trump had an announcement. "That night, Eric and I told the whole family I was pregnant with Luke, with our son," Lara said. "It was just a very special memory that we will always have."

Hearing the loud exclamations, Barron came rushing back into the dining room. He was sweating and huffing and puffing. Out of breath. "What happened? What happened?" He was juggling both worlds: the grandkids, where he reigned supreme as the favorite uncle, and the adults, who were busy changing the world from the White House State Dining Room.

"It was so peaceful and so beautiful," Lara said. "The family was all together. It was just magic. We had been through so much. There had been so much pain and accusation. It had really been shocking. It had been a long, bitter, divisive campaign, but now the nightmare was finally over. The country would come back together as it always did. There was so much to do."

"Okay?" Barron asked, waiting for an answer. Was that it? Was there more? Were the announcements over? "Okay?"

The kids were calling from the East Room of the White House, where they had found new, foolproof places to hide. Uncle Barron was needed elsewhere.

★ 10 ★

BLOWING IT UP

*"Watching the media meltdown and Martha Raddatz crying
on television, well, it was just a little bit too much."*
—Donald Trump Jr.[1]

On January 21, 2017, while the Trump family was attending
the traditional inaugural religious service at the National
Cathedral, the Grammy Award–winning recording artist
Madonna was taking to the podium of the Women's March to make a
solemn declaration. "Yes, I'm angry," she said. Carefully looking back
down at her index cards with her talking points. "Yes, I am outraged.
Yes, I have thought an awful lot of blowing up the White House . . ."
The crowd cheered.[2]

Some of the Trump family members were in a motorcade back to
the White House when they spotted her comments on their Twitter
feed. Family text messages jumped from car to car.

"It's interesting," Donald Trump Jr., told me in his description of
the day. "People on the left have been portrayed by the national media
as 'tolerant.' There is nothing tolerant about the American Left. Even
among themselves. If one of their own makes even the slightest slip
from orthodoxy, they will viciously turn on them."

From the beginning, Donald Trump and his family had been a magnet for public criticism. Some of this was pure partisanship. Or just plain tribalism. The Red team against the Blue. Some was animated by money that members of the establishment feared they might lose if Trump won the election and made progress in reforming the government. And some of it was just crazy as in the *Philadelphia Daily News* comparing Trump to Hitler on its front page.[3]

Still, none of that fully explained the vitriol directed at this family, including its most innocent and defenseless members. Perhaps this was because "the Donald" was tough, he could take it, and since he seemed impervious to the most outlandish attacks, the best way to hurt him was possibly through the people he loved.

The viciousness of the attacks was without parallel.[4] For example, on the morning of the inauguration, Stephen Spinola of Comedy Central tweeted that ten-year-old Barron looked like a "date-rapist-to-be."[5] In a follow up tweet he ridiculed the young man's genitals.[6] A writer for the NBC show *Saturday Night Live* tweeted that the president's son would be America's "First Homeschool Shooter."[7] (Barron was not homeschooled.)

Attacks on the first lady were equally vicious. When she appeared radiant in a blue coat and long blue gloves on Inauguration Day, the attacks only intensified. A *New York Times* reporter, Jacob Bernstein, made the claim that she had been a "hooker." It was the sort of sexist claim that high school boys make of young ladies whose beauty and brains are a threat. The *Times* responded by saying that "the comment was not intended to be public."[8] Bernstein apologized but was not fired.[9]

Meanwhile, the UK *Daily Mail* took the story public, claiming that First Lady Melania Trump had once worked for an escort service. Not only was it wrong, but the newspaper subsequently lost a lawsuit over its attack and publicly admitted that its claims about the first lady were not true. They had to pay out $2.9 million.[10]

When Donald Trump complained about the rapper Snoop Dogg threatening him with a gun in a video, the rapper "Bow Wow" (Shad

Moss) tweeted back the threat that he would make the first lady a sex slave.[11] "Shut your punk ass up talking shit about my uncle," Moss said, "before we pimp your wife and make her work for us."[12]

When news came that Jared Kushner and his wife, Ivanka Trump Kushner, would work in the White House, Trevor Noah from *The Daily Show* promoted the slur that Trump wanted to commit incest with his daughter.[13] He urged television viewers to hashtag this idea on Twitter.

When news leaked that Lara Trump was pregnant, the celebrity Chelsea Handler led a public attack on the unborn child.[14] "Just what we need. Another person with those jeans [*sic*]. Let's hope for a girl."[15] Handler, stung by criticism that she couldn't spell correctly, attacked the Trumps again in the fall, declaring "Is there anyone dumber than @realDonaldTrump? Besides his children, and Melania?"[16]

Examples of such ferocious attacks go on and on. In May 2017, the comedian Kathy Griffin arranged for a picture of herself holding the severed, bloody head of President Trump.[17] In June, the actor Johnny Depp posed a question to his audience at the Glastonbury Festival in Somerset, England: "When was the last time an actor assassinated a president?" He then added, "Maybe it's time."[18]

Chelsea Handler's curse on Lara's unborn baby didn't work. And it was a boy. Eric Luke Trump was born on September 12, 2017. A second baby, Carolina Dorothy Trump, was born August 19, 2019, to become the tenth grandchild of the president.

SELF-INFLICTED MURDER?

While Hollywood and some publications were more extreme in their obscene hostility, the campaign of the television networks against the new Donald Trump administration was just as pronounced. The networks were dependent on their corporate sponsors, which were, likewise, dependent on a system that naturally favored some companies and not others. Donald Trump, the outsider, himself a billionaire, could not be legally bribed by lavish political donations. In his independence, he became a disrupter as he worked to bring some sanity to the nation's economic woes. And that was most unsettling to those who for decades had drawn sustenance from the rich world of crony capitalism.

No matter how successful the president's true record may have been, with the stock market up and unemployment down, the media's hostility toward Donald Trump and his family was toxic. It was having its impact on the public. His popularity hovered around 40 percent. To be sure, the media itself paid a price for their bias. A Gallup poll showed that only 20 percent of Americans had a "great deal" of confidence in TV news, which put it lower than newspapers, which registered an anemic 23 percent.[19]

The active media campaign against Trump sometimes defied logic.

At first, the economic success of the Trump administration was ignored. One study showed that during a four-month period, less than 1 percent of all television news coverage monitored concerned the economy.[20]

When the rebounding numbers were too massive to dismiss, critics suggested that while there might have been some economic growth, it was benefitting only the rich friends of Donald Trump. But this, too, was a difficult argument to make. Billionaire elites had overwhelmingly supported Hillary Clinton and the Democrats in the election.[21] Likewise, the unemployment numbers undercut the premise that Trump and his economy were hostile to women, blacks, and Hispanics. The government's own numbers soon showed the lowest unemployment rate in history for blacks and hispanics and the lowest in half a century for women.

Late in the second year of Donald Trump's presidency, when wages were up for the poorest of Americans, the Democratic and media critics fashioned a new explanation. In September 2018, former president Barack Obama, speaking at the University of Illinois, suggested that the economy was indeed growing, but it was because of him. He claimed that the emerging good news was due to his own economic policies finally kicking into gear.[22] Obama, who had wondered aloud how candidate Trump was going to get those new jobs he had promised, was now taking credit for them.

The story of a weakened ISIS experienced a similar metamorphosis. First it was denied. Then it was ignored—and then reluctantly acknowledged with an increasingly familiar new twist. It was all thanks to former president Barack Obama, whose policies had only needed time to cook in order to have their impact.[23]

Some television networks shamelessly advanced all three theories simultaneously. At any given moment, a pundit might be declaring that the growth was not real and ISIS was not defeated. Meanwhile, another would argue in a subsequent segment that the recovery benefited only the rich. And yet another would say that the economic boom was real and ISIS had, indeed, been defeated, but that it was the work of Barack Obama.

Others may have reluctantly come to the conclusion that the economy was indeed booming, and maybe even Trump was responsible—but they didn't care. They still didn't like Trump. It was not really about poor people, after all, it was about their team winning. The comedian Bill Maher spoke for many of Trump's opponents when he wistfully hoped out loud for a recession.

When Van Jones interviewed Jay-Z on CNN he asked the obvious question. Does Trump have a point? "He's one who is saying look, 'I'm dropping Black unemployment. Black people are doing well under my administration. . . . Maybe the Democrats have been giving us good lip service but no jobs?"

Jay-Z, a Clinton supporter and popular rapper, with an estimated net worth of $900 million, answered by saying, "No, no, that's not the point. Money does not equate to happiness."[24]

Trump was the enemy, even if he was right.

Not only were the president and the first family targets, the media began to grow angry at anyone, public or private, who supported the Trumps. This included the Republican establishment, which had once been a dependable member of the opposition.

That first summer of Trump, a gunman opened fire, attempting to murder Republican congressmen on a baseball diamond in Virginia.

Scott Pelley, the calm, erudite, understated anchor of *CBS Evening News*, wondered aloud to his television audience whether the attempted murders were "foreseeable, predictable and, to some degree, self-inflicted."[25] The gunman was a Bernie Sanders supporter.

Being a Trump Republican was now worthy of death.

NO HONEYMOON FOR THIS GUY

Historians often refer to the first few months of a new administration as the "honeymoon period" of a presidency. The public, the media, and members of Congress will give the new administration the benefit of the doubt.[26] But the media, having failed to accurately call the 2016 election, was in no mood to be accommodating. When the economy took off like a rocket, this time defying the economic experts, the media and its allies became almost hysterical and desperate in their opposition.

A Harvard University study on the president's first one hundred days in office could not find a single major area of media coverage on Trump that was more positive than negative.[27] According to the Harvard study, no other president had experienced such negative coverage.

A 2018 review of more than one thousand television news stories showed that 92 percent were negative, while only 8 percent were positive.[28] Trump's use of social media to speak directly with the American people was likewise under attack. Pro-Trump YouTube channels were allegedly targeted by Google. It was also claimed that subjects and information on search engines were skewed.[29]

The former Speaker of the House Newt Gingrich said that "no president since Abraham Lincoln has faced the kind of unending bias and hostility from the media that President Trump is living through."[30]

Madonna's remarks about blowing up the White House signaled a new era of violent protest. On January 20, 2017, even before the swearing-in had taken place, protestors armed with hammers and crowbars broke Washington, DC, storefront windows and set a limousine on fire. The owner of the limousine, a Muslim, was a small-business entrepreneur. At the time, almost all of his drivers were

Pakistani-born immigrants, also Muslim. He was shaken and confused by the mob. Later, I spoke with many of his drivers. Never mind, they were told. It was the symbolism of the burning limousine that mattered. They would have to take the loss stoically.

"I remember reading about the Muslim businessman," Don Jr. said. "He apparently spent his life savings to start his business. It was really a great American success story. But the rioters burned his car.

"There's a great irony here. Again, the Left preaches tolerance, but it's really only tolerance if they say it is. They can withdraw their credentials at any time if it serves their purpose."

The street protestors, described as "well-organized" by the *Washington Post*, had come prepared with medics and an attorney from Colorado to assist those who were planning to be violent or get arrested. The protestors—or perhaps more correctly, the organized rioters—came from twenty-six states and the District of Columbia.[31] They gathered in parks downtown, where their experienced street fighters stood on benches and gave detailed instructions on what to say and do to get the most television coverage. I lingered on the fringes of some of these prep sessions. "Use your mask," one leader exhorted. "It has a purpose."

As events would have it, aside from the fiery, burning limousine, which filled the television screens, the demonstrators actually gained little traction on Inauguration Day. Instead, several hundred thousand Trump supporters filled the grassy mall that stretched from the Capitol to the Lincoln Memorial to celebrate and witness the swearing-in of the new president.

It was the next day, the day that Madonna took to the stage, that the same mall was filled with hundreds of thousands of women. The women would be wearing what they called pink pussy hats, symbolic of female genitalia. It was explained, in an article in the *Detroit Free Press*, that the hats would be abandoned by organizers at future women's events on the grounds that they excluded "transgender women, as well as women of color whose genitals are more likely to be darker colors than pink."[32]

CNN would later say that Madonna's "blowing up the White House" statement was taken out of context.[33] But then, CNN would not provide its audience with the context. Madonna's speech had been filled with profanity and F-bombs.. By anyone's standards, there was no denying that "the long nightmare" that some members of the Trump family had thought was finally over was now only morphing into something even worse.

A conversation between the Trump White House and the media would soon dissolve into a tooth-and-claw debate about just how many people had attended the inauguration. Many of Trump's supporters felt that the new administration needlessly wasted equity on the discussion. Meanwhile, leaders of the Women's March claimed that their event would be the largest demonstration since the days of the 1970s and the protests against the Vietnam War.

HOW THE RESISTANCE GOT ITS NAME

In retrospect, right after the 2016 election, there had been no immediate, massive, grassroots street reaction to the Trump victory. The Left had not expected Trump to win. The outrage had come from the national media and Hollywood personalities, some even weeping over the election results. Journalists who had remained professional and stoic on 9/11, as the World Trade Towers collapsed over their shoulders, now turned bitterly angry at their own television audiences, many of whom had voted for Donald Trump.

Donald Trump Jr. remembers watching the election-night moment unfolding at Trump Tower. "They wouldn't call it. I thought, 'What's going on? What are they trying to do? Can others see this?'

"You could sort of see, you know, everyone's trying to draw this out. They were hoping and praying that miraculously, something would happen.

"Watching the media meltdown and Martha Raddatz crying on television, well, it was just a little bit too much. Remember, she had been the moderator of the second debate. Imagine?

"Before we went upstairs, we were in the war room downstairs on a split screen. We were all simultaneously watching it all. I love the mix tapes that have been put together since then, but we saw bits and pieces of all of that stuff as it was happening.

"Here are these journalists, who had been telling us with a straight face that they didn't have a favorite, they just wanted to get to the real news. I just want you to know, the whole world could see, they were visibly shaken. In some cases, they were in tears. They didn't cry over caskets coming back to Dover Air Force Base, they didn't cry over 9/11, but when their big bosses lost control of power? They cried. This was happening before their very eyes. It was just sort of amusing to watch.

"The irony of all of it is that Democrats had been warning the nation for months that elections have consequences and that you had to accept the will of the people and Donald Trump better not make a fuss when he loses, the country needs to have unity, it needs to come together. Hillary harped on this.

"The truth of the matter is that our people wouldn't have liked it if we had lost, but there would never have been a single rioter in the street. I would have gone back to work the next morning, getting back to doing what we do.

"I'm not saying I would have been happy about it. I think leadership under Hillary Clinton would have been a total disaster. You would have perpetuated the same nonsense and made it, frankly, even worse. The swamp would have loved it. The lobbyists were already invested in the Clinton Foundation, in Congress, in each other. But I wouldn't have spent the next two years moaning about it.

"With the media it's always, 'Do as I say, not as I do.' That's the reality, save the environment but make my private jet rentals an exception. Don't allow guns except for me and my bodyguards. Make sure you meekly accept the election when Hillary wins. That's the right thing to do, except she didn't win and the media immediately expected the street mobs to get with it."

RIOTS IN PORTLAND

The only immediate reaction on the ground happened in Portland, Oregon, the day after the election. This was the antifa crowd, who some critics claimed were sponsored by the leftist billionaire George Soros. Antifa, a moniker for "antifascist," included some experienced street agitators, previously trained in the Black Lives Matter organization. As paid protestors, they could be reliably turned out with a few phone calls.

These beginner protests in Portland, Oregon, continued throughout the week, breaking out into violence that Friday evening. Groups of anarchists dressed in black, head to toe, carried baseball bats. Nineteen cars at a Toyota dealership were damaged, and windows were smashed at storefronts in Portland's central Pearl District. Police said the demonstrations had turned into a full-scale riot.[34]

In Chicago, a group of young African American men pulled a white man out of his car and viciously beat him for "voting for Donald Trump."[35] This story was too graphic for television networks to show, although Fox News aired it once. Television producers may have considered the footage politically counterproductive to feature. The man "had his arm put through a back window with the window rolled up, trapping his arm inside the car. The car was driven through traffic, dragging the man's body with it."[36]

There were a few protests in numerous other places across the country, including in front of Trump Tower itself in New York City. Protestors used the hashtag #NotMyPresident across social media.

In San Francisco, an online effort began urging consumers to boycott Ivanka Trump's product lines, going under the hashtag #GrabYourWallet. The idea was to economically punish Ivanka, the president's daughter, for not speaking out against her own father.

In New York, residents of certain apartment buildings insisted that the Trump name be removed from the marquees of their buildings. Professional basketball teams tried to avoid staying at Trump-named hotel properties.[37]

Keith Olbermann, the sportscaster turned leftist political pundit, had an online broadcast for *GQ* magazine throughout the 2016 election year. The show was called *The Closer*. On November 9, the day after the election, Olbermann sent out a tweet saying, "Let the resistance begin." He gave his show a new name. From now on it would be *The Resistance*.[38]

The national media apparently liked the idea and liked the name. Violence was good for ratings. "The Resistance" echoed the heroics of World War II and the French Resistance to the Nazis. For young people, it mirrored the name of the New Republic forces battling the evil and fascist-looking forces of the First Order in the fictional Star Wars universe. In both cases, it positioned "Resistance" members as opposing fascism and afforded them a touch of romance.

One of the overt acts of resistance came from a source well-schooled with framing narratives and romance: Hollywood. In a video released under the auspices of a movement called "Unite for America," an assortment of television actors appealed to members of the Electoral College to select anyone other than Donald Trump. The actor Martin Sheen, who portrayed the fictional US president Josiah Bartlet in the television drama *The West Wing*, kicked off the video and was followed by Debra Messing of *Will and Grace* fame. Sheen and Messing were joined by numerous stars of the small screen.

Interestingly enough, the campaign made it especially clear, they were not asking electors to vote for Hillary Clinton. There was already a modest, heretical school of thought emerging that wondered if Trump's victory was partially due to his flawed opponent. Rather, this new project was an attempt to force the presidential selection into the US House of Representatives. (This is the procedure described in Constitution when there is a deadlock in the Electoral College.) It was an "anyone but Trump" appeal.

It failed.[39]

THE STREET GANG BECOMES A MOVEMENT

On the heels of the third Trump-Clinton televised debate in late October, a woman from Maine, Libby Chamberlin, started a Facebook page called Pantsuit Nation. The name came from Hillary Clinton's penchant for pantsuits. The page initially urged women to wear pantsuits to the polls on November 8, as a sign of supporting Hillary Clinton. By November 8 the page had exploded, boasting nearly three million members.

On November 9, a Pantsuit Nation member named Teresa Shook posted to the group that there should be a "Women's March on Washington." The idea took off rapidly and a website, womensmarch.com, was created. While the concept was initiated by upper-middle class white women, it was quickly appropriated by other groups as well.

Marie Berry and Erica Chenoweth, research professors at the University of Denver, describe these groups as "tributaries." Beyond the Pantsuit Nation women, one of the Women's March tributaries was the Occupy movement. Occupy Wall Street was perhaps its best known demonstration, but the organization had many offshoots and causes. Its involvement with the women was significant. Occupy was focused on its enemy, the wealthiest "1 percent" in America. Occupy members never really warmed to Hillary Clinton; their members were much more likely to have supported Senator Bernie Sanders during the Democratic nominating process.

The initial organizers of the Women's March, who were more likely affiliated with the Pantsuit Nation, came under increasing criticism from other #NotMyPresident and #Resistance activists. They were criticized for not sufficiently considering "intersectionality." This was a view that gender oppression needed to be elevated to the level of race and class oppression and include oppression of the LGBTQ community. It was a criticism of early feminists, who were predominantly white and heterosexual. The Pantsuit Nation community was also less experienced in the art of street activism and organizing rallies.

Eventually, the leadership of the Women's March was passed to activists with more experience on the streets, people who had learned how to provoke confrontations and how to set up events for sympathetic media. New leadership came from the ranks of the Black Lives Matter and immigrants' rights tributaries, including Muslim activists. It was these leaders who were in charge by the time Madonna mused about blowing up the White House.[40]

While some of these leaders urged a passive resistance modeled after Martin Luther King Jr., they were increasingly joined by people from groups such as antifa that led to some of the violence seen in Portland and the burning limousine on Inauguration Day.

Borrowing tactics that had been used successfully by ISIS terrorists, antifa became well known for posting videos of its members, usually clad in all black, including face-covering balaclavas, punching alleged white supremacists in the face. Videos of such punches were put to music and posted on social media.[41]

Things had moved from wearing pantsuits to punch a Nazi in the face as a form of activism. But further research found that some of their targets were not white supremacists at all.[42] They were simply white people caught in the wrong place at the wrong time.

In early January 2017, *Rolling Stone* magazine described a coalition of odd bedfellows forming as the "Resistance." Not just street protestors and anarchists, but established Left organizations such as Planned Parenthood, the American Civil Liberties Union (ACLU), the Human Rights Campaign, joining with John Weaver, a Republican political consultant, who had advised the presidential campaigns of Senator John McCain and Governor John Kasich.

Also identified as a Resistance leader was Evan McMullin, a former CIA agent who ran against Trump as an independent for president. McMullin placed third among Utah voters. He had previously worked on Capitol Hill as a Republican House staffer. The article quoted Stuart Stevens, a longtime Republican strategist who had led Mitt Romney's presidential campaigns in 2008 and 2012 as well as Bob Dole's presidential campaign in 1996.[43] There was Elizabeth Kübler-Ross, the famous Swiss American psychiatrist, who first came up with the five stages of grief: denial, anger, bargaining, depression, and acceptance.[44]

A DEATH BLOW FOR MANY

Donald Trump's 2016 election victory was like a death blow to many. For millions, it meant the death of the dream of the first female president in their lifetime. It killed the dream of a third or even fourth term of an Obama-like administration. For some, it meant the death of the dream of demography being destiny, the belief that an increasingly multicultural America would never again elect a Republican president, certainly not an America First president like Donald Trump.

It was a devastating defeat to members of the Left, to the socialists. It was a blow to American academia, which was codependent with China, a nation that was sending masses of full-paying students to their universities. It would mean the postponement of "free education," which would allow the federal government to pay for college tuition. It would postpone legislation to wipe out the student loan debt in the United States. It would be a setback for the idea of "reparations"—that is, government grants to descendants of American slaves—a cause endorsed by almost all of the future 2020 Democratic presidential candidates.

Finally, and perhaps most significantly, the election of Donald Trump represented a setback and an unknown future for many corporate, globalist monopolies. It would force them to wait him out, or to tilt, God forbid, to more supply-and-demand and free markets until he could be thrown out of office. These monopolies depended on insider deals and sometimes quick, cheap money direct from the Federal Reserve and other devices to finance growth.

In some cases, these companies were also the engines that ran the American media. Their advertising dollars kept the media functioning and paid the salaries of the TV anchors. Some companies had pieces of ownership, both directly and indirectly. Meanwhile, their grants to think tanks paid the salaries of the earnest guest pundits and experts who dominated the airwaves. Incredibly, even beyond television talking heads, this elite corporate community was willing to ally themselves, at least temporarily, with street thugs and members of the Left to mount a substantial opposition to Trump and to block his planned reforms.

To use the language of one of its own, there would be no honeymoon, no moving on to bargaining, depression, and acceptance. The "Resistance" insisted on staying in the stages of denial and anger. "Not My President!" they declared. And then there was Madonna's famous line: "I have thought an awful lot about blowing up the White House."[45]

Many of the sixty-three million Americans who had elected Donald Trump as president looked on in stunned disbelief. Several million of them had voted twice for Barack Obama, feeling a great sense of pride in electing the first African American president. Now they were being attacked and berated for having voted to make America great again.

In June 2018, Representative Maxine Waters called for open harassment of anyone even associated with Donald Trump. "I want to tell you," she said, "these members of his Cabinet who remain and try to defend him, they won't be able to go to a restaurant, they won't be able to stop at a gas station, they're not going to be able to shop at a department store. The people are going to turn on them. They're going to protest. They're absolutely going to harass them until they decide that they're going to tell the president, 'No. I can't hang with you.'"[46]

If you were not in the Resistance, it was best to keep quiet, keep your head down, and let the storm pass over.

11

RUSSIAN ROULETTE

"What they did was treasonous, okay? It was treasonous."
—DONALD TRUMP[1]

Some inside the Trump family, and many who had voted for and supported Donald Trump for president, believed that the American corporate media had never really accepted the 2016 election results. Rather than admit that their views and opinions had been rejected by the public, they chose, rather, to promote the idea that the 2016 election was fraudulent. Television anchors and pundits who had predicted the election of Hillary Clinton were now recovering from their shock and contending that they had not been wrong after all. Secretary Clinton would have won, they now suggested, if it had been a fair election. Donald Trump's victory was the result of a Russian conspiracy to cheat the voters and help him win.

Soon, major media organizations, including CNN and the *New York Times*, were promoting stories and personalities that were claiming Donald Trump was a Russian spy. If true, this would be the greatest moment of its kind in world history. This would rank with the assassination of Julius Caesar, the French Revolution, and the landing of a man on the moon.

There was no shortage of former Obama government officials willing to give this remarkable theory credence. Citing a *New York Times* report, one commentator noted that "a former Department of Justice spokesman believes this may prove once and for all that Vladimir Putin is Trump's handler, and Donald Trump is a Russian spy."[2]

This was, of course, a ridiculous story. In their international travels, the Trump children were often pulled aside by heads of state. "Please tell your father how sorry we are that he is going through this Russian nonsense," they would say. "Tell him we are thinking of him."[3]

These stories gave me a very different perspective. Of course, the head of state of any nation, friend or foe, would immediately want to know the answer to this question. Israeli prime minister Benjamin Netanyahu would have called in the head of Mossad the very day the *New York Times* ran their first story. Netanyahu, who had personally known the Trumps for years, would have asked the head of Mossad, "What is going on here?"

In fact, the heads of state of France, the United Kingdom, and Saudi Arabia, or any nation in the world would want to know. Our enemies and rivals in China, North Korea, and Iran had to know. Imagine the ramifications for trade and mutual defense. The directors of all of the world's 120 intelligence agencies, from the American CIA to the French DGSE, would be expected to explain this story to the leaders of their countries. The American media could drag the discussion out for two years, to create as much political damage as possible, but no world leader could let a single day pass without knowing the truth behind this American media conspiracy theory.

One can only imagine the laughter in the Kremlin when Vladimir Putin slid a copy of the *New York Times* down the conference table before his assembled intelligence leaders. "Well, which one of you did this?"

The fact was that in the years leading up to the 2016 election the Clinton campaign had far more links to Russia than anything the inventive American national media could find with Trump. No one was suggesting that Clinton was a Russian spy; they were just questioning her integrity. In 2010, the US State Department, headed by Secretary of State Clinton, had signed off on permission for a Russian company to purchase a Canadian company named Uranium One. Since the Canadian company owned significant mining rights in the United States, it required US approval.[4]

Five years later, the Russian government decided to "acquire a majority stake" in the company.[5] Weeks later, a Russian investment bank with ties to the Kremlin had paid the Democratic nominee's husband, Bill Clinton, $500,000 to give a speech.[6] What followed was a massive infusion of money to the Clinton Foundation. The money came from Russian oligarchs and friends of President Putin. Before they were done, the Russians had donated $145 million to the Clinton Foundation.[7] The media virtually ignored the story.[8]

Instead, night after night, for two years, the major television networks led with what they promised viewers would be the most astonishing story in world history. Donald Trump, the American president, was a Russian spy. The most tangible "proof" of this stunning moment in history, promoted with a straight face by anchors and pundits on American television, was an investigation that revealed that persons and organizations in Russia had purchased $200,000 worth of Facebook ads harmful to the former secretary of state Hillary Clinton. Never mind the reports that the founder of Facebook and all of its top stockholders, officers, and executives had openly supported Hillary Clinton for president and had donated thousands of dollars to the Clinton Foundation. An article in *The Hill* proclaimed that "Clinton is largest beneficiary of Facebook donations."[9]

ORIGINS OF THE RUSSIAN CONSPIRACY THEORY

In July 2016, FBI director James Comey held a press conference in which he declared the end of the inquiry into Hillary Clinton's use of private email servers. She had used the private servers for government business and then destroyed their contents after they had been subpoenaed. Her own employees had been instructed to smash and destroy their cell phones with hammers. The suspicion of critics was that Clinton had been operating a massive pay-to-play scheme. Nations and companies would donate millions to the Clinton Foundation and get special favors in return.

Comey's investigation had been called "Midyear Exam." In the press conference, Director Comey took the unusual step of declaring that there was nothing to prosecute. Usually this was a decision left to officials in the Justice Department, not the director of the FBI.

Later that month, FBI investigators, some who had worked on "Midyear Exam" were reassigned to a counterintelligence investigation called "Crossfire Hurricane"—an investigation into the Trump campaign and possible collusion with the Russian government. Quite a contrast in names, "Midyear Exam" versus "Crossfire Hurricane."

"I was born in a crossfire hurricane" is the opening lyric of the Rolling Stones song "Jumpin' Jack Flash." Many Trump campaign rallies end with the Rolling Stones song "You Can't Always Get What You Want."

Notably, one of the FBI investigators was Peter Strzok, deputy assistant director of the Counterintelligence Division. He had served on "Midyear Exam" and would later join the team of Special Counsel Robert Mueller. Strzok was having an extramarital affair with an FBI colleague named Lisa Page. She was an FBI attorney who also worked on both investigations. Strzok was removed from Mueller's staff after a report from the Department of Justice Office of the Inspector General revealed private text messages between Strzok and Page deriding Donald Trump and his supporters. Strzok and Page's personal relationship also violated FBI employee rules.[10]

In an August 15, 2016, text message, Strzok told Page: "I want to believe the path you threw out for consideration in Andy's [Andrew McCabe, the deputy director of the FBI] office that there's no way Trump gets elected—but I'm afraid we can't take that risk. It's like an insurance policy in the unlikely event you die before you're 40."[11]

Later, in congressional testimony, Strzok and Page would argue that they were debating the speed of the Trump-Russia investigation. If Trump were not elected, they could take their time and not spook the Russians. But could they take that chance? What if Trump were elected and the Trump staffers who may have colluded with Russia were given positions in the new administration?

When the texts became publicly known, they both denied that they were referring to a plot to go after the president-elect.[12]

Following the release of the embarrassing texts between Strzok and Page, the FBI dug in hard, refusing to release any further information demanded by Congress. It was information sensitive to national intelligence, they insisted. This only aroused greater congressional and public curiosity. While Fox News covered the unfolding drama, most of the national media ignored the story.

When yet another Strzok-Page text became public, it was harder to avoid the obvious. "Just went to a Southern Virginia Walmart," Strzok wrote to his girlfriend, Page. "I could SMELL the Trump support."[13] "Smell" was written in capital letters. Coming from such bias, the "insurance policy" now sounded ominous.

JOHN McCAIN STRIKES BACK

Shortly after Trump's November 2016 victory, US senator John McCain, the senior Republican from Arizona, attended an international security conference in Halifax, Nova Scotia. It was a regularly scheduled conference he had attended before. While there, McCain was approached by Sir Andrew Wood, a retired British diplomat. Wood told Senator McCain and one of his associates about a report "that Wood had not read and conceded was mostly raw, unverified intelligence." It had been prepared by a former MI6 officer named Christopher Steele. McCain observed, "This was too strange a scenario to believe, something out of a le Carré novel."[14]

In his book *The Restless Wave*, McCain described the bizarre scene. "Our impromptu meeting felt charged with a strange intensity. No one wise-cracked to lighten the mood. We spoke in lowered voices. The room was dimly lit, and the atmosphere was eerie. Wood described Steele's research in general terms. He had not read it himself, but vouched for Steele's credibility. I was taken aback. They were shocking allegations."[15]

McCain arranged for his associate David Kramer, a former State Department official, to travel to London to meet with Steele. Kramer was working at the McCain Institute for International Leadership at Arizona State University at that time. Kramer met with the former MI6 officer in England and deemed him credible. The senator agreed to receive a copy of the now infamous Christopher Steele dossier.

Today it is widely reported that Steele had been paid to put together his famous dossier by GPS, an opposition research organization created by a former *Wall Street Journal* reporter. GPS was paid for the research by Perkins Coie, a powerful law firm contracted by both the Hillary Clinton presidential campaign and the Democratic National Committee (DNC). Observers concluded that the Clinton campaign used the intermediaries of Perkins Coie and GPS to pay Steele for the dossier.

We don't know if McCain was given a paper copy or perhaps a flash drive, but we do know it took a physical form since, the senator states, he kept the dossier in a safe until he could deliver it to James Comey, the director of the FBI. Why not just send an email, since it was just opposition research and not classified information? Perhaps all the cloak-and-dagger international travel made the dossier more credible?[16]

The fact was, while Senator McCain's associate Kramer made his exciting trip to England to pick up the Steele dossier, the file had already been in the United States for months. Steele had first given the dossier to an FBI official stationed in Rome, Italy, in August 2016.

Weeks later Steele shopped the dossier to American news outlets and continued to do so throughout the fall of 2016, trying to have it published before the election. Steele had even given it to a State Department employee in October. None of the news outlets ran with the unverified information.

The dossier included salacious, unverified stories of Trump supposedly cavorting with prostitutes in a Moscow hotel. There were descriptions of "golden showers," urinating on the bed that Obama had once used. Supposedly the Russians were holding this material and would be able to use it to blackmail the American billionaire turned politician.

There was no proof to any of the allegations, and many of the details surrounding the narrative were easily proven false. After meeting with Steele in October, Kathleen Kavelec, Obama's State Department deputy assistant secretary, sent officials at the FBI an email questioning Steele's credibility and pointing out claims in his research that were likely false.

THE CALCULATIONS OF JAMES COMEY

Meanwhile, the FBI leadership, apparently convinced that Hillary Clinton was headed toward election as the next president of the United States, used the Steele dossier for a Foreign Intelligence Surveillance Act (FISA) warrant request to the FISA court on October 21, 2016.

Director James Comey was well aware of the Steele dossier. Comey had it on his mind after the surprise election upset, when he started to interact with the new, president-elect. According to James Baker, the FBI general counsel at the time, Comey and Baker were concerned that briefing president-elect Trump on the dossier would evoke actions taken decades ago by FBI Director J. Edgar Hoover, who had a reputation for keeping files on prominent people and using them as blackmail when it suited him.[17]

Even so, Comey went forward.

During presidential transitions, the time between the general election and the inauguration, US intelligence agencies start to brief the president-elect along with the outgoing president. It is a standard procedure, designed to make sure the new president is up to speed the moment he or she is sworn into office.

On Thursday, January 5, 2017, after an Oval Office intelligence briefing to President Obama, Director Comey, Deputy Attorney General Sally Yates, National Security Advisor Susan Rice, Vice President

Biden, and President Obama had a "brief follow-on conversation." Susan Rice wrote an email to herself to document the conversation:

"President Obama began the conversation by stressing his continued commitment to ensuring that every aspect of this issue is handled by the Intelligence and law enforcement communities 'by the book'. The President stressed that he is not asking about, initiating or instructing anything from a law enforcement perspective. He reiterated that our law enforcement team needs to proceed as it normally would by the book.

"From a national security perspective, however, President Obama said he wants to be sure that, as we engage with the incoming team, we are mindful to ascertain if there is any reason that we cannot share information fully as it relates to Russia."[18]

A long section of the email follows with redactions, presumably for security reasons. Then Rice finishes the email:

"The President asked Comey to inform him if anything changes in the next few weeks that should affect how we share classified information with the incoming team. Comey said he would."[19]

Rice wrote this email to herself on January 20, 2017. Fifteen minutes after the inauguration ceremony for Donald Trump had begun.

The day after the Oval Office "follow-up conversation," Director Comey arrived in New York to visit with the president-elect at his office in Trump Tower. This was where transition business was being conducted. Comey was there for the scheduled regular intelligence briefing for the incoming president.

It was Friday, January 6, 2017. A two-page summary of the Steele dossier was presented to president-elect Trump. It was also provided that day to the so-called Gang of Eight, the congressional leaders of both parties, who are briefed on sensitive intelligence and national security matters.

Until that time no news organizations had published the Steele dossier's allegations. No one deemed them credible enough to run. There is an old maxim in media relations that if you have bad news you put it out on Friday—that way the story has time to die over the weekend.

If you have good news, you put it out on Tuesday, so the story has time to be picked up and repeated many times during the rest of the week.

Four days later, on Tuesday, CNN was reporting that the president-elect had been briefed on a summary of the dossier's information. Their story came from "multiple US officials with knowledge of the briefings." The CNN byline was by four of their top reporters, including Carl Bernstein, who had helped break the Watergate scandal and had coauthored *All the President's Men*. Information in the dossier was not deemed newsworthy before, but intelligence officials briefing an incoming president on the same information would pass the test.[20] Soon after, *Buzzfeed* published all thirty-five pages of the Steele dossier. News outlets picked up the intelligence briefing story and included links to the *Buzzfeed* story.[21]

Where did *Buzzfeed* get its copy?

Apparently it got its copy from David Kramer, Senator McCain's transatlantic traveling associate. This was revealed in a libel suit filed in a British court by Russian companies that had been mentioned in the dossier. In that case, under oath, Christopher Steele admitted that the allegations in the dossier were "unverified."[22]

DONALD TRUMP CALLS IT TREASON

So it was that the national media, stung by the embarrassment of the 2016 election, now began promoting the idea that the Russians had "colluded" with Donald Trump to win an unlikely election. They had done it, the media alleged, so they could blackmail the new president into doing what they wanted. Soon Democrats and their media allies began promoting the idea that Donald Trump was a Russian spy.

Once in office, Trump had immediately ordered the modernization of the nation's nuclear deterrent. He had increased military expenditures. He had increased sanctions against Russia. He had taken a strong stand against Syria and Iran, Russian-supported states. He had forced NATO nations to increase their military commitments. He had campaigned against Nord Stream 2 and Germany's reliance on a gas pipeline from Russia. It was pretty hard to understand how or why the Russians would want their spy to take such actions.[23]

It didn't matter. In May 2017, a special counsel investigation into Russian collusion began. Former FBI Director Robert Mueller was tasked to lead the probe.

In my conversations with the president, he readily conceded that the attacks from hostile media had preoccupied him and harmed his presidency. "Anybody else would be unable to function under the kind of pressure and distraction I had. They couldn't get anything done. No other president should ever have to go through this. But understand, there was no collusion. They would have had to make something up.

"The interesting thing out of all of this is that we caught them spying on the election. They were spying on my campaign. So you know? What is that all about?"

He turned to Sarah Sanders, his press secretary. "Sarah, they were spying."

Then he turned back to me. "I have never ever said this, but truth is, they got caught spying. They were spying!"

And then, in case I didn't understand what he was saying to me, he added just who it was who he thought was doing the spying.

"Obama," the president said.

He let that sink in for a moment before continuing. "Think about that for a minute," the president said. "They were spying. Remember? Two years ago. I mentioned this thing about Trump Tower? I put out this thing?"

In March 2017, he had claimed in a tweet that he had been wiretapped at Trump Tower. The national media had mocked him. This was absurd, they said, although in 1993, the new first lady, Hillary Clinton, had claimed something similar. She and Bill Clinton had moved into the White House. At the time, Hillary suspected that their predecessor, President George H. W. Bush, who had once been director of the CIA, was having them bugged. Hillary didn't trust the Secret Service, which she feared was loyal to the former president, so she called for the FBI to do a sweep. When they failed to find anything, she tasked the Secret Service and even later the CIA to search for eavesdropping devices. When nothing was found, she set up her own internal White House personnel security office, staffed by two workers from the political campaign.

"It turned out I was right. By the way," Trump said. "In fact, what I said was peanuts compared to what they did. They were spying on my campaign. They got caught and they said, 'Oh we were not spying. It was actually an investigation.' Can you imagine an administration investigating its political opponents?

"What they did was treasonous, Okay? It was treasonous."[24]

12

SUNDAY EVENING AT JARED AND IVANKA'S HOUSE

"In politics, we find that people who talk, don't do,
and people who do, don't talk."
—JARED KUSHNER[1]

I t was a cold, dark Sunday night in January 2019. The residential streets of this Georgetown neighborhood were so crowded that my wife, Myriam, and I had to park a couple of blocks away and walk to the house. The sidewalks that lined the narrow streets curved and wound up and down hills, making it feel more like San Francisco than suburban Washington.

We were told that former president Barack Obama lived nearby. This meant that the Secret Service had double duty in this neighborhood, with two families to protect. It also explained why there were so many police SUVs lined up, their flashing red lights a jarring interruption to the blackness of the cold night. Police and Secret Service officers were out on the streets, mingling and talking among themselves. We felt like strangers, outsiders, passing through a neighborhood block party.

The Kushners' three-story house was large, well-lit, and white. There was no front yard, and the house itself was on a slight incline, which made it appear to jut straight up out of the sidewalk. The lower floor and garage were at street level; a two-story staircase led up to the main entrance.

Secret Service agents quizzed us as we approached out of the darkness, their faces appearing and disappearing as the red lights flashed. They asked for our names and then sent us up the stairway to the front door.

Inside, Jared, Ivanka, and their children greeted us warmly. The children appeared happy, confident, outgoing, and polite, needing little encouragement from their parents. "Make sure you shake Mr. Wead's hand."

We were ushered into a living room, where two comfortable-looking couches faced each other. Like Ivanka's office, the room was minimally furnished. There were no exotic artifacts from foreign countries, no zebra skins, no massive family portraits on the walls, and, if there was any artwork, I can't remember it.

Inside a fireplace at the end of the room, a fire crackled, popped, and hissed throughout the evening. This was the real thing: no cluster of ceramic, fake logs, heated by piped gas.

Jared and Ivanka sat side by side on one of the couches, facing us. Myriam and I sat on the other. There, for the next two hours, we interviewed one of America's most enigmatic and mysterious couples. Throughout the evening, a young man brought us drinks—we drank only water—and hors d'oeuvres of avocado toast.

POLITICS IS A STRANGE BUSINESS

From the beginning, Ivanka had told me that I needed to sit down with Jared Kushner, her husband. After speaking with him for a few minutes, I could see why. He is scary bright. He often sees things that others miss. The storyline held that, when the president encountered an impossible problem, he passed it to Jared Kushner to see what he could come up with.

Most of the books written about the Trump White House have been driven by colorful stories about political infighting, with Kushner often the target. Having written about numerous presidents and their White House operations, and having served as a senior staff member at the White House, I knew well why Jared Kushner had become the target of bitter vitriol—and why he had survived.

He had survived, of course, because he was the president's son-in-law and his loyalty was unquestioned. If the president were to fail, so would Jared Kushner.

And he had become a target because it was much easier to blame him for any in-house political defeat than it would have been to blame the president, which would have amounted to political suicide. Thus, an attack on Jared Kushner would be the last stop on the train, the last station before the train would leave the White House altogether. Any attack on Kushner was an attack on Trump.

During this first interview in January 2019 and in the one that followed at the White House that summer, Kushner never said a negative word about anybody else. He appeared to be without guile. Clinical. Taking none of it personally. When we confronted him with salacious stories from books and articles that depended on anonymous sources for their material, he only smiled. At one point, he looked at Ivanka and said, "In politics, we find that people who talk, don't do, and people who do, don't talk."

When we raised some of the criticisms that Chief of Staff John Kelly had leveled against him, he refused to take the bait.

Later in the conversation, he said, "In general, people in politics seem to develop their strategies around their personal ambition and then decide on their objectives. For me, the first step is to define the objective and then develop the strategy."

Later that night, on our drive home, my wife and I talked about this. Maybe Jared didn't get the point. For most people in politics and in government, achieving their personal ambitions *was* the objective. Jared Kushner's goal may very well be justice reform, or finding common ground in the Middle East, or reworking the North American Free Trade Agreement (NAFTA). But the people he was dealing with wanted power. At one time, they, too, may have cared about policy. It may have even been what initially attracted them to politics. But most had long since concluded that they couldn't do anything good unless they were to advance.

They cared about policy only to the extent that it helped them destroy the person who worked in the next cubicle or who was higher up the ladder. Some of these rivals, these enemies, were people they had met for the first time only a few months before. A year before, they hadn't even known they existed. Now they were willing to risk their whole career and cause the nation to suffer just to bring them down. Such were the creatures that evolved from the swamp that Trump had vowed to drain.

This partially explained why Jared and Ivanka were able to get so many things done. They already had power. They also had fame and money. They could pursue policy for its own sake. Meanwhile, loyalty came naturally to them. Betraying the president would not bring them any more wealth or fame or power; it would bring only pain.

Their challenge was to find others who would help them—like-minded people who would focus on similar objectives. Sometimes they would be outsiders to government and politics, and sometimes they would be exceptional persons from inside the government who, for their own complicated reasons, had crawled out of the swamp onto higher ground. Jared and Ivanka needed allies who would fix on the same objectives and help them attain the right results.

Some journalists and activists misunderstood the role that Jared and Ivanka played in the Trump administration. They saw them as ideological advocates, arguing for liberal positions inside the White House bubble.

In my interviews, I would find that they played a much different role. Yes, they sometimes advocated for a more liberal view on a given issue, but not as a means to dictate policy. Instead, it was to make sure that every side of a question was fully understood. From their New York experience, even their Jewish experience, they often had perspectives that had been missing from other Republican White Houses. But once any issue had been fully vetted, once the president had been given all the facts and made his decision, they were fully on board.

HOW JARED AND IVANKA GOT THEIR WEST WING OFFICES

We started by asking about the 2016 campaign. As discussed in earlier chapters, Jared and Ivanka had played prominent roles.

Then we asked about the Trump administration's first days in the White House. When had Jared and Ivanka taken their first walk through the West Wing? I imagined that they would have returned to Trump Tower with a map of the White House in hand, discussing who would have which office, where and why.

I asked Jared how he had decided on his office. Is it next to the president's? Between the Oval Office and the chief of staff's office? Was there a fight for the territory? Were there big discussions? Did the president insist on that?

"We just took the offices we were given," Jared said.

That was a surprise. I later learned from an administration official that Reince Preibus, the former chairman of the Republican National Committee who became Trump's first chief of staff, had mapped it all out. It had nothing to do with Jared or Ivanka.

There had been a tweet by the *New York Times* correspondent Maggie Haberman saying that Ivanka's office had been set aside for her months in advance.[2] That seemed unlikely, and if it was true, Ivanka apparently knew nothing about it.

There had also been an incredible account from Vicky Ward's book *Kushner, Inc.* I wanted to know if President Trump had, indeed, hired John Kelly as chief of staff and ordered him to "get rid of my kids; get them back to New York."[3]

According to the story, prominently reported in the American media, Kelly told the president that it would be difficult to fire them, "but he and the president agreed that they would make life difficult enough to force the pair to offer their resignations, which the president would then accept."[4]

Jared laughed.

Peter Mirijanian, speaking for the Kushners' lawyer, said of Ward, "It seems she has written a book of fiction rather than any serious attempt to get the facts. Correcting everything wrong would take too long and be pointless."[5]

Media critics were promoting the idea that the Kushners were so powerful that Trump and General John Kelly conspired in fear and trembling in the Oval Office on ways to bring them down.

How much money does Jared Kushner make in his new White House job?

"We have both waived our salaries," he answered. "We are volunteering for this country."

I wanted to know what happened right after the election. What were their first reactions? What surprised them? I had learned from my own sources in the Secret Service that the agency had had few plans in place for a Trump win on Election Night. Nearly all the planning had been based on a Clinton win.

"No, no, the Secret Service was great," Jared said. "The surprises were all political. After the election Trump reached out to Hillary Clinton. And Ivanka reached out to Chelsea. But the next day, Hillary challenged the vote and demanded a recount."

This was a story that had never seen the light of day. The Trumps had extended an olive branch, but it had been spurned.

THE UNEXPECTED ADVANTAGES OF THE RUSSIAN WITCH HUNT

The release of the Mueller report, with its findings on the theory of a Russian collusion conspiracy, was expected any day. The tension was great. Critics were predicting that there would be multiple indictments. Don Jr. would go to prison. In fact, the Mueller report would not appear for another two months. What was it like in Trump world? Waiting for Mueller? Living with these constant accusations all over television?

"I told Trump, 'You are as innocent as you could ever be,'" Jared Kushner joked. "So, in that sense, it is good." Jared, like his father-in-law, always tried to see the best in any given situation.

"Because of the Russian investigation they [the members of the news media] did not cover the policy changes we were making," he said. "The cutting of regulations could have been big stories. Instead, they were blind to what we were doing, and we were able to jump-start the economy.

"The Russian investigation made the White House team tighter," he said.

"But it hurt, didn't it? You couldn't have wanted it?" I said.

"The process of the investigation is itself the punishment," Jared said.

An exception to this trend was how the media reacted to the Trump decision to withdraw from the Paris climate accord. Even Russia could not distract them from this issue. Years before, well-meaning journalists and environmentalists had tried to persuade US officials to ratify the Kyoto Protocol, but that idea had been killed by the Byrd-Hagel Resolution of 1997. This resolution disapproved of agreements that forced the United States to pay for cleaning up the environment in China, India, and other nations without requiring those nations to do something significant to limit their own emissions. The argument from the developing countries was that Americans had become rich by manufacturing on a massive scale, polluting the world in the process. It was only fair for other countries to build up their own manufacturing base, even if that too meant massive pollution. America, they insisted, had an obligation to follow behind and clean up in their wake. The US Senate had soundly rejected this idea, passing the Byrd-Hagel Resolution 95–0. Even Senator John Kerry, a Massachusetts Democrat and an environmentalist, had voted for it.

Obama was more subtle in his approach. When the Paris accord was signed in April 2016, the American media was ready to provide him with cover. Details about the accord were reduced to one single theme: It was good for the environment. Period. Don't ask any questions. Who could be against that?

To make sure that the discussion would go no further, Obama made it clear that America's support for the accord required no congressional action. This was not a treaty, he insisted; it was a nonbinding "agreement."[6] With Obama's signature, America joined.

Without any public discussion, an issue that had once led to a 95–0 vote in the Senate was now reversed. The American public hardly noticed. By the time Trump was challenging the Paris accord, a Yale survey showed that 70 percent of Americans wanted to stay with the agreement.[7]

Members of the national news media were outraged when Trump pulled out. They highlighted the reaction of world leaders, promoting the idea to the American people that Trump's decision made the United States a pariah to the rest of the world. Trump was apparently unfazed. "I was elected to represent the citizens of Pittsburgh, not Paris," he said.[8]

I later raised this subject in an interview with the president. "Of course they don't like me," he said, referring to some of the nations that had signed on to the accord. "They like the idea of American citizens giving them money. This amounts to a massive redistribution of American wealth to other countries."[9]

Publicly, Trump said the agreement would cost "America $3 trillion in economic activity and 6.5 million in industrial and manufacturing jobs."[10]

IF IT'S IMPOSSIBLE, GIVE IT TO JARED

Donald Trump had built his fortune, established his fame as an entertainer, entered the political arena, and won the ultimate prize. He was not going to change his methods now. One of those methods was to empower people to do great things, even when others objected and other people were deemed to be better qualified.

In 1980, when Trump tapped Barbara Res to build Trump Tower, she became the first woman to oversee a major New York City construction site.

During his 2016 political campaign, Trump had picked his daughter-in-law Lara Trump to run his campaign in North Carolina. Many observers believed that his election chances hinged on the outcome of that one battleground state. Lara had no political experience, but she knew the people there and wanted to make it work.

North Carolina went for Trump.

In 2016, to the surprise of many seasoned political operatives, Trump appointed Kellyanne Conway as his campaign manager. She went on to become the first woman in US history to lead a presidential campaign to victory.[11]

Of course, it didn't always work. One could even argue that it often failed. But the times it succeeded were instructive. If people were really passionate about something, Trump believed, they would be good at it.

Savvy Trump-watchers were not entirely surprised when the story broke that President-elect Trump had asked Kushner to lead the administration's effort to solve the Middle East crisis.[12] "I would love to be the one who made peace with Israel and the Palestinians," Trump told the *New York Times*. "That would be such a great achievement."[13]

Kushner's assignment was met with disbelief, followed by outrage and ridicule. But that was not even half of the story. Eventually Kushner would be made the president's "point of contact for over two dozen countries."[14]

Kushner would eventually meet with Iraq's prime minister to talk about the war with ISIS. He would lead the White House Office of American Innovation, working with the technology entrepreneur Elon Musk, Apple president Tim Cook, and Microsoft founder Bill Gates. He would use this same platform to "modernize the Department of

Veterans Affairs," to seek solutions for the opioid epidemic, and to "develop ideas for Trump's upcoming infrastructure proposal."[15]

Perhaps most notably, Kushner would take the lead in enacting criminal justice reform, meeting with senators on both sides of the aisle and forcing activists to quit squabbling and instead funnel their solutions into a workable "first step."

It was sometimes difficult to know when Ivanka's work ended and Jared's began, or the other way around. Both were involved in the planning of the president's 2017 speech to the joint session of the US Congress, with Ivanka reportedly taking the bigger role.[16] It was widely heralded as a positive, bipartisan speech—one that stunned Democratic leaders, who had been anticipating something altogether different.

MOVING THE AMERICAN EMBASSY TO JERUSALEM

I wanted to know how President Trump had made the decision to move the American embassy from Tel Aviv to Jerusalem. One by one, a succession of recent American presidents, including Bill Clinton, George W. Bush, and Barack Obama, had made it a campaign promise. Some had chastised their predecessors for failing to take that action.[17] Bush had promised he would order the move on his first day in office. But, once in power, each president had dropped the idea. How did Trump do it? Did he just grit his teeth and make the decision? Why had other presidents failed to deliver? What was it like trying to take this action?

"If you want to do something tough," Kushner said, "you're always going to have opposition. The question is, what kind of opposition? Is it big opposition, small opposition? Is it vocal opposition or nonvocal opposition? And I think that the president just went with his gut on a lot of these issues.

"I do think we ran a very good process to show him all of the risks of the people who are concerned about this. That includes intelligence assessments. In the end, the president believed that it was something he had promised to do and it was something that he wanted to do.

"You know, even though people said things could go badly, if it happened, he also said, 'Look, it's a time of relative stability in the region.'

"The key word there was 'relative.' He said, 'I may never again have a chance to do this.'

"So when the waiver came up, he wanted to do it. He took the decision. He said to the peace team, 'Look, I do want to try to take a real shot at the peace agreement. You know, how will this help us or hurt us?'

"We said, 'Look, in the short term, it will hurt you. Because, again, we do think this will drive them away from the table. But in the long term, we think that it helps because you have to start slaying some of these sacred cows. We're a sovereign nation with the right to recognize the capital of another sovereign nation. We shouldn't allow people to bully us into not doing that. The more people see that you keep your word and that you show strength, the more people will believe in you. This is something that will reverberate and show people that you're not like the other presidents who didn't move the capital but who also didn't make peace. They didn't have either one. It's almost like, sometimes, you have to break a leg to reset it.'

"The president saw that this was really something he wanted to do. Again, he wants to keep his promises. And so he kept this promise. But it was close.

"You know, in government, you have to distinguish between what's a real headwind, what's a real problem, and then what's a weak whimper. Sometimes they kind of sound the same. So, he just trusted his gut to know which it was.

"He's not afraid to make tough decisions. If it turns out badly, he can backtrack a little bit. But he's going to try things. He trusts his gut. He trusts his instinct. He's pretty fearless.

"Donald Trump doesn't say, 'Let me take decisions that will make me more popular, or they'll get me reelected.'

"He's saying, 'What can I do that will help me make our country stronger and do the things I promised I would do?'

"I can look at two examples. One is tariffs. Before he did the steel tariffs, a lot of people were telling him that the market was going to crash. He was told that it was going to be a disaster. The whole world will fall apart. Gary Cohn was warning him about this. 'You're going to lose all of your allies.'

"The president basically said, 'Look, I've been wanting to do this for thirty years. I've been saying that this is the right thing to do. I campaigned on it. I got elected on it. I want to see if it's a real problem, I can always backtrack.'

"It turned out that he did it. And it really wasn't that big of a deal. He was able to accomplish a lot of what he wanted to accomplish. The market price is correcting now, and it has been an investment for America. It has added productivity and a lot of jobs.

"The president saw that through."

Kushner said the same thing occurred when it came to dealing with China. "I had a friend come to me. He said, 'You know, what he's doing is very brave. Because the true benefits of fixing our trading relationship with China will probably not be felt in his presidency. But the detriments and the cost of trying to rebalance things for America will be totally incurred now, during his administration.'

"The president's view is, 'Look, I promised I was going to do it. I want to fix this thing. If I get it right, then it's good. Hopefully, the people will recognize that and they'll reelect me. If not, I'll go and I'll live my life.'

"His view is, while he's here, he's going to do everything possible to make as much progress as he can on the issues he thinks are critical to our country's long-term viability and strength."

WARS AND RUMORS OF WARS

Though many columnists in the mainstream media predicted war would break out in the Middle East if the US embassy were moved to Jerusalem, they were proven wrong.

French president Emmanuel Macron and Turkish president Recep Tayyip Erdoğan made an effort to try to get Trump to back down.[18] "Were you surprised by the reaction?" I asked Kushner. "There was much less of an uproar than anyone expected."

"It showed that, on this issue, a lot of people had moved on," Jared said. "A lot of these Arab leaders used their hatred of Israel and the demonization of Israel for the last seventy years. They could blame all of their problems on Israel. But it was really about deflection, because they had a lot of domestic issues at home."

The fact was that citizens in many countries in the region had limited property rights. The people's lives were not getting better. Some of this was due to mismanagement of the national economies. Some of it was because of the overemphasis on radicalization, and the perversion of a great religion.

"What would happen if they focused on how to make people's lives better?" Jared asked. "How can you help your people? How can they live better lives as opposed to blaming Israel for everything?"

When Trump moved the US embassy to Jerusalem, massive demonstrations ensued; more than fifty-eight Palestinians were killed. But "the war" never materialized.

"So, yes, people do care about the Palestinian cause," Jared said. "People want to see it going in the right direction. But people have been lied to on that issue for so long. These issues have become bigger in the public eye than they actually are. We need to find a way to resolve them and get through them."

As a writer and speaker, I have traveled internationally for thirty years. I wanted to know if Jared and Ivanka ever got away together on any of their foreign trips. Especially during any of their Middle Eastern trips. Did they have any fond memories of a café somewhere? How did they travel?

"Ivanka really only joined me on the trip for the opening of the new embassy in Jerusalem," Jared said. "My trips are usually last minute. You're just on the plane going from place to place."

Do you sleep on the plane?

"Either on the plane, or I'll catch a couple hours wherever I am. But my trips are pretty intense. Most of the pilots are military, and they say they've never seen trips like this. The people they carry come in and do their meeting and see the sights. The teams I'm with come in and do meetings all day long. They actually need to put on an extra pair of pilots for us sometimes because we're on the move, trying to get things done."

One advantage for Kushner was that he had no counterpart to meet with on foreign trips. There was less protocol. Things moved quicker.

Another advantage was the fact that he was family. Many governments understand the concept of family. They trust it. They know that people come and go in the world of politics, but family endures.

"They know that I have the president's interests at heart," Jared said. "They realize that I was there before and I'll be there after."

LUNCH AT THE KING DAVID HOTEL

We talked about historic comparisons. There is a long list of presidential children who have become ambassadors. They tend to make long-lasting friendships. Many become ambassadors long after their fathers have left the White House. John Eisenhower and Caroline Kennedy are modern-day examples.

Kushner was dispatched to the Middle East soon after President Trump came to power. He paved the way for the president's first successful trip to Saudi Arabia and Israel.

"It's interesting, I'm able to meet at a very high level," Jared said. "And in a way where there's not a ton of protocol. We don't have to take pictures or read talking points. We can just sit down on the same side of the table and say, 'Okay, this is our problem. Let's brainstorm together on how we should go about solving it.' It allows us to be much more honest.

"There's another thing: They've seen that nothing's ever leaked from the discussions we've had. So they're able to be more open and trusting.

These are issues where the leaders know what they want to accomplish, but the foreign ministers are just afraid to get yelled at. So they just stick to the party line that they know will never be accomplished.

"The informality of these meetings [has] allowed us to discuss different viewpoints," Kushner said. "People also appreciate being brought in at the front end and having their opinions solicited. We are able to really develop solutions based on this feedback."

"There are a lot of very thoughtful, smart people who are the rulers in a lot of these countries who want to see an issue finally resolved. They see their region moving forward. They think there's a lot of potential if we can get through the most intractable issues."

Ivanka and Jared both traveled to Jerusalem and delivered speeches for the dedication of the new embassy. The event had a profound significance on Jared Kushner, who was accompanied by his older sister, Dara.

"For Ivanka and I, a big part was my sister coming to the dedication. My older sister came by the hotel beforehand to see me and rode over with me. It was a thrill to be able to think about the fact that we were grandchildren of Holocaust survivors," Jared said. "The Nazis had tried to kill the entire Jewish people and kill our family. A lot of our family died. And now here we were, together, in Israel, in a Jewish state, on the day where we were dedicating the new American embassy in Jerusalem. We were representing the president of the United States, and we were there with the secretary of the treasury, and with the prime minister of Israel. That was a very, very, very, significant moment in our lives.

"I was able to make a speech. I don't speak publicly very often, but this was a real honor to be able to be there presenting and trying to give a message of hope and unity. A message about how it is important for the world to recognize truth and reality. That we're only going to move forward if we start acknowledging the truth."

It was a historic moment, I said. The dedication of the new embassy.

"It was something that should have been done a long time ago," Kushner replied.

During the trip to Jerusalem, Jared and Ivanka Kushner stayed at the famous five-star King David Hotel. I had my own fond memories of stays there. I also have an autographed photo of Menachem Begin, the deceased former prime minister of Israel, who as a member of the Jewish resistance had ordered the bombing of the hotel that had left ninety-one people dead. The Middle East is a complicated business.

"The day of the ceremony, Ivanka and I had lunch in the dining room of the King David," Jared said. "We were joined by Senator Lindsey Graham, Senator Dean Heller, Senator Mike Lee, and Senator Ted Cruz. It was a great lunch with a bunch of senators, and there were all kinds of people who were so excited to be there. So many of them have now become good friends."

The event's organizers had blocked off the room and arranged one of those famous Israeli luncheons. There was a spread of grilled chicken, falafel, olives, pita, hummus, and all the good things that make dining in Israel a memorable experience.

"There were a lot of laughs, and people were really just very, very excited about what was about to happen," Kushner said. "They were appreciating and understanding the historical significance of this day that had been long overdue. People understood the political courage that the president had shown, in not only keeping his promise, but in going forward and wanting to recognize right from wrong. The president was really fighting for progress and trying to make sure that he was doing his part to move the world forward."

Our evening had gone on way too long. The fire, once ablaze, now smoldering embers. The children had made an early appearance in their pajamas, and Ivanka had retreated for a time to put them to bed. When Myriam and I finally said good night to Jared and Ivanka that cold Sunday evening in January, we thanked them both for the work they were doing.

Ivanka was kind and radiant. One again, Jared Kushner was self-effacing. "Well, we are privileged to serve our country," he said.

★ 13 ★

THE GREATEST
JOBS PRESIDENT
GOD EVER CREATED

"The election was not a right-versus-left contest, it was the
outsiders versus the insiders."
—Jared Kushner[1]

In three separate conversations with the president, the red-hot
American economy came up. He was fascinated by the media's stubborn refusal to recognize what was happening. In normal times,
the economy was big news, a regular feature that often led newscasts.

New jobs numbers and unemployment figures were always announced. Entire networks had been created to meet the public's demand
for detailed economic information. At last count, fifteen business channels were available to American viewers, including Bloomberg, CNBC,
Sky News Business Channel, and Fox Business Network.

Yet the great American economic miracle, the longest-running
boom in US history, was largely ignored. It was as if it hadn't happened.
It wasn't news. Stung by the election of Donald Trump, the media was
now stung again by his economic success.

"The world is collapsing," the president said in one of our 2019 conversations. "And yet America is booming. We alone are growing stronger. It's amazing. Great numbers came out again today on Wall Street. They do not even talk about it. They won't admit it. They never say anything."[2]

One study tracked television news coverage during the four months leading up to the 2018 midterm elections. It showed that 92 percent of the stories about Trump on ABC, CBS and NBC were negative and fewer than 1 percent of them dealt with the economy.[3]

For the record, as I write this chapter, during the summer of 2019, the Trump administration has created six million jobs. More Americans are employed than ever before in American history. Some 400,000 new manufacturing jobs have been created. It was once thought that manufacturing in America was over. Jobless claims have dropped to the lowest levels in fifty years.

Under Trump, Americans enjoy the lowest rates of unemployment among African American workers since the government began keeping records.[4] Likewise, America is experiencing the lowest unemployment rates for Hispanics and Asians and the lowest rates of unemployment for women in half a century.[5]

DONALD TRUMP'S PROMISE

In June 2015, when Donald Trump announced his candidacy, he declared that he would be "the greatest jobs president that God ever created."[6] No one paid much attention. But a year later, as the campaign was heating up, and after Trump secured the nomination, his repeated claims about creating jobs began to irritate the incumbent, President Obama.

During a 2016 town hall meeting, televised by the Public Broadcasting Service, an incredulous Obama openly mocked Trump in front of the audience. A participant had asked about Trump's jobs claim. "When somebody says . . . that he's going to bring all these jobs back, well, how exactly are you going to do that?" Obama asked. "What magic wand do you have?"[7]

Obama wasn't the only one annoyed by Trump's displays of self-confidence. He and the world's best economists had tried to find more jobs and there weren't any left in the cupboard.

When then-candidate Trump issued a proposed budget promising economic growth exceeding 3 percent, perhaps even 4 percent, it was met with near-universal derision. Economic experts across the board, both Democratic and Republican, said it couldn't happen. Not only were American economists in agreement, the opinions were nearly unanimous in Europe and across the Pacific Rim.

Obama's White House Council of Economic Advisers had predicted 2.1 percent growth for 2017 and 2.3 percent growth for 2018.

Larry Summers, who had been the treasury secretary under President Bill Clinton and the director of the National Economic Council under Obama, warned Americans to "plan for the worst."[8] Summers said Trump's plan would work "if you believe in tooth fairies."[9]

Robert Brusca, a former professor at Baruch College's Zicklin School of Business and chief economist of the Food and Agricultural Office at the United Nations, was dismissive of Trump's claims. "No, pigs do not fly," he said.[10]

Online fact-checkers ridiculed Trump and helped correct the record for researchers who might have otherwise been tempted to believe his economic forecasts. The Federal Reserve Bank of San Francisco estimated that "real" economic growth would be closer to 1.5 percent, or maybe 1.7 percent.

"It's time to embrace the malaise," declared the *Financial Tribune*. "The era of greatness is done."[11]

Moody's Analytics produced an exhaustive, well-documented assessment of what would happen to the economy under Trump.[12] There would be a severe recession. Unemployment would rise to 7 percent.[13] One of the authors of the report was Mark Zandi, who had advised Senator John McCain during his 2008 presidential bid.

Even four months into his presidency, after Trump's positive talk and deregulation campaign had ignited a stock market boom and stronger economic growth seemed possible, economists across the board, Republicans and Democrats, maintained a united negative voice. They appeared to be buoyed by each other's dark opinions and frightened to break ranks and risk facing ridicule from colleagues.

On May 19, 2017, in an analysis for the *Los Angeles Times*, the Pulitzer Prize–winning columnist Michael Hiltzik quoted experts across all partisan and ideological lines and concluded that going beyond 2 percent growth was unlikely. "Making up the difference from 2% to more than 3% looks like a pipe dream," he wrote.[14]

According to many economics experts, the US economy under the Trump administration was going nowhere. Of course, the political elites had predicted that he could never win the presidency in the first place.

But Trump had a habit of doing what experts said couldn't be done. For the record, by his second year in office, the economy was growing at 4.2 percent.[15]

ERIC TRUMP'S EXPLANATION

Some of Trump's family members were equally astonished by what they saw as the media's denial. "It's amazing when you see what's going on," Eric Trump said. "Sometimes I think, 'Well, maybe I see it because I'm a business guy, or maybe because I run a company, or maybe because I am a math guy.' But then, why not report wage increases? Everybody feels that. At every level.

"There is just no arguing his success. There's no arguing the quantifiable metrics. If you actually get down to a serious conversation and you talk numbers and you talk employment, you talk wage growth and you talk consumer confidence, how can you not recognize what is happening?

"Look where we are with these trade wars? *Forbes* has been tracking it with some honest articles about China being down thirty-two to thirty-three percent."[16]

I scrambled to find a *Forbes* article by Kenneth Rapoza entitled "China Is Losing the Trade War in Nearly Every Way."[17] I passed it to Eric.

"Yes, this is it," he said. "There are some others that go bullet point by bullet point, breaking down the whole process. And when you watch *The View*, you have a bunch of talking heads attacking my father. I mean, it's incredible.

"I couldn't be prouder of him. I couldn't be happier for the American workers who are finding jobs and seeing their wages increased. We all fought so hard to get to this moment. And he fought so damn hard to achieve this."

Lara Trump wasn't surprised by the economic numbers. "I just knew before he became president that if anyone understood the way the economy works, it's a businessman," she said. "The guy who has dealt with money his whole life, who has made his name off of being a billionaire. He understood all the loopholes, all the things that didn't work, and the reasons why they were hurting the country.

"Listen, he has had ties all over the world. Forever. He's had all kinds of things manufactured and he had to go to China to get it done because we had no manufacturing left in this country. Before Donald Trump it was not competitive to manufacture here in the United States. So I knew he was going to be incredible for the economy well before he became president.

"Look at all the facts. Look at how he has rolled back regulations, giving small businesses so much more opportunity to hire people. My parents are small business owners. It's impacted them. The fact that he has been calling out the unfair trade deals around the world. Finally, someone is standing up and saying, 'Guys, this isn't fair. We've got to fix this.' And guess what? It wasn't easy but he's making a lot of progress. I think China's right there, ready to make some really good deals with him. He obviously did it with Canada and Mexico. It has allowed American businesses to thrive, allowing people to get back to work."[18]

Like his father, Eric Trump often brought the subject back to the national media and their glaring omissions. Fake news was about more than reporting false information; it was about ignoring important, true information, he said.

He singled out George Stephanopoulos, the former Democratic adviser and ABC News commentator and host. "During the campaign, Stephanopoulos was sitting in his ivory tower" in Lincoln Square, across the street from ABC News's headquarters. "People in the media weren't getting the movement; they weren't getting the people that were left behind in this country. So it makes sense they didn't see it as newsworthy when these people started to get jobs.

"I mean, we would go to this town that had the most beautiful factory that you had ever seen other than the fact that the windows were boarded up, the parking lot had a chain-link fence around it, and there were no cars. There would be no lights on. It was a ghost town. But you could see the beauty of the building. You could see the beauty of the manufacturing and the commerce that had taken place there. This factory was dead and you still had a town surrounding the factory. It had once employed ninety percent of the people in this town, and that town was dead. Every single one of those people in that town were forgotten because of stupid deals like NAFTA. Because our politicians didn't give a damn.

"There was this woman in Iowa, she goes, 'I get seven hundred dollars from Social Security. The problem is, I spend a thousand bucks every month on insulin shots.' She has stage II diabetes. She continued, 'So I cannot afford to eat. I can't afford anything. I'm lucky I have a son and he has a job. He doesn't do very well, but just enough to make up the difference and get me a little food.' She said she was living in his living room.

"You want to cry when you meet these people," Eric Trump said. "These people were truly forgotten. The media doesn't care about these people. They never do stories on them. It doesn't fit their narrative. The media has its own agenda. And these people don't fit. As far as they are concerned, these people don't exist. But my father works every day for these people. We were out there and we met them and we heard them and we think about them every day. All these new jobs you hear about? He's doing it for those forgotten men and women."

STEPHANIE GRISHAM'S GRAND ARRIVAL

From the beginning of this book project, my access to the Trump White House passed through the offices of Bill Shine and Sarah Huckabee Sanders.

After Shine stepped down as director of White House communications in March 2019, I operated exclusively through the office of Sanders, who was serving as the White House press secretary. In the hot summer of 2019, all of that changed. Sanders resigned. She had been a highly respected staffer with a reputation for intense loyalty to the president. Her emails had opened the way for my interviews with administration staff.

Now my hope for continuing access, my connection to finish this book, ran through the office of a new White House press secretary, Stephanie Grisham. I knew Grisham by reputation from her work in Arizona politics. She was known for being fiercely loyal to whomever she worked with. Previously, she had worked as press secretary to the first lady, Melania Trump.

Stephanie landed in her new job in spectacular fashion. On a presidential trip to Asia, she impressed the cynical, jaded White House press corps by fighting for their right to cover the president's impromptu walk into North Korea. It was a singular moment of history. Trump was stepping across this contentious border, where guards had shot at each other and soldiers had been killed. It marked another seminal moment in the relationship between Donald Trump and Kim Jong-un.

Seeing Grisham, an assertive American woman, fighting off North Korean security bullies, brought smiles and cheers from all Americans. There she was, pushing open a path for the White House press corps to ensure they could cover the story.

It was instructive that the announcement of Grisham's appointment had come from the first lady. Stephanie would have multiple assignments. She would do the jobs that had previously been done by both Bill Shine and Sarah Sanders, White House communications director as well as press secretary. She would also keep her old job, as press secretary to the first lady.[19] The president was reconfiguring the White House staff, creating "super aides."

MICK MULVANEY, THE MAN WITH TWO JOBS

On July 9, 2019, I interviewed White House Chief of Staff Mick Mulvaney. He is the twelfth White House chief of staff I had met and one of the most impressive. Mulvaney is vivacious, quick, and decisive—traits that any chief of staff must have to survive. We talked for a moment about others who had held this difficult, powerful position. He said he had just met with and talked to John Sununu, the former governor of New Hampshire and chief of staff to President George H. W. Bush. Sununu had been my boss when I worked in the White House.[20] He was a strong leader, the prototype for a chief of staff.

Mulvaney said that many former chiefs of staff, both Democrat and Republican, had been available to him, and he called on them frequently. But he was in unchartered territory. No other chief of staff had served simultaneously as director of the Office of Management and Budget, which Mulvaney had been doing since day one of the Trump administration.

The president apparently liked what he saw and kept Mulvaney in both places. It was similar to the arrangement Trump had made for Grisham, although Mulvaney's positions carried greater power and greater potential consequences. If somebody showed that he or she could do a job well, Trump apparently liked to give that person even more responsibility.

All that made Mulvaney a rare, if not endangered, species. I say endangered because he was integral to the red-hot, high-octane Trump economy. That, in turn, was key to the success, maybe even to the survival, of the Trump White House.

The office of the chief of staff is a suite of rooms located at the southwest corner of the West Wing. One could say that this is the "west wing" of the West Wing, both in terms of its location and of its power. It is right down the hallway from the Oval Office, near Jared Kushner's office. On the other side, headed in the other direction, one passes the vice president's office.

The chief's suite includes an office for the deputy chief of staff, Emma Doyle, and spaces for Mulvaney's administrative assistants.

I wanted to get the story behind Trump's economic success and knew that, other than the president himself, no one else could give me a better start. Mulvaney was the perfect person to talk to. We sat down around a coffee table in his office.

"So how did the Trump White House do this?" I asked. "What brought back this economy? And how do you respond when people say, 'Well, it's just Obama delayed?'"

That last question literally brought Mulvaney out of his chair.

"I keep a couple of my favorite graphs here," he said, fishing for a folder off his desk and then sitting back down and plopping it open onto the table between us. "This is it."[21]

He spread pages and charts across the table. "Obama's last budget and their economic assumptions going forward show exactly what they expected," he said. "This is what they thought they would be able to do."

He showed their predictions for the gross domestic product for years into the future. They were all in the range of 2.3 percent, which matched what they had been saying publicly at the time. "This was the new normal," Mulvaney said. "In fact, if you look at other budgets that they wrote, the out years were as low as 1.9, 2.0. They knew that they couldn't get out of this rut. That is why they started talking about 'the new normal.'"

That phrase reminded me of one used by President Carter, who in 1979 blamed the then-failing economy on the attitude and ambitions of the American people. He gave a national address talking about a "crisis in confidence" among the American people.[22] Pundits dubbed his address "the malaise speech," although it never contained that word.

Referring to the Obama team, Mulvaney said, "They talked about the graying of the nation. They talked about the slowdown in productivity. They were trying to lessen expectations. It was really about managing the decline of the nation, without actually using that language. They were saying that the nation was no longer a three-percent-growth nation. We had ended that cycle of our history. We were now in a low-growth mode.

"Of course, they looked all across the world, at least at the developed nations, and they saw that. They saw it in Europe. They saw it in Japan and they figured, 'Okay, that's the way everybody else is going. So there we go as well.'

"That's why I think it's just outrageous when they try to take credit for something that they didn't think could be done and wouldn't have known how to do even if they had finally believed it possible."

Mulvaney cited *New York Times* columnist and Nobel Prize–winning economist Paul Krugman for having coined one of his favorite phrases on the economy. "He was asked if three percent GDP was even possible; this was in March 2017. He said, 'No, you could make me total dictator to do everything I think would work and it still wouldn't get you up more than a few tenths of a percentage point.'[23]

"Actually, that may be one of the few times that Paul Krugman was right. If he was a dictator, and he did everything he knew to do, he still couldn't get growth because he wouldn't know what to do.

"So, it's just absurd for the Obama intelligentsia to be taking credit for where we are now, because they knew they couldn't do what we're doing. They didn't even think it was possible. They couldn't even conceive of three percent, four percent growth. They just didn't have the same type of vision."

HOW THE TRUMP TEAM TURNED IT ALL AROUND
So, how did the Trump team achieve something that the Obama team didn't think was possible?

"We deregulated and we fundamentally changed the way that we tax capital production, the creation of wealth," Mulvaney said. "So, when we deregulated, that was a structural change.

"One of the things people say is that you guys are just using lower taxes like a sugar high. Or they'll say you increased spending last year. That's a sugar high.

"I'm like, 'Okay, those two things are true. But deregulating is a structural change; it pays benefits every single year. If it's now easier to open a business, it's going to be easier for you to open your business this year and easier for me to open my business next year. It's a structural change. If we do a stimulus, for example, it's just a one-time thing. But deregulation is the gift that keeps on giving towards growth.'"

Ah, but wait. Democrats say that you are getting rid of regulations that are needed. How do you answer that?

"There are literally thousands of old regulations that have never been cleared off the books, and others that urgently needed clarification," said Mulvaney, who cited the "waters of the US" rules and the Corporate Average Fuel Economy (CAFE) standards as examples.

Mulvaney said he once ran a small business and was stunned at the level of regulation involved. "The government would dictate how big the font was on my menu boards, what I had to tell people about the food, and how often I had to do various things in the store. That's the kind of stuff that people don't see. It adds only a marginal, very marginal, cost to the way we live around here. But, when you add thousands upon thousands of regulations and red tape, it does make a real difference.

"I never had a small businessman or -woman come into my office, in my six years in Congress, and ask me, 'Please, lower my taxes.'

"They came in and said, 'Please, get the government off my back.'

"That's what we've done. That's a structural change.

"The other thing that we've done is we changed the way that that we invest and produce capital. We have made it easier for people to create things, to produce them and to supply them to the market."

How have you done that? I asked.

"By allowing them preferential tax treatment to invest in their own businesses. If you would make a capital investment in your business, you get to immediately deduct that investment.

"What has that done? It's done a couple of things. First of all, it's dramatically increased productivity.

"Look, the GDP is a mathematical equation that you can tie back to many different factors. One of the ways you can deliver GDP is the number of people working times their individual output. Okay, that is the gross domestic product. They produce.

"There are two factors in that equation, the number of people working, and their personal output. Now, we have had some success that people didn't think we could have in terms of the number of people working. Our critics said, 'Oh, the country is graying and you terrible Trump people are never going to increase immigration enough, so you're never going to be able to increase the number of people working.' We did it by encouraging people to come back to the workplace who had given up under the Obama administration.

"Then we focused on something else that Democrats never thought possible. We increased productivity again. They thought that those days were behind us. We said no. If we can get businesses to invest in capital, then people are more productive.

"That's indeed what we see. Productivity has gone up. For example, we gave business an incentive to buy new and better pieces of machinery. What followed was more productivity, more output for that person.

"The GDP goes up. But not only is GDP going up, the economy is growing. It's done so in what we consider to be a supply-sided growth, which is why we don't have any inflation.

"Keep in mind, you and I are old enough to remember what inflation is. It is loosely defined as too much money chasing too few goods. In four years in Washington, Democrats and other Keynesians would think, 'Every time the economy heats up, we have the risk of inflation. People are taking home more money. There will be more demand for goods. Inflation.'

"How do you solve that? You make more goods.

"Go back to the system we created, which encouraged capital investment, encouraged productivity, and encouraged the output of things. You don't have inflation. You don't have too much money chasing too few goods. More goods keeps inflation at bay. That is the supply-side phenomenon that people have been talking about since [the influential American economists] Milton Friedman and Arthur Laffer.

"You know, a long time ago, back in the eighties, with Ronald Reagan as a candidate, it was the supply-side revolution that they kept talking about. Well, we were able to do it.

"So, you've got an increase in productivity, an increase in GDP, and an increase in wages, because wages tend to go up as productivity goes up. We've done all of that without inflation."

TALKING JOBS WITH JARED KUSHNER

Avi Berkowitz, a deputy assistant to the president, had run *Trump Tower Live*, the Trump campaign's Facebook online news report. A Harvard Law graduate, Berkowitz met Kushner in 2017 during a game of pickup basketball at a Passover celebration in Phoenix, Arizona. They clicked, and he soon was regarded as Kushner's right-hand man.[24]

I met Berkowitz in the Eisenhower Executive Office Building, an ornate structure located next to the White House. Built in the late 1800s during the Grant administration, it once housed the State Department, the War Department, and Navy Department—all rolled into one.

It is considered part of the White House grounds. Many presidents—Richard Nixon, for example—worked in a suite of offices there while reserving the Oval Office for ceremonial purposes. Eisenhower used the Indian Treaty Room, located in the East Wing of the Eisenhower Executive Office Building, for news conferences.

Berkowitz escorted me to Jared Kushner's office in the West Wing of the White House, between the Oval Office and the chief of staff's suite. As a student of history who had once worked in the White House and knew the West Wing, I had long been curious about its

configuration under Trump. This was prime real estate. I knew that
Kushner's office would be small, even tiny, but I didn't know just how
cramped and dark it would feel.

I should explain that the White House is always changing. While
load-bearing walls remain in place, that is not the case with others. It is
not unusual for a White House denizen to return to the building after a
weekend away and find that a whole new wall has been built, complete
with crown molding and illuminated by newly installed chandeliers. It
might look like it could have been built one hundred years ago.

At the entrance to Jared Kushner's office, we met Cassidy
Dumbauld, special assistant to the president and Kushner's gatekeeper.
Cassidy, has an outer, windowless office with two large-screen televisions on the wall behind her desk. She chatted amiably with us for a
few minutes before we were invited into Jared's space. Just as Ivanka
had done in her crowded office upstairs, Jared had made room for a
conference table in his.

Jared Kushner picked up right where he had left off four months
prior, during out last interview, in his Georgetown home. I had the
notes right in front of me. He didn't. So, it was a little surprising that
he remembered the exact place where that conversation had ended.

"So, the economy was a very big focus for the president," Kushner
said. "One of the first things he did during the transition, and also
during his first weeks and months of the administration, was to start
bringing in CEOs. He just wanted to talk with them and get other
perspectives. The president wanted to know what they thought. What
needed to be done to allow them to create more jobs? He wanted to
know what competitive winds they were facing internationally. What
were the issues during the last administration that hurt their ability to
grow their businesses here in America?"

Kushner noted that a big issue for President Trump was bringing
corporations back to American soil, and he explained this. "One of the
big issues during the campaign was inversions. A lot of companies were
starting to become domiciled offshore. There were tax advantages to

do that. The regulatory environment was such that that it was hard for them to make investments in capital expenditures here in the United States.

"So, reviewing regulations was a big focus and an important part of the president's ability to turn around the economy. Of course, the president believes that we should have some regulations, but not to the point of choking businesses out of existence and destroying entire communities."

Other members of the administration brought up this same issue. There was a need for balance between cleaning up the environment and creating a chance for businesses to thrive. America's ability to clean up the environment stems directly from its wealth. This was why other nations coveted American involvement in the Paris accord and other such agreements. Our science, technology, and money were needed to clean up the environments in China, India, and developing African nations. These countries were becoming manufacturing giants and the world's worst and most toxic polluters.

But there is a limit to how much of a tax burden the American middle class can shoulder without having an opportunity to create wealth for themselves. If America's wealth were drained, if its roads and bridges were crumbling, if its middle-class tax engine were depleted, how could it help the world battle pollution?

"It's interesting," Jared observed. "When it comes to the environment, many companies want to do well and others, obviously, don't care and need to be reined in."

During the previous two administrations, this whole process had become a hotbed of legalized corruption. Though one of the administrations was led by a Democrat and the other by a Republican, they followed similar paths when it came to regulating tax inversions. Some companies were held to high standards; others were given exemptions that were inserted into stimulus bills. Such companies essentially paid for their "privilege to pollute" by donating to members of Congress. This process grew during the Great Recession and was justified in the name of job creation.

Some companies bought millions of dollars of in advertising, promoting their corporate commitment to the environment, assuring themselves good media coverage, even though some of them were exempted from laws protecting the environment. They were too big to comply.

Trump's deregulation effort moved the whole process to a more even playing field and revived free enterprise. It allowed small businesses to get into the game, businesses that couldn't afford to make massive political donations or big advertising buys on the television networks. And yet the newly invigorated businesses generated jobs.

"So, we started doing a lot of strategic deregulation," Jared said. "The president rolled back a lot of the overreaches of the federal government. He believes in a smaller federal government."

Trump's deregulation process represented a major change in the way of doing business in America. In some cases, it meant that small businesses could challenge entrenched monopolies. As the mounds of regulatory paperwork required for new businesses were cut, new businesses opened in greater numbers. That, too, meant more jobs.

Perhaps the most significant consequence of deregulation was America's surprise emergence as an energy-independent nation.

Early in my career as a writer, my conversations with Presidents Ford and Carter sometimes turned to the energy crisis. Both men faced the challenge of what to do about the dependence of the United States on nations in the Middle East, sometimes at moments of great international peril.

For them, the goal of an energy-independent America must have seemed like an impossible dream, and that dream must have continued throughout the Reagan years. Seven presidents were unable to achieve it. Under Donald Trump, once the chains of regulation were cut, America moved rapidly and naturally toward energy independence.

Jared Kushner was impressed at how quickly the change occurred, and how profoundly it has affected the nation. "Within the first two years, America had become energy independent," he said. "It was critical, both because it developed a substantial industry but also because it decreased our reliance on foreign oil. That dependency had been a major vulnerability for our country. Being energy independent gave America a lot more power. It also brought a lot more wealth into the country."

MORE ON HOW RUSSIAN COLLUSION SAVED THE ECONOMY

The president expected major challenges to this process. The established monopolies, protected by Democrats and Republicans alike, and, more importantly, by their allies in the national news media, had been years in the making. There were still spats over particularly onerous regulations that punished the more outrageously partisan business enterprises, but since the end of the Cold War, this new arrangement had become solidified.

It was international. Some companies in Europe and the Pacific Rim also depended on hobbled American competitors. This "new world order," as President George H. W. Bush and Soviet leader Mikhail Gorbachev proclaimed it in 1990, had only become more entrenched with each successive president.

The expectation in the White House was that each step Donald Trump took toward deregulation would be challenged. After all, deregulation would disrupt monopolies that had been years in the making. The news media would focus narrowly on isolated examples of suffering or damage, thereby stoking outrage until the process reached a boiling point. There would be no explanation or understanding of the advantages of a free market, and no news coverage about the creation of new jobs. Any moves toward further deregulatory measures would be universally denounced and blocked. The whole process would end.

For the Trump administration, the trick was to eliminate as many of the worst regulations as quickly as possible before the national media, backed by their corporate sponsors, began their campaign.

Then, as painful and as unfair as the situation may have been, the Trump administration's deregulatory process was saved by an unlikely new actor: the Russian collusion conspiracy.

Jared Kushner had talked about this to me during our conversations at his Georgetown home the previous January. "The fact is that the media didn't focus on deregulations one way or the other because they were so obsessed with the palace intrigue, and the Russian nonsense," he said.

The result?

"We had a very aggressive deregulation agenda. It was historic. I think, over the first two years of the administration, we had a net decrease in the cost of regulation. We had a big decrease in the pace of the Federal Register. It was something that hadn't happened ever. So that was a very, very big push from the government. Deregulation. It led to a lot of investment from companies and the creation of many jobs here in America."

DONALD TRUMP'S "BIG, BEAUTIFUL CHRISTMAS PRESENT"

America had tax cuts under George W. Bush. Over the years rates had gone up, rates had gone down. But there had been no tax reform bill since Ronald Reagan, and even he hadn't been able to accomplish it until his second term.

On August 2, 2017, less than seven months after Trump took office, *Newsweek* ran an article titled "Tax Reform: Why Trump and the Republicans Will Fail."[25] The writer warned "It's going to be much, much harder this time, and Donald Trump is no Ronald Reagan."

Nevertheless, on December 22, 2017, during his first year in office, Donald Trump signed into law the largest tax-reform legislation in more than three decades. Trump called it a "big, beautiful Christmas present."[26]

"The corporate tax cuts and the personal income tax cuts really helped America be competitive globally," Jared Kushner said.

"It gave companies a lot of strategic advantages to be here. America has the most advanced and developed private sector in the world. We had the best rule of law in the world and the best democratic system. So, companies want to be here, but we were making it cost prohibitive for them to do so. That's why they were moving overseas."

The president had been a relentless cheerleader for American business. From his first day in office, his words seemed to ignite the stock market. Trump made it his business to praise or scold every business leader who visited the White House about job creation; on every trip abroad, he included a shameless pitch for American business.

"The president used his voice to focus on business," Jared said. "Celebrating business and telling them that he wanted them to be successful. The last administration had a war on business, where they were demonizing CEOs and demonizing their business."

But Trump's approach was nuanced, promoting those businesses that were helping the economy, and going after those businesses that were closing factories. "The president's voice was two edged. So, while he would promote some businesses, he would publicly go after other companies who were closing factories and moving them overseas," Jared said.

Trump's approach had an impact.

"You had a lot of CEOs that were afraid to close factories and close production and move them overseas now, thanks to the president's carrot-and-stick approach," Jared said. "He was a great cheerleader for the market. He was able to unleash the animal spirits of the American industry that had really been hobbled and deflated after years of the last administration."

NOW THE PRESIDENT GETS A DAILY TRADE BRIEFING

From time to time in my interviews, I unexpectedly stumbled onto items that were not publicly known. This happened during my conversations with Jared Kushner about the economy.

"Another thing he's done to rebuild the American economy is to focus on our trade deals," Jared said. "After the Second World War, we were the wealthiest country in the world. We tried to create a new world order by protecting everybody and paying for a global defense. At the same time, the United States gave sweeter deals to its trading partners than it got in return. Of course, we did that to rebuild the rest of the world and to build democratic allies. That was very successful. But in the eighties, and especially after the Cold War, we probably should have rebalanced all of that. We never really did."

Kushner told me that he and others in the White House noticed that the president got a daily threat intelligence briefing, but he never got extensive trade briefings and economic briefings.

"We changed that," he said, noting that Trump believes that national security and economics are tied together. "You can't be a safe country if you don't have a strong economy," he said. "And you can't pay for a big military if you don't have a strong economy. So the president focused much more on economics, on trade deals, than probably any president in history. He speaks to his trade rep every day. He's focused on doing a lot of different deals at one time. And he's trying to rebalance things, to make sure that we're bringing a lot more jobs and a lot more industries back to America.

"Conventional thinking had held that free trade creates a global supply chain, which lowers the cost of goods for consumers, and everyone benefits," he said.

"But that's not how it works," he added. "The reality is that, in free trade, you have winners and losers, and the costs of free trade are that factories are closing in different communities. The costs are very concentrated. You'll have a factory in Baltimore that will go out of business and you have a thousand people laid off. Some people can get new jobs, and some people can't. Some go on government programs. Some experience great poverty. There is an increase of crime, there are addictions, drugs. The families pay the consequences.

"So, there is a downstream effect of free trade that has brought a huge cost to our society. And it's been disproportionate in terms of how it has impacted. This is why the president is trying to protect American industry."

TRUMP'S SECRET ECONOMIC MOVES

While members of the news media have largely ignored the big stories of economic success in America under the Trump administration, they have also shown little interest in writing about any of the more nuanced advances the White House was making, Jared said.

Jared cited important work by Ivanka to help people get jobs.

"This retraining initiative is something that Ivanka has taken a lead in," Jared said. "She has really taken a lead in trying to make sure that we're reskilling the American workforce for the future," he said.

"Our education system has not evolved. We have a big focus on college degrees. Meanwhile, we have a lot of great careers that are within reach [to people without college degrees]. They require just a little vocational training. We've got a ton of unfilled jobs, as we have a growing economy."

Jared noted that business leaders tend to look far into the future to identify—and take steps to avoid—problems that may be coming down the pike. "In politics, you really only get credit when you solve problems where there is a crisis," he said. "But businesspeople get rewarded by making sure that you don't have problems in the first place. A businessperson is thinking of things that will prevent problems and create future opportunities."

"Ivanka's retraining initiative is an example of this administration taking steps to prepare the US workforce by looking far down the road," he said. "So, we see the reskilling effort as something that helps us in the short term but will also help us avoid displacement of workers in the long term," he said. "It will make sure we have the right skill set to deal with the economy as it's evolving. That's a great thing."

"At present, the president is focusing on the industries of the future, such as the nation's many great innovators, including the internet companies," Jared said. "That, too, requires a long view. We have to make sure that we have an industrial plan to be globally competitive for the next thirty years. The president is very focused on that. We are talking about 5G [fifth generation cellular network technology] or major investments in artificial intelligence, quantum computing, and synthetic biology. These are areas that are very important for the future of our country."

Some of this work goes unrecognized, and much of it is thankless. If the media will not even credit Trump for the economic advances he has already achieved for the nation, what chance is there that the media would credit the president for decisions he is making for the nation's future?

One of the administration's big decisions concerns what to do about the nation's decaying infrastructure. Long before he became president, Trump was bemoaning the sorry state of America's roads, highways, and bridges. He remembers when American airports were the marvel of the world. Today, foreign visitors are stunned by what they find.

This was one of the major issues that had driven Donald Trump into public life in the first place. He could see with his own eyes the collapse of America. It is what inspired his America First policy. It wasn't that America had no responsibilities worldwide, it was that it was losing its battle at home.

"One thing I'll say is that when the president laid out his vision for a lot of these issues, people thought it was impossible to accomplish any of it. You had a lot of people in the last administration saying two percent growth was the new normal.

"The president had a campaign outline for what he was going to do. He brought in the right advisers when he got here. He was able to put a lot of these things in place. If you look at the Council of Economic Advisers and a lot of their estimates, we've been spot on. We've actually been more accurate than the CBO [the nonpartisan Congressional Budget Office] with the past administration about what was possible."

As a result of Trump's policies, "what you're seeing now is workforce participation growing. We're bringing a lot of people off the sidelines. We have productivity growing as well, which means you're getting higher wages for the first time in many years."

THE OUTSIDER PRESIDENT

At times, Jared seemed amused by the president's fearless leadership in the face of such establishment headwinds. Old Washington hands told him that other presidents had operated differently. "What they say about this president," he told me, "is that he's not looking at polls. He's not saying, 'Oh, should I make this decision or that decision?' And he's not saying to himself, 'Oh, this guy gave me money, so should I decide one way or the other?'

"He truly was elected as an outsider president. He brought a lot of people into the administration, and we're not part of the establishment. He's brought in a whole new crop of people.

"The election was not a right-versus-left contest; it was the outsiders versus the insiders.

"One of the smartest things the president did was not allow people who publicly criticized him during the campaign [to] come in and work in his administration. There were a few exceptions to that. He also tended to avoid the experts who were wrong about predicting the election. He saw that as a sign of bad judgment, and it revealed a little bit about the circle they lived and worked in. It was a way to filter out who was part of the old establishment class.

"So he brought in a whole new crop of people. Maybe they didn't have the traditional résumés for doing their jobs, but many of them shared his vision. It took a little bit of time to figure out who were the right people and who were the wrong people.

"Basically, there were two types of people: those who thought Trump was saving the world and those who thought they were saving the world from Trump. Over time, we got rid of a lot of the latter.

Eventually, the president got a really good team, a really coordinated team. And he was able to start empowering his whole administration.

"He's not afraid to make decisions. He's action oriented, and he's telling everybody, 'Do your job.' Not surprisingly, the metabolism of this government is just far higher than I think any government before. People are working really hard to keep up with all the different things that are happening. Some are focused on price transparency, others on electronic medical records interoperability, still others on all the different regulations we're putting in place that really help business.

This was a story that never got reported. While the Trump administration eliminated many onerous, unnecessary regulations, as well as regulations that helped create monopolies for some chosen corporations, it was also, revising and modernizing needed government rules. It was replacing outdated regulations that were only defeating their purpose.

"The FDA [Food and Drug Administration] has approved more generic drugs for the first time ever. The prices of drugs have gone down. You've got all these accomplishments that are happening all across government. But people don't really notice, because they have nothing to do with Russia."

★ 14 ★

THE ISIS HORROR STORY

*"We're going to beat ISIS very, very quickly folks.
It's going to be fast."*
—Donald Trump on the campaign trail in 2016[1]

During the 2016 election campaign, the narrative presented by candidate Donald Trump on American foreign policy was widely belittled by academics, members of the news media, and State Department experts. Political professionals derided his chances of winning the election. Economists laughed at his plans and projections for the American economy. And foreign policy doyens mocked his ideas about America's place in the world.

While the savviest observers agreed that Trump had correctly identified North Korea's emergence as a nuclear power as the preeminent, long-term strategic danger to the United States, the bulk of the nation was focused on the immediate threat posed by the Islamic State of Iraq and Syria (ISIS). The soldiers in this black-clad, murderous army were proponents of radical Islam.

The terrorist organization had conquered 35,000 square miles of territory, carving out its proclaimed caliphate in the Middle East. ISIS controlled massive swaths of land, including the major cities of Raqqa, Syria, and Mosul, Iraq.

Americans had to watch as their own armored vehicles, with black ISIS flags waving from their turrets, proudly raced across the deserts of the Middle East, massacring villagers and subjecting thousands of civilians to slavery. Entire Christian and Yazidi communities of men, women, and children were herded into open-air pens without shade, food, water, or sanitation and then, over a period of days, systemically slaughtered. Some of the Christians claimed that they could trace their heritage back to the first century. They and the Yazidis, an ancient, persecuted religious minority, had lived in peace for generations with their Muslim neighbors.[2] They were now disappearing. Members of families who escaped the ISIS net spoke with horror of seeing decapitated bodies littering the streets.

On the night of April 14, 2014, a group of terrorists called Boko Haram, who would later align themselves with ISIS, kidnapped 276 girls, most of them Christian, from a government school in Chibok, Nigeria. A few days later, in a proof-of-life video sent to CNN, the Boko Haram commander laughed into the camera. "I've got your girls," he said. "I've got your girls."[3]

Two years later, I interviewed some of the girls and young women who escaped Boko Haram. Their harrowing stories are hard to forget.

In 2014, ISIS forces overran the town of Sinjar in northern Iraq. It had been a safe haven for Yazidi women and children while their husbands battled the terrorists. No longer. ISIS slaughtered the children and took thousands of the women as sex slaves. The United Nations declared it a genocide.

THE OBAMA DOCTRINE

The concern of the Obama administration had been that the appeal of ISIS was spreading. The group was attracting allies in Yemen and parts of Africa. In February 2015, the Islamic terrorists took twenty-one

Egyptian Coptic Christians to a coastal Mediterranean beach in Libya and beheaded them there in a videotaped ritual. The killers chanted sacred passages from the Koran during the bloody sacrifices. One of the victims on the beach cried out, "Jesus, help me!"[4] The next day, Pope Francis denounced the killings.

In March 2015, the BBC reported that in Nigeria, Boko Haram had set up roadblocks on major highways. Truckers reported that non-Muslim "infidels" were pulled from their vehicles and beheaded on the spot with chainsaws.[5] The squeamish American media largely ignored the story.[6]

Before the year ended, ISIS could boast an annual budget of $2 billion. It had thirty thousand troops on the ground in the Middle East. It operated in eighteen countries.[7]

On April 20, 2016, two months before Trump announced his run for president, Boko Haram announced that it was collaborating with ISIS and pledged to follow its leadership in creating an Islamic state that would stretch into Central Africa.[8]

The implications of the ISIS campaign were clear: We will do what we want with impunity. We will kill men, women, and children at a whim. And we will do it with your guns, your armored vehicles, and your grenade launchers. And no one can do anything about it.

The message of ISIS to America was menacing: Eventually, someday soon, we are coming for you.

In the United States, the public was puzzled over how the terrorists had seized American guns and armored vehicles in the first place. It was embarrassing to the Obama administration and politically harmful to Hillary Clinton, the former secretary of state and Democratic presidential candidate.

Perhaps out of respect to Obama-Clinton, online editors and television producers in America largely passed on the story.[9] Much of the public assumed that US military forces had abandoned the equipment, which wound up on the black market, where the terrorists bought it.

In fact, some of the equipment was new, and the dates on the weapons showed that some of them had been purchased by ISIS fewer than sixty days after they were manufactured.[10]

President Obama's strategy was to defuse the whole idea of war with Islam. His administration refused to use the phrase "Islamic terrorism." This strategy was popular with the more liberal leaders of Europe, especially in France, where large pockets of Muslim immigrant neighborhoods exist.

Obama often seemed to be speaking more to the Islamic world than to his own American audience. On March 6, 2007, Obama was quoted by *New York Times* columnist Nicholas Kristof as saying that the Muslim call to prayer was "one of the prettiest sounds on Earth at sunset."[11]

At the 2015 National Prayer Breakfast, Obama compared ISIS to the Crusades. "Unless we get on our high horse and think this is unique to some other place," he said to a ballroom full of three thousand stunned religious officials, "remember that during the Crusades and the Inquisition, people committed terrible deeds in the name of Christ."[12]

It must have been a bit disconcerting to most in his audience, who not only questioned his historic conclusions but were struck by the fact he had been forced to retreat eight hundred years to find anything comparable. He seemed to be inadvertently making the point of his critics. This was something from another century, and it was barbaric.

In contrast to Obama's approach, then-presidential candidate Trump's declarations against ISIS were graphic and direct. At a 2015 rally in Fort Dodge, Iowa, Trump was asked about the terrorist group.

"I'd bomb the shit out of them," he said.[13]

In April 2016, on the campaign trail in Connecticut, presidential candidate Trump promised, "We're going to beat ISIS very, very quickly, folks. It's going to be fast. I have a great plan. It's going to be great."[14]

His Democratic opponent, Hillary Clinton, mocked this promise. In their first head-to-head presidential debate, Clinton jabbed at

Trump's declarations about ISIS. "He says it's a secret plan, but the only secret is that he has no plan."[15]

DONALD TRUMP'S VICTORY

In hindsight, it looked easy. Trump had promised on the campaign trail that he would take care of ISIS quickly, and that appeared to happen. By November 2017, during Trump's first year in office, the terrorist organization had been practically wiped out.

But the American media, obsessed with their campaign to convince the public that Donald Trump was a Russian spy, was in no mood to award him another victory. They insisted that ISIS had not been defeated at all. ISIS forces were still there, they said, even if they had lost most of their territory.

The media compared the Trump administration's enthusiasm over the defeat of ISIS to President George W. Bush's declaration in 2003 that major combat operations in Iraq had ended. As he spoke, viewers could see a banner behind him that read MISSION ACCOMPLISHED. But the war in Iraq was not nearly done and would resurface in deadly fury. It would be the same with ISIS, the media promised.

At first, Trump was careful not to declare ISIS as finished, but by the end of his first year in office, the group's forces had been bottled up inside just a few square miles of territory. Voices in the Pentagon were saying that it was all but over. Trump began saying that it was "virtually defeated."

Even then, Trump's detractors wouldn't let go. CNBC ran a story in November telling readers that "experts warn the terror group is still a serious global threat."[16]

By December 10, 2017, ISIS's remaining fighters were trapped in a small enclave a few miles wide. "Has ISIS Been Defeated in Syria, as Trump Claims?" asked one headline.[17]

Pundits on CNN and MSNBC now insisted that ISIS was not dead at all, because its ideas were still alive. It was like arguing that the Allies had not won World War II because Nazism still existed. On December

22, 2018, CNN correspondent Arwa Damon expressed contempt for the idea that ISIS had been defeated. "It's so naive," she said.[18]

But by March 2019, MSNBC and CNN had to face reality. Trump had chalked up another victory. There was no way around it. ISIS was dead. "It ended, in the Syrian farming hamlet of Baghouz, as little more than a junk yard about the size of Central Park, filled with burnt-out vehicles and dilapidated tents,"[19] Robin Wright reported for the *New Yorker*. The once great terrorist organization that had once attracted legions of young recruits was now a cesspool of urine and feces. They had been reduced to making soup from boiled grass. The organization's warrior families, who had once been willing to blow up themselves, their children, and any hated nearby infidels, now surrendered meekly. They begged for water and food, seeking the luxury of prisons over the promises of paradise that they had used to entice their recruits.

Ironically, the last word out of ISIS did not come from a fearsome warrior making a heroic, suicidal stand. It came from a young woman, Hoda Muthana, a three-time ISIS bride. She surrendered to authorities and then promptly announced that she was a citizen of the United States from Alabama and wanted to go home. "I believe that America gives second chances. I want to return and I'll never come back to the Middle East," she promised.

Her lawyer passed information to ABC News and the Associated Press. Hoda had traveled to the Middle East, where she had married three ISIS warriors. She had lived with the terrorist organization for four years. Her Twitter feed had exhorted, "Go on drivebys, and spill all of their blood, or rent a big truck and drive all over them."[20]

Muthana was interviewed on CBS's *Face the Nation*, after which a blogger, Karen Townsend, observed, "It sure seems like the intention is to make Muthana into a sympathetic character."[21]

Thus ended the story of ISIS, not with a bang but with a whimper. A twenty-four-year-old mother with a baby was all that was left as a spokesperson. Her first two husbands had been killed in battle, she explained. Her third husband had divorced her. She wanted to go home.

ISIS had dominated a large portion of the public discussion during the 2016 election campaign. Now Trump's war was being called "the most successful unconventional military campaign in history"[22] by Elizabeth Dent, a nonresident scholar with the Middle East Institute's Countering Terrorism and Extremism program.

But media critics said the credit belonged to Barack Obama.[23]

Donald Trump, the master brander, closed the book on ISIS by giving them a new name. "While on occasion these cowards will re-surface, they have lost all prestige and power. They are losers and will always be losers."[24]

The fact was that no one—except, perhaps, Donald Trump himself—had expected it to be that easy. It was this expectation of failure that had left so many in the media trapped into the position of denying its success. After the victory was finally established, it was quickly forgotten. There were no colorful documentaries produced, no interviews given, and no history books written. It was like a magic trick. Once members of the public had learned the secret behind what Donald Trump had done, they were no longer interested. But I was interested.

INSIDE THE CAMPAIGN TO TAKE DOWN ISIS

In the late summer of 2019 I was told that the White House was setting up another meeting for me with the president. If it happened, it would be my fourth. We had never talked about ISIS, so I was planning to ask plenty of questions about it.

To prepare myself, I stopped by the White House to check in with some of the administration sources who had already been so helpful. They advised me to contact Secretary of State Mike Pompeo and his predecessor, Rex Tillerson. They said I should speak to former national security adviser Lieutenant General H. R. McMaster and his successor, John Bolton. They mentioned former Secretary of Defense James Mattis, and a long list of others.

The president had suggested that the whole government would be available to me, and Sarah Huckabee Sanders was diligent in contacting any of the sources I needed but the response was mixed. Some of them did not respond at all, and others could not provide the answers I needed. When I finally found the person who had the inside story I needed, he would only talk from the position of anonymity. I had taken pride in writing a book that was on the record, with personalities that had never spoken openly before, but the information I was offered was too valuable to pass up.

It was a good thing I didn't. My final conversation with the president was interrupted by world events. What I gained instead was someone who was in the room with the president and saw it all unfolding in real time and best of all, was willing to talk about it if I would only protect his identity.

"When the president first came into the White House," my source said, "He started assembling the different experts from the National Security Council and from the military. He started asking a lot of questions about the status quo. What had been tried? What had failed?"[25]

"When was this?" I asked. "When did the president take on ISIS? When did he get started?"

"Right away. The first day. It was, 'Let's focus on this, let's focus on that.' I think the president just came in and wanted to start doing everything immediately.

"General McMaster realized that the president had a lot of ambition; that there was a lot he wanted to accomplish and quickly. So he took the initiative to say, 'Well, let me try to put this into a national security strategy. Let me take all of your ideas and instincts and put them into an operational plan.'

"He did a very, very good job of doing just that. You've seen our national security strategy document that was released? General McMaster did a fabulous job with that. What McMaster was able to do was to take all of the president's ideas, and all of the things he wanted to achieve, and put them together into an organized document. I give General McMaster a lot of credit for that. Then, through the interagency process, we were able to get feedback from everybody. The strategy paper made it easier to develop action plans and then make sure we coordinated outcomes in all of these different areas. It was very helpful."

How soon did all of that take place? What was the timing?

"This whole process probably took about four months or so."

How long did it take for the president to get it all assigned and carried out?

"Well, it took about a year to put the final product together. But we knew what we were doing after a couple months. It just took time to get the teams in place and to find the right people."

The national security presidential memorandum was dated January 28, 2017, and titled "Plan to Defeat the Islamic State of Iraq and Syria."[26] The document called for a new plan to be submitted within thirty days. The president wanted to know if there should be any changes to the rules of engagement.

He wanted to know what international laws applied regarding use of force against this enemy. He wanted to identify cyber strategies to isolate and delegitimize ISIS and its ideology. He wanted to recruit new coalition partners to help in the fight. He wanted to shut down ISIS's financial support, cutting off money transfers, oil revenue, revenue from human trafficking, and sale of looted art and other sources of revenue.

"With regards to ISIS in particular this was a very big focus for the president," the White House source said. "He spent a lot of time on it. What more could we do to expedite the campaign? He wanted to take care of it. People were suffering, people were dying."

WHAT TRUMP DID DIFFERENTLY

Obviously, America's handling of ISIS had not been working. What did Trump do differently? Some of his tactics, the source told me, remain secret and sensitive. But some simply involved establishing a different relationship with his men in the field.

"The generals made recommendations," my source told me. "The president immediately gave them whatever authority they needed. He

asked a lot of questions. He constantly challenged the different assertions, and we eventually started to make a lot of progress."

Secretary of Defense Mattis said Trump "delegated authority to the
right level to aggressively and in a timely manner move against enemy
vulnerabilities." [27] This meant troops on the ground could sometimes
call in an air strike, something that would have been undoable in the
Obama-run war.

In March 2017, when an American-backed fighting unit asked
for immediate air transport to conduct a surprise attack on an ISIS-
controlled dam, the request was carried out smoothly and quickly. [28]
Again, an outcome that would previously have been impossible to
achieve was happening because of Trump's new orders.

Another major shift was to do more than simply win battles. Now,
instead of driving the enemy out of a city and then moving on to the
next enemy stronghold, military forces surrounded the enemy forces
and annihilated them. The result was that ISIS fighters could not retreat and fight again another day in another location. Instead, they
were eliminated.

To carry out this mission, Trump gave US Special Forces more
freedom to engage the enemy on the ground. They were no longer just
support personnel whose actions were subject to approval from higher
authorities. With their participation came more independent action
supported by sophisticated air power and drones.

Donald Trump Jr. saw this as an important change in strategy.
"The president was more than happy to let the generals on the ground
make decisions," he told me. "They would have a much greater understanding of the battlefield, and the threat, than a lawyer bureaucrat
back in Washington.

For example, he said, friends working in SEAL teams told him they
were not able to complete their mission because they had to check with
Washington first. "As an example, I have friends in the SEAL teams,
and they have said, that they have actually had targets in their cross-
hairs, but with the time difference in DC, they had to wait for approval

and lost the opportunity," he told me. "Imagine, they needed that kind of approval from DC? By the time the guy wakes up in Washington, shows up to office at nine thirty in the morning, goes through a full assessment of the situation, obtains the approval, children have moved into the target area and the team on the ground have literally lost the opportunity to take out a high-value target."[29]

There is no question that the empowerment of the Pentagon and soldiers in the field to make split-second decisions helped advance the war on ISIS. That same kind of empowerment applied to other practices, which remain unknown publicly.

When the Trump team moved into the White House, the newly appointed CIA director, Mike Pompeo, invited some of the president's staff over for lunch. They met with the agency's top five staff members.

Someone from the White House asked about the major differences between the Trump administration and that of its predecessor. Was there something the Trump folks could be doing better?

One answer given was that in the last administration, everything was being run from the White House. The president's staff was very operationally involved. If the CIA wanted to buy furniture in one of its foreign stations, it might require the White House to sign off on the purchase.

"What the president did and what Mike did, as well," my White House source told me, "was to decentralize a lot of the control. Giving it back to the experts in the field, who are now tasked to make these decisions. The most important decisions are still passed up [through the chain of command]. A lot of the others can be made closer to the action. We've got all of these great people throughout the government. The new Trump theory was to let them make choices. If they're not making those decisions themselves, then we can always pull it back up. So that was the first thing.

"Next thing they said was that, in the previous administration, they spent a lot of time in the White House doing nonstop PC [political correctness] meetings. They would have a meeting every week, and at the conclusion of the meeting there was always the suggestion, 'Let's meet again in two weeks.'

"Nothing was ever resolved. Nothing was ever good enough.

"They said that one thing about this White House is that there are a lot of decisions being made. They sensed that the president was not afraid to make decisions. They wouldn't always agree with every decision he made, but they appreciated the fact that he was willing to ingest the information, get briefed on it, and then decide one way or the other."[30]

NO EASY CHOICES

My source taught me that one of the challenges from the beginning was for the president's team to get him all the information he needed on a wide variety of issues, from domestic policy to foreign policy. He had to be properly briefed. But when he had enough information, he made decisions quickly.

"That was where some of the conflicts with some of the campaign people came in," I was told by my key White House source. "They just wanted him to do what they wanted him to do. The big conflict that people like General McMaster had was that now we were in the White House, we were in government, we were playing with live ammunition. This was different than being in a campaign. If the president wants to change his mind on something, and he's a very fluid thinker, he ought to be able to do it."

Some people in the White House told me they saw the president as more of a pragmatist than an ideologue. Just because he had said during the campaign that he was going to do something, once he was in the White House, he did not have to make it happen. First, he needed to revisit the issue to make sure he had the most current, pertinent information.

The wiser heads on senior staff wanted to present him with all the facts. They wanted to present him with all the arguments in favor of or against any given decision. After looking at all sides, then they would offer him a range of ways to accomplish the same goal.

"We had a lot of people here initially who just wanted him to take quick decisions that weren't properly thought through," my source told me. "We paid a price for that. There were some instances where they were able to get decisions through that later backfired."

The national media was overwrought by the turnover of personnel in the Trump White House, sometimes faulting him for letting Obama Justice Department officials go. A high administration source expressed frustration over that. "Imagine your predecessor, from a different political party, gets to pick your staff for you," the source said. "Why have elections if the new president can't pick his own people?"

During my time on senior staff at the White House, back in the eighties, I was told that the average length of stay was 1.5 years. It hasn't really changed. Turnover remains common.

Ronald Reagan had four chiefs of staff. So did Bill Clinton. Barack Obama had five. George W. Bush had five secretaries of the treasury. Jimmy Carter had six secretaries of state, confirmed or acting, during his four years in office.[31]

As a businessman, Donald Trump had always been quick to hire and fire, depending on the job he wanted done. He has continued this practice as president, and it has paid off.

"I admire the way that the president has developed his team and the process for decision making," my source told me. "He has run up the learning curve so quickly, on so many topics. He's done a good job of shuffling staff, in and out, and really getting the right team around him. At least for the most part.

"He's now in a position where he's not afraid to take tough decisions. That's where we are today. He's normally very, very well briefed before he takes a decision. He understands the magnitude of the decisions he's taking, but he's not afraid to do it. He's amazing.

"Look, there's very few situations that come to the desk of the president that are clear cut. No one can just say, 'This is the right answer, and this is the wrong answer. This is the good option, and this is the bad option.'"

"If there are easy decisions, they are already made before they get to the president's desk. He gets the hard ones."

★ 15 ★

AMERICA'S SHAMEFUL SECRET

"We do not pay ransom in this country, at least, not any longer!"
—PRESIDENT DONALD TRUMP

S oon after becoming president, Donald Trump stumbled onto one of America's most shameful secrets. More than one hundred Americans were being held hostage around the world. They were in addition to the three thousand Americans imprisoned outside the United States, many of them charged with violating drug laws or involvement in human trafficking.[1] Some of these convicted prisoners were innocent or facing exaggerated sentences simply because they were from the United States and were thus targets of monetary or diplomatic blackmail. In the face of this crisis, America, with all of its wealth and power, sometimes appeared as a weak, stumbling giant, unable to defend its children.

In 2015, President Barack Obama actually apologized to families of hostages, telling them, "We will do better."[2] This shame was being handled in the shadows, far from the glare of media attention and with little public negotiation by the government.

That process was informed by the hostage crisis of 1979, when Iran seized fifty-two US diplomats and citizens at their embassy in Tehran and held them for 444 days, making the United States look helpless.

In researching my book *The Iran Crisis*, I had met with former president Jimmy Carter. He had a brilliant mind and was deeply troubled by the plight of the hostages. But the president's critics believed that the more attention given the story, the harder it was to get the Americans released. For many policy makers, this was the lesson learned. The more celebrated the hostages, the greater their value to the hostage takers.

It was a valid point for the American government to make, but within time it morphed into something more high-handed. Families of hostages were told that their chances of seeing their loved ones return home would increase if they kept quiet and let the US government negotiate unseen. In addition, government officials encouraged news agencies to ignore hostage stories and, when they did surface, withheld information reporters needed to keep the stories in the news or on TV.

This prevailing practice hardened under recent Republican and Democratic administrations. This was the protocol adopted by Presidents George W. Bush and Barack Obama and it was one that families of victims tended to accept.

The rise of Islamic terrorism, which led to dramatic kidnappings and beheadings forced the issue from the shadows. Desperate families, perhaps feeling that they no longer had anything to lose, began to openly plead the case for their loved ones. During the last two years of the Obama administration, some hostage families began to suspect that the American government wanted such tight secrecy to cover for their own inaction. Government investigators were unseen and unaccountable; no one could measure their progress—or lack thereof.

Relatives of the journalist James Foley, who was kidnapped in northern Syria in 2012, were frustrated by officials of the Obama White House. "I was surprised there was so little compassion," his mother,

Diane Foley, told reporters. "We were told we could do nothing . . . meanwhile our son was being beaten and tortured every day."[3]

Diane Foley was told to trust the government, "that the way they were handling things would bring our son home."[4] The Foley family had to beg the Obama White House for information. "We were an annoyance, it felt, at some level. They didn't have time for us."[5]

James Foley was beheaded by ISIS terrorists on August 19, 2014, in Syria.

The case of Otto Warmbier, a University of Virginia student on tour in North Korea, marked a change in strategy, not by the American government, but by the family of a victim. The Warmbier case became a highly visible story.

The young man was arrested in January 2016 at the Pyongyang International Airport, as he was about to leave the country. He was accused of stealing a propaganda poster off a wall of his hotel in North Korea. He was sentenced to fifteen years of hard labor.

When Donald Trump assumed the presidency in January 2017, he was confronted with the Warmbier case and ninety-nine others. Trump was horrified by what he learned and determined to try something different.[6]

In April 2017, Trump secured the release of Aya Hijazi, and Egyptian-American humanitarian worker, from an Egyptian prison.[7] "We called the president of Egypt," Trump said, "and he released her. She was there for a long time—three years. And the previous administration was unable to get her out. A fantastic young woman. And she was released."[8]

In June 2017, after Trump opened a dialogue with North Korean dictator Kim Jong-un, Warmbier was finally released from a North Korean prison, where he had apparently been tortured. Otto was unable to see or speak when he arrived in the United States; he died days later.[9]

In November 2017, three members of the UCLA basketball team were arrested and detained in Hangzhou, China. Charged with shoplifting from a Louis Vuitton store, each man faced ten years in prison. Trump intervened and secured their release and return to the United States.[10]

In May 2018, Pyongyang released three US citizens. President Trump and the first lady journeyed to Joint Base Andrews, in Maryland, to meet them upon their arrival at three a.m.[11]

During the ceremony, Trump offered "warmest respects to the parents of Otto Warmbier, who was a great young man who really suffered."[12]

Two weeks later, Trump helped secure the release of Joshua Holt, who had been arrested in Venezuela, and imprisoned there for nearly two years without trial.[13]

By this time, Trump was beginning to develop quite a track record of releases. "You were a tough one, I have to tell you," he told Holt. "That was a tough situation. But we've had 17 released, and we're very proud of that record. Very proud. And we have others coming."[14]

By June 2019, other countries were asking Trump for help in getting citizens of their countries released from foreign prisons. Even the once condescending Canadian prime minister Justin Trudeau was seeking the American president's help.[15] Trump's reputation as a negotiator, once a source of amusement among diplomats, was now becoming an accepted reality. If you want something done, go to the Donald. But you may have to be willing to offer something to America in return.

Was Trump succeeding in ways that previous presidents had not? Were the circumstances different? What was he saying and doing to get hostages released?

SEIZING ANDREW BRUNSON

One of the more intriguing examples of a Trump rescue involved the safe return of Andrew Craig Brunson from a prison in Turkey. Brunson was the pastor of the Resurrection Church in Izmir, on Turkey's Aegean coast. Thanks to a green light from the president, access from Sarah Huckabee Sanders, and a phone call from the president's friend Paula White, I was able to talk to Brunson at length and get his story firsthand.

An American citizen, Andrew Brunson was arrested in October 2016, just before the presidential election. In July of that year, an attempted coup against Turkish president Recep Tayyip Erdoğan failed, and the reaction was a massive roundup of military personnel, academics, educators, and any other public figures that authorities deemed suspicious.

In all, more than 100,000 people were deported or arrested. Some languished in prisons without charges or explanation. Erdoğan was using the occasion to rid the country of political opposition.

Just how Brunson ended up on Erdoğan's list was not known to US officials for several years. Requests from the American government for information were ignored. In violation of the Vienna Convention on Consular Relations, Turkey denied Pastor Brunson a meeting with a US consulate representative and refused to allow members of his church to provide him with food, water, or clothing. Brunson didn't gain access to an attorney until two months after his arrest. Meanwhile, the Turkish government labeled him "an armed member of a terrorist organization."

Pastor Brunson was accused of crimes that included links to the Fethullahist terrorist organization. The leader of this group, Fethullah Gulen, was living in exile in the United States. Gulen was Erdoğan's public enemy number one.

Brunson was also accused of aiding the Kurdistan Workers Party (PKK). He was accused of political or military espionage, attempting to overthrow the government, attempting to overthrow the Turkish Grand National Assembly, and attempting to overthrow the constitutional order.

It was impossible for Brunson to refute any of the charges, since the Turkish government offered no evidence. Brunson himself was not even interrogated, which was alarming to some at the American embassy in Ankara. It appeared obvious that the Turkish government was looking not for facts, but for a guilty verdict.

Years later, when the case finally came to trial, the American authorities were able to fully understand what the Turkish government was doing. An unidentified witness testified that Brunson was guilty because a light had been on for four hours in a room on the second floor of the Resurrection Church. This was part of the Turkish government's proof.

There was no window on the second floor of the church.

Another unidentified witness testified that a contact named "Jacqueline" had sent a video of a popular food dish composed of meat, rice, and vegetables and named *maklube* to Pastor Brunson's phone. Maklube was served at religious gatherings of the Fethullahist terrorist cells. It turned out that Jacqueline was Brunson's own daughter. And, yes, she was indeed guilty of liking maklube.

A third unidentified witness, code-named "Prayer," argued that all US churches and their missionaries were connected to a plot to undermine the Turkish government. Prayer argued that Mormon missionaries, who provide missions to the Kurdish region, entered the Resurrection Church and spoke with Brunson. In the minds of the prosecutors, speaking with Mormon missionaries provided the evidentiary link between Brunson and the outlawed PKK.

The sixty-two-page indictment against Brunson was littered with circumstantial evidence and ever-changing and contradictory testimony. Meanwhile, Brunson was denied any chance to provide for his own defense. His ten defense witnesses were all declared "suspects" by the Turkish court, although none were ever charged. Still, with this designation, their statements clearing the pastor of any wrongdoing were inadmissible.

In the middle of this bizarre trial, Trump tweeted, "My thoughts and prayers are with Pastor Brunson, and we hope to have him safely back home soon!"

The Turkish government never stated publicly why it had imprisoned Brunson. He was a Christian living in an intolerant Islamic nation. As an American Christian, held in a Turkish prison, surrounded by fellow inmates, including anti-Western Islamic terrorists, Brunson was in an untenable situation. He and twenty other inmates were jammed into a cell that was designed to hold eight. Brunson lost fifty pounds. He was facing a life sentence.

TRUMP GETS INVOLVED

Donald Trump's involvement in the Brunson case began long before the trial. Upon taking office, he was given a review of the case, and he reacted immediately. A meeting with Erdoğan was set and, on May 16, 2017, the two leaders met in the Oval Office.

Publicly, Trump praised Erdoğan. "Today, we face a new enemy in the fight against terrorism, and again we seek to face this threat together,"[16] he said. Privately, Trump called for Brunson's release.[17]

Trump's high-profile interest in Brunson's case eventually saved his life. But the initial reaction of Turkish officials was to move the North Carolina pastor into solitary confinement. It was considered the ultimate punishment in prison. Turkish officials insisted they were protecting their hostage from possible assassination by another prisoner, but Brunson later had nothing but praise for his fellow prisoners. His only fear was of the government.

In July 2017, Trump held a surprise meeting with Erdoğan at the G20 summit in Hamburg, Germany. In the interview for this book, Andrew Brunson told me that he was following events from his prison cell. "President Trump asked for my release twice," Brunson said. "The president and Vice President Pence asked for my release at the meal they had after the summit, and I think they had maybe fifteen or twenty minutes with Erdoğan. They later attended a press conference and yet another meal. While they [television broadcasters] showed all these events, I was in prison watching. Erdoğan appeared to refuse my release by basically not answering the president. We don't know exactly what he said, but clearly, it wasn't positive."[18]

In the summer of 2017, prison officials allowed Brunson to leave his cell for one hour a week. His wife, Norine, was allowed short, periodic visits, during which she was separated from him by a pane of glass and they spoke by telephone.

Their daughter, Jacqueline, was also permitted a visit. "It was hard to see my father so broken, so thin, so desperate," she said. "I'm still waiting for my wedding. I'm still waiting to wear the wedding dress that I got almost a year and a half ago. I'm still waiting for my dad to walk me down the aisle. I'm still waiting for that father-daughter dance."[19]

In September 2017, Erdoğan suggested that Brunson be exchanged for Fethullah Gulen, the Islamic preacher living in exile in America. The US State Department rejected this idea out of hand. Should Brunson, an innocent American Christian who shouldn't have been arrested in the first place, be free to return to America and Gulen, a Muslim who had violated no American laws and was living freely in the United States, be turned over to the Turkish government for likely torture and execution?

In July 2018, with Brunson now facing trial, the White House raised the issue anew. Pence, calling for the release of Brunson, threatened Turkey with "large sanctions," and Trump lauded the pastor as a "wonderful human being."

"He is suffering greatly," Trump said. "This innocent man of faith should be released immediately!"[20]

On July 19, the president tweeted: "A total disgrace that Turkey will not release a respected U.S. Pastor, Andrew Brunson, from prison. He has been held hostage far too long. @RT_Erdogan should do something to free this wonderful Christian husband & father. He has done nothing wrong, and his family needs him!"[21]

ASKING FOR HELP FROM NETANYAHU

Trump then tried to broker a deal through a third party. In exchange for Brunson, President Erdoğan requested that a twenty-seven-year-old Turkish citizen, Ebru Özkan, be freed from an Israeli prison and repatriated to her homeland. It would be an act of good faith, Erdoğan said.

Trump reached out to Israeli prime minister Benjamin Netanyahu. It would be a tough political decision to make. Özkan had been arrested in Israel for links to a terrorist organization. But then, Trump and the United States had done many favors for Israel. The next day, she was released from prison, and within the week, she was on a plane back to Turkey.

The White House now expected Brunson's release. The long ordeal was over.

Except it wasn't. On July 25, 2018, the Trump administration was notified that the hostage had not been freed. In fact, the trial process was going forward. Brunson would face judgment and sentencing. The news hit the White House like a thunderclap. It was seen as a betrayal.

Erdoğan insisted that it had all been a misunderstanding. "We told the Americans that they could help us with getting Ebru, but we never said, 'and in exchange, we will give you Brunson.'"[22] he said.

Trump was unimpressed. "I think it's very sad what Turkey is doing," he told Reuters. "I think they're making a terrible mistake. There will be no concessions."[23]

Then Trump offered a warning. "I like Turkey, I like the people of Turkey very much," he said. "Until now, I had a very good relationship, as you know, with the president. I got along with him great, I had a very good relationship, but it can't be a one-way street."[24]

Brunson was following this drama from his prison cell in Turkey, hoping that it would lead to a breakthrough. "President Trump had asked Netanyahu to release a Turkish woman being held in Israel," he remembered. "But that was really the icing on the cake. Other agreements had been privately reached. The Turks basically then asked for more."[25]

Citing Brunson's deteriorating health and now aware of the pastor's high profile worldwide, the Turks moved him out of prison and into home detention, pending final judgment. The fifty-year-old pastor and his wife predicted to friends that a guilty verdict would come with a life sentence.

At the time, two US citizens were also being held captive in Turkey: Serkan Golge, a NASA physicist, and Ismail Kul, a college chemistry professor.

After his release, Andrew Brunson had been briefed by American officials and had learned more about the details surrounding his captivity and the extraordinary measures that had been taken to win his freedom.

"There were several agreements that were made that the Turks backed out on," he said. "And when I say Turks, it all goes back to

President Erdoğan. He had the complete authority, and no one would make agreements without his approval. So there were several times when an agreement was reached, and they would back off, trying to get more."

While former Obama officials acknowledged that the Brunson affair represented a human-rights violation, some in the American media were critical of the White House's dealings with Turkey under Trump. Turkey was a NATO ally, they insisted. An irate Turkish foreign minister tweeted, "No one dictates to Turkey."[26]

The next month, while Brunson awaited sentencing, Trump slapped sanctions on two Turkish officials, Minister of Justice Abdulhamit Gul and Minister of Interior Suleyman Soylu. They had both been involved in Brunson's apprehension. Then, the US Department of the Treasury's Office of Foreign Assets Control invoked the Global Magnitsky Act, thereby blocking both officials' access to US assets and halting their ability to do business with US entities.

Erdoğan was unimpressed. In retaliation, Turkey levied sanctions on US Interior Secretary Ryan Zinke and Secretary of Homeland Security Kirstjen Nielsen.

TRUMP'S KNOCKOUT PUNCH

The White House solicited involvement from the US public, a move that translated into congressional action. Senator Thom Tillis from North Carolina and Senator James Lankford of Oklahoma, both Republicans, and Senator Jeanne Shaheen of New Hampshire, a Democrat, led a bipartisan group dedicated to returning Brunson and others like him to the United States.

A total of seventy-one senators signed a letter to Erdoğan citing "anonymous accusations, flights of fantasy, and random character assassination" and demanding Brunson's release.

Meanwhile, Trump urged the State Department to brief NATO and the European Parliament on the case. By the third day of the Brunson trial, ninety-eight members of the European Parliament had sent an open letter to remind Erdoğan of "the European and International commitments of the Republic of Turkey in regard to freedom of religion, to the prohibition of arbitrary detention, and to the right to a fair trial."[27]

At the same time, the Trump administration maintained its pressure on Halkbank. The Turkish state-owned bank had been identified as aiding Iran in an attempt to evade US sanctions and was facing billions of dollars in possible fines.

After the Trump administration declined to clear Halkbank in exchange for Brunson's release, negotiations ended in a stalemate. But Congress continued to exert pressure, with Senator Tillis introducing a bill rejecting international loans to Turkey. "If the Turkish government continues to detain Pastor Brunson," said Senator Bob Menendez of New Jersey, "as well as locally employed staff, journalists, and civil servants, then the United States cannot continue to support loans to Turkey from International Financial Institutions."[28]

Still, Erdoğan was unmoved. He also appeared to be puzzled that Trump and the Americans were willing to risk so much over one person whose significance appeared minimal. Speaking to an audience in the Black Sea resort city of Rize, he said, "If the US is turning its back on us . . . choosing a pastor instead, sorry. We continue our path with decisive steps. This treatment by America of its strategic partner has annoyed us, it has upset us."[29]

But still, Erdoğan made it clear that Brunson would not be released.

Trump understood money and he understood markets, maybe better than any president before him. He knew that power is fueled by money. For the first time in his life, he was able to wield both in excessive amounts. The question was how far was he willing to go to secure the release of an American hostage.

On August 10, 2018, with Turkey in the middle of an economic crisis, Trump hit the country hard. "I have just authorized a doubling of Tariffs on Steel and Aluminum with respect to Turkey as their currency, the Turkish Lira, slides rapidly downward against our very strong Dollar!" he tweeted. "Aluminum will now be 20% and Steel 50%. Our relations with Turkey are not good at this time!"[30]

Hovering around 3.7 to the dollar, the Turkish lira had started 2018 on shaky ground. Coupled with US political sanctions and political unrest between Turkey and the United States, the Turkish lira climbed to 4.7 by the middle of July. Waiting for a political victor to emerge, investors anxiously sat on the sidelines watching the political drama unfold.

Investors responded immediately to Trump's tweet by exiting the stock market, and the Turkish lira plummeted from 4.7 to the dollar in July to almost 7.0 by mid-August. Billions of dollars had been lost within days.

The Turkish government responded with sanctions of its own. In retaliation against the tariffs levied by Trump, Erdoğan approved tariff increase on American cars, alcohol, and tobacco. Responding to the tariffs and the rapid decline of the lira, Erdoğan appealed to his fellow Turks for support. "If you have dollars, euros or gold under your pillow, go to banks to exchange them for Turkish lira," he said. "It is a national fight."[31]

Back in his prison cell, Brunson was watching as the brinksmanship played out. "Turkey's economy already had systemic problems," the pastor told me. "There were serious problems. They were headed toward a crash. But when Trump imposed the sanctions and the steel and aluminum tariffs were doubled, that was the signal to the market and many people to get out. Also, it was the straw that broke the camel's back.

"When it came to my release, there had been several times when an agreement had been reached, and they would back off trying to get more. So, they were already teetering, and the economy was going to go. They had serious problems. Also, the Turkish stock market lost forty billion dollars immediately. The lira going up to seven was a big shock to the economy.

"Yet in spite of that, Erdoğan doubled down and would not let me go.

"I was very upset and my family was very upset. Very significant steps had already been taken. 'If this won't do it, what will do it and can the United States even do any more?'"

Worldwide headlines captured the moment. In the UAE *National*:

"Trump Hits Turkey with Doubled Tariffs as Lira Tumbles."[32] In the UK *Telegraph*: "Trump's New Tariffs Send Turkey's Currency Crashing."[33]

FREEDOM FOR THE HOSTAGE

It was now clear that there would be no further decisions regarding Brunson until the Turkish court reconvened in October 2017.

The world now had a clearer picture of what had been going on inside Turkey. The pro-government media was heavily invested in the process. They had labeled Brunson an American spy and had been working closely with the prosecutor's office. The media and the prosecutors had fed on the stories and rumors of the other, driven on by popular opinion. The facts were what they wanted them to be.[34] But the whole world was now monitoring the process and listening to the prosecutor's narrative, following his evidence, seeing how the court refused any explanation from the defense. It might have been enough in Turkey, where Christians were considered by many to be "infidels," but it did not work for any objective observer.

The Turkish economy was in shambles. For what? The man they were trying to put in prison for life was seen by the world as innocent. On September 6, 2018, the head prosecutor was removed from the case.

The crisis had reached an impasse. On October 12, 2018, in the city of Aliaga, Turkey, better known as the final destination of the 1970s television series *The Love Boat*, a three-judge panel prepared to deliver its verdict.

For the first time, Brunson was allowed to speak for himself. He appeared shaken. He had already tasted life for two years in a Turkish prison. He knew what lay ahead. "I am an innocent human being," he proclaimed. "I love Jesus, and I love Turkey." Brunson's whole body convulsed, tears and sweat covered his face. He embraced his wife in preparation for the impending verdict.

Following five hours of deliberation, the three-judge panel made their announcement.

Guilty.

Now awaiting the judges' sentence, Andrew Brunson and his wife, Norine, clung to each other in anxious stillness. The crime? Aiding terrorism. The sentence? Three years, one month, and fifteen days. As a result of Pastor Brunson's good conduct, the judge reduced the sentence to time served.

Norine described the scene in the courthouse. "We just got on our knees in the courthouse; we didn't care what anybody thought."

Donald Trump tweeted from the White House, "My thoughts and prayers are with Pastor Brunson, and we hope to have him safely back home soon!"

Brunson was euphoric. "This is the day our family has been praying for," he said. "I am delighted to be on my way home to the United States. It's been an extremely difficult time for our family and we want to express our appreciation to the millions of people around the world who have faithfully prayed for this day."[35]

TIC TACS IN THE ROOSEVELT ROOM

President Trump welcomed the Brunsons to the White House on October 12, 2018. "From a Turkish prison to the White House in 24 hours, that's not bad," Trump said.[36]

During my interview with Brunson in the summer of 2019, I asked him about his visit with the president. "What we remember, Doug, is that the president is very friendly. Norine said that he has a big heart. That is the feeling we get from him. Just a big heart; that he is genuinely caring about people."

They met first in the Roosevelt Room in the West Wing. "So, we were standing there," Brunson said. "President Trump walked over and greeted us. He pulled out a box of Tic Tacs, breath mints, and he offered me some, and I said, 'No, no thank you.' Then I thought, 'Wait, if the president is offering you some, I better take them.' So he gave me three and poured them out in my hands."

They then moved to the Oval Office, which was packed with reporters.

"The one thing that I remember most from that experience," Brunson said, "is the thought that only twenty-four hours before I had been convicted of supporting terrorist groups. And within twenty-four hours, within one day, I was meeting with President Trump in the Oval Office.

"I had another thought. Only seventeen months earlier, President Trump had a summit with President Erdoğan of Turkey. And he sat in the same yellow chair that I was sitting in. The pictures showed President Trump and Erdoğan, sitting in those same yellow chairs. And I just thought that was a wonderful story of redemption."

Video from the meeting showed Branson getting out of his chair and kneeling to pray for the president. The scene was carried around the world.

"I asked, 'Would it be okay for me to pray for you?' And he said, 'Sure.'

"'Can I do this right now?'

"He said, 'Yes, go ahead.'

"So I went over to his chair and I knelt, and I put my hand on his shoulder. It is what many, many Christians do when they pray for someone, they will put their hand on you, just as a way of blessing. The truth is, we believe in impartation," the pastor explained, referring to the giving and receiving of spiritual gifts. "And we are hoping that God will give a blessing through that."

Was the prayer something he had coordinated with the White House ahead of time?

"No. When we were coming over on the plane, I'd asked Tony Perkins—he was on the flight with us—if he thought the president would mind if we prayed for him." Perkins is an evangelical Christian leader.

"He said he thought President Trump would be open to that. And so, I had just jotted down three or four things I wanted to pray for him so that at the moment I would not forget them. So, I just prayed some of those things over him, and then Norine jumped in and prayed after I did.

"We didn't realize it at the time, but what we've been told that it is unusual for someone to pray for the president. I know there are prayers said, for example, at inaugurations and when Congress convenes. But somehow, praying for him and having that broadcast out, all the words of the prayer, is more of an unusual thing, which we did not know at the time."

Trump followed the prayer with a provocative query of his own. "Could I ask you one question? Who did you vote for?"[37]

There was laughter.

"You," Norine Brunson said.

Pastor Brunson smiled. "I sent in an absentee ballot from prison."

During the Oval Office visit, a reporter asked, "Mr. President, what do you do different than other administrations? You talked about the 19 people that you've seen—Americans held abroad that you've seen released. What did you do differently than previous administrations?"[38]

"They are tending not to take them out of our administration," Trump responded. "And I think I could tell you why, but I won't. But they tend not to take them out of our administration. And you know what? It's going to stay that way."[39]

NO RANSOM

In 1979, I had met with President Jimmy Carter and Ronald Reagan, the former California governor who would wrest the presidency from Carter in an election the following year. At the time, one of the biggest issues before the electorate was the Iran hostage crisis. Our embassy officials and other US citizens had been taken hostage by Iranian street mobs, encouraged by the Iranian government.

Once in the Oval Office, Reagan redefined American policy. "America will never make concessions to terrorists," Reagan said. "To do so would only invite more terrorism. Nor will we ask nor pressure any other government to do so. Once we head down that path, there will be no end to it, no end to the suffering of innocent people, no end to the bloody ransom all civilized nations must pay."

A Presidential Policy Directive (PPD) states, "The United States Government will work in a coordinated effort to leverage all instruments of national power to recover U.S. nationals held hostage abroad, unharmed. The United States will use every appropriate resource to gain the safe return of U.S. nationals who are held hostage. But the United States Government will make no concessions to individuals or groups holding U.S. nationals hostage. It is United States policy to deny hostage takers the benefits of ransom, prisoner releases, policy changes, or other acts of concession."[40]

In my conversations with President Trump, I came away feeling that this policy had softened over the years and that the United States was, in fact, selectively violating its own stated dogma. "We do not pay a ransom in this country, at least any longer," President Trump stated during his meeting with Brunson. "It started in a different administration, we took it over, we inherited it."

When I asked about hostages, Trump was emphatic. "We don't pay money to ransom innocent men and women to the countries. And terrorists that take our people. But believe me, they pay."

And I believed him. The Turkish economy had been practically ruined over its government's insistence on imprisoning an innocent man. Mostly to save face with pro-government media and government prosecutors, driven by religious and cultural bias.

Brunson told me he is convinced that Trump, personally, made the difference in his release. "So, this is what happened," Brunson said. "I really believe, in my mind, God was the one that did this, but he used President Trump, and if he had not taken those steps, I don't think that the Turkish president Erdoğan had any intentions of letting me go. It was really the unprecedented personal attention by President Trump, his leadership that led to my liberation."

★ 16 ★

THE FOREIGN POLICY PRESIDENT

"I don't know, but they're telling me that I might be more of a foreign policy president. What do you think?"
—DONALD TRUMP, IN AN INTERVIEW WITH THE AUTHOR

As a candidate, Trump's frequent refrain was "America First." We should take care of our own problems, he said, before meddling in the business of other nations. But the words "America First" were also a reminder that other countries were competing for our attention and our resources. One reason Trump had entered politics was his long-felt frustration over the nation's trade deficits and defense arrangements, which he believed had led to the economic bloodletting of the American middle class. Were Americans being taxed to take care of the rest of the world? Trump had also complained that massive regulations, especially onerous to homegrown American businesses, had chased companies and jobs out of the country.

The challenge for Trump was determining how to take this on. Those jobs were going somewhere. Those trade deficits were benefiting someone. Our massive military expenditures were protecting other nations, freeing them to spend their money on other things.

The tax dollars that had fled America under Bush and Obama, on a massive scale, were now funding other nations' government programs. They were building highways and airports in the capitals of other nations. An American president who had promised to make his country great again would have to pry loose those American dollars from the clutches of nations that had become addicted to them and that would not give them up willingly. America was not alone in the world. If Donald Trump was really going to put America first, the rest of the world was going to howl.

And it was even more complicated than that. The world of commerce had grown so international and interconnected that most big American banks and companies had also found a way to benefit from the money flowing to other countries. "America First" would be resisted not only by a long list of nations that were sucking from the teat of the American middle class, but also by many of America's corporate giants, many of which were major advertisers and owners of the American media.

Trump was in for the fight of his life.

Our biggest trade deficits were often with countries that manipulated their currencies and stole American intellectual property, including top-secret military technology. Much of this, especially the key relationships of major American corporations with China, was driven by insider deals and a vast maze of "legalized" corruption. Many of those companies also sponsored the US news organizations whose stories promoted those same policies to the American people.

All of those companies gave massive donations to the Democratic and Republican parties and to key legislators. They financed many well-intentioned special-interest groups that promoted regulations that caused economic hardship for small businesses, conveniently resulting in monopolies for themselves. They financed think tanks that commissioned scholars to write papers and conduct studies to justify the status quo.

America's universities, addicted to foreign students who were paying full tuition, openly advocated globalism and funded supporters such as Senator Elizabeth Warren, a Massachusetts Democrat, who was reportedly paid $350,000 by Harvard University to teach a single class.[1] This is the same woman who conveniently promoted the idea of government-paid, free college education. It was hard for some to see Harvard University, which had a $37.6 billion endowment, in need of further government subsidy.[2]

In a conversation with the president, I brought up these issues. "When you were first elected and took office, you obviously began to learn details that the rest of us don't know," I said. "You had all of these ideas for years, decades really, ideas about the world and about trade and corruption. You've given speeches about it. How did all of that change when you became president? Was it as bad as you thought?"

"It is even worse," the president said. "It is far worse than I thought.

"The good news," he added, "is that we have great potential. We are turning it all around. And that's one of the reasons this country is rebounding.

"I can give you twelve countries right now. You would be shocked! How about Germany? How about Saudi Arabia? These are great countries. These are rich countries. Some of the richest countries in the world.

"So, we defend Saudi Arabia and they don't pay us, okay?"

The president shifts in his chair, preparing me for his impersonation of an actual conversation. You've got to love this; remember, Trump is an entertainer.

"So, I told the king, 'You've got to pay. Okay, king? You've got to pay.'"

The president then pursed his lips to mimic the dignity of King Salman bin Abdulaziz al Saud of Saudi Arabia. "And the king says, 'Yes, and how much would you like?'

"Imagine? Imagine?" Trump said. "The Saudis have been doing this for years, but nobody ever asked them to help pay for it. Saudi Arabia wouldn't exist if it weren't for American support. It is the most incredible thing I have ever seen. Our roads are falling apart, our bridges are in danger, our airports look like they are in developing countries, and you have years and years of us protecting the world while they all grow rich. Doug, I hope you can see right now how crazy this is."

He impersonated King Salman once again, pursing his lips. "'Yes, and how much would you like?'

"I say, 'Hasn't anybody ever asked you before?'

"He says, 'Well, no. Nobody ever asked us.'

"This is how America was run. For years. For years. And there is so much I could tell you. It's worse than I thought."

DONALD TRUMP'S WINNING FOREIGN POLICY

In November 2016, just before the Clinton-Trump election, fifty leading Republican foreign policy experts signed a letter warning of the dangers of electing Trump as president. "Donald Trump is not qualified to be president and commander-in-chief," they wrote. "Indeed, we are convinced that he would be a dangerous president and would put at risk our country's national security and well-being."[3]

Two years later, according to *Investors Business Daily*, "even former Obama administration officials were admitting that, while Trump's methods were certainly unorthodox, he was getting results that those . . . experts could only dream about."[4]

Politico, one of Trump's fiercest critics, was asking aloud, "Doesn't Trump deserve some credit?"[5] Ivo Daalder, ambassador to NATO under Obama, described Trump as a "disrupter" who "is leading to some very healthy debate about what are our goals."[6]

When Trump demanded that NATO nations pay their delinquent dues, token amounts of money that they had agreed to pay to provide for their own defense, the American national media erupted. He was trying to weaken NATO, they claimed. He was a Russian spy. The media insisted this with a straight face.

Trump did not back down. "This has been going on for decades, by the way. Under many presidents," he said. "But no other president has brought it up like I have."[7]

He was right.

In fact, within two years, the NATO secretary general insisted that Trump's confrontational approach to member nations had made the organization stronger than it had ever been. The call for increased participation from allied nations was "having a real impact."[8] It was long overdue.

"Here is the ultimate example of American stupidity," Trump told me. "We buy billions and billions of dollars' worth of missiles. Then we give them away to our allies, our rich allies.

"So I challenge that. I say to the general, 'Why are we doing that?'"

At this point in the conversation, Trump once again adopted the persona of a character in his story. He straightened up like a soldier and declared solemnly, speaking in the monotone, emotionless, staccato voice of his general, "Sir! They are our ally. They are our friends. Sir!"

Then Trump's demeanor relaxed. "I say, 'They are not our friends. They are ripping us off.'"

The president straightened up again, becoming the general. "'Sir, they are our ally. Sir!'

"The worst part of this is the realization that the people who treat us worst are our allies. And you've heard the story with South Korea with the missiles system, with the THAAD anti-missile system?"

The president was referring to the Terminal High Altitude Area Defense system, which became operational in South Korea in May, 2017. It is designed to intercept any incoming North Korean missiles.

"We give so much," Trump said. "We give so much. We get nothing. Many times, we can't even get votes in the United Nations."

Trump immediately corrected himself, declaring defiantly, "Well, I get votes. You know what I do any time I want a vote?"

He is talking about the United Nations.

"They say to me, 'No, we don't need to vote on this issue. We are not voting for you.'

"I say, 'Okay, good. Tell them we are cutting off all aid.'

"We get a call back about two minutes later.

"Suddenly they say, 'We've decided to vote for you.'

Apparently, the president doesn't always employ this strategy or it doesn't always work, because after his brief burst of empowerment he returned to his lament. "We don't even get votes in the United Nations, and we give hundreds of millions of dollars to countries you have never even heard of."

Why? I asked. Why does the American media defend this and even promote it? Why does the establishment promote it? Why did it take him to expose it?

"It is part of the deep state," he said. "It is part of the system." And then he adds that mischievous chuckle he makes, which is hard to describe, "It is also stupidity, to be honest. I think a lot of it is stupidity."

PRIME MINISTER SHINZO ABE OF JAPAN

My anonymous foreign policy source, a fly on the wall during the president's most important deliberations, insisted that—behind the scenes, at least—Jared Kushner's imsight was sometimes crucial. He knew the president and saw his personality as an asset. During the campaign, when his father-in-law was considering tapping Mike Pence to be his running mate, Kushner recommended that the two men play golf together. And that pattern was replayed, at Kushner's suggestion, with Prime Minister Shinzo Abe of Japan.[9] The prime minister was coming to Washington, so Kushner recommended that Trump host him in a round of golf. Apparently, it was a success. The two men played twenty-seven holes.[10] According to my source, "They had a blast together."[11]

Donald Trump's philosophy on trade and its impact on the United States was carefully laid out in a 1990 *Playboy* article. "I'd throw a tax on every Mercedes-Benz rolling into this country," Trump said. "And on all Japanese products, and we'd have wonderful allies again."[12]

Prime Minister Abe had prepared for his visit with Trump by reading the decades-old article. The question remained: What could they do to reduce America's $67.6 billion trade deficit?[13]

Invoking Kushner's idea of personal diplomacy, Trump used his personality to the fullest. "They flew down to Florida together," my source told me. "It gave them time to relate to each other. It was something more than having to read talking points and talk about issues. The president likes those relationships. And that's very important."

They met again in May 2019 for a ceremonial visit in Japan, where the friendship deepened. There was a dinner at a hibachi restaurant with First Lady Melania Trump and Akie Abe, the wife of the prime minister, joining their husbands. The two world leaders played golf. The American president presented a trophy to the winner of a sumo wrestling tournament,[14] and Donald Trump became the first head of state to meet Japan's new emperor, Naruhito.

PRESIDENT XI AND THE MAGIC OF MAR-A-LAGO

The new president's relationship with China was one of the most significant issues in the opening weeks of his administration. During the transition, Trump said he was not willing to recognize the One China policy, which does not recognize the Republic of China, which rules from the island of Taiwan. Trump's position rattled the Chinese. As a result, President Xi Jinping did not make a congratulatory call to the newly elected Trump. For the moment, China and the United States were not talking to each other.

At staff level and at a diplomat level, the American and Chinese teams were meeting about trade and designing strategies for moving things forward, but the process was labored. The Chinese were saying all the right things, but their presentations at meetings consisted of their diplomats reading long scripts. "When they finished a script, they pulled out another one, and then they'd have yet another," a senior administration source told me. "So we soon realized that their diplomats were more like fax machines. They were conveying messages, but they didn't really have the ability or the authority to explore changes."[15]

Some on the American side concluded that the Chinese were happy to leave things as they were; they had no motivation to change anything.

Jared Kushner had an inspired idea to break the deadlock. If the president could find a way, within himself, to acknowledge the One China policy, keeping in mind that he could always reverse himself later if he so desired, then he could use the change of policy as an exchange for President Xi coming to the United States to meet.

It worked.

Once again, the White House would put the president's personality to maximum use. The event would take place at his compound in Florida—not the White House. It would be described as a two-day bridge-building summit. The whole schedule was planned to give the two leaders concentrated time together.

The first meeting, on the first day, was fifteen to twenty minutes of casual greeting. It was just the two of them with their translators. Later, Jared and Ivanka Kushner introduced their six-year-old daughter, Arabella, who sang some Chinese poems and songs in Mandarin.[16] The world watched this moment with fascination. It was warmly received in China, where Arabella became an online star.

Finally, Trump and Xi sat for an hour and a half. It was at this point, observers say, that the conversation really started to open up. They began talking about North Korea, trade, and many other issues. The two men appeared to be developing a good relationship.

That night, President Trump and the First Lady and President Xi Jinping and Madame Peng Liyuan had a dinner that lasted a number of hours. Trump began by asking his counterpart questions about Chinese history. Once the conversation started, it kept going, leading to more questions. This was a side of the president that tended to surprise people to whom he revealed it. His conversations were never one-way. He had an insatiable curiosity, and he was a good listener.

As it happened, during the Xi visit, the United States responded to the use of chemical weapons by Syrian president Bashar al-Assad's on his own people. It had been a festering issue, since Assad had used chemical weapons against his own people years before—during the Obama administration.

In 2012, Obama had famously warned that the use of chemical weapons would represent a red line that Syrian could not cross without incurring "enormous consequences." But, the following year, Assad ignored the warning and used chemical weapons anyway. In response, Obama backed down and did nothing.

"I was sitting at the table," Trump said, describing the moment. "We had finished dinner. We are now having dessert. And we had the most beautiful piece of chocolate cake that you have ever seen. And President Xi was enjoying it.

"And I was given the message from the generals that the ships are locked and loaded. What do you do? And we made a determination to do it. So, the missiles were on the way.

"And I said, 'Mister President, let me explain something to you . . . we've just launched 59 missiles . . . heading to Syria and I want you to know that.'

"I didn't want him to go home and then they say: 'You know the guy you just had dinner with just attacked [Syria].'"[17]

By the early fall of 2019, the United States and China were still in the grips of a major trade negotiation that could succeed or fail. Even so, the personal relationship built between Trump and Xi has endured and is seen by the policy makers I spoke with as a foundation for those talks to go forward. For the first time in many decades, the two countries have a chance to resolve some of the hard problems they must face.

ANGELA MERKEL: "GREATEST LEADER IN THE WORLD"?

Two months after he announced his run for president, Donald Trump was praising Germany's chancellor, Angela Merkel. "Germany is, like, sitting back silent collecting money and making a fortune with probably the greatest leader in the world today, Merkel. She's fantastic . . . highly respected."[18]

It was not just a moment of praise for the German chancellor, it was also criticism of American foreign policy, which some argued had offered up the middle class of the United States as the piggy bank to the world.

Two months later, when Merkel welcomed massive Syrian migration, Trump's praise turned sour. They were trying to get a grip on international terrorism, sponsored in the Middle East. They were spending a fortune and planning to spend more. Trump, ever the businessman, wondered at the absurdity of spending more money to combat terrorists from the Middle East and then suddenly allowing undocumented migrants from that region to pour into Europe.

Trump said that he understood safe zones for people, but "what's happening in Germany?" he asked. "I always thought Merkel was, like, this great leader. What she's done in Germany is insane. It is insane."[19] Later, on the campaign trail, Trump compared Merkel to Hillary Clinton, his Democratic rival.

After the election and Trump's surprise win, the first meeting between the two heads of state was set for March, 2017. In preparation, Chancellor Merkel read Trump's book *The Art of the Deal* and watched episodes of his reality show *The Apprentice*.[20] She told friends that she had never prepared more for such a meeting.

At a joint press conference with Merkel, Trump joked, "As far as wiretapping by this past administration, at least we have something in common perhaps."[21] The Obama administration had been caught red-handed eavesdropping on the German chancellor and, days before, Trump had quoted a lawyer on television who suggested that Obama had wiretapped Trump Tower.

Trump's accusations about wiretapping were met with widespread ridicule and outrage in the American media, but as the president himself pointed out, later events would show them to be not nearly as far-fetched as they appeared at the time.

The same month as the Trump-Merkel meeting, Hillary Clinton's former campaign manager, Robby Mook, admitted that wiretapping was, indeed, likely going on in Trump Tower.[22]

How had the Trump-Merkel relationship evolved since those early, uncertain days? How do American diplomats see her? Top administration sources say that she has gotten a lot of political pushback on immigration. Her policies were probably driven by noble intentions, but they may have done a lot to disrupt the confidence and comfort of many people in Germany.

"I do sense that she's kind of thinking like she's at the end of her run," a source told me. "She may be trying to stabilize, solidify her legacy. It doesn't feel like she's looking to do a lot of the things that we think are necessary to reframe our bilateral relationship."[23]

Today, the American media hails the relationship between Merkel and Obama. She openly admired Obama, who was a rock star in Germany. But when the former American president asked her to back down from Nord Stream 2, the Russia-to-Germany gas pipeline, she demurred. When he asked her to increase Germany's spending for NATO, she ignored him.

Trump has been respectful, but more confrontational. His focus on the trade imbalance with Germany has been a big irritant to Merkel. She took a shot at Trump in May 2019 in a commencement speech at Harvard University. The German chancellor talked about "tearing down walls of ignorance and narrow-mindedness."[24]

A prominent source involved in the American-German discussions says that Trump and Merkel have had a good personal relationship; all their interactions have been fine. "But I think she's concluded, 'Let me just wait this out,'" the source said. "It doesn't feel like there's a great desire to make the concessions needed to rebalance the relationship."[25]

Secretary of State Pompeo visited with Chancellor Merkel and German foreign minister Heiko Maas in May 2019. A member of the German Bundestag said, "The German-American relationship could not be worse."[26]

Well into the president's third year in office my anonymous senior foreign policy source would tell me that "right now, the relationship is pretty asymmetric. We've got thirty-four thousand troops in Germany. We're doing a lot to defend them, allegedly, from Russia through NATO. And yet they're doing a gas deal with Russia. Which makes no sense. In addition to that, we have a huge trade imbalance.

"Germany, in general, is now starting to get a lot of pushback from the other European partners. They may feel that Germany is a very strong country who has done too well on trade as well as a lot on these different issues. Now I think there's a feeling that the wealth should be shared a little bit more fairly, they want some balance."[27]

After hearing opinions from others, I was eager to hear what Jared Kushner thought. A lot of Americans have been charmed by the German chancellor's initial interaction with Ivanka during her first visit to the Trump White House. How did Kushner see her? What lessons can we learn from her life?

"I think she's been a great leader," Kushner said. "I think what she's done for Germany economically has been amazing. She's got a strong morality, driven by her understanding of German history and her desire to make sure that Germany has a different place in the world from where it was before. There's no question that Chancellor Merkel is one of the more impressive people that we deal with. She's very meticulous.

"So, it's a complicated time. But I think that, again, Angela Merkel is fighting for Germany's best interests. We respect that. She is very good at it. She is very capable and she is very, very smart."[28]

"MACRON CAME IN WITH A LOT OF HOPE"

Like many Americans, Donald and Melania Trump were prepared to embrace France. In their positions as president and first lady, that meant getting along with their counterparts, Immanuel and Brigitte Macron, the president and first lady of France.

Both Donald and Melania had spent a good deal of time in Paris during their adult lives. The president had stayed for only a few days at a time, as a businessman. He had stayed at many hotels and properties. He had once stared out from the balcony of a room at the Hôtel de Crillon in the Place de la Concorde, which was bustling with traffic just below. In the distance, he could see the Eiffel Tower sparkling over the treetops.

Melania, on the other hand, had lived there much longer. She had been an upwardly mobile fashion model, racing across Paris on its rumbling Metro to auditions and living in a cramped apartment.

At times, each of them had passed by the American embassy; each of them had looked through the dark, tree-lined streets that led to Élysée Palace, the official residence of the president of the republic.

When they arrived in Paris in July 2017 to celebrate Bastille Day, they came as leaders of the most powerful nation on earth, and they came with better insights into what was really going on in France than most presidents and first ladies before them.

Critics argued that well-meaning French laws had unintentionally created Islamic terrorist enclaves in some French cities. Arrested criminals were released back into their own neighborhoods without having to post bond. The French police were reluctant to enter these enclaves, where Islamic law protected the people.

A concierge at the Sheraton Paris Airport Hotel and Conference Centre warned tourists not to take either of the last two trains back from downtown Paris. They weren't safe. In 2016, during his campaign, Trump picked up on this widespread sentiment, saying that his friend Jim "no longer goes to Paris on vacation."[29]

If Muslim immigration was affecting French culture, the elected government would not acknowledge it. French political correctness reigned supreme. A three-part, six-hour documentary, shown in America on Netflix, recorded the deadliest terrorist attack in Parisian history, with the deaths of 130 people and more than 400 injured. The elaborate production included interviews with forty persons. Throughout the narrative, people referred to "terrorists" and "attackers." What motivated these "terrorists" was never discussed. The word "Islam" was never mentioned.

Trump, with his warnings about Islamic terrorism and his attempted ban on travel from select countries he labeled as dangerous, struck mainstream French audiences as harsh. His war on ISIS was too direct. His story from the campaign trail about "Jim" rankled France's government-dominated media. It was one thing for the French to complain about their problems; it was something altogether different for an American to do so. The French media had gotten the memo from their American counterparts. The American first couple was treated with only measured civility.

Even so, some in the general public were fascinated. Melania and Brigitte were meticulously compared and lauded.[30] Everything they wore, from hats to shoes, was a source of endless discussion. If Melania was the target of adolescent jealousy by New York fashion magazines, she was still somewhat celebrated in France. *Paris Match* had had her on its cover numerous times.

"You're in such good shape," Trump said to France's sixty-four-year-old first lady. It sent the American media into spasms of horror, but it delighted the French.

The American president, for his part, was deeply impressed with the Bastille Day military parade down the Champs-Élysées. Why couldn't the United States, the most powerful nation on earth, have a parade like that? The American media hysterically compared Trump to Stalin, Hitler, and Kim Jong-un. Only dictators had military parades, they said, conveniently ignoring the fact that Senator Chuck Schumer, the senior Democrat from New York, had called for such a parade to honor the soldiers who fought in the War on Terror.[31] Not to mention the fact that the whole idea had been sparked by the politically correct French.

Trump left France impressed and convinced that he had a friend.

In April 2018, Trump and Melania welcomed the Macrons to the United States. America pulled out all of the stops. On a Monday evening, they dined at Mount Vernon, George Washington's home, where Trump showed off the key to the Bastille. It had been one of France's first gifts to the fledgling United States, which they had helped liberate from England. On Tuesday, the Trumps hosted the Macrons at the

White House for the first state dinner of their presidency. On Wednesday, Macron became the first French leader in a decade to address a joint session of Congress.

Macron had three goals: Persuade Trump to return to the Paris accords, to stick to the Iran nuclear deal, and to return to the Trans-Pacific Partnership. There was no way he could achieve them; it would have meant de-trumping Trump.

My senior administration foreign policy source said that "Macron came in with a lot of excitement and a lot of hope. I think he's taken on a lot of tough issues domestically, which is what he promised to do. He's tough, and he's going to try to ride them out.

"The president's team can't figure out why he refuses to reverse some of these policies that we see as no-brainers. Like getting out of the Iran deal. How to reverse that?

"We have not been able to get fully on the same page with him about some of the big foreign policy objectives. Yes, the relationship has been very good. I think there's a strong chemistry between the two leaders. And I think it's still very early. They both have more duration. And we'll see how it goes. There's a strong foundation from which to work with.

"Macron has the potential to be a great leader for Europe."[32]

But Trump made it clear that he was unimpressed with his French counterpart. I asked him how he would describe Macron. And he answered with one word: "Deceitful."

On June 6, 2019, Trump visited France to join in observances of the seventy-fifth anniversary of the D-day landing in Normandy. This time, the president's speech was carried live and the whole French nation looked on and appeared deeply moved. Many in the French public learned for the first time that Melania Trump had lived in Paris, that she was fluent in French and could speak five other languages.

Macron, deeply unpopular at home, was more willing to find common ground than he had been during their first meeting, and the relationship was back on track.

BORIS JOHNSON AND THE SLUMBERING GIANT

On May 24, 2019. British prime minister Theresa May stepped to the microphones outside Number 10 Downing Street to announce her resignation. "I will shortly leave the job that has been the honor of my life to hold," she said.[33] The normally stoic prime minister was fighting back tears.

Trump said he felt bad for her. "I like her very much, she is a good woman. She worked very hard."[34]

Hours before this drama unfolded, I was interviewing my foreign policy source at the White House, and the subject of Theresa May came up.

"I think she's got a tough job," the official said. "I think she's going through it."

My source brought up Boris Johnson, the populist UK politician who had served as foreign secretary and mayor of London. Johnson had grown frustrated with the negotiations over Brexit, the British process of leaving the European Union.

"I am increasingly admiring of Donald Trump," Johnson had said in June 2018. "I have become more and more convinced that there is method in his madness."[35]

"Boris Johnson had some great comments about Brexit." My source laughed, remembering that moment. "Where he said if the president were here, he would be throwing out ideas left and right. And everyone would be going crazy, screaming at each other, but we'd make a deal.

"So Prime Minister May is different from a Boris or a Trump. I think she's doing it her way. We're hoping that she's successful, but she's in a very, very tough position.

"The relationship between her and Trump is pretty good. And whatever happens in the United Kingdom, we are happy to do a trade deal with them that will help us both, if they get out.

"A big part of the coming state visit is to hopefully show that we've been great allies for a long time. We want to continue that, to be their friend, regardless of what they decide with Brexit."

On July 24, 2019, Boris Johnson became the new prime minister of the United Kingdom. "We are once again going to believe in ourselves, and like some slumbering giant we are going to rise and ping off the guy ropes of self-doubt and negativity,"[36] he said upon the announcement.

THE RISE OF MATTEO SALVINI IN ITALY

The Trump administration also saw a potential ally in Italy, where the colorful politician Matteo Salvini emerged. At the height of the Syrian Civil War, Italy was growing frustrated with European neighbors who were welcoming immigrants from the Middle East but expecting them to transit through Italy, where they would be fed and vetted. Hungary promptly shut down its borders. Austria's citizens overwhelmingly voted in a right-wing government. England, via referendum, voted to leave the European Union, with many of its citizens resolved that their country should not be run by autocrats in Brussels.

Meanwhile, Italy, a Catholic nation with compassion and sensibilities for immigrants was soon on the verge of being overwhelmed by the sheer numbers. It had become the hospital and security clearinghouse for immigrants spreading all across Europe. It was one thing to be hospitable; it was something else for a country to lose one's culture, language, religion, and nationality.

By the time Trump came to power in the United States, Italy was experiencing even more immigration challenges. While France was perfectly willing to continue to loot the natural resources of its former African colonies, it was refusing to take their impoverished migrants as new French citizens.

While accusing America of being racist for trying to limit entry into the country of hundreds of thousands of illegal immigrants from Central America, French diplomats left their own French-speaking African former colonists waiting in Italy.

The desperate migrants traveled from French-speaking African nations across the deserts of Libya, now a stateless nation thanks to Obama's foreign policy, into Italy, the closest European nation.

In 2018, Italy's antiestablishment 5 Star Movement party and right-wing League party formed a government, promising to control immigration.[37] They did so by closing their ports to rescue ships from non-profit organizations and ending collaboration with other European countries' humanitarian efforts. These immigration policies were led by Interior Minister Matteo Salvini, whose additional goals were to establish Italian migration centers in Libya to stem the tide of the illegal crossings through the Mediterranean.

Salvini had caught American attention with his "Italians First" message. "This is something that the Trump White House understands," a friend of the president told me. "He can work with someone who makes his intentions clear."

THE WAR THAT HASN'T HAPPENED YET

As of early fall 2019, a hot war with Venezuela or Iran is possible. But, three years into his administration, Donald Trump has emerged as the first American president in nearly forty years to avoid involving America in a new war.

During our conversations, Presodent Trump has shown that he is a man of great patience and a willingness to negotiate. He has also shown that, if and when that soft touch fails, he would not hesitate to strike with full and decisive force.

This is a possible outcome for America's relationship with Iran. Long before taking office, Trump marveled at the American government's self-deception about this hostile country. Obama's solution had been to deliver to Tehran $1.7 billion in cash, on pallets in the night, like illicit drug money. Cash. So no future American president or Congress could halt bank transfers and undo the deal.[38]

Most critical of all, Iran was granted the right to eventually build a nuclear bomb.[39]

As the crisis with Iran has moved into each new critical phase, Trump, through his restraint and wisdom, has surprised critics. In July 2019, Iranian forces shot down an American drone. They seized British ships. They arrested what they claimed were seventeen American CIA spies and sentenced some of these alleged agents to death. Trump countered the report of the agents as totally false.[40] He held his fire.

The apparent objective of the Iranian government was to force a breach between the United States and its European allies. But Trump's steady, restrained reactions have given him a heavy hammer to wield when he is ready. Panicked critics say that Iran has the power to shut down the Strait of Hormuz, affecting oil shipments from Saudi Arabia, Kuwait, Iraq, the United Arab Emirates, Qatar, and Iran itself. Almost 26 percent of the world's liquefied natural gas volumes passed through the strait in 2018.[41] But if Iran were to do that, Trump's defenders say, it would only further enrich the United States, which is now energy independent.

"Iran doesn't know where they are," President Trump said. "They are a very mixed-up country. Their country is in turmoil. . . . Whatever it is, I'm just going to sit back and watch." Then he added, "We're ready for the absolute worst."[42]

★ 17 ★

THE MONROE DOCTRINE REVISITED

"We're going to have a real border, because
we're going to have a wall."
—DONALD TRUMP[1]

The Monroe Doctrine of 1823, which, among other things, prohibited any further colonization in the Western Hemisphere by European nations, is America's most enduring foreign policy position. Mostly written by John Quincy Adams, then the secretary of state to President James Monroe, it committed the will of the United States to protecting the new nations of North and South America.

Presidents since have leveraged the policy to keep everybody out of the Western Hemisphere. And the policy has been vigorously invoked by American presidents as justification for military actions.

The doctrine all but atrophied under presidents George W. Bush and Barack Obama. The former was arguably bankrupting the nation for a war in Iraq while the latter was committed to empowering Cuba and normalizing relations with that Communist country.

With great gusto, President Donald Trump has jumped back into Latin American issues with both feet. While it is unlikely that he will see the full manifestation of his Latin American policies while he is still president, his obvious objective in the region is to stymie the spread of radical socialism that flourished during the Obama presidency and to counter Cuban-sponsored repression in the region. He clearly is committed to blocking the initiatives and activities of the so-called troika of tyranny: Cuba, Nicaragua, and Venezuela.

In the most recent episode of saber rattling, Cuba put boots on the ground in Venezuela. There were reports that Cuban-trained mercenaries were serving as personal bodyguards to Nicolás Maduro, the socialist dictator of that country who knew he couldn't trust his own countrymen to protect him.[2]

There was another great irony playing out in this story. Russia was propping up Maduro. In December, 2018, Russia sent two Tu-160 bombers, nuclear-capable jets, to Venezuela.[3] In March 2019, it sent military advisers to the country.[4]

In addition to the blatant violation of the Monroe Doctrine, Russia's military presence created a bizarre juxtaposition. On the one hand, the Democrats and the American media were insisting that Donald Trump was colluding with Russia. On the one hand, they claimed that he was a Russian spy, and on the other hand, they left him unsupported in invoking the Monroe Doctrine to keep the Russians out of the Western Hemisphere.

Some Democrats who were advocating socialism for the United States were embarrassed by the broad failure of the socialist economy in Venezuela. Senator Bernie Sanders, a Democratic presidential candidate, refused to call Maduro a dictator, insisting on CNN that there were "still democratic operations taking place in their country."[5]

President Trump's strategy on Venezuela called for rallying the Organization of American States (OAS) and getting it to actively vote against Venezuelan human rights abuses.

I was in the middle of an interview with President Trump when he was interrupted by a call. "Sorry," he said. "Working on Argentina now. That's my new project." Trump's calls to and from Latin America were part of an ongoing effort. He would eventually organize forty-three nations of the world in support of Juan Guaidó, the opposition leader in Venezuela, who human rights activists insisted should be legally recognized.[6]

There was also an economic component, a hallmark of Trump foreign policy. He never misses a chance to use money to strengthen his case. Since 1996, US presidents had waived enactment of Title III of the Helms-Burton Act, but now Trump put it back into play..[7] Trump's decision not to waive Title III allowed lawsuits against companies that used property that had been confiscated by the Communist government of Cuba.

Would it work? There were just enough unknowns to discourage some foreign investment. The foreign policy of Donald Trump always had a bite. In this case, the message to Cuba was clear: Get out of Venezuela, stop trying to export Communism to Latin America, or the economic squeeze would get worse.

TRUMP AND MEXICO

During the months I worked on this book I was able to connect with Luis Videgaray, the former foreign minister of Mexico. My sources at the White House told me that he didn't give interviews, but with the president giving the green light to my project I was able to touch base with him during one of his short visits to Washington, DC.

Videgaray could tell me the whole, secret back story on Trump's private, ongoing relations with Mexico. He could also reverse-engineer the dismantling of the North American Free Trade Agreement (NAFTA) and how it had morphed into the United States Mexico Canada Agreement (USMCA). This new agreement was a clear win for all three countries—if Congress would approve it.

"I left office back in November 2018," Videgaray told me. "And since then [I] went completely private. I've had no interviews with any media in Mexico or abroad. So this is the first time I've done anything like this."[8]

There were so many questions Videgaray could help with. What did the presidency of Donald Trump mean to Latin America? What did it mean to Mexico? What did he think about immigration? About NAFTA?

"When Mr. Trump announced his candidacy in 2015," Videgaray said, "coming down the escalator, putting Mexico and Mexicans in the center of his initial statement, he was immediately unpopular in Mexico.

"No one believed he would be the Republican nominee, much less the president of the United States. So, as he began to survive the primaries it became more and more serious. I began to tell our Mexican president, Enrique Peña Nieto, 'You know, Mr. President, I think we should all think more seriously about Mr. Trump. We have no connections. He has apparently tapped into feelings of the American people. I think you should try to have a back-channel connection.'

"The president said, 'That's fine, so you do it.'"

As Videgaray explored his contacts in Washington and on Wall Street to find the best way to approach Donald Trump, Jared Kushner's name came up repeatedly. His first meeting with Kushner was in May 2016, held in a café at a nondescript hotel in Washington, DC. What was supposed to be a short introductory meeting ended up being long and substantive.

"I was immediately impressed by Jared Kushner," Videgaray told me. "I knew he was young. People told me that he was a smart guy, but I was still pleasantly surprised by his clarity. He came off as a well-meaning person who cared about America."

After several meetings and phone conversations, Kushner arranged a breakfast meeting with Donald Trump at the Bedminster Club in August 2016. Jared and Ivanka were present, and the meeting lasted two hours. "I found Donald Trump to be a very likeable person," Videgaray later told me. "He was very gracious. It was a fun conversation. My sense was that he wasn't anti-Mexican at all. He just wanted to change some things, primarily on trade."

Videgaray knew that it was a tough time for the Trump campaign, with the media and critics sniping at the candidate from every side.

Videgaray recalled Trump's words: "I am doing my best. We might not win. If I win it will not be bad for Mexico. There will be changes. We will negotiate. But I will be the first president in a long time who actually thinks about Mexico and cares about our relationship.'"

Videgaray summed up the meeting this way: "I left thinking, 'If he wins, we know one thing for sure: it's going to be very interesting.'"

Most important was that a back channel was now in place that would benefit all parties going forward.

A BETTER DEAL FOR ALL THREE COUNTRIES

When Donald Trump became president, the American establishment, both Left and Right, howled about Trump's challenge to NAFTA. The national media gleefully amplified the criticism. Trump was considered reckless, destroying the relationship with our biggest trading partners and our closest friends.

Conservative Republicans said it was an assault on free trade. Trump pointed out that the NAFTA agreement was 17,000 pages long—which makes it very unlikely that a single human being on earth has actually read it. Teams of lobbyists, special interest groups, politicians, and companies have read the one hundred pages that affected them or their industry, but who could claim expertise on all of it? Leo Tolstoy's *War and Peace* is only about 1,000 pages. Did it really take 17,000 pages to spell out the words "free trade"? Obviously the agreement was filled with qualifications and requirements for its participating member nations. Donald Trump contended that the final product was a maze of corruption and conflicting objectives. There needed to be fixes.

Jared Kushner's relationship with Luis Videgaray from Mexico, and with Prime Minister Justin Trudeau's chief of staff, Katie Telford, and his private secretary, Gerald Butts, in Canada, would prove critical. Time and again, the trade negotiations would reach a toxic level, with each side dug in. Kushner would break apart the various pieces and start rebuilding them again, in different ways, constantly seeking to look beyond the words and what was said, trying to find the real hot buttons. What were the most important, nonnegotiable issues? Discussions went on for hours.

Most in the American media railed against the process and denounced the final product. Thoughtful experts admitted that the newly created USMCA was better for American workers, which was Trump's objective.[9] The new agreement benefited American dairy farmers and manufacturers. It forced Mexico to end discrimination against women and underpaid migrant workers from Central America.

In October, 2018, Ambassador Robert Lighthizer, the US trade representative, appeared in the White House Rose Garden to announce the new deal. Lighthizer told reporters, "I've said before, and I'll say again, this agreement would not have happened if it wasn't for Jared."[10]

Most significantly, government experts in all three countries praised the final product. President Donald Trump, Prime Minister Trudeau, and Mexican president Enrique Peña Nieto signed the agreement on November 30, 2018, in Buenos Aires at the G20 summit.

Trump declared, "The USMCA is the largest, most significant, modern and balanced trade agreement in history."[11] It was not over. It still had to be ratified by the US Congress, where the House of Representatives was controlled by Democrats reluctant to give the president any more wins.

"Jared and I were both extremely involved in the renegotiation of NAFTA," Luis Videgaray says. "At first President Trump wanted to cancel NAFTA outright and start all over again, but the consequences would have been great for both countries."[12]

Was Donald Trump right to put the three countries through such an arduous and risky process? Was it worth the effort?

"I think he was right," Videgaray told me. "It is better for all of us. It was not an easy process. It was difficult. But he was right. He was being truthful. I can tell you that now, looking back and seeing what was changed."

THE IMMIGRATION CHALLENGE

The ultimate crisis in the Western Hemisphere is immigration. Not only illegal immigrants coming to the United States, but also floods of immigrants fleeing socialist Venezuela to neighboring countries.

The crisis in Central America is an example of how complex the problem can be. Under Bush-Obama, Honduras, for example, was given millions of dollars in aid, as well as military and law enforcement expertise to combat gangs of drug traffickers in the country. Today, critics say that the Honduran government has been successful in wiping out more than twenty-three narco-gangs that terrorized the country, only to have them replaced by the government itself. The Honduran president's own brother is now in American custody on drug charges.[13]

The chief source of hard dollars for the Honduran economy comes from two sources: its drug trade, which depends on masses of immigrant "mules" crossing illegally into the United States, and remittance income from immigrants, legal or otherwise, working in America and sending their money back home. The latter also involves a thriving sex slave operation. In both cases, the country encourages massive caravans of immigrants to pour across Mexico and into the United States.

Concluding that American aid money was going directly into the hands of drug traffickers, Donald Trump ordered it cut. Critics admitted that ending subsidies to some corrupt governments was long overdue but said that cuts to programs promoting the work of charities was harmful to the people. The myopic American media, refusing to report on the desperate conditions on the ground in Central America, nevertheless, attacked the president for his lack of humanity.

The driving force behind the immigration debate in the United States is the partisan contest between Republicans and Democrats. In 1979, I cofounded Save the Refugees. The organization morphed into Mercy Corps. I served as a founding board member of that organization, which has now donated several billion dollars' worth of food and medicine around the world.

Our challenge in the early eighties was Democrats opposed to immigration from Asia. Then-senator Joe Biden complained about American workers losing jobs.[14] California governor Jerry Brown tried to block the use of Travis Air Force Base in California as a port of entry for orphans from Vietnam.[15] They were the children of American servicemen and Vietnamese women. Their mixed race made them readily identifiable on the streets of Saigon, where they were sometimes murdered.

There was a very clear political reality involved. Asian immigrants tended to go into business. They opened restaurants and stores, and they eventually voted Republican. African and Latino immigrants, on the other hand, tended to require welfare assistance. They were more likely to vote Democratic to be assured of those opportunities.

The current open invitation from Democratic leaders, calling for no borders, for no restrictions, making any kind of entry into the United States legal, will shift the political power in America to the Democratic Party. According to some election models, Trump would have lost the 2016 election with a transfer of only 80,000 votes.[16] As I write this, in just one month (May 2019), US Border Patrol officers "encountered 144,000 undocumented immigrants on the southwest border of the United States."[17]

During the 2016 campaign, Donald Trump made building a wall on the border with Mexico a clarion call. And he said, "Mexico will pay for it."

This was one promise that the Democrats did not want Trump to keep. It went to the heart of their plan for political ascendancy. There was a short-term, tactical, cosmetic reason as well. Recent presidents were stung by the charge that they broke their promises. Presidents were seen as liars.

"Read my lips: no new taxes," George H. W. Bush had said.[18]

"I did not have sexual relations with that woman, Ms. Lewinsky," Bill Clinton had declared.[19]

"The British Government has learned that Saddam Hussein recently sought significant quanities of uranium from Africa," George W. Bush told the world.[20]

"You can keep your doctor," Barack Obama had promised voters.

Stung by Trump's record of promises kept, his political opponents fiercely opposed any moves toward finishing such a wall.

President Trump offered a deal on citizenship for children of illegal immigrants already in the country. He offered new programs to speed up legal immigration. The Democrats were not having it. There would be no wall. At a Democratic Party presidential primary debate on June 27, 2019, the candidates were asked to raise their hand if they supported government-provided health insurance for illegal immigrants.

Incredibly, every Democratic candidate raised his or her hand.[21]

NO COLLUSION, NO OBSTRUCTION

"How soon do you think Mueller knew there
was no collusion? Four days, maybe?"
—DONALD TRUMP JR.

The Mueller investigation slogged on under a universal premise. A good prosecutor could indict anyone, in any circumstances, regardless of his or her guilt or innocence. A former New York state judge had once declared he could "indict a ham sandwich."[1] Lavrentiy Beria, Stalin's chief of the secret police, once declared, "Show me the man and I will show you the crime."[2] In this case, the man was President Donald Trump, and an alliance of the national media and the Democratic Party were convinced that they could find him guilty of something. Eventually.

In the sixteenth century, Cardinal Richelieu, who was practically ruling France at the time, was quoted as saying, "Give me six lines written by the most honest man in the world, and I will find enough in them to hang him." The idea, if not the actual quote, captured a real sentiment. The special counsel Robert Mueller was the supreme master of the game. If Richelieu needed only six lines, what could Mueller do with 1.4 million pages of White House memoranda, and seventy hours of interrogating the president's own personal attorney?

The very idea of the Mueller investigation prompted many of the leading media figures to declare the Trump administration was all but over. How could anything be accomplished with this bearing down on them? The drumbeat began only three months after the presidential inauguration.

There seemed to be favorite words, talking points, which were repeated daily by different guests, even on different networks. "The beginning of the end for the Trump presidency," declared the MSNBC host Lawrence O'Donnell.[3] Presidential historian Douglas Brinkley said essentially the same thing on CNN.[4]

"Mike Pence might have to assume the office of the presidency," proclaimed Chris Stirewalt, digital politics editor at Fox News.[5]

"Another turn of the screw," said Norman Eisen to CNN viewers.[6] Eisen had been President Obama's ambassador to the Czech Republic.

"Do you think this is a tipping point?" CNN anchor Wolf Blitzer eagerly asked one of his on-air guests.[7] As if an echo from another building, a guest on MSNBC answered the question. "This is a tipping point," said Joel Benenson, a former Clinton campaign adviser.[8]

John Schindler, a former National Security Agency employee, claimed that he had received an email from a senior intelligence agent that began with these dark words about President Trump: "He will die in jail."[9]

Obama's CIA director John Brennan tweeted that the sum of Trump's actions "rises to & exceeds the threshold of 'high crimes & misdemeanors.' It was nothing short of treasonous."[10]

JAMES COMEY GETS THE BOOT

FBI director James Comey looked at the TV screens in utter disbelief. He was addressing the FBI employees at the Los Angeles field office. They were meeting in the communications room. He was facing the employees but could see a bank of big-screen televisions running live coverage behind them.

On one of the screens a large graphic appeared. COMEY RESIGNS. Knowing that he had not resigned, Director Comey was stunned and puzzled, thinking fast. Could this be a prank? Then the graphic changed. COMEY FIRED. The graphics were now regenerating on the other screens on different channels. The volume on the televisions was muted, but the graphics were screaming for attention.

The employees saw the expression on Comey's face and began to turn around to look at the wall. It was May 9, 2017. James Comey's time as FBI director had come to an end.[11]

Since that January 6, 2017, Trump Tower meeting when Director Comey had briefed President-elect Trump on the Steele dossier, the relationship between Trump and Comey had gone downhill.

The day after the inauguration, President Trump had invited members of law enforcement to a White House meeting. These were the people who had helped with security during the transition. The president wanted to personally thank them for their service. The list of guests included members of the Secret Service and the FBI. James Comey was reluctant to go. His political instincts and his appreciation for the power of the corporate media were urging him to stay as far away from Trump as possible. But when he learned that the head of the Secret Service was attending, Comey knew he could not decline.

The event was held in the White House Blue Room. Comey, wearing a dark blue suit, tried to blend into the blue curtain, hoping the president would not notice him. Hard to do for a man with a height of six feet, eight inches.

The president praised the head of the Secret Service, Joe Clancy, and asked him to come stand with him and the vice president. Then it was Comey's turn. The president called him forward. In his book, *A Higher Loyalty: Truth, Lies, and Leadership*, Comey describes this as a "complete disaster," being praised by the president in front of TV cameras.

Trump leaned forward and said into Comey's ear, "I'm really looking forward to working with you." In the corporate world, this was a nice gesture by an incoming boss to an executive who had been hired by someone else. Comey decided it was Donald Trump asking him "to come forward and kiss the great man's ring."[12]

Over the next few months, Trump and Comey had several private meetings, including a one-on-one dinner at the White House. Unknown to the president, Comey had started composing memos based on their private conversations. Comey had worked for two previous presidents. According to his own account, he had "never done something like that." He had never felt the need to reconstruct a conversation in a later memo. This had never happened with another president, or even "about encounters with any other person."[13]

One of the memos regarded a West Wing meeting in February 2017. Comey said that President Trump had asked him to stay in the Oval Office alone. The president wanted to talk about Michael Flynn, who had served as national security adviser to President Trump.

Comey claims the president said, "He is a good guy, he has been through a lot." Flynn had been fired for misleading Vice President Pence about private phone conversations with the Russian ambassador. The vice president had looked bad, innocently defending Flynn. The national security adviser had to go.

According to Comey, President Trump said, "I hope you can find your way clear to letting this go, to letting Flynn go. He is a good guy. I hope you can let this go."[14]

MICHAEL FLYNN: A CASUALTY OF A POLITICAL WAR

Lieutenant General Michael Flynn had a distinguished career and a rocky relationship with the Obama administration. He had served in command positions in both Iraq and Afghanistan. Early in Obama's second term, Flynn had risen to head the Defense Intelligence Agency (DIA). It was the Pentagon's chief intelligence agency, tasked with collecting information and analyzing the military capabilities of other nations. Heading the DIA is one of the highest positions in the US government's intelligence community.

Flynn disagreed with the Obama White House. Obama's national security team and others in the intelligence community felt that the death of Osama bin Laden signaled the end of the radical Islamic terror threat. Flynn was seeing the reports of the rise of ISIS and disagreed with the "cut off their head and they will die" strategy. Flynn believed America was fighting against an ideology, not an individual leader. When President Obama called ISIS the "JV team," Flynn said it was a mistake.

In 2014 Michael Flynn was asked to resign from the DIA. Reports were that Obama's director of national intelligence, James Clapper, was behind pushing Flynn out.[15] Flynn became a vocal critic of Obama's foreign policy. In the fall of 2016, in the middle of the presidential race, Flynn was one of the few former national security officials to openly support Donald Trump. He gave a speech at the Republican National Convention.[16]

Michael Flynn had also crossed swords with James Comey's FBI. Flynn had picked up the cause of Robyn Gritz, a former FBI agent with fifteen years of counterterrorism experience. She had filed a lawsuit claiming that the FBI had discriminated against her because she was a woman. Several other women agents made the same claims to Congress that male agents were given preference at the FBI. Gritz claims that the FBI ran her out of her job and revoked her security clearance for minor time card violations. Flynn publicly praised and defended Gritz: "She was one of the really, to me, bright lights . . . she was really a real pro."[17] It was a poke in the eye of Comey's FBI team.

During the presidential transition in late 2016, Flynn spoke by telephone with Russia's ambassador to the US. The subject of US sanctions placed on Russia by the Obama administration after the election was discussed. The Department of Justice, still staffed by Obama appointees, claimed Flynn had possibly violated the Logan Act.

The Logan Act, passed into law in 1799, was meant to prevent private citizens from negotiating with foreign governments against official US diplomatic positions. In over two hundred years, no one has ever been prosecuted under the Logan Act, probably because there are First Amendment questions with the law.

In any case, General Flynn was not acting as a private citizen in the phone calls with the Russian ambassador. He was part of the president-elect's transition team. It is standard for transition officials to interact with officials of foreign governments. It had occurred in some degree or another under every modern presidency. There was no Logan Act violation.[18]

Nonetheless, on January 24, 2017, four days into the Trump administration, Comey had two FBI agents visit Flynn at the White House to ask him about those phone calls.[19] One of those FBI agents was Peter Strzok, the married man whose mistress and fellow FBI colleague, Lisa Page, had asked him for assurance that Donald Trump would never be president. Strzok was the agent who had written to Page that he had just gone to a southern Virginia Walmart where he could "SMELL the Trump support."[20] Strzok had cryptically corresponded with Page about an "insurance policy" to guarantee that Trump would be taken out.

Under normal circumstances, if the FBI wanted to interview a member of the president's staff, it would notify the White House Counsel's office. The White House would have had a lawyer present. Flynn was assured that he did not need a lawyer and so met alone with the agents.[21]

Comey now claims that Flynn lied about the content of those phone calls.[22] Congressional testimony by Strzok indicates that at the time he did not feel Flynn had deliberately lied to them. Lying to the FBI is a federal offense. It was on the lying charges that Flynn was later indicted and pled guilty.[23] At the time of this writing, there is a chance that Flynn may change his plea, since his attorneys were not given the potentially exculpatory evidence of what the FBI agents at the meeting felt at the time, including their belief that Flynn had not deliberately lied.

THE REVENGE OF THE FBI

FBI director James Comey had written a memo about his January 2017 Oval Office conversation with the president. They had discussed Michael

Flynn; the president said he hoped that Comey could go easy on the war hero. Comey had carefully shared his memo with others at the FBI. He made two copies: one kept in the FBI files, and one kept at home. After he was fired, Comey no longer had access to the FBI files. He sent one copy of the memo to a friend of his, a law professor at Columbia University, and asked him to "share the substance of the memo—but not the memo itself—with a reporter." This was done on Tuesday, May 16, 2017.

Just as Comey later said was his intention, the strategic leak of the memo triggered the special counsel investigation into all things Trump, including, eventually, the whole false saga of Russian collusion.

Here's how Comey later explained it: "I decided that I would prompt a media story by revealing the president's February 14 direction that I drop the Flynn investigation. This might force the Department of Justice to appoint a special prosecutor."[24]

Just as Comey hoped, Robert Mueller, a former director of the FBI, was appointed as a special counsel, and the Mueller investigation began. They were coming after Donald Trump and they were going to take him out.

Usually, an investigation into public officials is overseen by the attorney general of the United States. That is why Obama's attorney general Loretta Lynch had oversight of the "Midyear Exam" investigation into Hillary Clinton's emails.

Why was a special counsel needed in the investigation of Donald Trump? Because Attorney General Jeff Sessions, formerly a Republican senator from Alabama and an early Trump supporter, had recused himself from all matters regarding the Trump campaign and Russia.

The president felt blindsided by Sessions. "He should not have recused himself almost immediately after he took office," the president said at a Rose Garden event. "And if he was going to recuse himself, he should have told me prior to taking office, and I would have quite simply picked somebody else."[25]

The newly announced special counsel, Robert Mueller, James Comey's longtime colleague and friend, promptly began to assemble his team.

The media quickly dubbed it the "Dream Team"[26] or the "All-Stars,"[27] terms usually reserved for sports. Andrew Weissmann was singled out for praise as part of the Enron corporate corruption task force.[28] Many articles failed to mention that several of the Enron convictions were overturned by the US Supreme Court for incorrectly applying the law. Weissmann went on to become general counsel of the FBI under Robert Mueller and later a law school professor in New York City.[29]

Other members of Mueller's team were clearly partisan and did not inspire confidence. Thirteen of the seventeen attorneys were registered Democrats. One of them, Jeannie Rhee, had been on Hillary Clinton's legal team, for lawsuits related to her email scandal. Rhee had also represented the Clinton Foundation. Many had donated to Democratic campaigns, and Andrew Weissmann had attended the 2016 Clinton Election Night party at the Javits Center.[30] Mueller also hired Peter Strzok and Lisa Page, who served until their text messages came out during an FBI inspector general investigation. They were quietly moved to other jobs at the FBI.

In a very sensitive and politically charged investigation, one would think Mueller would have made every effort to form a team that would, at least, appear unbiased. It does not seem that was important to Mueller.

Donald Trump would pay a big price for firing James Comey. The revenge of the former FBI director would be costly, not only to the president, but to the nation.

CNN STRIKES BACK

For twenty-two months, including over the stretch of the midterm elections when Democrats took back the majority in the US House of Representatives, new "revelations" would surface. Each was greeted by the media as the impending end of the Trump presidency. Time after time, the stories would prove to be untrue.

On December 9, 2017, for example, CNN offered a breathless, sensational report declaring that during the 2016 presidential campaign

Donald Trump Jr. had been sent an email giving him access to the WikiLeaks emails stolen from the Clinton camp. This, before they had gone public. Had the Russians helped it along?

As the journalist Glenn Greenwald later wrote in *The Intercept*, "Within an hour, MSNBC's Ken Dilanian, using a tone somehow even more unhinged, purported to have 'independently confirmed' this mammoth, blockbuster scoop."[31]

After agitated, hyperventilating news anchors expounded on this crime for hours it was finally learned that the timeline on the purported email did not match the reported claim. The email was sent to Donald Jr. days after the same information had been made available to the general public.[32]

According to Greenwald, "CNN and MSNBC deleted most traces of the most humiliating story from the internet, including demanding that YouTube remove copies of their own telecast."[33]

Another story held that Anthony Scaramucci, a one-time Trump ally and a short-lived director of communications for the president, was reportedly under investigation for ties to an entity called the Russia Direct Investment Fund. Surely this showed Trump-Russian collusion! It was also fake news. The next day CNN apologized to Scaramucci. Three CNN journalists were forced to resign.[34]

The Guardian reported that Julian Assange, the founder of WikiLeaks, had been visited by Trump's campaign manager Paul Manafort at the Ecuadoran embassy in London, where Assange had lived since seeking asylum there in 2012. They had met not just once, according to the news source, but three times! Numerous media sites picked up this news. Surely this was proof of collusion. But this story was also false. Assange was being watched by British law enforcement and multiple worldwide intelligence agencies. There was no Manafort connection. *The Guardian* never followed up on the story and did not answer requests asking from where it had come in the first place.[35]

Michael Cohen, Trump's former attorney, would testify that Donald Trump knew in advance about the infamous "Trump Tower meeting."

A meeting that had been asked for by a Russian attorney during the election. Supposedly she would give the Trump campaign dirt on Hillary Clinton from Russian sources. Campaign chairman Paul Manafort, Jared Kushner, and Donald Trump Jr. had met her in Trump Tower. She talked about an entirely separate issue—Kushner even texted his assistant asking her to get him out of the meeting because it was a waste of time. President Trump had long said that he knew nothing about the meeting.

The Cohen story was also incorrect. Michael Cohen would testify that Donald Trump did not know about the meeting in advance. The source of the story had been Lanny Davis, Cohen's attorney and a defender of Bill Clinton during his impeachment. Compounding the error, CNN denied that Davis was their source for the bad information. Davis later confirmed that he had indeed, been CNN's source.[36]

Despite all of these false reports, or perhaps because of them, Robert Mueller was raised to the level of mythic hero. A hero who could slay the dragon. Roman Catholics use votive candles with images of various saints during times of devotion and prayer. Votive candles with the image of Robert Mueller were marketed online.[37] Saint Robert would slay the Trump dragon!

The December 1, 2018, Christmas episode of *Saturday Night Live* featured the women of the cast singing a parody of "All I Want for Christmas Is You." With a picture of Robert Mueller in a Santa cap descending behind them, the ladies sang that they just want one thing for Christmas: "Mueller please come through / because the only option is a coup."[38]

DEMOCRATIC EXPECTATIONS

As the top Democrat and current chair of the House Permanent Select Committee on Intelligence, Representative Adam Schiff of California had been the point man for the Democrats throughout the investigation. In December 2017, he appeared on CNN's *State of the Union*.

"The Russians offered help," Schiff said of the Trump team. "The campaign accepted help, the Russians gave help, and the president made full use of that help, and that is pretty damning, whether it is proof beyond a reasonable doubt of conspiracy or not," Schiff said. "Can you prove beyond a reasonable doubt, will be Mueller's question to answer."[39]

A year later Schiff's confidence had grown incrementally. "There's clear evidence on the issue of collusion," he said in a CNN interview on January 10, 2019. "But whether it amounts to conspiracy beyond a reasonable doubt, I think, we still have to wait for Bob Mueller's work."[40]

On November 17, 2018, Democratic Senator Richard Blumenthal told MSNBC host Chris Hayes, "The evidence is pretty clear that there was collusion between the Trump campaign and the Russians." Hayes asked if it really was that clear. "The evidence is there," Blumenthal insisted. "Whether they have enough of it to bring criminal charges is another issue."[41]

A few days before Mueller delivered his report, the Connecticut Democratic senator delivered an ominous prediction. "There are indictments in this president's future," Blumenthal told MSNBC. "They're coming. Whether they're after his presidency or during it."

CNN interviewed Representative Jerry Nadler, a Democrat from New York and the House Judiciary Committee chairman, on November 30, 2018. Nadler saw collusion. "The fact that Manafort and Trump Jr. met with Russian agents who told them they wanted to give them dirt on Hillary as part of the Russian government's attempt to help them, and that they said fine," Nadler said. "I mean, it's clear that the campaign colluded, and there's a lot of evidence of that. The question is, was the president involved?"

From the beginning, one of the strongest Democratic Party voices for impeachment had been that of Representative Maxine Waters of California. At a town hall meeting of the Congressional Black Caucus Foundation in Washington, Waters urged activists to press for impeachment. "Here you have a president," Waters said, "who I can tell you, I guarantee you, is in collusion with the Russians to undermine our democracy. Here you have a president who has obstructed justice and here you have a president that lies every day."[42]

With the Mueller report pending, there was a bandwagon of expectations developing. A *Newsweek* headline declared "Why Donald Trump Jr. Will Be Indicted by Mueller . . . And Will Help to Ensnare His Father."[43]

Lanny Davis, the former Clinton lawyer and counsel for Michael Cohen, was publicly promoting the same idea. "I do suggest, respectfully, that Donald Jr., based upon signing a hush money check for his father—out of a trust fund, by the way, that was set up to prevent any money being spent that would help Donald Trump while he was president—out of that trust fund is where the Donald Jr. check was written, that is a crime."[44]

Meanwhile, Natasha Bertrand, a journalist for *The Atlantic*, insisted that Donald Trump Jr. was privately telling friends that it was going to happen. She made her remark following an appearance on HBO's *Real Time with Bill Maher*. It happened during an online-only segment aired live on YouTube after the show.[45]

"I think that Don Jr. is probably in more immediate jeopardy," said Ms. Bertrand. "He has been telling his friends and associates that he expects to be indicted, and he's been saying that for the last couple months."[46]

I was interviewing Donald Trump Jr. during this time and asked him about reports that he feared indictment. Was he worried? He laughed and rolled his eyes. "Well, why don't you refute it?" I asked.

"We did. We said it was one hundred percent false. Do you think anybody wants to hear that?"

I eventually found a story with Don's refutation. "A spokesman for Mr. Trump, 41, disputed the reporter's comments."[47] But the insistent perception of the American national media and their allies in the Democratic Party was that Don Trump Jr. was headed to prison.

THE MUELLER REPORT LANDS WITH A THUD

Finally, on March 24, 2019, twenty-two months after beginning, the Mueller investigation issued its report. The investigation had lasted three months longer than the entire Trump presidential campaign they were examining. Reports on its cost varied and depended on the book-keeping methods, but a *Washington Post* story showed expenditures of $16.7 million in its first ten months alone.[48]

The report read, "The investigation did not establish that the Trump campaign conspired or coordinated with the Russian government in its election interference activities."[49]

There were no new indictments.

A prosecutor who can supposedly indict a ham sandwich couldn't find anything on Donald Trump.

A headline in the *New York Times* proclaimed, "A Cloud over Trump's Presidency Is Lifted."[50] Two CNN personalities admitted on air that Trump "had been vindicated."[51] But this burst of fairness wouldn't last long. Soon enough, the media would be back with new outrage, but the fact that it would be reported at all was stunning.

"This all goes back to the same thing," Don Trump Jr. told me. "They just keep wanting to redo the 2016 election. As it relates to Mueller? In the end, they were able to do the damage that they wanted to do. They were able to hold that over my father's head in midterms.

"Even so, basically, he had one of the most successful midterms in recent history. You know, we basically lost some in the House and picked up some in the Senate. Obama's midterms were catastrophic by comparison.

"We were able to have that kind of result, despite having this cloud overhead when you knew all along that there was no collusion. They were able to keep that going. With no evidence. Ridiculous assertions. It was very effective in doing, at least, part of what they wanted to do. They could keep the investigation going for many months more than they needed. It was bullshit from moment one.

"Afterward, all of a sudden, Muller went from being the Democratic savior, the media savior, he was the messiah, he was going to be the guy, to a great disappointment. It went from collusion to obstruction, and now what do they call it again? A cover-up. It's really bullshit. It's all bullshit.

"When do you think that Mueller knew there was no collusion?" Don Jr. asked. "In the first four days, maybe?'

The Democrats and the national media put on a brave face. There had been earlier indictments; they could still point to that. Dozens of Russians had been indicted for election tampering, but these were largely symbolic charges. They had nothing to do with Trump. There had been a long list of the same kind of culprits when the Chinese had tried to pour money into the Clinton reelection campaign of 1996. Russia, China, and the United States do not have extradition treaties. The Russians were unlikely to face American justice. There was the galling fact that their illegal acts had taken place when Barack Obama was president.

Trump's former campaign chairman Paul Manafort was also indicted and convicted on charges relating to his business dealing in Ukraine. But those were activities that happened twelve years before the campaign. Trump's former attorney Michael Cohen pled guilty on charges related to non-Trump businesses in New York City and Trump campaign violations having nothing to do with Russia. The political consultant Roger Stone was indicted on obstruction and witness tampering charges. None of the Stone charges were for crimes committed during the campaign.

Part two of the Mueller report declined to reach a legal conclusion on obstruction of justice. Attorney General William Barr and Assistant Attorney General Rod Rosenstein, who had oversight of the Mueller Investigation, wrote that "the evidence developed during the Special Counsel's investigation is not sufficient to establish that the President committed an obstruction-of-justice offense."[52]

WHEN TRUMP GOT THE NEWS

Chief of Staff Mick Mulvaney was actually with the president and first lady when the Mueller Report came down. I wanted to get his inside take on what happened and how they reacted.

"There were several different days," the chief of staff said. "The first day was when the summary report came out. I think that was on a Friday. Of course, we could not see it. Then Attorney General Barr put out his own summary on a Sunday."

That was the big one. William Barr's summary was made public. It was March 24, 2019. Reports said that the president and his staff were at Mar-a-Lago. That morning he had played golf with his chief of staff and others.

"For that trip I remember specifically asking that Pat Cipollone and Emmet Flood be with us. These were our two lead lawyers. Cipollone was White House counsel and Flood had been taken on to help specifically with the Mueller report.

The William Barr summary was relayed down to them at 3:50 p.m.

"I remember standing there, along with Cipollone and Emmet, going over the four-page memo, line by line, with the president. We were able to digest that. Then we actually went back into the president's suite, with the first lady. We were discussing the memo ourselves while we watched television and heard others commenting on the memo, all of this was happening in real time."

"What was the president's reaction?" I asked.

"Obviously, very positive, very positive."

"Did he smile or laugh?"

"Well, I remember we went through it line by line and there were two parts that drew his attention, one of which was the language that said the decisions in the report were made without regard to the special consideration for the president.

"There is a policy over at DOJ that says, constitutionally, you might not be able to indict a sitting president. So what that language told us was that this policy was not a factor. They were not withholding indictments because of this consideration. They were withholding indictments because they were not warranted. That was a huge win for the president.

"Obviously, the findings in the first half about, you know, where it says there is no evidence, at all, of collusion, I can't remember the exact language, or perhaps it said, 'not a single piece of evidence for a single instance of collusion,' those were the highlights that caught the president's attention."

Stunned by the summary released by Attorney General William Barr, the media and the Democrats took a day off before regrouping and saying that the actual, full report would be damning. Just wait. The attorney general had mischaracterized the details.

White House chief of staff Mulvaney's team could take nothing for granted. "The final time was right here, in this office," Mulvaney said. "We knew that the full report was coming out that day and so we had set up a war room. As soon as it came out, we broke it up into pieces. We had about ten people, and everybody was going to read forty pages. So we assigned everybody different forty-page sections. We were trying to learn as quickly as we could what was actually in the report both times.

"I was extraordinarily proud of the work that the communications department, the press department did at that time. Of course it was Sarah Sanders, but not just her. It was the entire team.

The day that the Barr summary came out and the day the Mueller report actually came out, itself, we had six or seven scenarios gamed out. If it says this, then this is where we'll go with our response. If it says that, then we'll go here instead.

"In both cases, I remember, we had sorted out a range of scenarios with the very best possible outcome to the very worst possible outcome. So, there was the whole spectrum of scenarios. As it turned out, we were able to use our very best possible outcome on both days. So I was very pleased with the advance work that the communications and press shops had done. Because we were ready very, very quickly. I thought we were very right on message. Of course, we had great stuff to work with because the report was so favorable to the president."

THE "KEEP IT GREAT" RALLY IN ORLANDO
Despite the warm summer weather in Orlando, Florida, people had

started lining up for the Trump rally days in advance. Twenty thousand excited supporters waited, many dressed in iconic Trump campaign red. Across the crowd one could spot various versions of the "Make America Great Again" baseball cap. The basketball arena where the Orlando Magic play was packed to maximum capacity.

Thousands more, who were not able to gain entrance, watched on huge projection screens outside. They were eagerly anticipating the official launch of the president's reelection campaign. It was Tuesday, June 18, 2019. Just a few short months after the release of the Mueller report.

After a warm-up speech by Vice President Pence, the president and first lady entered the arena to the sounds of wild cheering and Lee Greenwood's patriotic anthem "God Bless the U.S.A." Melania, dressed in a bright yellow pantsuit with flowing sleeves, introduced her husband to the crowd. Just a few minutes into his speech, the president summarized, from his view, what happened with the Mueller investigation:

"We went through the greatest witch hunt in political history. The only collusion was committed by the Democrats, the fake news media, and their operatives, and the people who funded the phony dossier: Crooked Hillary and the DNC.

"It was all an illegal attempt to overturn the results of the election, spy on our campaign, which is what they did, and subvert our democracy. Remember the insurance policy just in case Hillary lost? Remember the insurance policy.

"They appointed eighteen very angry Democrats to try and take down our incredible movement. After two years, 1.4 million pages of documents, five hundred search warrants, five hundred witnesses, 2,800 subpoenas, and forty FBI agents working around the clock, what did they come up with?" he asked the crowd.

He answered for them, "No collusion, and the facts that led our great attorney general to determine no obstruction. No collusion, no obstruction. And they spent forty million dollars on this witch hunt; forty million dollars."[53]

There would be no "bombshell" on Russia collusion. There would be no treason. There would be no walls closing in. There would be no resignation from office. No slaying of the dragon.

Instead, there would be a reelection campaign.

The motto this time: Keep America Great.

★ 19 ★

GOD AND THE SUPREME COURT

"Paula, you're praying!"
—DONALD TRUMP TELLING HIS FRIEND WHAT HE WANTED
HER TO DO ON INAUGURATION DAY

I t has been said that Donald Trump's legacy will be "conservative judges who will dominate US law for decades."[1] His reshaping of the Supreme Court was not as easy as it looked. Thirty-seven times in American history a Supreme Court nominee had been unsuccessful. Eleven times the nominees had been withdrawn by the president himself, sometimes after great public pressure. Even George Washington had withdrawn a name. Another of Washington's nominees had been rejected by the Senate. Indeed, Donald Trump would be severely pressured to withdraw both of his nominees, not only by his political opposition and the national media but by some within his own political party. He never wavered.

Meanwhile, throughout his presidency, Donald Trump's appointment of federal judges operated like a factory assembly line. He was reshaping the American judiciary. By January 2019, "Trump had appointed 30 circuit court judges, a rate unparalleled by his recent predecessors."[2]

One report claimed that "Trump had already appointed more judges in his first two years than the five previous presidents at the same point in their presidencies."[3]

Neil Gorsuch was nominated to the Supreme Court during Trump's first month in office. His confirmation hearing was an unsettling, bruising business, but nothing compared with the fight that was to come. Gorsuch was finally sworn in as a justice on April 10, 2017.

The Democrats, consistently unable to win statewide referendums for their cultural agenda, even in the most liberal of states, had turned more and more to a combination of the courts and the national media to promote their issues. In a tradition that hailed back to Dwight Eisenhower and continued during the Reagan-Bush years, they had relied on an occasional gift of a more moderate-to-liberal judge nominated to the Supreme Court from a Republican president. Thus, Democrats nominated liberal justices. Republicans nominated conservative justices but also a few liberals of their own. In recent years, Reagan had given them Justice Anthony Kennedy, a so-called swing vote. George H. W. Bush had given them Justice David Souter, who was soon considered by the modern, neoconservative movement to be a liberal.[4]

On July 9, 2018, after the resignation of Associate Justice Anthony Kennedy, Donald Trump announced Brett Kavanaugh as his second nominee. Kavanaugh was a Catholic and a Yale Law School graduate who had already been confirmed by the Senate to serve on the Court of Appeals for the District of Columbia Circuit. But Brett Kavanaugh was another conservative. There would be fireworks.

The national media and the Democratic Party reacted with horror. A Republican president had appointed two Supreme Court nominees and they had both been conservatives.

"What's the big deal?" Trump asked me in one of our interviews. Democrats nominate liberal justices; Republicans were elected to nominate conservative justices. "That's why people voted for me."

On the very day that Kavanaugh's nomination was to be decided by the Senate Judiciary Committee and sent to the floor of the Senate,

Democratic ranking member Dianne Feinstein of California interrupted the process by introducing allegations against the nominee.
Feinstein had been sitting on the story for months. According to a
summary of the allegations, "36 years ago, as a 17-year-old high school
student, he groped and tried to force himself on a 15-year-old girl at an
underage beer party."[5] Kavanaugh vehemently denied the story.

The unfolding drama escalated into a circus. Michael Avenatti, the
attorney for a porn star who went by the name Stormy Daniels, now
represented new clients who came forward to make their accusations
against Kavanaugh. Avenatti was being encouraged by journalists to
run for president himself, so they gave his allegations some credence at
the time. The story was that Brett Kavanaugh, during his high school
years, did "cause girls to become inebriated and disoriented so they could
then be 'gang-raped' in a side room or bedroom by a 'train' of boys."[6]

Avenatti's claims were soon contradicted by his own witnesses,
and the bitterly personal, unproven attacks on the nominee began to
backfire politically. Brett Kavanaugh was sworn in as a Supreme Court
justice on October 6, 2018.

A few days later, Avenatti's claims were beginning to crumble.
NBC, seen by many as a leading media opponent to Donald Trump's
administration, ran a story entitled "New Questions Raised about
Avenatti Claims Regarding Kavanaugh."[7] Avenatti's star witness was
now saying that it hadn't been Kavanaugh at the party.

By 2019, Michael Avenatti, the man who had become a darling of
the national media, had been indicted in two jurisdictions. Federal
prosecutors in New York were saying that he had "concocted a scheme
to extort over $20 million from sports giant Nike."[8] One news report
stated that "the combined maximum for all charged crimes is 97 years
in prison."[9]

The Supreme Court nomination process had been a brutal, bloody
business. But it was something that Donald Trump had to do. It had
been a political promise. He had promised to bring balance back to
the courts. He was achieving the appointments and that balance at a

rate that the great Ronald Reagan could not match. He had made his promise to conservative Catholics and to white evangelical Christians and, surprisingly, to a small but critical percentage of black evangelical Christians who had swung back to the Republican column in 2016. It was a promise that revealed a side of Donald Trump that very few ever saw or knew existed. In a sense, he had fulfilled a promise to himself.

There was more to Donald Trump than met the eye.

TRUMP'S SECRET SOURCE OF VOTES

Donald Trump's more savvy political friends must have wondered at his luck. Given the same set of circumstances, they may have imagined that they, too, could have won the Republican nomination and ultimately the presidency. They would have told themselves that, during the process, they certainly would have been less self-destructive than Donald Trump. His success had all been a question of timing. Oh, the whimsical vagaries of fate.

The fact is, there was much more than luck behind Donald Trump's mystical rise to the presidency. He was playing with cards that few even knew he had.

One of his most important political cards was his unseen, underreported, long-standing relationship with white evangelical Christians. On Election Day 2016, they would be the largest, most cohesive sociocultural group captured by exit polling data. And yet the Democrats would give them to Trump without a challenge. He would be staked the evangelical vote. "Here, you can have them." Of the final tally in 2016, 1 percent of the voters would be Muslim, 12.9 percent would be African American, 17.6 percent would be Hispanic, 23 percent would be Catholic, and 26 percent would be white evangelicals.[10] The latter was gift wrapped by the Clinton campaign and handed to Donald Trump on a silver platter.

The problem with winning the white evangelicals was that for every vote they gave you, they took one away. Hollywood, academia, and the national media all held very deep and strident antipathy toward Christians. ABC had once proposed a sitcom with the title "Good

Christian Bitches."[11] One can imagine the reaction if the word "Chris-tian" had been substituted with any other religious or social group. The week before the 2016 election, celebrities supporting Hillary Clinton in California gathered in a recording studio and produced a musical video that ended with the words, "Jesus f— Christ, please vote."[12] The video is still online; as of this writing, it has more than a million views. While YouTube would later be criticized for censoring conservative commentary, this anti-Christian profanity on behalf of Hillary Clinton is still, apparently, perfectly acceptable. Once again, one can imagine the reaction if activist members of a major American political party had used the name of the prophet Mohammed as a curse word to motivate their voters.

Strategically, the solution for a Republican candidate was to get to evangelicals early and with strength, when the media was less observant, so that the candidate could reach out to other, more media-acceptable and media-approved voter groups during the home stretch. Historically, the Republican political landscape was littered with candidates who had waited too late to secure their evangelical base and had gotten caught in the media headlights during the actual election year. It had happened to both Senator John McCain in 2008 and to former governor Mitt Romney in 2012, the former having to take Sarah Palin onto his ticket to try to mitigate the problem.

Democratic candidates had it much easier. They didn't have to win the evangelical vote; they merely had to make a token effort and they would automatically get a piece of it. Some evangelicals were "liberals" and predisposed to vote for a Democratic candidate. These voters believed in gun control. Or they worried about the environment. Some were even pro-choice. Every modern Democratic president since Jimmy Carter had made the effort to reach this bloc, including Bill Clinton and Barack Obama. The latter appointed a young Assemblies of God pastor to head up what was called "the Joshua project," an outreach to evangelicals.

After the 2016 election, Michael Wear, a former White House aide to President Barack Obama, wrote an op-ed in the *Washington Post* entitled "Why Did Obama Win More White Evangelical Votes than Clinton? He Asked for Them."[13]

Donald Trump's long, quiet relationship with evangelical Christians had allowed him time to fully understand the value of their numbers. It is something that numbers on a page cannot convey. It has to be personally experienced, especially for a resident of New York City who can live and die without ever meeting an evangelical in the flesh. But it had also allowed him the time to be burned by the deep animosity evangelicals provoked in other groups. With the right word dropped here or there, he could see their sheer numbers pad his book sales, his television audiences, and later his social media accounts. But throughout the 2016 GOP primary season, he always kept one eye on the coming general election, allowing another candidate to be closer to the evangelicals than himself, and thus attracting some of the more bitter media antireligious animus.

Donald Trump's private connection to the evangelical Christian community protected him in the Iowa caucuses, where two other prominent, public, evangelical candidates, Senator Ted Cruz and the neurosurgeon Ben Carson, would split that vote. It allowed Trump to show well, coming in second place, with a respectable piece of the evangelicals himself. He would win the next week in New Hampshire, where evangelicals were scarce. Eventually, Trump's personal link to the group would help him emerge as the frontrunner and sweep up other GOP delegates in the South.

It was in the general election that Donald Trump's connection to evangelicals would be tested. When the *Access Hollywood* tape emerged, which contained the candidate using lewd and offensive language, his political support appeared to collapse. The Republican establishment openly broke with him. But as the voters absorbed the story and as his evangelical friends began to consider the alternative, Trump's support began to slowly come back.

The national media was perplexed. How could evangelicals support a brash, egotistical New Yorker who used such offensive language? It was all about the Supreme Court, some said. It was the flawed candidate on the other side, others contended. Some felt it was a reaction to an insistent Hollywood and a perceived bias in the media. The more celebrities and the media pushed them to Hillary Clinton, the more they inclined toward Trump. Part of that, or even all of that, may have been true, but the fact was that unseen, unknown, Donald Trump had his own shared history with evangelical Christians. It was not a recent invention born out of political expediency. It had been born nineteen years before. And it was personal.

When I asked the president for names of friends whom I should talk to, people who could help tell his story, people who understood him, the following name came back in an email from the White House press secretary Sarah Huckabee Sanders:

Paula White.

PRAYING WITH PAULA

It turned out that the Reverend Paula White, a striking blonde, was a televangelist. She was the pastor of the twenty-thousand-member New Destiny Christian Center in Apopka, Florida. And in fact, while this was her home church, she served as an overseer of multiple congregations all across the country.

My wife and I caught a plane to Florida in March 2019, where we sat down with Paula White and her husband, the rock musician Jonathan Cain, who just happened to be in the Rock and Roll Hall of Fame as a member of Journey. It turned out that Paula White offered a much more complicated side of Donald Trump than we had anticipated.

"This happened about eighteen years ago," she said.[14] "I was sitting in my home office and my executive director called and said, 'Mr. Trump is on the line.'

"I said, 'Yeah, sure, right.'

"He said, 'Paula, this is for real. Mr. Trump is on the line.'

'We were always having fun on staff and I was just sure he was pulling my leg a little bit but he said, 'No pastor. This is real.'

"He comes on the line and he says, 'You are fantastic. You have the *it factor*.' He started to quote almost verbatim three of my sermons on the value of vision. So immediately I was quite impressed. I was still, I think, a little bit in shock and awe. When I say verbatim? I have pastored now for thirty-four years. This wasn't someone just saying that you spoke on this message and it was meaningful. This was different. He really got into it. This was a three-part series, and he was telling me the details of my sermons, and that was pretty impressive. I was thinking, 'None of the people in my congregation listen this well.'"

She laughed.

"He told me how he was confirmed as a Presbyterian and grew up in Norman Vincent Peale's church. He talked about some of Norman Vincent Peale's sermons. It was very detailed. Telling me how Peale had influenced his life."

Dr. Norman Vincent Peale had been the pastor of the Marble Collegiate Church, also on Fifth Avenue, about thirty blocks south of Trump Tower. Peale's book *The Power of Positive Thinking* was published in 1952 and dominated the *New York Times* best-seller list for three years, eventually selling fifteen million copies in forty languages.[15] Long before Trump Tower ever existed, the Fred Trump family would often attend the church, along with Donald Trump, just a young man. It was in this church that he would later marry his first wife, Ivana, and it was there that he would meet his second wife, Marla Maples. Yes, that's right. Donald Trump met Marla Maples at church.

According to Paula White, the powerful preacher Norman Vincent Peale, with his "positive Christianity," had stirred something deep inside the young Donald Trump, and it had never been fully resolved. After the death of Dr. Peale, Trump had tried to attend other churches and listen to other pastors, but his increasing celebrity status made such visits bothersome. And none of the sermons touched him as had Dr. Peale's. He would quickly become bored and the church service would become a drudgery. Donald Trump found it easier to hide in the privacy of his own home, tucked away in Trump Tower, where he could pick and choose among the television preachers. Over the years the questions and ideas about faith only accelerated. By the time he discovered Pastor Paula White, a televangelist whose positive message apparently resonated with him, his pent-up spirituality fairly erupted.

"This was our very first conversation," Paula White remembers. "And he shared everything about his faith. He had seen Dr. Billy Graham as a young man and had been deeply moved. But he liked to watch many of the others, some you wouldn't expect, like Jimmy Swaggart. It was so interesting to hear him describe their sermons. In some respects, deliverywise, Graham and Swaggart both had this fiery passion, this booming voice that Donald Trump apparently liked. But the messages were quite different. One was grace, the other hellfire and brimstone. And then Dr. Peale was such a contrast to both of them."

Paula White was impressed with the relationship between Peale and Trump. "I think a lot of people underestimate the role that Norman Vincent Peale played in American faith. They underestimate the depth of his message. It was the right time and the right place. New York City, coming out of a period of depression and hopelessness. It impacted people who were struggling to hold on to something. The proof of that is the influence it had on Donald Trump. Norman Vincent Peale is now gone, but his messages took root in that young life, and the youth who was listening would become president of the United States.

"Donald Trump had watched hours of Christian television," Paula said. "And not just watched it, but really listened to the messages. He had retained what he had heard. He could bring it back and repeat it to me. He would say what it meant to him. So that first conversation was very much about the impact that his faith had had on his life."

MOVING INTO TRUMP TOWER

Trump asked Paula White if she ever visited New York.

"I told him that actually I was doing a Bible study for the New York Yankees with George Steinbrenner. He said he would love to meet with me and my family. So on my next trip up to the city I ended up in his office, meeting Rhona Graff and Keith Schiller and many of his staff. The very next time after that, we had lunch at Jean-Georges."

It was a Donald Trump ritual. Special friends were hosted at the four-star restaurant on the lobby level of the Trump International Hotel at One Central Park West. In his book, *Let Me Finish*, Governor Chris Christie described a dinner at Jean-Georges with Donald Trump at which the businessman grew impatient with a fan wanting a picture. Paula White's experience was different.

"You know, in all the years I have been with Donald Trump, I have never seen that. Now, it's true that when he walks into a room he owns it. But it's not arrogant. In fact, it is quite charismatic and humble. Everybody knows who he is.

"Actually, I have seen him wait patiently for pictures and autographs, at great inconvenience. Even that afternoon I noticed he went in through the lobby of the hotel, just to make sure he had shaken hands and said hello to everyone on staff. He would look every one of them in the eye.

"I was just getting to know him. He showed me the wine list but I declined, not knowing at the time how deeply he felt about alcohol. Throughout the afternoon he talked about his children, about Don Jr., Ivanka, Eric, and Tiffany. And he talked about his deep faith.

"Right from the beginning he started introducing me to others as 'his pastor.' So, as in any other case, with a pastor, he started asking me to pray for things. He would talk and share his heart. I have always protected that. I will never betray that. But I can say that it became very clear how deeply he loved his children; his admiration for them, his concern for them, was always at the forefront of his prayers. Like any other parent. That was usually what he wanted me to pray about."

During this time, the Reverend Paula White's regular trips to New York City centered on intensive Bible studies for the Yankees baseball team. She became the unofficial, unpaid chaplain for the franchise.

"Christina Steinbrenner had started attending my church in Tampa. She was married to Hal Steinbrenner at the time, and so one thing led to another. Yankees outfielder Gary Sheffield started coming to the Bible studies. Later Alex Rodriguez would become involved. Darrell Strawberry began attending my church in Florida. He and George Steinbrenner were very close."

Eventually, some of the relationships became quite close and intertwined. Both Paula White and Alex Rodriguez would have homes in Trump Tower. And over the years, the Reverend Paula White would become a bit of a celebrity herself. In 2003, Michael Jackson would invite her to his ranch in California "for spiritual support."[16] In 2010, Kid Rock would invite her to a party on Second Avenue that became a national story.[17] Rival religious leaders criticized Paula White for attending the event, at which the booze flowed, even though she quietly sipped on a Pepsi.

GOD AND MONEY

Money was never a part of the relationship between Donald Trump and Paula White. But on one occasion she brought in a Christian woman leader who was working with young ladies caught up in human trafficking. The victims were trying to break free from drugs and find a way out.

Trump was amazed, and then he suddenly switched into high gear. "Now, this is really helping people," he said. "This is the real deal."[18] He immediately sat down and wrote a check out for the woman's ministry. He then proceeded to strongarm a group of businessmen who happened to be in his office. "Come on, write her a check, right now. Get out your checkbook. This is really helping. Let's go. Give her some money."

A Southern Baptist pastor in Florida remembers Donald Trump and his entourage showing up late for a church service and sitting near the back. Later people in the congregation told the pastor what had happened, laughing as they told the story. When it came time for the offering, Trump had pulled out a stack of twenty-dollar bills and started passing them out to nearby parishioners. "Here, put this in the offering. You too. Everybody should be giving something."

On every visit Paula made to the city, Trump's office would call, and he would say, "Please stop by, come by." Sometimes he would ask her to come by to pray for his staff.

"On one occasion he asked me to stop by for the production of *The Apprentice*, his popular television show. He said, 'Come in and pray over everyone.' So he walked me through, and it was a lot of people; I mean, he had a total of three hundred and fifty people working on the show, and probably a hundred were actually there. I was mesmerized. Remember, I have my own television program, but he had a tech, for the tech, for the engineer. My own faith was increasing, my own vision was increasing. This man was a big thinker with a meticulous knack for boring in on the details when that really mattered.

"Anyway, he asked me to come in and pray for them. All of them. He called them together. He said, 'Paula, I want you to pray for each one. So, I just started praying over people. I've always had a boldness to lay hands on people. I pray in the name of Jesus. I pray the way I am and the way I know. He always had a respect for that and understood."

Paula White's relationship with Trump was different from other religious figures or charity fundraisers, and she treated the relationship differently from a visit with Michael Jackson or an MVP New York Yankees baseball player.

"I had a feeling about Donald Trump. Right from the beginning. I felt that God had a special purpose for him. I remember an unusual moment in his office. Now, I can't tell you what provoked this, but I said, 'Sir, I don't want your money. I have enough of my own. I don't want your fame. I have enough of my own.'

"Then I said, 'I want your soul.'

"At that point I literally got up and walked out of the office. I know that sounds kind of wild. Later, we laughed about it. I think either he thought, 'This woman is just totally crazy,' or 'Boy, she is bold.' But you can also look back on it and see that even then, many years ago, there was this special feeling about Donald Trump and his destiny. This was not the King of Pop, or a Hall of Fame home run king, but God had a very definitive destiny for this man. It was different from anyone else. And I could feel it."

RUNNING FOR PRESIDENT

Did he ever talk to her back then about running for president?

"This had come up before, but it was very tenuous. He would say something along the lines of, 'Paula, pray about the idea that one day, I might think about running for president.'" She laughed. "So, how do you pray about that?

"Then suddenly, in 2011, he got more certain. He said he wanted me to go into serious prayer about whether or not he should run for president. Keep in mind, he never asked me to pray for something that he wanted for himself, like a business deal or more money or some advantage over someone. It's true that sometimes he would ask for very specific things for his family and his children, but never for himself. If it was about him, the prayer he wanted was a prayer for the will of God."

Trump decided not to run for president in the 2012 election cycle, but he was back again to ask for Paula's prayers for the 2016 election cycle.

"On one occasion he had me bring Christian leaders to Trump Tower just to pray. This may have been around 2014. This wasn't about asking for their support, this was just for a time to pray about the 2016 election. He came in the room once or twice during this. Once he sat with us for about an hour. Again, he didn't want to talk. He just wanted to sit there with us while we were praying. A pastor or a religious leader won't sit still that long. They will come for a few minutes of prayer and then leave. In their minds they have more important things to do. But he seemed to find some peace being there."

Was he manipulating these Christian leaders? In 1993, soon after his inauguration, Bill Clinton had a succession of private, pastoral counselors fly to the White House, each unknown to the other, praying with him monthly. This was before the Monica Lewinsky scandal. This was before the publicly announced counselors he would later, so famously, engage. I had served as a religious adviser to the Bush family and knew how intricate and sophisticated outreach to various religious groups could be. There was much more to the art of presidential politics than the layman would ever imagine.

I raised this with Paula White. "Did you ever think he was trying to reach only out to establish a political connection? That his spirituality was bogus?" I asked.

"Doug, I have been courted by politicians," she said. "I went with Franklin Graham to Mitt Romney's house. I sat on a blanket with Barack and Michelle Obama and Oprah at their house. I was invited to events with the Bush family. Smart politicians reach out to all constituencies. And smart religious leaders know when it is happening. Donald Trump's faith is very real.

"Later, in the 2015–2016 campaign years, we would have meetings with Christian leaders. It is a way to show respect and to reassure them that they will be included, they will be heard. But this was something else. This was something truly personal and spiritual."

Maybe so, but if Trump was so religious, why did he use the F word in his conversations? Why was he so ignorant of biblical language, referring to "Two Corinthians" during an appearance at Liberty University?

At the Family Leadership Summit in Ames, Iowa, in 2015, the moderator, Frank Luntz, asked Donald Trump if he had ever asked God for forgivingness. "I'm not sure I have," Trump answered. "I just go on and try to do a better job from there. If I do something wrong, I think, I just try and make it right." Then Trump talked about his Presbyterian communion service, taking the cup of wine and eating the cracker, saying, "I suppose that is a form of asking for forgiveness."[19]

"Well, he is certainly not religious," Paula White said. "He is no theologian. But he completely understands the concept of redemption, and I know his spiritual life is real and personal and it has been ongoing for years."

For his swearing-in ceremony on Inauguration Day, Trump would use a Bible given to him as a child in 1955 by the Presbyterian Sunday

School Board. It had been preserved by his grandmother. He would also use Abraham Lincoln's Bible. When the Washington, DC Museum of the Bible later said they were planning a display, along with bibles belonging to Presidents Harry Truman, Dwight Eisenhower, George H. W. Bush, and George W. Bush, a staffer at the White House called back for more details. Cary Summers, then president of the museum, said that they would place the Trump Bible just above the others in the showcase. The White House staffers said, "Good call."[20]

"His mother was a very strong Christian woman," Paula said. "She had a lot of influence on him. He was filled with stories about her. He talked a lot about her. The part about no drugs, no alcohol? I got the impression that it came from his mother. She would pray about her problems and then just give them over to God. She had a lot of influence over his father."

His brother Freddie had died early from alcoholism.

"Sometimes, when he would talk about Freddie, his whole face and voice would change. His demeanor would change. He would talk about his brother with a tenderness. He obviously believed that his brother could have been a great achiever. That was a word he would use often in our discussions. 'Achiever.' He would talk about how smart his brother was and how alcohol had ruined things for him and eventually taken his life."

"PAULA, YOU'RE PRAYING!"

In the days following the 2016 election, Paula White was called into the office of President-elect Trump at Trump Tower. There was a crowd. Steve Bannon, Reince Priebus, and a host of other staff were in the room, all in animated conversation.

When Trump spotted Paula, he looked up and shouted everyone else down. "Paula, you're praying!" he declared. He was talking about the swearing-in ceremony for Inauguration Day. It was not a question. It sounded like the one easy decision Trump could make.

Paula White knew her friend. She had anticipated that this would be coming. Conservative Southern Baptists would never accept a woman offering the prayer. Mainstream Protestants and evangelicals expected that someone in the Graham family would get the nod, like Franklin Graham or Billy Graham's up-and-coming grandson Will.

Some in the liberal national media didn't want a prayer at all. Others had been specifically attacking Paula White for months. She was an evangelical, they didn't like that, and in a hilarious bit of contortionism, they had suddenly assumed the mantle of arbitrators of Christian doctrine. Now, in addition to dictating who the American people should vote for in elections, they were now telling them what their religious doctrines should be, if they had to have any. She was a heretic, they said, married three times, a preacher of the "prosperity gospel."

Donald Trump, who was a billionaire, who had also been married three times himself, was not impressed by the new theological expertise of the American media.

When Paula tried to offer a suggestion, he shouted her down. "You're praying." That was final.

"Well, Mr. Trump, sir," she said gently, "I think I have a truly Trumpian idea for the inaugural prayer." She then proceeded to lay out the concept that was eventually accepted. There would be multiple preachers. Black, white, Catholic, Protestant, Eastern Orthodox, and Jewish. There would be Franklin Graham too. They would all pray.

Steve Bannon and Reince Priebus were enthusiastic about the idea. The president-elect smiled. The woman who had been leading teams of praying people for Donald Trump for eighteen years didn't mind sharing the stage with others. It would be Paula White who insisted that Pastor Jeffress preach the Trump family church service at Saint John's Episcopal Church the morning of the inauguration.

Jared Kushner, ever bright and observant, had not missed the fact that his father-in-law had tapped into a significant sociocultural religious bloc of voters, one that the national media despised, but one that no successful politician in America could ignore. On a trip to Liberty University, where they would meet with Jerry Falwell Jr., he pumped Paula White for explanations about how the various theological traditions evolved and what distinguished the denominations and why.

"SO WHO DO YOU WANT ON THE SUPREME COURT?"

Punch and cookies in the Roosevelt Room of the White House had been about as far as evangelicals ever seemed to get. Conservative Catholics and Mormons excelled, not because they were media favorites but because they had long been interested in government and had been willing to work inside the process.

This had been one of the big complaints from evangelicals during the Reagan-Bush years, the lack of representation among federal judges. While the national media promoted "diversity," it systematically excluded 40 percent of the American population who claimed to be born-again Christians. In 1988, while working on the George H. W. Bush presidential campaign I was given a study claiming that out of 749 federal judges surveyed, fewer than four identified themselves as born-again Christians. At the time, political figues routinely listed their religions in official biographies. In this case, four judges were representing almost half of the American population. Evangelicals argued that the absence of judges who understood their faith was leading to misunderstandings in the application of law, particularly to non-profit laws and the chuches' relationships with the IRS.

The Constitution makes clear that there should be no religious test for office, which was exactly the point that the evangelicals were making: If there was no test, why were they not getting appointments? Why had they been systematically excluded?

Before his death, Justice Antonin Scalia, a Catholic, bemoaned the fact that the Supreme Court was so unrepresentative of the American people and wondered if there shouldn't one day be an evangelical.[21] Six justices were Catholic, three were Jewish. Five were from the greater New York City metropolitan area, two from California. Four went to Harvard, three to Yale, and two to Stanford.

With Trump in office, evangelicals were hopeful that if they had no judges in the pipeline, they would at least be consulted and be part of the process. As chief executive, Trump "issued an order enforcing First Amendment protections for religious liberty." He restored "the freedom of military chaplains to espouse biblical morality." He essentially reversed President Obama's transgender military policy. He revoked the Education Department's order that public schools allow gender-confused males access to girls' restrooms and locker rooms. He cracked down on sex trafficking, signing a law allowing states to move against sex advertisement on internet sites that trafficked in children.[22]

Jerry Falwell Jr., the president of Liberty University, and the televangelist James Robison said they were experiencing greater access to Trump than any other president. Falwell, one of Trump's earliest supporters, told the *Washington Post*, "I think Trump is more one of us. He's not an elitist. He doesn't look down his nose at evangelicals and Christians and conservatives. I'm very shocked by how accessible he is to so many. He answers his cellphone any time of the day or night."[23]

In February 2017, President Donald Trump convened a meeting of national leaders to discuss his upcoming appointment to the Supreme Court. Representatives from every group of people, of all sexual orientations and racial backgrounds, were invited into the White House. For the first time in years, evangelicals were not excluded.[24] Sitting to the president's right at one of the most important meetings was Paula White. Members of the national media were hysterical. Trump didn't seem to care.

★ 20 ★

TIFFANY'S TALE

"No matter the ridicule, you must stay true to what you
believe is in the best interest of everyone."
—TIFFANY TRUMP[1]

A s I reached the end of my work, I knew that my door into the
Trump family would soon be closing. There was still some
unfinished business, and I felt a greater urgency to get it done.
I wanted to start a discussion within the family about the legacy of
President Donald Trump and his administration and, perhaps just as
important, a discussion about the legacy of the Trump family. When
I learned that Tiffany Trump would be willing to answer questions, it
seemed like a perfect moment. She had spent her childhood in California, raised separately from the others. She would have a unique
perspective on the Trumps of New York and on the story of her father's
rise to the presidency.

Tiffany Trump was famous for never giving interviews. That is
never as in "never." She was the Garbo of the Trump children. The first
lady, Melania Trump, had given more interviews than Tiffany. If she
would agree to answer my questions, it would represent her first public
conversation since her father had been elected president.

Her discretion had not protected her. It had created a vacuum. As a result, she was the subject of constant fake stories. Journalists roamed freely, knowing that she would not venture out to correct them. According to one July 2019 headline, "Tiffany Trump Just Got Snubbed by Her Dad in a Big Way."[2] It was a story alleging that the president didn't want her help in the 2020 political reelection campaign. It was false. The fact was that working day to day on the campaign would mean giving up law school, something she didn't want to do. Her father totally agreed and said he would welcome her help on free weekends and when she was available for special rallies.

Other stories suggested that she didn't like her father and didn't want to be involved in his work. The stories alleged that she shunned her father's policies. These too were false. She is proud of her father. Their love for each other is strong.

In one of her last interviews, conducted the night before the 2016 election, Tiffany told Sean Hannity of Fox News, "It's hard but we know who our father is, and I think no tabloid can spread anything that will make us doubt that. We know the truth."[3]

Almost all the stories about Tiffany were accounts based on anonymous sources, claiming to be coming from her close friends. Meanwhile, inside the Trump family the bond was strong. The outside hostility only made it stronger. The two sisters, Ivanka and Tiffany, are especially close. Ivanka has often reached out a hand to her younger sister. Thanks to Ivanka, Tiffany had done modeling. She had made a connection at *Vogue*. Eric Trump is her buddy. And touchingly, as I would learn, Tiffany adores her little brother, Barron.

THE CALIFORNIA TRUMP

Tiffany Trump was born October 13, 1993, in West Palm Beach, Florida. She is the president's only child with his second wife, Marla Maples, and the fourth child in the Donald Trump family. Tiffany and her mother are best pals. In fact, I caught up with Tiffany on a return trip from Mallorca, Spain, where the two had been vacationing together.

I wanted to know how much this presidential business had been a part of Tiffany Trump's life. Could she name an exact day or time that she first became aware of her father's intention to run for president? Did she have earnest conversations with him like Don Trump Jr.? Did she remember him reading newspapers with exasperation like Eric? Or did she remember the family summit at Bedminster that Lara had talked about?

"It's a conversation that has been going on within my family all of my life," Tiffany said. "But speaking about it is far different than when it becomes a reality. I don't think there was any way to tangibly and mentally prepare for the impact my father's announcement would have on our lives.

"My dad's announcement came at the time that I was going into my senior year at the University of Pennsylvania, and being on a college campus during this time led to both positive conversations and challenging surprises amongst my friends and fellow students."

Life for a presidential candidate's son or daughter at a university cannot be easy, especially for the child of a Republican. American academia has been notoriously liberal for many years. One of the Nixon daughters was reportedly spit on by fellow students as she walked across campus.

George W. Bush had once expressed to me his concern about his own daughters being on campus during a presidential campaign. I had talked to him on the telephone in 1997 when he was the leader in the latest presidential preference poll. I asked him what he was going to do.

"I'm not going to run," he answered.

"Why not?" I asked. "You are at the head of the pack."

"Because of the girls," he said. He was referring to his twin daughters, Jenna and Barbara. "They would be in college then and it would ruin their lives."

"Did it ruin your life?" I asked.

"No," he said. "It made my life."[4]

How did being the daughter of Donald Trump, a controversial and unconventional political figure, affect the world of Tiffany Trump, the young student, at a time when campuses were more politically radical than ever before? According to many reports, free speech was now limited on many campuses.[5] Even beyond the classroom and academic discussions, how was her life impacted socially?

"Technology was a factor," Tiffany said. "And the growing influence of social media and online platforms played a large role in the impact it had on my family and my own life.

"One of the most challenging experiences for me," Tiffany said, "was even seeing friends I had in elementary school in California quickly judge me for simply supporting my father. Early in the campaign I chose to delete my Facebook account.

"Growing up as the daughter of Donald Trump I was accustomed to uninvited attention in the past, given his fame, but I had learned to protect myself from public exposure. Although at times it was difficult to handle the lack of anonymity, I adjusted. Instead of allowing external forces to rattle me, I focused on what I could control: pursuing my education and ensuring the authenticity of my own actions. However, when my father decided to run for president, the nature of the attention directed toward me shifted from curiosity to contempt and from interest to judgment."

BECOMING A PUBLIC FIGURE IN ONE DAY

Tiffany Trump's rebirth as a celebrity happened suddenly, without time to prepare. It was a jolting experience. She delivered her speech to the Republican National Convention and suddenly, with the flip of a switch, she was known to millions of people. She could not walk down the street or into a restaurant without being recognized. For the millions who missed that televised moment, there were many others on the street nearby, curators of public life, who could whisper, "Do you know who that is?"

She was living in New York City at the time. "I had been taking the subway alone to work," Tiffany said. "However, after the Republican convention it began to become a little more difficult to fly under the radar. I was instructed to take extra precautions for my security, which meant much longer commutes and less time simply walking in the city that I love."

If she had lost her anonymity, her career trajectory was also suddenly knocked off kilter.

"After my speech at the RNC I feel like there was more of a focus on me and what role I would have," Tiffany said. "The RNC was the first time I truly spoke about my father's run for president.

"I had an internship in New York City during this time. It was a great opportunity and truly exciting but now more eyes in the office were turned in my direction. I was being watched both out of curiosity and sadly out of blind contempt. It was clear that my life had changed forever."

What were her emotions and feelings on Election Night? Did she believe the early reports that her father would lose? At what point did she finally conclude he would win?

When it came to crunching the numbers, Tiffany turned out to be one of the more insightful members of the family. "I've grown up with the mentality that anything is possible and that things can change in a split second," she said. "I didn't believe the early reports, as I think it is nearly impossible to predict outcomes when there are so many factors at play."

What was she feeling backstage at the Hilton? Just before the whole family marched onstage? America's new first family?

"It's hard to really put my feelings in words, but it was both very humbling and surreal, as we didn't know exactly how our lives would change but it was clear that they would. What so many thought was the 'impossible' became reality."

THE LEGACY OF THE TRUMP FAMILY

How do various members of the Trump family feel about his legacy? How do they feel about the future of their own family brand? What has kept them together through all the pressure? What has kept them from familial rivalries?

"Eric, Ivanka, and I are in the same age group," Don Jr. says.[6] "We always had a bigger understanding. We've been lucky. I think we've seen what happens when something is driven into the ground by ego. This is true in a family or in a business. Perhaps there's an irony here because in our family you can see the importance of having an ego. You have to be driven to get anything done, but I think we also have had to keep an eye on its disastrous effects.

"A family-run business is really binary. It's rarely just okay. It's either good or it's terrible. More often than not, it's terrible because of divisions. So, yes, we have many of the Trump characteristics, we have a lot of competition, and yet I think we've always had a big picture of what those kinds of rivalries would do if left unchecked.

"Again, speaking for Eric, Ivanka, and myself, I think from a young age, we were exposed to a lot of media viciousness. Going through my parents' divorce when I was twelve years old. Watching it play out on the front pages of the New York City tabloids for a month. You know, I think it really created an us-versus-the-world scenario. For all the bad things that it caused it also brought us together. We just sort of defended ourselves and took care of ourselves.

"So, while we're not perfect, we may not agree on everything, I think we understand what the pitfalls of going to the mattresses would mean. We've always been able to speak together. We've always been pretty vocal about what we were thinking. We talk it out and sort it out.

"People are certainly trying to pit us against each other," Don Jr. said. "But it just doesn't work that way. It goes back to our youth. We experienced some of the cruel realities of the world. We know that many of the things that might divide us, many of the rivalries, are created by nonsense. We've always had a unique ability to stick together, to be that childhood unit that we were when I was twelve, Ivanka was eight, and Eric was six. I think Eric will tell you that I was a big mentor to him growing up. We've always had that sort of relationship, where we're really as close as you can be as a family, and that's the way it's always been."

I asked Eric Trump how often he gets back to the White House. How often does he check in with the president? "I'm there once every couple of weeks. I speak with my father often. He has placed tremendous trust in me, and we have long been very close."

How has power affected the president? How has it affected the family?

"That day in the elevator," Eric said, "that day that Don talks about. When my father told us, 'We are quickly going to know who our real friends are,' he was right. I still chuckle thinking about all the text messages that came in the day after we won. It took most of the day just to respond to them. I got messages from people I hadn't heard from in six months, saying, 'Congratulations, buddy. I was there the entire time. I just didn't want to disrupt you. I knew how busy you were.'

"It's funny. 'You're right. I didn't hear from you. Now you want to be on the winning team.' The world is a fickle place."

I asked Donald Trump Jr. how the White House years had changed the family.

"We are just trying to experience some of the amazing things that we now have access to that we will never have again. Even my father said, 'Whether it's the best or the worst presidency in history, you have a finite window to be able to see this piece of America. You should try to experience what you can, because it is truly incredible.'

"That's how I feel," Don Jr. said. "This is the greatest nation in the world. To be able to see things and experience things at this level is truly amazing. To be able to roam the White House, to campaign across the country. To be able to see the results of our father's hard work. To see the dreams he's had for this country coming true. To see, every day, hardworking Americans getting those new jobs, well, it makes all the adversity, all the hell, all of the media lies, even the witch hunts against my father, it makes them all worthwhile.

"I can tell you, my father, the boy from Queens, is still amazed to this day that he is president. He does not take it lightly. He believes in the magnitude, the gravity of what he has to do. He is still moved by the fact that people elected him. He is not jaded. He is totally focused on doing what is right, no matter how it is misinterpreted by others.

"He is impressed by America. He loves the American people. He is so happy to see the jobs come back, so happy to see minorities and the disenfranchised now experiencing the American dream, so happy to see those people in Pennsylvania, Michigan, Wisconsin, and Ohio who had been forgotten now turning things around. He feels the responsibility to do more, and he is working constantly to find more jobs to help more Americans."

TIFFANY AT THE WHITE HOUSE

If the White House had interrupted the family business adventure in New York City, it had curiously brought Tiffany Trump full circle, back to her father and the center of the Trump family. Now attending law school in Georgetown, she is only blocks from Jared and Ivanka's house and her little nephews and niece. She is only blocks from the White House and her father and her little brother.

"I tend to go to the White House to see my dad and stop by to say hi to Melania and Barron about every week. It's nice that my law school is so close that I'm able to stop by and see Barron playing soccer in the yard after school.

"Being a student at a law school university definitely comes with a lot of curiosity from my peers. The past two years have been filled with some awkwardly funny moments and other more serious and scrutinizing moments."

I asked Tiffany if she could describe the disconnect between public perceptions about the Trumps and the reality. There had been so many false stories, filled with false quotes. On the evening of January 20, 2017, right after the inauguration, a *Time* magazine reporter, Zeke Miller, wrote a story claiming that the new president had removed the bust of Martin Luther King Jr. from the Oval Office.[7] It was false. The disinformation never stopped. Two years later, Ian Bremmer, a New York University professor and columnist for *Time* magazine, posted a tweet with Trump saying, "Kim Jong Un is smarter and would make a better President than Sleepy Joe Biden."[8] It was a false quote, of course, but the professor defended it saying it was "kinda plausible."[9] He later deleted the tweet.[10]

How was the Trump family different from the distorted image created by the Democratic-corporate media propaganda? What surprised people who got to know the family?

"We really are compassionate people," Tiffany said. "I wish that everyone had a chance to know each of us as individuals so that they could see the *true* us, which is different from many preconceived notions.

"What most people don't know is that I am the product of many divergent economic, religious, and social circles. The divide between the two sides of my family is striking. While my father is an affluent businessman from New York, my mother's family is from rural Georgia, where many of my relatives have been forced to forfeit jobs due to the high cost of gas.

"Similarly, I was not raised to identify with one religion: I was exposed to two. My mother took me to synagogue on Fridays and Saturdays and to church on Sundays. I grew up eating kosher and observing the Sabbath, while also reading the Bible and singing Christian hymns."

What secrets of success has she learned from her father's rise to power?

"The importance of having a clear vision and focusing your energy on tangible ways to make that goal a reality—no matter the ridicule, you must stay true to what you believe is in the best interest of everyone.

"To achieve success, you truly have to care about what it is you are doing, why you are fighting for it, and for whom you are fighting."

I asked Tiffany the question I had asked her brothers: What keeps the Trumps together as a family? Many families have deep divisions. FDR, a Democrat, had a son who opposed his reelection and years later became a big supporter of Ronald Reagan, a Republican. And Reagan had a son who spoke at the Democratic National Convention.[11]

"Having a common understanding and knowing who we are as a family continues to make us grow closer," Tiffany said. "Everyone in my family works very hard and has busy schedules, but although that may cause divides for many, for us, I believe our work ethic makes us closer and illustrates how similar we are."

What are her dreams and hopes for her life? For America?

"I dream that the citizens of the United States can find common ground and unity. There's too much division in the world we live in, and I believe it is crucial for everyone to listen to each other in order for us to become more united.

"My experiences, both private and public, have provided me with a heightened awareness of the necessity to treat everyone with dignity by seeking to understand others' opinions without judging their character. As I look to the future, I seek to play a role in healing the divides that have surfaced by being a voice of reason and a peaceful bridge builder. I hope to use my knowledge of the legal system as a tool to advocate for what I believe in and for those in the world who cannot do so for themselves.

"I look forward to the opportunity to define myself through my own actions, my own successes, and my own informed opinions—always listening, always learning, and always seeking to identify commonalities among differences."

TAKE ME TO BUCKINGHAM PALACE, PLEASE

On June 3, 2019, President Trump and the First Lady were hosted by Queen Elizabeth II and Prince Philip at a formal state dinner that was six months in the planning. A long list of administration officials made the trip to London with the president and were present at the royal event, including US ambassador Woody Johnson; the president's chief of staff, Mick Mulvaney; the US secretary of the treasury, Steve Mnuchin; the president's national security adviser, John Bolton; the White House press secretary, Sarah Huckabee Sanders; counselor to the president Kellyanne Conway; and many others.

The media was scandalized that the president had taken along his own family even though Jared and Ivanka Kushner were White House aides and had become indispensable to the administration. The media seemed to begrudge the Trumps any personal pleasure or honor, even if it was the natural consequence of their legitimate duties. Journalists were sure that no such thing had never happened before. As the author of *The Raising of a President* and *All the Presidents' Children*, I started getting calls from reporters.

No, it is nothing new, I assured them. They were disappointed. Theodore Roosevelt had dispatched his daughter Alice to meet with the empress dowager of China while the whole world watched transfixed. In 1933, newly elected president Franklin Roosevelt sent his son Jimmy, who was an insurance salesman, to meet alone with the prime minister of England and then on to meet with the president of France at the Élysée Palace. Before he had finished his diplomatic jaunt, Jimmy traveled on to Rome, to meet the pope and then huddle with Italian dictator Benito Mussolini.

In 1991, President George H. W. Bush made sure his own children got to attend a state dinner and personally meet Queen Elizabeth when she visited the United States. None of the children actually worked in government; the president simply wanted them to experience the moment. The eldest son (and future president), George W. Bush, grabbed headlines when he quipped to the queen, "I'm the black sheep in my family, who's yours?"

"None of your business," the queen tartly replied.[12]

Even with that history, the 2019 state dinner with Queen Elizabeth hosting the Trumps was something altogether different. There was great political and public controversy for extending such honors to Donald Trump. In the fall of 2017, the *Evening Standard* had made it clear that Trump would not be meeting the queen anytime soon.[13] It would not be proper. There would be demonstrations in the streets.

Some British pundits concluded that the unique Anglo-American relationship, especially in light of Brexit, was too important to play with. Her Majesty the Queen, they insisted, must bite her tongue and go ahead with it.

Other sage observers who knew the queen had long ago predicted that her avid curiosity and mischievous temperament would never have allowed her to miss hosting a Trump state dinner.[14] It was inevitable. A privately conducted name recognition poll allegedly showed, for better or worse, Donald Trump was the second-most-famous person on earth, after Jesus.[15] If the Trumps wanted to meet the queen, well, most likely the queen wanted to meet them too, although she could never admit it to anyone, not even to her corgis. It would be a superb moment for history.

This moment would see the coming together of two very different persons and families, representing very different sociocultural experiences. One family was staid and entrenched, the other brash and provocative. And yet both were masters at building and maintaining brands. On that subject, the queen was perhaps the only person in the world from whom the Trumps could still learn a thing or two. And the queen, who had met so many colorful world leaders and celebrities—well, it would have been a shame to miss the Trumps. They may be only flashing meteors passing overhead, but oh how brightly they shine! To add the trophy of their faces to her vast collection of the world's most famous and infamous personalities who had dined at her table was a nice win for history. She needed Donald and Melania, but she needed Ivanka and all the other Trumps, too.

That night, Donald Trump raised his glass to the queen. "On behalf of all Americans, I offer a toast to the eternal friendship of our people, the vitality of our nations, and to the long, cherished, and truly remarkable reign of her majesty the queen."[16]

What no one knew is the informal way in which the Trump kids arrived at the event. It wasn't in a fairy tale, golden carriage pulled by six white horses or even in a presidential motorcade of limousines, with drivers in smart uniforms.

"During the state visit in the UK"—Tiffany laughed as she recalled the memory—"my siblings and I took a large van or bus to Buckingham Palace. It was fun as we were all in gowns and tuxes and piled into the bus. It was as if we were in a carpool, but our destination was quite more extravagant than going to school!"

★ 21 ★

MELANIA'S REVENGE

"The problem is they're writing history and it's not correct."
—MELANIA TRUMP TO SEAN HANNITY[1]

As in the case of her husband, Donald Trump, the first lady, Melania Trump, did not come to the White House via a traditional path. Most first ladies arrive as the wife of a politician or a general. The latter was often synonymous with the former, for it takes great people skills to rise to the top in the military. Melania was the wife of a businessman and was herself a career woman with dreams and plans and products she launched.

Melania was born and raised in Slovenia, an enchanting, small country in the Balkans, with a narrow, tentative link to the Adriatic coast, which they proudly celebrate. Its capital city, Ljubljana, has a castle on a hilltop in its center. Melania is only the second first lady in history to be born outside of the United States, the other being Louisa Catherine Johnson, the wife of the sixth president, John Quincy Adams. Louisa Catherine was born in London.[2]

The Slovenia that Melania knew as a child was a part of Yugoslavia, a Communist country that walked a high wire between the two

towering Communist nations, the Soviet Union and the People's Republic of China. I visited Ljubljana on several occasions and tried to
pick up on some of the unique culture and customs.

Slovenia was an atheist state at the time of Melania's birth on April
26, 1970. Posters of the Yugoslavian dictator, Josip Tito, were everywhere.[3] There were no Christmas trees, although it was permissible to
buy a "New Year's tree." Easter was known and sometimes practiced
quietly at home but not by persons in prominent positions. The director
or foreman at a factory, for example, could lose his job over such care-
lessness. Still, it was an improvement on life in the Soviet Union, where
both Christmas and Easter were strictly forbidden. In the seventies,
schoolteachers often teased their children to find out which families
might be privately practicing Christianity at home. If discovered, they
would be reported to the state. The day after Easter, a teacher might
ask the classroom, "Children, did anyone have any special cakes or
food yesterday?" The Christian could be ferreted out and the family
identified. In a Communist country, one learned to keep one's mouth
shut. Especially in front of children.

Melania's father, Viktor Knavs, was a member of the League of
Communists of Slovenia, but he nonetheless, arranged for Melania to
be secretly baptized as a Roman Catholic. After Jacqueline Kennedy,
she is the second first lady in American history to practice the Catholic
faith, although several presidential daughters have been Catholic.

Life in a totalitarian state, where neighbor often spied on neighbor, and each block had its own political monitor, may have prepared
Melania for the vicious political and media attacks that have come her
way as first lady. They also give her a perspective on America that no
other first lady has ever had.

Growing up in Slovenia, Melania saw the United States as a place
where anything was possible. In America, "your dreams could come
true," she said. "You could do a lot of things. Whatever you decide
to do."[4]

Melania Trump speaks six languages fluently: English, Slovene, Serbo-Croatian, Italian, German, and French. In addition, White House sources told me that she can conduct simple conversations in many other languages.[5]

She has worked as a model in Milan, Italy, and Paris, even living for years in an apartment there. The media predictably ignored this story, but when she made her second trip to France as first lady, she was captured on television speaking French to the people of that country, and it made an indelible impression. My wife, who is French, was at home visiting her family when she saw the first lady on French television and heard the people of her tiny village exclaim with pride that the American first lady could speak their language.

Predictably, journalists and academics have expressed skepticism about the first lady's linguistic talents. They apparently fear it is a credit to her intelligence. Mastering such diverse languages—Slavic languages, Latin languages and then German and English, which are connected to neither of the former language families—does show remarkable skill and further provides Melania Trump with an understanding that no other first ladies have had. Federico Fellini once said, "A different language is a different vision of life."[6]

WHAT KIND OF FIRST LADY?

In 1999, when business tycoon Donald Trump was talking about running for president, his girlfriend, Melania Knavs, was asked by an ABC News reporter, Don Dahler, if she could picture herself as first lady. "Yes," she answered, saying that she would support Donald Trump and stand by him.

What kind of first lady would she be?

"I would be very traditional, like Jackie Kennedy and Betty Ford," she said.[7]

Melania Knavs Trump is not the only first lady to have developed an independent career of her own before coming to the White House. Lady

Bird Johnson was a successful businesswoman who ran companies, including media properties. When her husband died, she ran them alone, with her daughters. Nancy Reagan had been an accomplished actress. Hillary Rodham Clinton was a lawyer. Laura Bush was a librarian. Nevertheless, Melania Trump comes to the White House with a unique set of skills. As a fashion model she learned how to look, how to dress, how to obscure her own personal feelings and project confidence. She brought to the White House something that every first lady desires to project: poise and elegance.

Some say that the role of first lady should be changing because the role of women is changing. And thus a first lady who deals only with ceremonial and domestic chores is diminished when compared with a career woman, one who enters public life on her own merits, with her own political ambitions.

This is a thorny business. A president's wife is not elected. The German people voted for Angela Merkel as their leader. Should her husband serve as a co-leader? Is he diminished as a man if he does not assert himself in her government?

When Bill Clinton said, "You get two for the price of one," meaning that Hillary was going to help him run the country, it was not well received. Hillary eventually had to establish her own identity and political success, separate from him.

The modern role of first lady is further complicated by the fact that it has grown in responsibility. In the United Kingdom, there is a monarch. In France, and in many other nations, there is a prime minister who runs the government day to day, giving its president greater freedom to fill the ceremonial role. In the United States both responsibilities fall on the shoulders of the president. This is where first ladies can play a critical role.

Add to that discussion the fact that many first ladies have also been mothers of small children. It was a role that Jackie Kennedy played and that Michelle Obama performed as well. It is a role that Melania

Trump, with her devotion to her son Barron, has made preeminent. She is devoted to the upbringing of her son and defies any criticism of that role.

It has been my humble privilege to work with six of our American first ladies. I co-chaired a charity event with Lady Bird Johnson, who was efficient and businesslike. I did the same in an East Room reception with Rosalynn Carter. She was bright and passionate. I co-chaired four events with Nancy Reagan, three in the White House, one afterward. She was a strong lady and one of impeccable taste and a sense for public relations. I co-chaired a charity event with George and Barbara Bush, with whom I later developed a long friendship. Barbara was a passionate reader who turned something she enjoyed into a cause. And later I co-chaired a charity event with George W. and Laura Bush. Some of these events involved many weeks of planning and preparation, and in the case of the Reagans, a chance to get to know them.

One can appreciate Melania Trump's wisdom by her choice of causes. Lady Bird was ridiculed for ignoring the plight of the poor and making her cause the spread of wildflowers along American highways. Nancy Reagan was laughed at for being naive, telling drug users, "Just say no." Both Barbara and Laura Bush were criticized for making literacy their cause, when there were so many life-and-death issues. But while the media despised the new President Trump, and so were prepared to reject his first lady, they could hardly knock her cause.

When Melania Trump launched her "Be Best" campaign, taking up the issue of internet bullying of children, the media turned their ferocity on her, claiming that her husband was the biggest internet bully of them all. How dare she speak out on this issue?

The first lady responded with grace. In March, 2018 she slipped into a White House roundtable meeting with technology executives, dropping the comment, "I am well aware that people are skeptical of me discussing this topic. . . . But it will not stop me from doing what I know is right."[8]

Meanwhile, the wisdom of Melania Trump's choice of a cause became increasingly apparent. How could the media attack her issue of cyberbullying without proving her point?

MELANIA AND A HOSTILE MEDIA

Even in 1999, the media seemed to be seeking to divide the couple, asking questions about Melania's motives in their relationship and then invoking Donald's controversial lifestyle. "They don't know me," Melania said of the critics then, describing Donald Trump as "very kind" and "very charming."[9]

A reporter asked her at the time if she was "in love" with Donald Trump. Yes, Melania said.

She seemed to know instinctively that the media was something with which she would have to live. "I like to have my private life, too. Yes, but I'm always open. I'm not shy of the media. I'm not shy about the camera. That's my business. That's my modeling career. But it sometimes could be very tricky and unpleasant, unfair."[10]

In this interview, twenty years ago, the future first lady was already showing signs of wariness about journalists. She talked about being "misquoted" in past stories. Even then, Melania was using her poise and her beauty to deflect questions that could have stirred controversy. "Media can be very tricky sometimes," she said. "You need to be very careful."[11]

What kind of president would Donald Trump make? "He would be a great leader," Melania said. She thought his business skills would work to his advantage.[12]

Don Jr. sees the recent attacks on the first lady as a means to hurt the president. It is shades of the old movie plot in which the villain realizes that he can't break the hero so he turns his wrath on the hero's family. "Give me what I want or I will hurt the person you love."

"Most of the attacks on her are just to hurt him," Don Jr. said to me. "Since they can't break him, they turn their guns on her, someone who is innocent. So maybe he can take it, but does he really want to see her get hurt by this, too?

"At first you got some ludicrous stories. 'Oh my God, she is being held captive in the White House.' They were giving her a chance. 'Denounce your husband and we will go easy on you, we won't blame you. It's not your fault.'

"The problem with that approach is that they in fact have a very good relationship. They always have had a good relationship. So when the media realized that they couldn't divide them, they turned on her with a vengeance."[13]

Lara Trump is equally sanguine about the first lady. "She's an incredibly smart woman, and people don't give her nearly enough credit. When you look at the past first ladies, there is a totally different standard. The media criticism is so overdone that it actually backfires."[14]

White House press secretary Stephanie Grisham fought back with an op-ed. Responding to a historian's criticism of the first lady, she pointed out that Melania had recently "hosted a successful state dinner and dozens of holiday events at the White House. She has led restoration and preservation efforts in the residence. She has welcomed numerous foreign heads of state to the White House. And, most recently, she has represented the country at a state funeral."[15]

Grisham followed with a credible list of work the first lady had accomplished, trips she had made to suffering Americans and troubled children, victims of hurricanes and flooding, and the families of victims of school shootings. Where there has been pain in this country, the first lady has been the first on the scene.[16]

While the president respects his wife's independence and does not often publicly wade into the media's treatment of her, he is surely aware of what they are doing. We got into a discussion about it during our lunch. President Trump and I were talking about the comparisons between himself and President Andrew Jackson, when Jackson's wife, Rachel, came up.

"Tell me about her," Donald Trump said.

"Well, you know the story?" I asked.

"Tell me," he insisted. I got the very clear impression that he knew the story full well but still wanted my version. This was one of those occasions I had been hearing about. I had been told that Donald Trump could be a patient listener. Jared Kushner had talked about the meeting with President Xi at Mar-a-Lago, when President Trump had asked questions and then listened for the longest time to stories about Chinese history.

So I told Donald Trump the story. Rachel Jackson's first husband had disappeared and after many years was declared dead. She had subsequently remarried, this time to Andrew Jackson. But years later, when the presidential election heated up, it was learned that her first husband, while deceased, had actually been alive at the time of her second marriage.

Newspapers had a field day. Rachel Jackson was blasted as an adulterer and a bigamist.

Fortunately, she knew nothing about it. She was protected at the Jackson homestead, the Hermitage, carefully shielded from the political carnage. When Andrew Jackson won the election of 1828 and was the nation's president-elect, Rachel and her lady friends made the joyous trek into Nashville to buy a new dress for the inaugural ball.

Rachel's girlfriends were under strict orders to keep her away from any old publications laying around. But the old newspapers were stacked up in all the dress shops of Nashville, and Rachel was soon devouring every line of the salacious stories that had been hidden from her during the campaign.

Deeply religious, even saintly, Rachel Jackson was mortified. She went into a deep depression, stayed in bed, and eventually died before the inauguration. She was America's first lady, but she never set foot in the White House and she never wore the beautiful dress she had purchased that day in Nashville with her girlfriends.

At this, President Trump looked thoughtful and didn't say a word.

MELANIA AND DONALD, A LOVE AFFAIR

Donald and Melania Trump were married January 22, 2005, in Palm Beach, Florida, at the church Bethesda-by-the-Sea. Bill and Hillary Clinton were among the stellar list of celebrity guests. Billy Joel sang to the couple. Wedding guests would have been forgiven if they had whispered to their partners, "Just remember, when you shake Hillary Clinton's hand, you will be shaking the hand of the first woman president in American history." Donald and Melania spent their honeymoon at the Mar-a-Lago resort. Barron, their baby son, was born a year later.

Sources told me that in almost any conversation with the president, he will mention his wife, Melania. That happened at our luncheon. I was surprised by this. Perhaps I had been unwittingly influenced by the critical media narrative of everything Trump, including the interpretation of their marriage. The image of the first lady that came from my own interactions with the president showed a woman very much invested in the legacy of her husband and his administration. This was a close couple who faced the unprecedented outside hostility together. The first lady was very much in the game, which, of course, made sense. How could the success of any of the other members of the Trump family, including Melania, survive the one? The president himself? For good or bad, they were linked.

This is not to contradict the idea of her fiercely contested independence. "I have my own voice and my opinions," she says, "and it's very important to me that I express how I feel."[17]

She has been known to speak up and sometimes in political matters. "I don't always agree with what he tweets, and I tell him that," she said.[18]

Before the famous announcement for president in 2015, Lara Trump remembers a big discussion at the Trump family compound in Bedminster, New Jersey. "Well, I'm sure you've heard how the first lady has always told him he would win. That's so true. There was never a doubt from her. She believed in him. From day one, she always believed in him."[19]

"We had dinner on the president's birthday two days before he announced he was running for president," Lara Trump told me. "And we all talked about it as a family. He said, 'You know, this is something that's going to happen. If anybody has any thoughts on it, let's talk about it now. They're going to come after us.'

"Of course, we didn't know how bad it was going to be. But I remember that night, he turned to Melania, and he said, 'Honey, what do you think?'

"She goes, 'If you're going to run, you're going to win.' It was just like that. Matter of fact. And she was always consistent about it, even with all of the ups and downs on election night."

Lara described the drama at Trump Tower. "You remember me describing how we were all gathered around televisions on the fourteenth floor and then we moved up to the private apartment. And finally into the kitchen. Here was this big crowd of people gathered around watching all the final results from Michigan and Pennsylvania, coming in on this tiny TV. And even before they called the election Melania had officially declared it to the family. 'I told you. I told you.' She was right and she had known it from day one."

Journalists often try to look for a wedge between the first couple. The president was known for calling out, "Where's my supermodel?" Was this demeaning? Melania was once asked.

She only smiled. "It's his sense of humor."[20]

Other members of the Trump family insisted that the two, the president and the first lady, were often playful in their repartee. For example, while outwardly, officially, the various Trump family members would talk about what a privilege it was to serve their country, and you could ask them how they were holding up to the scurrilous public attacks and they would all answer back graciously, the fact was that privately, it was a nightmare, and they all knew it. No first family in recent memory had gone through what they were going through. It was much worse than Donald Trump's original warnings back at the family meeting in Bedminster, New Jersey.

The president would occasionally ease the tension by teasing the first lady, saying, sarcastically, with puffed up importance, "Melania, honey, look at this incredible journey I have brought you on."

"It's like a joke between them at every dinner," Lara says. "Everyone is attacking all of us and she's smeared for no reason other than pure jealousy and he says, 'Hon, isn't this amazing? This journey that I have allowed you to come on?'

"And she's like, 'Oh yeah, thank you so much.'

"It's hilarious. I love it."

THE TRIP TO AFRICA

In 2018 First Lady Melania Trump visited Ghana, Malawi, Kenya, and Egypt. It was her first major solo foreign trip, and it was a rousing success. She said that she wanted "to show the world that we care."[21]

It worked.

"Mrs. Trump has always envisioned her first international trip would be Africa," said Stephanie Grisham, her press secretary. "So, we've known we would be doing this since the very beginning."[22]

The trip focused on humanitarian issues, including healthcare, conservation, and education. There was also an emphasis on tourism, a major source of hard currency for many economically challenged countries of Africa.

In Ghana, Mrs. Trump toured the Cape Coast Castle, where slaves were held before their transport to North America by the British. She was deeply moved. "This is a very special place," she said. "I will never forget the incredible experience and the stories that I heard."[23]

When Mrs. Trump visited the pyramids outside Cairo, journalists and photographers had a field day, taking hundreds of pictures and describing every piece of her clothing for fashion websites. During a rare press conference, Mrs. Trump was continually asked questions about her wardrobe, "You know what?" she said. "We just completed an amazing trip. We went to Ghana. We went to Malawi. We went to Kenya. Now here we are in Egypt. I want to talk about my trip and not what I wear."[24]

Still, the president was pleased by the favorable international press. "The first lady did a tremendous job representing our country in Africa—like no one has before," Trump said. "She got to know firsthand the people of Africa, and they loved and respected her everywhere she went. Melania told me about her trip in great detail, and I'm so proud of the job she's doing on behalf of children everywhere. She works so hard, and does it all out of love."[25]

Melania's compassion has led to projects far beyond her antibullying campaign and unexpectantly touched the lives of private and public figures. Such is the story of Eric Bolling.

Bolling, the former host of the hit Fox News show *The Five*, was headed home on a beautiful Friday night. He and his wife, Adrienne, had just enjoyed a nice dinner together. It was approximately ten thirty. His cell phone rang.

"As a parent your stomach drops," he remembers. He was expecting a call from his son. "The girl on the other line was crying. I don't know why I immediately went there but I said, 'Kayla'—it was a girl he was dating at the University of Colorado—'is he still alive?' And through her tears she said, 'No.'"[26]

Adrienne had heard that word—"No"—from the cell phone. She immediately pulled their car over to the side of the road and let the speeding traffic pass by. Their son had purchased what he thought was a real Xanax tablet on campus. They would later learn that it was "a Chinese knockoff laced with the deadly fentanyl drug."[27]

Donald Trump called him the next day. "Eric, Melania, and I are so sorry. We will do what we can to help." Bolling and his wife were in shock.

The Thanksgiving holiday came two weeks later. "We were headed to the Thanksgiving dinner table," Eric remembers. "That empty seat was looming ominously. I swear to you, the phone rang as we were approaching the table. It was President Trump and the first lady calling to send their love and support, knowing that the holidays were going to be rough. They were right."

Eric Bolling launched a fifteen-city tour to talk about the dangers of opioid drugs. First Lady Melania Trump joined the tour and soon became the preeminent spokesperson. People waited for hours to see her and tell her their own tragic stories, which often ended in weeping.

The first lady determined to be proactive and make the cause preventative. She told audiences how she had shared the dangers of the crisis with her son Barron and urged other mothers and fathers to "have the talk" before it was too late. Texts and testimonials came in with countless stories of brokenhearted parents, and many of them thanked her for speaking so freely about the issue.

On May 7, 2019, Eric Bolling stood in the Rose Garden of the White House and spoke to Melania Trump. "First Lady, you've raised awareness about a deadly killer. You've helped lift the stigma, which will save countless of lives going forward. Best of all, you're saving our children, our babies, as young as ten, eleven, and twelve years old. We are losing thousands of them. We love them. America thanks you, First Lady.

"When the history books are written," Bolling said, "there should be a special chapter reserved for our first lady. Many first ladies have focused on making our lives better, and they have. But you, First Lady Melania Trump, have gone one step further and saved lives."[28]

In Melania Trump we may be witnessing the unfolding story of one of America's greatest first ladies. She has carved out a unique role as a champion for children, an advocate for victims of the opioid crisis, and the president's quiet diplomat. She moves graciously and silently from one hospital bed to the next, like an American version of Lady Diana, but she does so unheralded and unseen. Her "Be Best" anticyberbullying campaign has gone viral. Bolling calls her "The most important and accomplished first lady in American history."[29]

GRACE UNDER PRESSURE

One of Melania Trump's greatest gifts to the nation has been her gracious response to the media and the political vitriol directed at her. One could argue that the more outrageous and unfair the criticism, the more remarkable and impressive has been her elegant response. She holds her head up high and soldiers on. Her poise and her kindly confidence infuriate Donald Trump's opponents.

Late-night comedians mock her accent. April Ryan of CNN shamelessly declared that Melania was "not culturally American."[30] MSNBC anchor Nicolle Wallace suggested that both first lady Melania and first daughter Ivanka had to be "paid off." "Are they just the most stoic human beings, are they numb, are they dead inside, are they paid off, I mean, what's their deal?" Wallace asked.[31]

CNN reporter Brian Stelter saw sinister issues behind the fact that the first lady was not in the public eye for several days at one point.[32] In truth, she was recovering after a five-day hospital stay for treatment for a kidney condition.

The television personality Joy Behar said that before coming to America, the first lady "was in Slovenia doing nothing."[33]

Sometimes the mean-spirited snub of Melania Trump bordered on schoolgirl immaturity. At a 2017 event, Anna Wintour, the editor in chief of *Vogue*, ignored repeated questions about the beautiful and fashionable American first lady, Melania Trump, and insisted peevishly that Michelle Obama "was the best ambassador this country could possibly have in many ways, obviously, way beyond fashion."[34]

Melania had been impressed with Mrs. Obama. After their first meeting, President Donald Trump had tweeted, "Melania liked Mrs. O a lot!"[35] Months later, when the Trumps showed up at the White House for Inauguration Day, Melania had brought Mrs. Obama a present wrapped in a Tiffany blue box. Mrs. Obama held her fire, refusing to criticize Mrs. Trump but not hesitating to attack her husband.

On June 17, 2018, former first lady Laura Bush wrote an op-ed condemning the separation of children from parents who had been arrested illegally entering the United States. She called the policy cruel and immoral, and said that "it breaks my heart."[36] The national media went crazy with approbation. The Trumps were pilloried. Lost in the circus was the fact that Mrs. Trump had also argued against the policy, that the president himself was trying to get Congress to change the law, and the fact that such a policy applied to all violations of the law, including those that occurred to people arrested under Barack Obama and George W. Bush, Laura's husband. In fact, the majority of the photos and videos that the national media were using to illustrate their stories came from the Obama era.

What also went unmentioned by the media and the former first lady was the fact that her husband, President George W. Bush, had invaded Iraq on what some historians see as false pretenses, claiming that there were weapons of mass destruction, and in the process killed 110,600 people in Iraq alone, including an estimated 20,000 children.[37]

Months after the former first lady's attack on the Trumps, the Bush family gathered in Washington for the funeral of former president George H. W. Bush. The Trumps, including the first lady, opened their hearts and the White House to the visiting former first family. The Bushes, their children, grandchildren, and siblings were all hosted in Blair House like heads of state.[38]

"I gave the order," Donald Trump told me. Trump knew that I had once worked for George H. W. Bush and had coauthored a book with him. "I wanted to make sure that the Bush funeral had every possible courtesy extended," he said. "The use of the planes, for example, to make the funeral a worthy state event, a truly memorable one for history."[39]

George W. Bush once confided to me how hurt he and his siblings had been by the fact that the Reagans had shut them out of the private quarters of the White House when their father was serving as vice president.[40] But Melania Trump, who had only months before seen her husband strongly criticized by the former first lady, offered every kindness to the Bushes and their children. Melania gave the whole Bush family the tour that the Reagans had not and allowed them the pleasure of revisiting all of the old rooms and places that had once been their home, sharing their memories with grandchildren, cousins, and other extended members of the family who had heard the stories but never seen many of the private rooms of the White House.

When Melania Trump was asked by a journalist why she had taken up the cause of cyberbullying and created her "Be Best" campaign, she smiled thoughtfully and said, "I am the most bullied person in the world."[41] In response to the false and acerbic media stories that assail her daily, she holds her head high and continues to reach out to the suffering.

Meanwhile, to the exasperation of her husband's critics, she remains his most loyal counselor. Remember that Christmas 2018, the one described in the introduction to this book? When Donald Trump told his family that he wouldn't be coming to Mar-a-Lago, that he would remain alone in the White House? And at the last minute, Melania raced back to the White House to be with him? On Christmas night they would travel to Iraq to visit the troops.

She would not let him go into a combat zone without her. All the insistent and authoritative lectures that the Secret Service could give could not dissuade her. Very few first ladies had ever done this before. It was a short visit, anyway. It was not necessary. The media would not care or give her any credit for the trip. It was immensely dangerous. None of that mattered. If he was in danger, she would share that danger with him. She would not let him go alone.

Many said that she had not wanted this life, they had enjoyed a good life before. She had implored him, "Why do you want to do this?" But Donald Trump had chosen to run for president. She had known all along that he would win. They were partners, lovers. She would do her duty and see it all through to the end. Honorably and loyally.

History will soon forget the bitter, angry voices of Melania's critics. Unfortunately for those antagonists, the stories, the photographs, and the video record of this remarkable first lady will survive and be witnesses against their pettiness and jealousy. Future generations will be able to see for themselves this elegant woman who glides softly through the angry storm of critics who try to hurt her and her son. There will be the future equivalent of entire bookshelves full of stories about this enigmatic and mysterious first lady. The envious and spiteful critics who snap at her and who are tormented by her power and poise will be long forgotten. History will provide Melania's revenge.

★ 22 ★

YOU CAN CALL HIM GREAT

*"The more my father succeeds, the more his enemies
hate him but they will never stop him from doing
what he knows is right."*
—Eric Trump[1]

How does Donald Trump compare with other American presidents? What will be his legacy? Presidents are ranked based on a long list of criteria, but it is safe to say that they are primarily judged on their handling of the economy, on wars, on their ability to communicate, and on their personal intelligence. As of this moment, at this writing, on the basis of this remarkable economic boom alone, even should there be a recession and a war in his last year in office, even if there should be an impeachment, history would have to say that Donald Trump is one of America's greatest presidents.

Traditionally, the economy towers over all other factors in rating a president. For example, Jimmy Carter is one of the most intelligent persons to have held the office. A graduate of the U.S. Naval Academy, he pursued graduate studies in nuclear physics at Union College in Schenectady, New York.[2] Yet he is usually ranked as a poor president. George W. Bush is hailed by some as a great "warrior president," having decisively defeated Iraq in a volatile region of the world, but he too is increasingly ranked poorly. First for the dubious rationale for his war and second because it practically bankrupted the country. In both cases, Carter and Bush, the US economy suffered greatly, hurting the reputations of an "intelligent president" and "a warrior president." On the other hand, Bill Clinton was impeached, yet his balanced economy offers him remarkable historical resiliency.

Donald Trump's war record may be an inverse credit to his account. While it is still very possible that we will have a war with Iran during his last year of his first term, as of this writing, he is the first president in forty years to avoid involving the United States in a new hot war. Trump, for all the fear he engenders in a hostile American media, is a president of peace.

When it comes to communication, another of the metrics of presidential greatness, historians look for soaring rhetoric that can be etched in marble. Jefferson, Lincoln, FDR, Kennedy, and Reagan come to mind. But Donald Trump has been a transformational communicator. His use of social media has changed American politics forever. Indeed, world politics and international diplomacy will never be the same again. In 2019, when I talked with him about Andrew Jackson and how that president had organized his alliance of pro-Jacksonian newspapers, Trump only smiled and said, "I've got Twitter."[3]

When it comes to intelligence, critics are loath to credit Donald Trump, on the grounds that he arrogantly claims it for himself, but one must ask how was he able to see what every great economists in the world had missed. Was it luck? Was getting elected luck? Was creating jobs luck? Was he lucky in bringing back hostages that other presidents had left languishing in foreign prisons? Was defeating ISIS so easily just luck?

Of course, it is much too early to be having such conversations. The presidency of George W. Bush, which had an approval rating of 90 percent in 2001, collapsed into utter failure his last year in office.[4] With the economy in free fall, Bush, a so-called conservative Republican, did what only a socialist government in Europe would do. He nationalized the banks.[5] Before he left office, his approval rating was registering an anemic 25 percent.[6]

Then there is the question of whether or not the American national media and Euro-American academia will even allow Donald Trump to be considered great, no matter what he does or doesn't do in his remaining year in office and what he should achieve in a second term. Numbers be damned. If the American media can insist with a straight face that Donald Trump is a Russian spy and maintain that assertion, without evidence, for three years, they should have little trouble promoting the idea that he is a bad president in spite of what he has done to reduce poverty and economic misery for masses of Americans. They will simply inflate a market correction and turn it into an economic crisis. They can easily stack the historical deck against him. Didn't Napoleon himself once quote the adage that "history is but a fable agreed upon?"[7] Since when do numbers speak louder than the subjective opinion of the world's elites? Why would they want to honor a man who has diverted their monopolistic streams of income to masses of people who are only lower middle class or even poor? The people who FBI agent Peter Strzok said "smell"? The people whom Hillary Clinton threw into a "basket of deplorables"?

The answer is that none of that matters to me. My job is not to anticipate what will please wealthy media elites or academic critics but to write what I heard and found in my unique journey inside the world of Trump. That's all. And to offer my own opinion, without shame, based on what I have seen and heard, regardless of how it resonates.

TRUMP'S ECONOMY IN HISTORY

Herbert Hoover was everything the modern media seems to desire in a president. He was erudite, measured, politically correct, even courtly. He was also demonstratively compassionate, having saved Europe from famine after World War I. Hoover was a brilliant engineer. The Hoover Institute is a proud fixture of Stanford University. But Herbert Hoover is ranked as one of the worst presidents in American history. He led the nation into its most devastating depression. Hundreds of thousands of Americans lived in hunger and suffered from malnutrition. There were squalid cities of homeless people that sprang up near garbage dumps across the country. They were called "Hoovervilles." They had no water or sewage. Mothers made soup for their children by boiling the roots of weeds. People scavenged for food among the garbage.

This is the suffering that a bad president brings to a country.

Donald Trump is the anti–Herbert Hoover president. He is direct, tough, controversial, and decisive. He has rough edges and can say and do outrageous things. He is not politically correct. But in his first three years in office, he has presided over one of the greatest, longest economic booms in American history. Everything that socialist engineers and liberal politicians have ever wanted for the poor or the disenfranchised, the persecuted minorities, has apparently happened through free markets on Donald Trump's watch. Since he took office, more than 6 million Americans have been able to get off food stamps.[8]

By the time Trump announced for reelection, June 19, 2019, America had added over six million new jobs. The stock market was up 55 percent. Wages were up. Unemployment was down. Records were being broken among every demographic: African American and Hispanic unemployment had reached record lows. Youth unemployment was the lowest since President John F. Kennedy. Costs of health care were down, and prescription drug prices were declining for the first time in forty-six years.[9]

Moments that economists thought America would never see again were now starting to happen. A *Forbes* magazine study found that in Trump's first two years his economy had added 467,000 manufacturing jobs. Such numbers were considered an impossibility only a few years before. In Trump's first two years he had created six times more manufacturing jobs than Obama's economy had created in any of his best two years.[10] Economists were now anticipating that Trump's renegotiated version of NAFTA would create another 176,000 manufacturing jobs.

During the Great Depression, fifteen million people were out of work. By Trump's third year in office there were seven million unfilled jobs in America.[11]

The American Left, prominently featured by the corporate media, promotes the idea that only the wealthy benefit from Trump's economic miracle. It is not true. According to the IRS, 90 percent of Americans saw an increase in their take-home pay.[12] Even so, the media message was effective. Only seventeen percent of Americans were convinced that they were seeing that increase.[13]

Donald Trump's most obdurate enemies hold out the possibility that in the last year of his first term as president, things could go horribly wrong with his "miracle" economy. Senator Elizabeth Warren, a Democratic candidate for president, openly predicted a coming economic catastrophe.[14] A *New York Times* headline read "Are You Ready for the Financial Crisis of 2019?"[15] On August 8, 2019, HBO comedian Bill Maher, who had openly "wished" for a recession the previous year, doubled down and called for it again. "Sorry if it hurts people."[16]

Some experts believe that it is likely that there will be a stock market correction in the last months of Trump's term in office.[17] That's what markets do, they go up and they go down. The fact that Trump's stock market, for example, has continued to ratchet upward, with only short interruptions, throughout his presidency is an anomaly.

Even so, the momentum of his economic success is so broad based and now so diverse, any serious economic collapse is unlikely. All indicators are sound. The experts who once predicted Trump couldn't do what he wanted to do are now saying that it cannot be easily undone. Even with the worst of news, Trump will have presided over the hottest economy in the world and, arguably, the longest-running boom in American history. It has all happened at a time when the world's other great economies, such as those of China, Germany, and Japan, are all suffocating.

On the other hand, if the Trump miracle keeps right on chugging, if he pulls off a deal with China, if wages rise even more, if poverty continues to disappear, new jobs continue to be created, right up to the last days of his first term in office, then Donald Trump should easily be ranked as one of America's great presidents. This, based on the economic numbers alone. Either that or history will have to apologize to Herbert Hoover, Jimmy Carter, and George W. Bush. Hoover and Bush presided over the worst depression and worst recession in American history, respectively. Carter presided over inflation of 13.5 percent his last year in office.[18]

If the economy doesn't matter, then the whole list of ranked presidents will have to be reshuffled. The professors will have to hurriedly rewrite their history books and change the rules. Indeed, that may actually happen. Academics, like Olympic judges and football referees, can cheat. But it will lead to some awkward moments for professors in classrooms, as new textbooks are rushed into print and sold to compliant students and Google manipulates its searches to cover its tracks.

THE PRESIDENT OF PEACE

As mentioned, historians delve deeply into a president's prosecution of war. To put it bluntly, wars define a presidency. Donald Trump's robust reaction to Syria's use of chemical weapons showed a leader who was willing to act quickly and decisively, while shunning a protracted conflict. Likewise, Trump's annihilation of ISIS was so quick and so decisive that the media could hardly catch its breath. Americans are used to long wars. Senator John McCain, Donald Trump's political nemesis, once suggested that the United States could be in Iraq for one hundred years.[19] Long wars have supporters. They make money for companies, lobbyists, and politicians.

In Trump's case, both military actions, the Syrian missile strike and the campaign against ISIS, involved inherited crises. Aside from these early flashes of force, Trump has been remarkably adept at avoiding armed conflict. As of the early fall of 2019, Donald Trump is the only American president in recent memory who hasn't committed the nation to a new military conflict during his term in office.

As he urgently pointed out to me, a war with North Korea was a very real possibility when he came into office. He chose diplomacy instead. In comparison, Barack Obama had his war in Libya that turned badly and arguably helped allow the rise of ISIS. George W. Bush invaded Iraq, insisting that it had secret weapons of mass destruction. His war upset the social and religious equilibrium of the region and turned the Middle East into a killing field. Earlier in this chapter I quoted an Associated Press estimate of deaths in Iraq, but by some other respected estimates 400,000 people died in the whole region.[20] Bill Clinton committed the United States to the war in Kosovo. George H. W. Bush invaded Panama. Ronald Reagan invaded Grenada. Critics like to portray Donald Trump as reckless, but there is no basis in policy for that portrayal. He may one day be seen by historians as a man of peace who will have finished his first term in office without a hot war—something no other recent president can claim.

Even if war comes in the last year of Trump's first term—a war with Iran or North Korea, for example—the president will have set the stage and given the United States the moral advantage. In Sun Tzu's philosophy of leadership, the side with the moral or "character" advantage is the side that will eventually win in a given conflict.[21] Trump will have shown a willingness to negotiate with both countries. His tempered reaction to Iran's hostile attack on an American drone, the seizure of British tankers, and the Iranian-Yemeni attack on a Saudi oil refinery will allow him to respond with decisive force to any further provocation and still keep the respect of many diplomats. It will be said that "he tried."

Jared Kushner sees the president's legacy in broader strokes. He has been redefining America's role in the world. "This is the first president, really, since the Second World War," Kushner told me, "to have new ideas on what America's place in the world should be for a new time. The world has changed a lot. We need a different strategy. What the president is trying to do, in creating reciprocity and fair trade deals, is to lead by example. This is how you get other people to do more."[22]

At the end of World War II, America was pouring money and investment into all the other countries devastated by war, especially the countries that had been defeated, such as Japan and Germany. The idea was partly humanitarian but partly to rebuild the world's economy to our own benefit as well. We made refrigerators, but we needed customers.

These struggling nations had no money for their own defense, so we paid for that too. But time has caught up with us. We are like a successful father who always picks up the tab for dinner. There is a problem. The kids are grown, they are making more money than we are, and we are struggling but unwilling to forfeit our honorific role. America is a proud nation. We are still, always, paying for dinner.

The American national media portrays Trump's America First policy as selfish. He sees himself as realistic and as someone who cares about the American middle class, which has had to carry the rest of the world on its shoulders. He sees the Democrats and their corporate media allies as willing to take the money from the American middle class and use it to clean up the environments of China, India, and South Africa. To use it to defend Germany and NATO nations. To give them the freedom to use their own money to build airports, high-speed trains, highways and improve their education.

"The whole notion of us being entangled in all these foreign wars is not sustainable," Jared Kushner points out. "The president realizes that everyone else is being competitive economically, and so we should be competitive, too. Sure, we want to help everyone around the world. We are the most generous nation on earth, but we also need to help our own citizens.

"So, this is part of his legacy. He has brought a balance of new ideas. It has involved slaying a lot of sacred cows and figuring out how we put America on a new course. Look at the definition of America First. Look at his first speech during the campaign at the Mayflower Hotel on foreign policy. Follow through to his speech in Saudi Arabia, his speech in Warsaw, and all his other foreign speeches. Read the speech in South Korea. If you follow his foreign policy, you will see he is really rewriting what America's role in the world should be for this century.

"That could be a great legacy—if future leaders will really follow that model and hopefully not revert back to some of the old ways, because the old ways are not sustainable. This is hard medicine for some people to take on a lot of fronts. But Donald Trump is courageous enough to lean into these fights and really push people to do things the right way."

Jared didn't flinch when I broached the subject of political defeat in 2020. He pointed out that its impact would not only be domestic. "A lot of countries are now waiting for the next president so they can get a better deal. They don't want to have to pay to clean up their own environment or to provide for their own security. They can just wait until they get a Democratic president or a weaker Republican president and then America will go back to paying for everything again."

REINVENTING POLITICS AND COMMUNICATION

Donald Trump, like all presidents, will leave a political legacy as well. Critics bemoan his childish nicknames of opponents and his branding slogans ("Make America Great Again"). But no future effective politician will be without them. In his own unique and colorful way, President Trump has been a great communicator.

The evolution of American-style politics has been ongoing from the birth of the republic. When political parties emerged, George Washington was in dismay. Heated divisions began immediately. Jefferson's partisan supporters used pamphlets to broadcast Alexander Hamilton's affair with a married woman and his subsequent blackmail.[23] Hamilton's supporters accused Jefferson of fathering children with an underage African slave.

When Andrew Jackson ran for president he was depicted in lithographs. For the first time someone could actually see for whom they were voting. It was the first art many people on the frontier ever had. They would nail the poster up on the interior walls of their log cabins.

Critics were outraged. Good old, fat, bald John Quincy Adams would never have been elected if lithographs had been available a few years earlier. What's more, Jackson was cheating by showing himself on horseback leading troops into battle. Critics said it was a false depiction.

President William Henry Harrison, "Old Tippecanoe" introduced music bands, and critics bemoaned the idea that the presidency would soon be reduced to whoever had the best band. Harrison, whose vice-presidential running mate was John Tyler, also dabbled in a bit of pre-Trumpian branding of his own, telling voters they could vote for "Tippecanoe and Tyler too." The intellectual elites were mortified.

These inventions occurred constantly all throughout history. In modern times there was Richard Nixon's 1972 campaign, which registered the largest plurality victory before or since, more than the reelections of FDR or Ronald Reagan. That campaign taught the importance of voter identification and turnout.

In 1988, kindly, old George H. W. Bush, of all people, taught us the power of negative campaigning when he ran against Massachusetts governor Michael Dukakis. Bush's supporters ran advertisements about Willie Horton, a murderer who happened to be African American. He had been released from prison by his opponent's state furlough program, only to commit further crimes, including rape. I worked for Bush at the time. We encouraged him to let others tell the story.

Bill Clinton's 1992 campaign taught the importance of a rapid response to negative attacks. It was like the World War II tank as the solution to the World War I trench. This was when the fax machine affected the political world.

Barack Obama mastered social media in new ways. In 2012, Democratic congresswoman Maxine Waters said that Obama had created a "kind of database that no-one has ever seen before. With information about everything, on every individual."[24] It was promised that with this power, the Democrats would never lose another election.

According to Obama's 2012 media analytics director, Carol Davidsen, Facebook executives came to the Obama offices and "were very candid that they allowed us to do things they wouldn't have allowed someone else to do because they were on our side."[25]

Finally, in 2016, Donald Trump taught us powerful lessons in branding. It will be a part of his legacy and will likely be a permanent part of any other future politician's success. Trump can do big things with only a few words. With Twitter and social media, he is communicating directly with his audience and his political base.

Jared Kushner sees the president's style as a key to his success and a way he has affected the science of politics. "From a communications point of view, he's changed the whole game. Again, I think he's had a whole new notion of communicating with the public and of being available. People are starting to copy his style.

"He also has a lot of authenticity. That's something that people love. They want to know who he is and that he's not pretending to be somebody he is not. People know he is fighting like hell for this country. That's something that a lot of people respect and love."

Jared sees something deeper than new technology or style. "He has increased the metabolism of Washington. Things happen faster. For example, he has this sharp focus on a metric of jobs for American workers and for increasing their wages. With that focus he has found new ways to get it done. But it didn't happen automatically."

THE BETTER POLITICIAN

White House Chief of Staff Mick Mulvaney told me a story about President Donald Trump and the day he learned that he was the better politician. It was in the hot summer of 2019. I was sitting in the chief of staff's office. Judd Deere, the White House deputy press secretary, was with us taking notes.

"Of course, everybody who's elected to Congress thinks they're a good politician," Mulvaney said. He was already chuckling about what he was going to tell us. "And I got elected to Congress four times. I was the first Republican in my district in 130 years, beating the sitting budget chairman by ten points," He was laughing now, setting us up for how this story would rebound against him. "My opponent was a twenty-eight-year incumbent. So I thought I was a damn good politician.[26]

"Anyway, I was President Trump's OMB director when this happened. I got invited up to Camp David for the weekend. It was a small group of about five of us. John Kelly and Kirstjen Nielsen were there. We were having dinner with President Trump in the dining room at the Laurel Lodge. It was a big room and a small table."

General John Kelly was then serving as White House chief of staff. Kirstjen Nielsen was the director of Homeland Security.

"The president turns to me and he says, 'Hey, Mick, what's that thing next week, that thing in Switzerland?'

"I'm like, 'Davos?'

"'Yeah, yeah,' he says. 'I'm thinking about going to that. What do you think about that?'"

Davos is a mountain retreat in Switzerland where the World Economic Forum had been held each year since 1971. It hosted many of the financial movers and shakers of the world. The Americans, under Trump, had stayed home from Davos in 2017, but the president's shadow had loomed over everything that had happened. World leaders had spent the week talking about what to do about Trump.

Inside the White House, the conventional wisdom held that the president should stay home from the 2018 forum as well. He would be ambushed by critics if he went. His "America First" policy was rankling the rich nations of Europe and the Pacific Rim. It would be like stepping into a hornet's nest.

"I gave him a frank answer," Mulvaney said. "Which is one of the reasons, I think, he likes working with me. I said, 'Mr. President, I think that's the shittiest idea I've heard all day.'

"He laughed. He goes, 'Why is that? Why is that?'

"I say, 'Mr. President, no one over there wants to see you and no one over here wants to see you go. It's a no-win situation.'

"Every time I say something that I know registers with him, he sort of pauses and he raises his left eyebrow. And he looks at me and he goes, 'No, no, you're wrong.' He turns to John Kelly and he says, 'John? I'm going. Set it up!'

"Now Kelly is kicking me under the table, because Kelly absolutely does not want him to go. He thinks it's a terrible idea. I'm thinking I have pissed off the chief of staff and somehow I'm going to be blamed for convincing the president to go to Davos and get fired.

"So Trump goes to Davos. It was a huge success. Even a media success. He gave a speech over there, and the key line that everyone remembers was 'America first is not America alone.'

"Okay." Mulvaney is laughing. "In hindsight, watching it on TV, I said to myself, 'Very clever. He just figured it out. He had a great line. He was looking for the biggest forum, with the biggest megaphone, so he could deliver that line to the whole world and that was it. It was a fabulous line. It was a fabulous trip.

"But that's not what I remember most. What I remember most is what happened a few days later. He gets back home. I'm working on something and I go into the Oval Office. Very often, I'll go in a few minutes before the meeting and just sit by the edge of the Resolute desk and work on my notes and my papers. This day, the president walks in behind me."

While he is telling the story, Chief of Staff Mulvaney jumps up out of his chair opposite me and starts acting out the scene. Judd Deere, who has been sitting there with us, taking notes, puts down his pen and paper and looks on, smiling but spellbound. The chief of staff is circling behind me while he is talking. Judd Deere can see what he is up to but I have my back to him, so I am reading Deere's face to anticipate what's coming. Suddenly, unexpectedly, Mulvaney slaps me hard on my right shoulder from behind.

Bam!

"And the president goes, 'You were wrong about Davos, weren't you?'

"I say, 'Yes, Mr. President, I was.'"

"So that was the day," Mulvaney says, laughing and sitting back down in this chair, "I realized Donald Trump is a better politician than me."

MEASURING THE INTELLIGENCE OF A PRESIDENT

Most presidential ranking systems make an accommodation for assessing the intelligence of a president. It is certainly not the most important criteria. As pointed out, both Jimmy Carter and Herbert Hoover were brilliant men who are routinely ranked poorly as presidents because of their handling of the nation's economy.

Journalists and some historians enjoy ridiculing the intelligence of the forty-fifth president. Trump defends himself as having "a very large brain," which prompts even more mockery from his enemies.[27]

In fact, journalists and historians love to portray presidents as dumb. Perhaps it offers some salve to their own failed lack of ambition or industry. One encounters a similar, petulant portrayal in literature. Giants are usually dumb. In motion pictures, beautiful women are often dumb. Many people find blonde women attractive, so many people make jokes about blonde women. It is a way to even the scales. Perhaps it is reflective of our own insecurities.

Even some of America's greatest presidents have been slapped with the label. Abraham Lincoln was referred to by one of his own cabinet members as "our dear imbecile." General George McClellan, the commanding general of his armies, called him an "idiot."[28] Oliver Wendell Holmes once called Franklin Delano Roosevelt "a second-class intellect."[29]

I have met and known six American presidents, and none of them were dumb. But they were all portrayed that way.

It was my privilege to entertain former president Gerald Ford in my home on two different occasions and talk with him about the Warren Commission and pardoning Nixon. He was so effectively branded by *Saturday Night Live* as dumb that I was shocked by my first conversations. Ford was a policy wonk and knew the details of issues that were far beyond my reach.

As a college student, Jimmy Carter apparently scored a higher on an IQ test than did John F. Kennedy.[30] That didn't stop *The Atlantic* from assessing his presidency with an article entitled, "How Stupid Is Jimmy Carter?"[31] It was my privilege to meet Carter on several occasions. He is a voracious reader. When we first shook hands in the Roosevelt Room of the White House, he said, "I read your book!" I had written an instant book called *The Iran Crisis*, and the problem it discussed was still lingering. After he left office, I met him again with his wife, First Lady Rosalynn Carter, in Atlanta. They sat down with me for an interview. I asked how it would have affected history if he had bombed Tehran. Rosalynn was sitting on a couch nearby. She jumped to her feet and said, "Jimmy would have been reelected president!"[32]

Christopher Hitchens once wrote an essay on "the stupidity of Ronald Reagan."[33] I would write the 1980 campaign biography for Reagan. My brother and I would have dinner with the Reagans in their home in Pacific Palisades the week he announced for president. Over the years he would tell me stories about "the Gipper" and jokes from the Soviet Union.

On one memorable night Reagan gave me his theory on what really happened to Ted Kennedy at Chappaquiddick. When the Reagans moved into the White House I would plan three charity events with Nancy Reagan, two in the East Room. And even more charity events with them both after they left Washington. Ronald Reagan was not dumb and neither was Nancy.

George H. W. Bush would give me his first published account of being shot down over the Pacific. We would sit in his White House vice presidential office in front of a warm fireplace. His staff, who had never heard the story before, soon gathered around, and the next appointments were postponed. I would later coauthor a book with him and serve on the Bush senior staff as special assistant to the president in his

White House. My family has notebooks full of wonderful handwritten messages from the president and first lady.

On one unforgettable night, they would take me off to the Nine Dragons Chinese restaurant at Epcot, where we sat and talked about books while the Disney World theme park was closing down and fireworks were exploding out over the lake just beyond our windows. George H. W. Bush was a brilliant man with a generous spirit. People insisted that he was dumb because he preferred Robert Ludlum over John le Carré.

Finally, I would know George W. Bush better than any of them. We would spend hours together on the road, on commercial airlines, on private jets, in car caravans and Winnebagos. We ended up talking about everything that two men talk about when they are alone on the road together, including money, government, baseball, God, and sex. Mostly sex.

In 1987, when the Bush twins were just little girls, I would take George and Laura and Jenna and Barbara for Mexican food in Corpus Christi, where we spent the night talking about George's future in Washington, DC. George W. Bush, newly retired from the oil business, was fascinated. The three ladies were bored.

One day, when George W. Bush was governor of Texas and thinking of running for president, I called him in a panic. "You were featured on *Saturday Night Live* last night," I said. "And they made you look really, really dumb."

There was a very long pause. At first I thought he had hung up. And then he finally spoke up and said, "Good."

"No, it's not good," I insisted urgently. "They are defining you."

He was not impressed by my argument. The fact is, he knew what he was doing.

There are some who believe that academia and the media purposely target Republican presidents and cover for Democratic presidents. The comedian Chevy Chase, star of *Saturday Night Live*, who portrayed Gerald Ford as a buffoon, admitted as much in an interview on CNN.

"Obviously my leanings were Democratic and I wanted Carter in and I wanted [Ford] out and I figured look, we're reaching millions of people every weekend, why not do it."[34]

Most of the American people loved Democratic president Barack Obama—even many who disagreed with his policies. The fact that the American people elected and reelected an African American president was a source of great pride. So, the media consistently covered for his lapses. When he referred to the "English Embassy" it was overlooked. When he toasted the queen in the middle of the British national anthem it was forgiven. When he claimed that America had built "the Intercontinental Railroad," no one was particularly upset.[35]

When Republican vice president Dan Quayle misspelled "potato," however, it was a national story. When Barack Obama misspelled "respect," it was considered a brain freeze moment that happens to us all.[36]

Partisan or not, most agree and the metrics clearly show that the American media is hostile to Donald Trump. A Harvard study illustrates this fact dramatically.[37] There is persistent criticism declaring Trump unfit to be president. But Trump was right about the economic numbers, and the greatest economists in the world were wrong. History has a way of sorting hysteria from fact. Leo Tolstoy once said that "wrong does not cease to be wrong because the majority share in it."[38] The numbers clearly show that the attacks on Donald Trump's performance as president are wrong. Future historians who wipe away the dust of collective bias will see those numbers etched in stone and will be able to judge without contemporary emotion.

If presidents are partly ranked as strong or weak based on their personal intelligence, then surely Donald Trump's ability to see what the greatest economists in the world could not see is an example of remarkable insight.

THE IMPEACHMENT GAME

Even before Donald Trump assumed office, even before the Russia collusion conspiracy theory was launched, his political opponents were calling for his impeachment.[39] What does history teach us about impeachment? How would it affect the Trump presidency, and what would it mean to his legacy?

The process of impeachment is brutal. President Andrew Johnson was impeached in 1868 but survived the vote in the Senate. His son, Robert, who worked in the White House and served his father like the chief of staff would serve today, died in an accident the very next year. Many believe it to be a suicide.[40]

Historically, impeachment is not an easy thing to pull off. President Richard Nixon would have likely been impeached and convicted, so he resigned. But Nixon was opposed by a Democratic House, a Democratic Senate, and arguably a Democratic national media. Most important of all, Nixon's "high crimes and misdemeanors" were eventually made very clear and obvious. They were not debatable, as in the case of the ongoing accusations against Donald Trump.

President Clinton was impeached but not convicted in the Senate. And Clinton had actually committed crimes and was eventually found guilty of them—perjury, for example. Clinton was also accused of rape, though no charges were brought against him. The Republicans who opposed Clinton controlled both the House of Representative and the Senate. And yet he survived.

The outcome of an impeachment hearing and trial is not easy to predict. Attacks on President Clinton were perceived as unfair. People didn't like the idea of overturning a recent election, and the economy was good. Bill Clinton won reelection in 1996.

This is the great fear of Democratic House Speaker, Nancy Pelosi, who throughout the summer of 2019 refused to launch impeachment proceedings against Donald Trump. She counseled fellow Democrats that by doing so, they would only be helping to reelect him in 2020. The Democrats had hurt themselves by calling for impeachment even before Trump had assumed office. It looked like anything they said and did was only an attempt to overturn the election. Meanwhile, the American economy under Donald Trump was at its peak.

In late September, pushed by radicals in her own party, Pelosi finally encouraged the Democrats in Congress to start the impeachment process.[41]

The national corporate media boldly led the charge, at a time when it had lost much credibility by its failed story on Russian collusion. Without any self-examination or accountability over its handling of past Trump "scandals," it now tried to convince the nation that this time, they had their facts right. Would the nation listen? Or would an ongoing impeachment process only reelect Donald Trump?

What will be the historical legacy of impeachment hearings? How would history see Donald Trump if articles of impeachment were passed by the House of Representatives? Much of the answer would depend on how it was done and if it were nonpartisan. The fact is, in recent years, impeachment has become a much more common political tool. Barack Obama, both Bush presidents, even Ronald Reagan have been threatened with the possibility of articles of impeachment. Only one president in American history has been effectively removed from office, and that is Richard Nixon. Yet even Nixon is favorably ranked by some historians, as is Bill Clinton, who was also impeached.

It is very possible that the preposterous Russian collusion story has successfully inoculated Donald Trump from any new scandals that the impeachment process can uncover. While Russian collusion was meant to be a knockout blow, it may, in the end, be his key to political survival.

HIS TOUGHEST CRITICS

Almost immediately after his election, Donald Trump was under attack from pundits and presidential historians. They lined up to join the aggrieved national media in bemoaning the rise of Trump. Jon Meacham described the period as "an odd and disconcerting moment, to say the least. My own hope is that when we look back on this it will simply have been a waste of America's time and not the beginning of a serious cataclysm."[42]

Doris Kearns Goodwin, who wrote a book about what makes a great president, said "Trump doesn't measure up."[43] Presidential historian Allan Lichtman suggested that the Democrats needed to impeach Trump if they hoped to beat him for reelection in 2020.[44]

Ken Burns, producer of popular television documentaries, compared Trump to Hitler.[45] Burns told an audience at Stanford University, "Asking this man to assume the highest office in the land would be like asking a newly minted car driver to fly a 747."[46]

Other's picked up on Burns's Hitler comparison, and the national news networks shamelessly ran such commentary without any irony. Steve Schmidt, a former political strategist for Senator John McCain, compared Trump to both Hitler and Stalin.[47] Nicole Wallace, the former communications director for President George W. Bush, announced on her show on MSNBC that Donald Trump was "talking about exterminating Latinos."[48] She later apologized for her mistake. Michael Beschloss warned television audiences that Trump "may be planning to become dictator for life."[49]

How reasonable persons could make such comparisons is difficult to comprehend. To think that such ideas would be promoted by scholars is baffling. To make an obvious point, dictators such as Hitler or Stalin controlled the press and the media in their respective nations. Does anyone seriously believe that Donald Trump controls the American media?

Dictators control academia. Hitler's government, for example, established the curriculum and approved the textbooks. Classroom lectures were monitored under both Hitler and Stalin. A professor who misspoke could end up in Dachau in Germany or be sent to a labor camp in Siberia in the Soviet Union. Does anyone seriously believe that Donald Trump controls academia in America? In many cases, conservative speakers and writers are not allowed on American university campuses. In some cases, free speech has been effectively silenced and conservatives are not allowed to speak in defense of the duly elected president of the United States.

Dictators control the cinema. Stalin personally read the scripts of major motion pictures before they could be produced in the Soviet Union. Joseph Goebbels had to personally approve of every actor or actress appearing in major films in Nazi Germany. Does anyone seriously believe that Donald Trump controls Hollywood? Yet this mind-set of calling Trump a dictator now dominates the media narrative in the United States. It has no basis in reality.

The president would tell me an amusing story. We were in his "real office" behind the Oval Office. He lowered his voice conspiratorially, and then said that soon after his election a very prominent presidential historian, one of those mentioned earlier in this chapter, had made the pilgrimage to Mar-a-Lago. According to the president, he had stayed for days, flattering him and angling to be given the nod to write the authorized book on his administration. "He kissed my ass for a week," the president said, his eyes twinkling, knowing that he was being naughty. "Now he is paid money to attack me on television."[50]

He may be crude. He doesn't pull any punches. He is surely colorful. But Donald Trump is no evil dictator. His rise to power offended the establishment of both political parties and their respective surrogates, including almost all of their writer friends. The Bush family will not soon forgive his trouncing of their last nominee, Jeb Bush, whom Trump labeled "low energy." Nor will they forgive his early opposition to the Iraq War, a point that the national media refuses to concede, even though everyone I found in Trump world would attest that he had, indeed, been opposed to that war throughout.

The president has his share of friends among the national media as well. He invoked the name of Sean Hannity several times in our conversations. He admires his fearlessness. He laughed happily when discussing Lou Dobbs, whom he counted as a friend who would support him to the end. He regretted a misunderstanding with Neil Cavuto, which he didn't explain, only adding, "I wish I could do that over." And he mentioned the hosts of *Fox and Friends* several times.

THE ART OF THE IMPOSSIBLE

The German statesman Otto von Bismarck once said, "Politics is the art of the possible." This is exactly what I have experienced and seen in the presidents and presidential candidates I have known. They focus on winnable, doable goals that they know can be achieved even before they publicly announce them.

Donald Trump the businessman approached the presidency in a totally different way. In his book *The Art of the Deal*, as a businessman, he argued that one tackles the most difficult problem first and then moves onto the next hardest. Thus, Donald Trump's first question to Obama was not "What can I get done quickly?" It was "What is the biggest problem this country faces?"

"North Korea," Obama had said.

So began the presidency of Donald Trump. It represents a new concept for government. Politics for Trump has become the art of the impossible.

He was elected in 2016 to take care of the two biggest issues of that time: Rebuild the American economy and defeat the seemingly unstoppable terrorist group ISIS. Like a good magician he kept his audience spellbound by his words. "I will be the greatest jobs president God ever created," he promised when he announced his run for president.[51] "We're going to beat ISIS very, very quickly folks. It's going to be fast," he boldly declared on the campaign trail in Connecticut.[52] Afterward, from his White House stage, Donald Trump, like a good magician, made it look easy. It is only now, much later, when we know how the trick works, that the fascination wears off and we forget and take the relative peace and prosperity for granted.

The true measure of Donald Trump's success may be seen in the policies and decisions he has made that will survive him and endure. While the media howled and criticized his demands on NATO, will anyone in the future want to do it any differently? Will they want to retreat from what he has achieved? Would some future president refund the tens of millions of dollars that Trump raised from his NATO partners? The organization is now stronger than ever before.

Will we go back to the now discredited NAFTA and abandon the new Trump treaty that all three countries, Canada, Mexico, and the United States, like better?

Will some future president give up the hard-won first steps with China? Work that will not be felt for years to come but work that had to be done?

Will a future United States allow North Korea to go back to testing nuclear weapons?

Will the American embassy be moved back to Tel Aviv? Will an America of the future withdraw support for Israel to occupy the Golan Heights?

Will the United States go back to the Bush-Obama era of silencing and shaming the families of Americans held hostage abroad? Or will the Trump Doctrine prevail and America keep bringing its innocent citizens back home from foreign tyrants?

Will America retreat from its carefully won energy independence achieved by President Donald J. Trump?

Will a future America raise taxes again on companies and drive them out of the United States?

Will America, once again, return to nation building, sending American troops back into wars all over the globe? Or will it mind its own business more? Will it put America first?

This will be a big part of his legacy. What has he done that will remain? What will stick?

Of course, eventually, some of what Donald Trump has done will be reversed by future political successors, but no matter how shrill and harsh the media has been, it is not likely that many of the great things he has accomplished will be reversed any time soon. The media feigned outrage at the time of his decisions, but they will remain quiet when his successors do the same thing.

The American people like balance. It is why they seldom give a president a Congress of the same party with which to work. It is why, over the years, the pendulum swings back and forth between Right and Left. It is how Donald Trump was elected in the first place, at a time when the establishment elites were practically hysterical in their support of his opponent.

As the years pass, the nation will once more swing back into a time of manic political correctness. When the bitter voices of a domineering American media are more carefully revered and obeyed. When they feel more secure and take on a less emotional and a more dignified tone. When voters and viewers retreat back into a somnolent, obedient state of compliance. When all the search engines are wiped clean and supplied with the approved information, in the appropriate order. When politicians once again talk without saying anything and no one stretches the boundaries of civility or excites the imagination. When the big monopolies feel that they are once more secure and can emerge from the shadows.

When those days return you will begin to see bumper stickers. Slowly at first. And then more and more. "Give us back our Trump," they will say. But by then, he will be gone. He will have passed into history.

Jared Kushner talked about that on that cold January night in 2019, when my wife and I visited him and Ivanka in their Georgetown home. The fireplace was ablaze, and Jared and Ivanka were on the couch opposite us. "There will come a day," Jared mused, "when people will miss him greatly. He goes for the big thing and he gets it done. Nobody can keep up with the spirit in which he leads."[53]

DONALD TRUMP ON THE PHONE

O f course, I want to thank my editor, Kate Hartson, but as it turns out, she got praise directly from the President of the United States.

During one of our interviews in the Oval Office, I reminded him that my editor, Kate, had told me only to get the facts, and to be nice to him. He laughed, obviously charmed, and asked for her name and phone number.

Then, before I could say a word or warn Kate what was coming, the president was on the phone with her via the White House switchboard, talking about my work on this book and some of her imprint's other books and authors such as Newt Gingrich, Judge Jeanine Pirro and Corey Lewandowski and David Bossie. They chatted for a few minutes, and the president thanked Kate for the fair coverage he'd always gotten in the books she published. She responded by thanking him for all he was doing for the country.

After he'd hung up the phone, the president offered some key insight into his day-to-day process.

"See, how I just got that done?" he said, "right while I thought about it? No need to have something nagging on a list somewhere. Get it done. Bam. It's done!

"By the way. When I promote a book it will go to number one," the President added. "You watch. Your book will be number one."

It inspires me even now to finish these acknowledgments.

Thanks to White House chief of staff, Mick Mulvaney, the boss, to Bill Shine, Sarah Sanders, Stephanie Grisham, Madeleine Westerhoust, Julie Radford, Avi Berkowitz, Brad Parscale, Judson Deere, Baxter Murrell, David Bossie, Katrina Pierson, Caroline Moore, Kimberly Benza, Janet Mondesi, Rachael Craddock, Lindsay Walters, Bridges Lamar, Paula White, Andrew Brunson and Giovanna Coia.

My thanks to my wife, Myriam, and children who helped me with this book. Thirty years ago my wife transcribed hours of taped interviews with George H.W. Bush for a book I co-authored with the 41st President. Now, three children and three grandchildren later, she was doing it all over again with President Donald J. Trump. My son, Joshua Wead helped research and write on foreign policy and edit corrections that came back from the Trump family. My daughters, Chloe Fuentes and Camille Castillo, organized the photographs. Another friend whose name must remain unmentioned for security reasons, helped organize the hours of voice recordings, helped write the chapter about the hostages and did all of the primary research on Melania Trump. Dan Godzich researched and helped write about the resistance and the Mueller Report. My sons Shannon and Scott, their spouses Janeen and Amy helped me. Thanks to Jesse Benton and Wesley Bishop. Finally, there is the long list of anonymous sources inside the Trump White House and the government who gave me a fly on the wall perspective of the most important moments of the first three years of the Trump administration.

Thanks to the versatile team at Foundry Literary for representing me. And thanks to Rolf Zettersten, Patsy Jones, Sean McGowan, and the sales team at Hachette Books.

Finally, most of all, thanks to the President and all of the Trump family members for trusting me and letting me inside to see and hear more than they probably should have. Thanks to the First Lady, Melania, to Don, Jr. Jared and Ivanka Kushner, Eric and Lara, Tiffany and Barron.

On occasion I felt like a time traveler, coming back from the future, encountering this remarkable family in the middle of their remarkable journey at the beginning of the 21st century. They are the Trumps. Not the Medici's or the Rockefellers or the Kennedys but they are ever much as colorful as any other family we have seen in history. While I had to labor and write for many days and months, sometimes I just sat back and enjoyed the voice recordings, listening as they told their stories. Another 400 unused pages lay on the cutting room floor. For a student of history, such as myself, there seems to be so much to hear and read and so little time capture it all.

NOTES

INTRODUCTION

1. Unless otherwise indicated, all quotes from President Trump come from conversations and interviews conducted by the author between 2016 and 2019.
2. Interview with White House staff member, January 10, 2019.
3. Doug Wead, *Game of Thorns* (New York: Center Street, 2017), 2.
4. http://www.businessinsider.com/hillary-clinton-endorsements-newspaper-editorial-board-president-2016-2016-9
5. https://www.bloomberg.com/news/articles/2016-09-26/billionaire-donors-led-by-soros-simons-favor-clinton-over-trump
6. https://www.alternet.org/2017/02/experts-agree-trumps-rosy-predictions-economic-growth-are-mathematic-impossibility/
7. https://dailycaller.com/2018/06/01/economists-trump-economy-numbers/
8. https://www.washingtontimes.com/news/2017/dec/31/trump-economy-false-predictions-left/
9. https://www.washingtonpost.com/news/wonk/wp/2017/05/23/larry-summers-trumps-budget-is-simply-ludicrous/?utm_term=.3b6ad044d2f5
10. https://financialtribune.com/articles/world-economy/78259/trump-is-dreaming-pigs-dont-fly
11. https://ntda.org/u-s-economy-tops-4-gdp-growth-in-second-quarter/
12. https://money.cnn.com/2016/10/24/investing/stocks-donald-trump-hillary-clinton/
13. https://www.usatoday.com/story/opinion/nation-now/2017/12/20/president-trumps-successes-have-been-underreported-gary-varvel-column-nation-now/968842001/
14. https://www.washingtonexaminer.com/washington-secrets/trumps-list-289-accomplishments-in-just-20-months-relentless-promise-keeping
15. https://twitter.com/realdonaldtrump/status/453956405389967360
16. https://thehill.com/blogs/blog-briefing-room/news/281936-obama-to-trump-what-magic-wand-do-you-have
17. https://foreignpolicy.com/2016/09/26/clintons-debate-take-on-trump-only-secret-is-he-doesnt-have-a-plan/
18. https://www.youtube.com/watch?v=-5jRHn153ZQ
19. https://www.haaretz.com/us-news/bill-maher-under-fire-for-ivanka-trump-incest-joke-1.5469269
20. Ivanka Trump to the author in 2018.
21. Unless otherwise indicated, all quotes from Eric Trump come from interviews with the author in 2019.
22. Unless otherwise indicated, all quotes from Ivanka Trump come from interviews and conversations conducted by the author from 2017 to 2019.
23. This story was related to the author by Ivanka Trump in 2019.
24. https://www.borgenmagazine.com/johnsons-war-on-poverty-speech-reaches-50/
25. https://www.usatoday.com/story/money/2018/01/19/year-into-trump-presidency-401-k-balances-looking-good/1045408001/
26. https://www.cnbc.com/2016/12/05/trump-effect-that-house-you-want-got-16000-more-expensive-since-he-won.html
27. https://dailycaller.com/2018/09/18/soros-kavanaugh-protesters/
28. http://time.com/5066679/donald-trump-federal-judges-record/
29. President Trump to the author.
30. https://www.vox.com/2018/4/15/17238568/syria-bomb-trump-obama-russia
31. https://www.vox.com/2018/4/15/17238568/syria-bomb-trump-obama-russia

32. Interview with Luis de Videagaray, January 2019.
33. https://www.usatoday.com/story/news/world/2019/01/27/nato-chief-credits-trump/2695799002/
34. https://www.foxnews.com/world/trump-american-hostages-home-policy-experts
35. https://www.census.gov/foreign-trade/balance/c5700.html
36. https://deadline.com/2018/12/donald-trump-christmas-eve-tweet-storm-border-wall-general-mattis-dow-plunge-jerome-powell-1202525594/
37. Interview with Jared Kushner, January 2019.
38. Unless otherwise indicated, all quotes from Lara Trump come from interviews with the author in 2019.
39. https://www.reviewjournal.com/news/politics-and-government/trump-first-lady-answer-christmas-eve-calls-from-children-looking-for-santa-1558683/
40. https://abcnews.go.com/Politics/melania-trump-returns-washington-trumps-attend-christmas-eve/story?id=60006016
41. https://www.nytimes.com/2018/12/26/us/politics/trump-iraq-troops-visit.html

1: NO NUCLEAR WAR ON MY WATCH

1. Unless otherwise indicated, all quotes from President Trump come from conversations and interviews conducted by the author between 2016 and 2019.
2. https://tradingeconomics.com/united-states/unemployment-rate
3. https://www.youtube.com/watch?v=Mi41C3gV9kw
4. https://www.latimes.com/politics/washington/la-na-essential-washington-updates-trump-warns-north-korea-of-fire-and-1502220642-htmlstory.html
5. https://dailycaller.com/2018/05/27/president-trump-freed-17-prisoners/
6. https://www.theguardian.com/world/2017/oct/13/trump-meet-parents-japanese-teenager-seized-north-korea-abductions-megumi-yokota
7. https://www.apnews.com/94fab8f77bcb4fb5864669026906bf60
8. https://dailycaller.com/2018/05/27/president-trump-freed-17-prisoners/

2: LUNCH WITH PRESIDENT TRUMP

1. https://www.latimes.com/politics/la-pol-updates-everything-president-trump-calls-kim-jong-un-little-rocket-1512093131-htmlstory.html
2. https://www.nytimes.com/2017/04/20/opinion/the-north-korea-trump-nightmare.html
3. https://www.theatlantic.com/international/archive/2018/06/trump-kim-korea-success/563012/
4. https://www.history.com/news/kennedy-krushchev-vienna-summit-meeting-1961
5. http://www.josephloconte.com/commentary/the-weekly-standard-fdr-stalin-and-the-tragedy-of-yalta/
6. https://www.usatoday.com/story/news/world/2014/01/03/newser-kim-jong-un-uncle-execution/4303319/
7. https://www.cnn.com/2017/02/27/asia/kim-jong-nam-north-korea-killed/index.html
8. https://www.mercycorps.org/articles/north-korea/food-north-koreas-families
9. https://www.newsweek.com/north-korea-starving-nuclear-missiles-641188
10. https://www.aol.com/article/entertainment/2019/02/18/donald-trump-melania-trump-at-oscars-a-brief-history/23672046
11. https://www.washingtonpost.com/blogs/erik-wemple/wp/2018/02/13/is-the-sound-of-clicking-cameras-at-the-white-house-nearing-extinction/
12. https://grabien.com/story.php?id=132091
13. https://abc.go.com/shows/this-week-with-george-stephanopoulos/episode-guide/2017-12/31-123117-us-closer-nuclear-war-north-korea-than-ever-before-former-joint-chiefs-staff-head
14. https://grabien.com/story.php?id=170957
15. https://www.youtube.com/watch?time_continue=23&v=4WGa1_TiT3o
16. https://www.breitbart.com/clips/2017/10/23/brzezinski-trump-wants-to-use-nukes-hes-excited-about-the-concept/

17. https://www.usatoday.com/story/news/world/2018/10/05/nobel-peace-prize-donald-trump/1508304002/
18. https://www.brookings.edu/articles/strategic-patience-has-become-strategic-passivity/
19. https://www.tmz.com/2018/06/12/dan-rather-trump-kim-jong-un-winner-summit/
20. https://pjmedia.com/trending/study-media-devotes-0-7-percent-of-coverage-to-booming-trump-economy/
21. https://www.washingtonpost.com/opinions/global-opinions/trumps-tweets-wont-stop-a-bloodbath-in-syria/2018/09/06/03af3c06-b13d-11e8-aed9-001309990777_story.html
22. https://www.businessinsider.com/melania-trump-asks-white-house-kitchen-staff-to-make-healthier-meals-for-president-2018-8
23. Interview with Jared Kushner, January 2019.
24. https://thehill.com/homenews/administration/393402-trump-media-coverage-of-north-korea-summit-is-almost-treasonous
25. Donald Trump, *The Art of the Deal* (New York: Random House, 1987), 28.
26. https://www.latimes.com/books/la-et-jc-michael-cohen-book-20180822-story.html

3: IVANKA'S WEST WING OFFICE

1. Interview with Ivanka Trump, 2018.
2. https://www.vox.com/2017/3/22/15005508/ivanka-trump-white-house-nepotism
3. https://www.nbcnews.com/politics/white-house/ivanka-trump-named-assistant-president-new-role-n740241
4. Doug Wead, *All the Presidents' Children* (New York: Atria 2003), 310.
5. https://www.nytimes.com/2017/03/29/us/politics/ivanka-trump-federal-employee-white-house.html
6. https://www.forbes.com/sites/denizcam/2017/11/01/why-ivanka-trumps-melania-as-a-worlds-most-powerful-woman/#3693db85732e
7. https://www.lifezette.com/2017/04/times-100-influential-people-list-includes-ivanka-donald-trump/
8. https://fortune.com/2017/08/17/40-under-40-bezos-zuckerberg-musk/
9. https://www.express.co.uk/life-style/life/833628/melania-trump-ivanka-trump-50-most-beautiful. http://www.freerepublic.com/focus/f-chat/3469091/posts
10. https://www.businessinsider.com/ivanka-trump-vs-north-korean-kim-jong-uns-sister-kim-yo-jong-2018-2
11. https://politicalwire.com/2018/03/12/in-ivankas-office/
12. Unless otherwise indicated, all quotes from Ivanka Trump come from conversations and interviews conducted between 2017 and 2019.
13. https://www.youtube.com/watch?v=Y5h8Sncv3Pk
14. https://www.youtube.com/watch?v=Y5h8Sncv3Pk
15. https://www.youtube.com/watch?v=hWGxWzFzdK4
16. https://www.msn.com/en-in/lifestyle/family/18-things-you-didnt-know-about-donald-and-ivanka-trumps-father-daughter-relationship/ss-BBzSPzL
17. Interview with Eric Trump, January 2019.
18. Interview with Ivanka Trump, White House, December 2018.
19. Interview with Ivanka Trump, White House, December 2018.
20. Interview with Ivanka Trump, White House, December 14, 2018.
21. https://www.opednews.com/articles/Beauty-and-the-Beast--The-by-Elayne-Clift-120504-209.html
22. https://www.politico.com/magazine/gallery/2017/02/ivanka-trump-magazine-covers-000711?slide=0
23. https://www.politico.com/magazine/gallery/2017/02/ivanka-trump-magazine-covers-000711?slide=2
24. https://www.politico.com/magazine/gallery/2017/02/ivanka-trump-magazine-covers-000711?slide=8

25. https://thehill.com/policy/finance/domestic-taxes/365956-ivanka-trump-corker-had-real-integrity-during-tax-negotiations
26. https://www.independent.ie/style/celebrity/celebrity-news/ivanka-trump-said-she-was-blindsided-by-viciousness-of-criticism-directed-at-her-family-35820697.html
27. https://www.businessinsider.com/ivanka-trump-steve-bannon-clashed-white-house-2018-9
28. https://www.youtube.com/watch?v=hWGxWzFzdK4
29. Ivanka Trump, *The Trump Card* (New York: Simon & Schuster, 2009), p. 128.

4: Donald Trump Jr. and Whispers on an Elevator

1. Unless otherwise noted, quotes by Donald Trump Jr. used throughout this book are taken from interviews with the author from May to September, 2019.
2. This story was related to me by Don Trump Jr. in 2019.
3. https://www.nytimes.com/2016/03/13/us/politics/donald-trump-campaign.html
4. https://www.youtube.com/watch?v=wBy1CAyH08w
5. https://www.nytimes.com/2016/03/13/us/politics/donald-trump-campaign.html
6. https://thehill.com/blogs/in-the-know/in-the-know/405143-michael-moore-trump-ran-for-president-because-he-was-jealous-of
7. https://www.nytimes.com/2016/03/13/us/politics/donald-trump-campaign.html
8. https://blogs.wsj.com/washwire/2011/04/06/wsjnbc-poll-a-donald-trump-surprise/
9. https://factba.se/transcript/donald-trump-interview-cnn-piers-morgan-live-june-1-2011
10. https://factba.se/transcript/donald-trump-interview-cnn-piers-morgan-live-june-1-2011
11. https://ijr.com/5-times-donald-trump-praised-socialized-healthcare/
12. https://www.mediaite.com/tv/george-will-i-hope-trump-runs-and-gets-shellacked-so-we-can-end-this-charade/
13. https://www.nbcnews.com/politics/2016-election/donald-trump-accepts-barack-obama-was-born-u-s-giuliani-n645371
14. https://www.newsbusters.org/blogs/curtis-houck/2015/07/02/chris-matthews-voters-trump-because-hes-comic-book-hero-and-sinatra
15. http://www.msnbc.com/transcripts/the-last-word/2015-06-15
16. https://www.youtube.com/watch?v=c-IA-CkLFVs&t=24s
17. http://www.centerforpolitics.org/crystalball/articles/republicans-2016-what-to-do-with-the-donald/
18. https://fivethirtyeight.com/features/podcast-totally-subjective-presidential-odds-early-august-edition/
19. https://www.theguardian.com/us-news/2015/aug/22/donald-trump-wont-win-republican-presidential-nomination
20. https://www.nytimes.com/interactive/2016/us/elections/presidential-candidates-dashboard.html
21. https://www.youtube.com/watch?v=c-IA-CkLFVs&t=24s
22. https://www.youtube.com/watch?v=c-IA-CkLFVs&t=24s
23. https://www.youtube.com/watch?v=c-IA-CkLFVs&t=24s
24. https://www.youtube.com/watch?v=c-IA-CkLFVs&t=24s
25. https://www.youtube.com/watch?v=c-IA-CkLFVs&t=24s
26. https://www.youtube.com/watch?v=c-IA-CkLFVs&t=24s
27. https://www.youtube.com/watch?v=c-IA-CkLFVs&t=24s
28. https://www.nytimes.com/2003/01/06/opinion/the-seven-dwarfs.html
29. https://time.com/3512769/in-the-latest-issue-10/

5: Eric Trump and the Journey to Trump Tower

1. Unless otherwise indicated, all quotes from Eric Trump come from conversations, emails, and interviews in 2019.
2. https://www.nytimes.com/1988/03/27/nyregion/plaza-hotel-is-sold-to-donald-trump-for-390-million.html

3. https://www.salon.com/2019/07/15/tell-all-book-shows-trump-manipulated-into-choosing-pence_partner/
4. https://www.businessinsider.com/trump-picked-pence-running-mate-he-said-nice-things-book-2019-7
5. https://www.salon.com/2019/07/15/tell-all-book-shows-trump-manipulated-into-choosing-pence_partner/
6. https://talkingpointsmemo.com/edblog/do-we-remember-that-manafort-pick-pence
7. https://www.hillaryclinton.com/feed/there-are-five-living-u-s-presidents-none-of-them-support-donald-trump/
8. https://www.nytimes.com/interactive/2016/upshot/presidential-polls-forecast.html
9. https://abcnews.go.com/Politics/clinton-vaults-double-digit-lead-boosted-broad-disapproval/story?id=42993821
10. https://www.youtube.com/watch?v=MBFbxx0XFmc
11. https://www.breitbart.com/the-media/2016/10/17/wikileaks-journalists-clinton-staff-homes-before-hillarys-campaign-launch/
12. https://www.breitbart.com/the-media/2016/10/17/wikileaks-journalists-clinton-staff-homes-before-hillarys-campaign-launch/
13. https://www.washingtonpost.com/world/national-security/how-the-russians-hacked-the-dnc-and-passed-its-emails-to-wikileaks/2018/07/13/af19a828-86c3-11e8-8553-a3ce89036c78_story.html
14. https://www.breitbart.com/the-media/2016/10/17/wikileaks-journalists-clinton-staff-homes-before-hillarys-campaign-launch/
15. https://www.cjr.org/first_person/podesta_emails_journalists_dinner.php

6: LARA TRUMP: "I CRIED ALL THE WAY"

1. Unless otherwise indicated, all quotes attributed to Lara Trump in this chapter come from conversations, emails, and interviews in 2019.
2. https://www.usatoday.com/story/opinion/2019/01/27/lara-trump-no-let-them-eat-cake-figure-editorials-debates/2695572002/
3. https://www.chicksonright.com/blog/2019/01/23/lara-trump-under-fire-over-controversial-remarks-on-the-government-shutdown/
4. Unless otherwise indicated, all quotes from Don Trump Jr. in this chapter come from conversations, emails, and interviews conducted in 2019.
5. https://pastdaily.com/2016/10/26/henry-kissinger-october-26-1972/
6. http://www.businessinsider.com/how-the-donald-trump-tape-got-leaked-2016-10/
7. https://abcnews.go.com/Politics/president-warren-hardings-love-child-confirmed-dna-testing/story?id=33060408
8. https://nypost.com/2012/11/25/the-many-loves-of-fdr/
9. https://potus-geeks.livejournal.com/694586.html
10. http://nymag.com/daily/intelligencer/2016/10/trump-campaign-final-days.html
11. http://www.businessinsider.com/donald-trump-women-video-apology-billy-bush-clinton-2016-10
12. http://heavy.com/news/2016/10/read-melania-trump-responds-to-donald-trumps-vulgar-2005-tape-what-did-reaction-billy-bush-statement-wife/
13. https://www.washingtonpost.com/politics/trump-recorded-having-extremely-lewd-conversation-about-women-in-2005/2016/10/07/3b9ce776-8cb4-11e6-bf8a-3d26847eeed4_story.html
14. http://www.businessinsider.com/paul-ryan-defend-donald-trump-campaign-2016-10
15. http://www.latimes.com/nation/politics/trailguide/la-na-trailguide-updates-south-dakota-s-thune-joins-chorus-1475946585-htmlstory.html
16. Doug Wead, *Game of Thorns* (New York: Center Street, 2017), 293.
17. Unless otherwise indicated, all quotes attributed to Jared Kushner in this chapter are taken from conversations or interviews conducted in 2019.

18. Chris Christie, *Let Me Finish* (New York: Hachette, 2019), 320.
19. http://www.cnn.com/2016/10/07/politics/donald-trump-campaign-crisis/

7: ELECTION NIGHT FOG

1. This quote of Donald Trump comes from Jared Kushner, overhearing his father-in-law during a phone conversation on Election Night 2016. Kushner relayed the conversation to me in a 2019 interview.
2. Interview with Brad Parscale, January 12, 2019.
3. This quote from Nick Ayers is attributed to him by Brad Parscale in an interview in 2019.
4. Doug Wead, *Game of Thorns* (New York: Center Street, 2017), 41.
5. https://www.newyorker.com/news/john-cassidy/why-is-donald-trump-in-michigan-and-wisconsin
6. https://www.gq.com/story/inside-donald-trumps-election-night-war-room
7. https://www.youtube.com/watch?v=SG1HVMd0Urs
8. https://www.dailywire.com/news/10611/bare-breasted-women-protest-trumps-polling-station-hank-berrien
9. http://www.nbcnews.com/card/clinton-arrives-new-york-polling-place-vote-n679621
10. https://nypost.com/2017/04/30/the-moment-hillary-clinton-was-forced-to-give-up-her-dream/
11. https://www.gq.com/story/inside-donald-trumps-election-night-war-room
12. http://pagesix.com/2015/07/08/if-hilary-makes-it-to-the-white-house-so-will-huma-abedin/
13. https://www.gq.com/story/inside-donald-trumps-election-night-war-room
14. https://www.gq.com/story/inside-donald-trumps-election-night-war-room
15. https://www.politico.com/story/2017/12/06/abc-data-trump-campaign-reprimand-284327
16. https://www.politico.com/story/2016/12/donald-trump-wisconsin-232605
17. https://www.gq.com/story/inside-donald-trumps-election-night-war-room
18. https://www.politico.com/story/2016/12/donald-trump-wisconsin-232605
19. Corey Lewandowski and David N. Bossie, *Let Trump Be Trump* (New York: Center Street, 2017).
20. I spoke with David Bossie in the green room at Fox News in Washington, DC, in February 2019.
21. Interview with Brad Parscale, January 12, 2019.
22. https://www.politico.com/story/2016/12/donald-trump-wisconsin-232605
23. Interview with Brad Parscale, January 12, 2019.

8: THE BIGGEST UPSET IN AMERICAN HISTORY

1. This quote was first given to me by Ivanka Trump, December 14, 2018, and confirmed by others present.
2. CBS Election Night coverage. https://archive.org/details/WTSP_20161109_000000_Campaign_2016_CBS_News_Coverage_of_Election_Night
3. CBS Election Night coverage. https://archive.org/details/WTSP_20161109_000000_Campaign_2016_CBS_News_Coverage_of_Election_Night
4. https://www.youtube.com/watch?v=iiBg7JbcYqA&t=366
5. https://www.gq.com/story/inside-donald-trumps-election-night-war-room
6. Unless otherwise indicated, all quotes from Brad Parscale in this chapter come from interviews in 2019.
7. CNN Election Night coverage.
8. CNN Election Night coverage
9. https://www.latimes.com/politics/la-na-pol-trump-polls-20161109-story.html
10. Unless otherwise indicated, all quotes from Lara Trump in this chapter are taken from conversations, emails, and interviews with her in 2019.
11. http://time.com/4563501/donald-trump-election-night/
12. https://archive.org/details/WTSP_20161109_000000_Campaign_2016_CBS_News_Coverage_of_Election_Night

13. This story and the quotes, including the president's quotes, were given to me by Brad Parscale and cross-checked with members of the Trump family.

14. This story came from a source within the campaign.

15. https://www.gq.com/story/inside-donald-trumps-election-night-war-room

16. Unless otherwise indicated, all quotes from Ivanka Trump came from conversations and interviews conducted between 2017-2019.

17. https://www.gq.com/story/inside-donald-trumps-election-night-war-room

18. Unless otherwise indicated, all quotes attributed to Eric Trump in this chapter come from interviews conducted in 2019.

19. https://www.bustle.com/articles/194235-transcript-of-john-podestas-speech-leaves-the-election-on-a-hopeful-note

20. Interview with Brad Parscale, January 12, 2019.

21. https://www.gq.com/story/inside-donald-trumps-election-night-war-room

22. http://mediamatters.org/video/2016/10/20/msnbcs-presidential-historian-calls-trump-not-accepting-results-election-absolutely-horrifying/213976

23. Hillary Rodham Clinton, *What Happened* (New York: Simon and Schuster, 2017), 56.

24. https://www.cnn.com/2016/11/09/politics/donald-trump-victory-speech/index.html

25. https://www.gq.com/story/inside-donald-trumps-election-night-war-room

26. https://www.gq.com/story/inside-donald-trumps-election-night-war-room

27. https://www.gq.com/story/inside-donald-trumps-election-night-war-room

28. https://www.bloomberg.com/news/articles/2016-09-26/billionaire-donors-led-by-soros-simons-favor-clinton-over-trump

29. https://www.chicagotribune.com/news/opinion/commentary/ct-clinton-foundation-investigation-russia-20171120-story.html

30. https://www.businessinsider.com/hillary-clinton-endorsements-newspaper-editorial-board-president-2016-2016-9

31. https://www.washingtonexaminer.com/what-media-bias-journalists-overwhelmingly-donated-to-hillary-clinton

32. This story was related to the author by Ivanka Trump.

9: MOVING INTO THE WHITE HOUSE

1. Interview with Lara Trump, January 2019.

2. Unless indicated otherwise, all quotes by Donald Trump Jr. in this chapter come from conversations, emails, and interviews in 2019.

3. From interviews with Lara Trump, 2019.

4. https://www.usmagazine.com/stylish/news/what-makeup-products-melania-trump-wore-on-inauguration-day-w

5. https://www.usmagazine.com/stylish/news/melania-trumps-inauguration-hairstyle-how-to-details-w462140/

6. https://nypost.com/2017/01/20/why-ivanka-will-be-the-most-stylish-first-daughter-ever/

7. https://time.com/4641208/donald-trump-robert-jeffress-st-john-episcopal-inauguration/

8. Unless otherwise indicated, all quotes from Tiffany Trump in this chapter come from a 2019 interview with the author.

9. Unless otherwise indicated, all quotes from Jared Kushner in this chapter come from 2019 interviews with the author.

10. https://www.businessinsider.com/ivanka-trump-plays-social-butterfly-at-obama-economic-conference-2009-3

11. https://www.businessinsider.com/ivanka-trump-plays-social-butterfly-at-obama-economic-conference-2009-3

12. Interview with Tiffany Trump, August 2019.

13. Interview with Tiffany Trump, August 2019.

14. https://www.episcopalnewsservice.org/2017/01/21/trump-inaugural-events-end-in-prayer-at-national-cathedral/

15. Interview with Jack Ford for the book *All the Presidents' Children*.

10: BLOWING IT UP

1. Unless otherwise indicated, all quotes from Donald Trump Jr. in this chapter come from conversations, emails, and interviews conducted with the author in 2019.
2. Madonna, Remarks at Women's March, January 21, 2017. available at https://www.youtube.com/watch?v=oKhVp--feJk
3. https://www.washingtonpost.com/news/the-fix/wp/2015/12/08/the-philadelphia-daily-news-front-page-goes-there-on-donald-trump/
4. https://rightwingnews.com/top-news/trump-nemesis-rosie-odonnell-slammed-speculating-whether-donalds-son-barron-10-autistic/
5. https://dailycaller.com/2017/01/23/comedy-central-guy-calls-barron-trump-a-date-rapist-to-be-with-a-small-pp/
6. https://dailycaller.com/2017/01/23/comedy-central-guy-calls-barron-trump-a-date-rapist-to-be-with-a-small-pp/
7. https://rightwingnews.com/donald-trump/snl-writer-posts-tweet-mocking-10-yr-old-barron-trump-americas-first-homeschool-shooter/
8. https://www.politico.com/blogs/on-media/2017/02/nyt-reprimands-reporter-for-calling-melania-trump-a-hooker-234962
9. https://www.politico.com/blogs/on-media/2017/02/nyt-reprimands-reporter-for-calling-melania-trump-a-hooker-234962
10. https://www.snopes.com/news/2017/04/12/daily-mail-melania-trump-libel/
11. https://pjmedia.com/trending/2017/03/16/rapper-threatens-to-make-a-sex-slave-of-melania-trump/
12. https://townhall.com/columnists/johnhawkins/2017/04/15/the-7-worst-liberal-attacks-on-donald-trumps-family-n2313730
13. https://www.washingtonpost.com/news/the-fix/wp/2016/01/08/too-far-the-daily-show-plugs-hashtag-donaldtrumpwantstobanghisdaughter/
14. https://townhall.com/columnists/johnhawkins/2017/04/15/the-7-worst-liberal-attacks-on-donald-trumps-family-n2313730
15. https://www.newsbusters.org/blogs/nb/tom-blumer/2017/03/21/chelsea-handler-upset-trump-familys-jeans-will-be-inherited-unborn
16. https://downtrend.com/71superb/chelsea-handler-calls-melania-and-baron-trump-among-the-dumbest-people-in-the-world/
17. https://www.washingtonpost.com/news/arts-and-entertainment/wp/2017/05/30/kathy-griffin-apologizes-for-severed-donald-trump-head-photo-after-backlash/
18. https://www.rollingstone.com/politics/politics-news/johnny-depp-when-was-the-last-time-an-actor-assassinated-a-president-195265/
19. https://www.investors.com/politics/editorials/media-trump-hatred-coverage/
20. https://www.investors.com/politics/editorials/media-trump-hatred-coverage/
21. https://www.bloomberg.com/news/articles/2016-09-26/billionaire-donors-led-by-soros-simons-favor-clinton-over-trump
22. www.marketwatch.com/story/obama-claims-ownership-of-uss-economic-recovery-as-he-blasts-trump-2018-09-07
23. https://www.vox.com/world/2018/1/30/16945312/state-of-the-union-2018-isis
24. https://www.youtube.com/watch?v=1GzEfh6MiCM&t=60s
25. https://www.washingtontimes.com/news/2017/jun/19/scott-pelley-cbs-news-anchor-asks-if-gop-shooting-/
26. https://www.realclearpolitics.com/articles/2017/01/13/trumps_honeymoon_over_before_it_starts.html#!
27. https://shorensteincenter.org/news-coverage-donald-trumps-first-100-days/
28. https://www.investors.com/politics/editorials/media-trump-hatred-coverage/

29. http://thefederalist.com/2018/08/17/screenshots-show-google-shadowbans-conservative-pro-trump-content/

30. https://www.realclearpolitics.com/2019/01/24/media_attacks_on_trump_worst_since_lincoln_464236.html

31. Peter Hermann, Keith L. Alexander, and Michael E. Miller, "Protestors Who Destroyed Property on Inauguration Day Were Part of Well-Organized Group," *Washington Post*, January 21, 2017.

32. https://www.freep.com/story/news/2018/01/10/pink-pussyhats-feminists-hats-womens-march/1013630001/; see also https://www.theblaze.com/news/2018/01/12/pink-pussyhats-of-the-anti-trump-womens-march-are-falling-out-of-favor-the-reason-is-quite-ironic

33. https://www.cnn.com/2017/01/23/entertainment/madonna-white-house/index.html

34. Jim Ryan, "Portland's Anti-Trump Protest Turns Violent, as Rioters Rampage in Pearl," *The Oregonian*, November 10, 2016.

35. https://www.youtube.com/watch?v=DoCyiQeHfZg

36. https://dailycaller.com/2016/11/17/heres-a-list-of-completely-substantiated-and-underreported-attacks-on-trump-supporters/

37. "The Trump Resistance Movement Builds," BBC News, November 17, 2016.

38. "#Resist," Know Your Meme, accessed June 11, 2019 at https://knowyourmeme.com/memes/resist

39. Michael Finnegan, "Trump's Electoral College Win All but Certain, but Hollywood Actors Urge Revolt," *Los Angeles Times*, December 15, 2016.

40. Marie Berry and Erica Chenoweth, "Who Made the Women's March?" in *The Resistance: The Dawn of the Anti-Trump Opposition Movement*, ed. David S. Meyer and Sidney Tarrow (New York: Oxford University Press, 2018).

41. Liam Stack, "Attack on Alt-Right Leader Has Internet Asking: Is It O.K. to Punch a Nazi?" *New York Times*, January 21, 2017.

42. https://dailycaller.com/2017/08/14/journalist-accused-of-looking-like-a-white-supremacist-by-anti-fascists/

43. Tom Dickenson, "Meet the Leaders of the Trump Resistance," *Rolling Stone*, January 13, 2017.

44. Elisabeth Kübler-Ross, *On Death and Dying* (New York: Scribner, 1963).

45. https://video.foxnews.com/v/5291959751001/

46. https://www.realclearpolitics.com/video/2018/06/24/maxine_waters_the_people_are_going_to_turn_on_trump_enablers.html

11: RUSSIAN ROULETTE

1. Interview with President Trump, January 24, 2019.

2. https://www.politicususa.com/2018/07/19/report-may-provide-proof-that-trump-is-a-russian-spy.html

3. Interview with Jared Kushner, 2019.

4. https://www.politico.com/story/2017/11/14/hillary-clinton-uranium-one-deal-russia-explainer-244895

5. https://www.nytimes.com/2015/04/24/us/cash-flowed-to-clinton-foundation-as-russians-pressed-for-control-of-uranium-company.html

6. https://www.washingtonpost.com/opinions/yes-the-clintons-should-be-investigated/2017/11/19/d88bb652-cb15-11e7-b0cf-7689a9f2d84e_story.html

7. https://www.washingtonpost.com/opinions/yes-the-clintons-should-be-investigated/2017/11/19/d88bb652-cb15-11e7-b0cf-7689a9f2d84e_story.html

8. https://www.washingtonpost.com/opinions/yes-the-clintons-should-be-investigated/2017/11/19/d88bb652-cb15-11e7-b0cf-7689a9f2d84e_story.html

9. https://thehill.com/policy/technology/279359-clinton-is-largest-benefactor-of-facebook-donations

10. Matt Apuzzo, Adam Goldman, and Nicholas Fandos, "Code Name Crossfire Hurricane: The Secret Origins of the Trump Investigation," *New York Times*, May 16, 2018.

11. Frank Miele, "Mueller 'Strzok Out' with his Whitewash Report," *Real Clear Politics*, April 19, 2019.

12. Philip Bump, "What the Strzok-Page 'Insurance Policy' E-Mail Was Actually About," *Washington Post*, March 14, 2019.

13. https://www.newsweek.com/peter-strzok-trump-smell-hillbillies-1020892

14. John McCain and Mark Salter, *The Restless Wave: Good Times, Just Causes, Great Fights and Other Appreciations* (New York: Simon and Schuster, 2018)

15. McCain and Salter, *The Restless Wave*.

16. McCain and Salter, *The Restless Wave*.

17. Tim Haines, "James Baker: Comey and I Worried about Creating Any J. Edgar Hoover Impression with Steele Dossier," *Real Clear Politics*, May 16, 2019.

18. Susan Rice, "Susan Rice January 20, 2017 Email to Self," *WikiSource* 2018, accessed June 12, 2019, https://en.wikisource.org/wiki/Susan_Rice_January_20,_2017_E-mail_to_Self.

19. Rice, "Email to Self."

20. Evan Perez, Jim Sciutto, Jake Tapper and Carl Bernstein, "Intel Chiefs Present Trump with Claims of Russian Efforts to Compromise Him," CNN, January 12, 2017.

21. Ken Dilanian, "FBI's Comey Told Trump about Russia Dossier after Intel Briefing," NBC News, January 12, 2017.

22. Caitlin Yilek, "Court to Unseal Christopher Steele Deposition," *Washington Examiner*, February 28, 2019.

23. https://www.theguardian.com/us-news/2018/jul/11/germany-and-russia-gas-links-trump-questions-europe-nord-stream2

24. This conversation took place between the president and the author in 2019.

12: SUNDAY EVENING AT JARED AND IVANKA'S HOUSE

1. Unless otherwise indicated, all quotes from Jared Kushner in this chapter come from conversations or interviews in 2019.

2. https://www.townandcountrymag.com/society/politics/a9168995/ivanka-trump-west-wing-office/

3. Vicky Ward, *Kushner, Inc.: Greed. Ambition. Corruption. The Extraordinary Story of Jared Kushner and Ivanka Trump* (New York: St. Martin Press, 2019) Also cited in this *New York Times* story: https://www.nytimes.com/2019/03/11/us/politics/ivanka-trump-jared-kushner-book.html

4. https://www.nytimes.com/2019/03/11/us/politics/ivanka-trump-jared-kushner-book.html

5. https://www.nytimes.com/2019/03/11/us/politics/ivanka-trump-jared-kushner-book.html

6. https://cei.org/blog/obama-claims-paris-climate-agreement-not-treaty-huh

7. https://www.theatlantic.com/science/archive/2017/05/most-americans-support-staying-in-the-paris-agreement/528663/

8. https://www.pennlive.com/news/2017/06/trump_i_was_elected_to_represe.html

9. Interview with President Trump, January 2019.

10. https://www.businessinsider.com/paris-climate-agreement-trump-why-us

11. https://personalliberty.com/sexist-donald-trump-empowers-women-white-house/

12. https://nypost.com/2016/11/22/trumps-thinks-kushner-could-help-broker-peace-in-middle-east/

13. https://www.nytimes.com/live/trump-at-the-new-york-times-the-tweets/

14. https://www.businessinsider.com/what-does-jared-kushner-do-in-trump-administration-2017-4

15. https://www.businessinsider.com/what-does-jared-kushner-do-in-trump-administration-2017-4

16. https://www.newsweek.com/donald-trump-ivanka-trump-address-congress-562664

17. https://dailycaller.com/2017/12/06/flashback-all-the-times-past-presidents-promised-to-move-us-embassy-to-jerusalem/

18. Interview with Jared Kushner, May 2019.

13: THE GREATEST JOBS PRESIDENT GOD EVER CREATED

1. Interview with Jared Kushner, May 2019.
2. Conversations with President Trump, 2019.
3. https://www.newsbusters.org/blogs/nb/rich-noyes/2018/10/09/study-econ-boom-ignored-tv-trump-coverage-hits-92-percent-negative
4. https://www.blackenterprise.com/black-unemployment-rate-falls/
5. https://www.whitehouse.gov/articles/americas-unemployment-rate-falls-lowest-level-almost-50-years/
6. https://nypost.com/2015/06/16/i-will-be-the-greatest-jobs-president-that-god-ever-created-trump/
7. https://thehill.com/blogs/blog-briefing-room/news/281936-obama-to-trump-what-magic-wand-do-you-have
8. http://larrysummers.com/2017/01/17/economy-under-trump-plan-for-the-worst/
9. https://www.washingtonpost.com/news/wonk/wp/2017/05/23/larry-summers-trumps-budget-is-simply-ludicrous/
10. https://financialtribune.com/articles/world-economy/78259/trump-is-dreaming-pigs-dont-fly
11. https://financialtribune.com/articles/world-economy/78259/trump-is-dreaming-pigs-dont-fly
12. https://www.economy.com/mark-zandi/documents/2016-06-17-Trumps-Economic-Policies.pdf
13. https://www.economy.com/mark-zandi/documents/2016-06-17-Trumps-Economic-Policies.pdf
14. https://www.latimes.com/business/hiltzik/la-fi-3percent-20170519-story.html
15. https://www.theguardian.com/business/live/2018/aug/29/markets-buoyed-by-trump-trade-deal-ahead-of-us-gdp-business-live
16. Unless otherwise indicated, all quotes from Eric Trump in this chapter come from conversations, emails, and interviews in 2019.
17. https://www.forbes.com/sites/kenrapoza/2019/01/14/china-is-losing-the-trade-war-in-nearly-every-way/#47d6631d7f03
18. Interview with Lara Trump, 2019.
19. https://www.japantimes.co.jp/news/2019/06/26/world/politics-diplomacy-world/first-ladys-spokeswoman-white-house-press-secretary/
20. My immediate boss was David Demarest, the director of communications, who answered to Sununu.
21. Unless otherwise indicated, all quotes Mick Mulvaney in this chapter come from an interview conducted in his White House office in the summer of 2019.
22. https://www.youtube.com/watch?v=cZ5dVBa3grw
23. https://www.businessinsider.com/jared-kushner-avi-berkowitz-trump-2017-3
24. https://www.newsweek.com/tax-reform-wont-pass-645118
25. https://www.theepochtimes.com/tax-reform-a-big-beautiful-christmas-present-says-trump_2363920.html

14: THE ISIS HORROR STORY

1. https://www.washingtonexaminer.com/trump-says-he-has-a-secret-plan-to-beat-the-islamic-state
2. https://news.nationalgeographic.com/news/2014/08/140809-iraq-yazidis-minority-isil-religion-history/
3. https://www.youtube.com/watch?v=pzNeadAezJ4

4. https://www.catholic.org/news/international/middle_east/story.php?id=58827
5. https://www.bbc.com/news/world-africa-31533391
6. PBS was an exception. https://www.pbs.org/newshour/world/boko-haram
7. https://www.newsweek.com/isis-release-2015-budget-projections-2bn-250m-surplus-296577
8. https://www.nytimes.com/2016/04/21/world/africa/boko-haram-and-isis-are-collaborating-more-us-military-says.html
9. https://www.csmonitor.com/World/Security-Watch/terrorism-security/2015/0206/Nigerian-military-recovers-weapons-stolen-by-Boko-Haram
10. https://www.wired.com/story/terror-industrial-complex-isis-munitions-supply-chain/
11. https://www.nytimes.com/2007/03/06/opinion/06kristof.html
12. https://www.ajc.com/news/world-govt--politics/obama-compares-isis-the-crusades-receives-heavy-backlash/GXNEQVOrHuYoqqMZxRaSUL/
13. https://www.businessinsider.com/donald-trump-bomb-isis-2015-11
14. https://www.heritage.org/middle-east/commentary/did-trump-really-beat-isis
15. https://foreignpolicy.com/2016/09/26/clintons-debate-take-on-trump-only-secret-is-he-doesnt-have-a-plan/
16. https://www.cnbc.com/2017/11/23/isis-finished-experts-warn-the-terror-group-is-still-a-serious-global-threat.html
17. https://www.theguardian.com/world/2018/dec/19/has-isis-been-defeated-in-syria-as-trump-claims
18. https://www.msn.com/en-us/news/video/damon-trump-naive-to-think-isis-is-defeated/vi-BBRjh5Z
19. https://www.newyorker.com/news/dispatch/how-trump-betrayed-the-general-who-defeated-isis
20. https://www.usatoday.com/story/news/world/2019/04/06/hoda-muthana-married-isis-fighters-so-trump-wont-let-her-back-usa/3350233002/
21. https://hotair.com/archives/2019/03/04/hoda-muthana-trump-study-legal-system/
22. https://www.mei.edu/sites/default/files/2019-03/The%20Unsustainability%20of%20ISIS%20Detentions%20in%20Syria_reduced.pdf
23. https://www.washingtonpost.com/news/posteverything/wp/2018/01/25/obamas-isis-policy-is-working-for-trump/
24. https://thehill.com/homenews/administration/435438-trump-isis-members-are-losers-and-will-always-be-losers
25. Interview with an anonymous White House source.
26. https://www.whitehouse.gov/presidential-actions/presidential-memorandum-plan-defeat-islamic-state-iraq-syria/
27. https://www.heritage.org/middle-east/commentary/did-trump-really-beat-isis
28. https://www.businessinsider.com/how-isis-lost-raqqa-capital-2017-10#the-syrian-democratic-forces-that-led-the-raqqa-campaign-is-a-coalition-of-various-militias-however-it-has-always-been-led-by-the-kurds-2
29. Conversation with Donald Trump Jr., 2019.
30. Interview with a high-level administration source who was present at the key meetings.
31. https://www.dailycaller.com/2018/11/15/donald-trump-white-house-turnover-fox-news/

15: AMERICA'S SHAMEFUL SECRET

1. https://www.washingtonpost.com/opinions/global-opinions/trump-gives-american-hostages-held-abroad-hope--and-also-takes-it-away/2018/12/23/965a5f28-046b-11e9-b6a9-0aa5c2fcc9e4_story.html
2. https://www.chicagotribune.com/nation-world/ct-obama-hostage-ransom-20150624-story.html
3. https://abcnews.go.com/International/government-threatened-foley-family-ransom-payments-mother-slain/story?id=25453963

4. https://abcnews.go.com/International/government-threatened-foley-family-ransom-payments-mother-slain/story?id=25453963
5. https://abcnews.go.com/International/government-threatened-foley-family-ransom-payments-mother-slain/story?id=25453963
6. This according to a source close to the president.
7. https://www.washingtonpost.com/politics/freed-egyptian-american-prisoner-returns-home-following-trump-intervention/2017/04/20/d569fe1e-2608-11e7-bb9d-8cd6118e1409_story.html
8. https://www.whitehouse.gov/briefings-statements/remarks-president-trump-meeting-u-s-citizen-freed-venezuela/
9. https://www.nytimes.com/2017/06/20/world/asia/otto-warmbier-north-korea.html
10. https://dailycaller.com/2018/05/27/president-trump-freed-17-prisoners/
11. https://www.nytimes.com/2018/05/10/us/politics/trump-korea-detainees-pompeo.html
12. https://www.nytimes.com/2018/05/10/us/politics/trump-korea-detainees-pompeo.html
13. https://www.nytimes.com/2018/05/26/world/americas/american-citizen-held-in-venezuela-released-trump-announces.html
14. https://www.whitehouse.gov/briefings-statements/remarks-president-trump-meeting-u-s-citizen-freed-venezuela/
15. https://www.ctvnews.ca/politics/trudeau-looks-to-trump-to-help-canadians-detained-in-china-1.4482222
16. https://www.nytimes.com/2017/05/16/world/middleeast/erdogan-turkey-trump.html
17. https://www.cnn.com/2017/05/16/politics/trump-erdogan-visit/index.html
18. Unless otherwise indicated, all quotations in this chapter of Andrew Brunson come from the author's personal interviews with the subject in 2019.
19. https://www1.cbn.com/cbnnews/world/2017/november/still-waiting-for-my-dad-to-walk-me-down-the-aisle-a-daughters-plea-for-imprisoned-father-to-be-freed-from-turkish-prison
20. https://www.dw.com/en/trump-demands-turkey-release-us-christian-pastor-andrew-brunson-or-face-sanctions/a-44842486
21. https://www.thehindu.com/news/international/trump-urges-erdogan-to-free-us-pastor-held-in-turkey/article24457853.ece
22. https://www.wktv.com/content/national/489452121.html
23. https://www.reuters.com/article/usa-trump-highlights/highlights-key-quotes-from-reuters-interview-with-trump-idUSL2N1VB111
24. https://www.reuters.com/article/usa-trump-highlights/highlights-key-quotes-from-reuters-interview-with-trump-idUSL2N1VB111
25. Unless otherwise noted, all quotes from Andrew Brunson in this chapter are taken from an interview in March 2019.
26. https://www.dw.com/en/trump-demands-turkey-release-us-christian-pastor-andrew-brunson-or-face-sanctions/a-44842486
27. https://eclj.org/religious-freedom/pace/open-letter-to-turkey
28. https://www.chattanoogan.com/2018/7/19/373144/Senators-Introduce-Bill-Demanding-That.aspx
29. https://www.reuters.com/article/us-turkey-politics-erdogan/erdogan-says-u-s-turned-its-back-on-turkey-upsetting-ankara-idUSKBN1KW0B3
30. https://www.nytimes.com/2018/08/10/us/politics/trump-turkey-tariffs-currency.html
31. https://www.france24.com/en/20180810-turkey-curency-lira-plunge-erdogan-trump-twitter-tariffs
32. https://www.thenational.ae/world/the-americas/trump-hits-turkey-with-doubled-tariffs-as-lira-tumbles-1.758702
33. https://www.telegraph.co.uk/news/2018/08/10/erdogan-tells-turkish-people-trust-god-lira-tumbles-us-row/

34. https://www.worldwatchmonitor.org/2018/07/hopes-dashed-for-release-of-pastor-andrew-brunson-as-trial-to-continue-into-october/
35. https://www.breitbart.com/national-security/2018/10/12/freed-pastor-andrew-brunson-this-is-the-day-our-family-has-been-praying-for/
36. https://www.washingtonpost.com/politics/trump-to-meet-evangelical-pastor-brunson-after-he-was-freed-from-turkish-jail/2018/10/13/352faf66-cef9-11e8-920f-dd52e1ae4570_story.html
37. https://www.whitehouse.gov/briefings-statements/remarks-president-trump-meeting-pastor-andrew-brunson/
38. https://www.whitehouse.gov/briefings-statements/remarks-president-trump-meeting-pastor-andrew-brunson/
39. https://www.whitehouse.gov/briefings-statements/remarks-president-trump-meeting-pastor-andrew-brunson/
40. https://obamawhitehouse.archives.gov/the-press-office/2015/06/24/presidential-policy-directive-hostage-recovery-activities

16: THE FOREIGN POLICY PRESIDENT

1. https://www.frontpagemag.com/fpm/233771/obama-and-elizabeth-warrens-big-lie-about-student-daniel-greenfield
2. https://www.harvard.edu/about-harvard/harvard-glance/endowment
3. https://assets.documentcloud.org/documents/3007589/Nationalsecurityletter.pdf
4. https://www.investors.com/politics/editorials/foreign-policy-trump-critics-successes/
5. https://www.politico.com/story/2019/02/05/trump-foreign-policy-afghanistan-1145766
6. https://www.politico.com/story/2019/02/05/trump-foreign-policy-afghanistan-1145766
7. https://video.foxbusiness.com/v/5808198024001/#sp=show-clips
8. https://www.breitbart.com/politics/2019/04/03/making-nato-stronger-again-alliance-chief-says-trumps-message-having-real-impact/
9. https://www.nytimes.com/2019/05/24/us/politics/trump-japan-abe-flattery.html
10. https://www.washingtonpost.com/news/worldviews/wp/2017/11/08/on-the-golf-course-japans-abe-did-a-ninja-stunt-and-trump-didnt-even-notice/
11. Interview with high administration source, 2019.
12. https://www.businessinsider.com/donald-trump-playboy-interview-trade-foreign-policy-japan-2017-2
13. https://www.thebalance.com/trade-deficit-by-county-3306264
14. https://www.usatoday.com/story/news/politics/2019/05/26/trumps-japan-trip-sumo-hibachi-north-korea-small-missiles/1243938001/
15. High administration source, May 2019.
16. https://mashable.com/2017/11/09/arabella-china-video-xi/
17. https://www.theguardian.com/us-news/2017/apr/12/trump-xi-jinping-chocolate-cake-syria-strikes
18. https://abcnews.go.com/Politics/trump-merkel/story?id=46198767
19. https://abcnews.go.com/Politics/trump-merkel/story?id=46198767
20. https://www.bustle.com/p/angela-merkel-prepared-to-meet-trump-for-the-first-time-by-reportedly-watching-the-apprentice-15539293
21. https://thehill.com/homenews/administration/324536-trump-jokes-that-he-and-merkel-were-both-wiretapped-by-obama
22. https://thepoliticalinsider.com/hillarys-campaign-chair-admits-trump-obama-wiretap/
23. Interview with top administration source, May 2019.
24. https://www.politico.eu/article/german-chancellor-angela-merkel-takes-aim-at-donald-trump-in-harvard-tear-down-walls-speech/
25. Interview with top administration source, May 2019.
26. ttps://www.politico.eu/article/mike-pompeo-hits-berlin-for-make-up-talks-with-chancellor-angela-merkel/

27. Interview with top administration source, May 2019.
28. Interview with Jared Kushner, May 2019.
29. https://www.cbsnews.com/news/is-trumps-friend-jim-who-no-longer-goes-to-paris-real/
30. https://www.dailymail.co.uk/news/article-4693482/First-Ladies-Brigitte-Macron-Melania-Trump-meet.html
31. https://downtrend.com/71superb/how-come-it-wasnt-fascist-when-chuck-schumer-wanted-a-military-parade/
32. Interview with high administration official, May 2019.
33. https://www.reuters.com/article/uk-britain-eu-may/brexit-brings-down-may-johnson-stakes-leadership-claim-idUSKCN1SU0UF
34. https://www.reuters.com/article/uk-britain-eu-may/brexit-brings-down-may-johnson-stakes-leadership-claim-idUSKCN1SU0UF
35. https://www.politico.eu/article/brexit-boris-johnson-donald-trump-all-sorts-of-chaos-says/
36. https://www.bbc.com/news/uk-politics-49084605
37. https://www.corriere.it/elezioni-2018/notizie/elezioni-2018-exit-poll-risultati-proiezioni-spoglio-eb21387e-1ff1-11e8-a09a-92b478235f6f.shtml
38. https://www.washingtonpost.com/news/fact-checker/wp/2018/03/01/was-obamas-1-7-billion-cash-deal-with-iran-prohibited-by-u-s-law/
39. https://www.politico.com/magazine/story/2017/09/22/iran-nuclear-deal-bomb-215636
40. https://twitter.com/realDonaldTrump/status/1153290669424807936
41. https://www.forbes.com/sites/daneberhart/2019/07/22/trump-has-put-iran-in-a-corner-now-what/#184ebc2c7875
42. https://www.usatoday.com/story/news/politics/2019/07/22/trump-denies-iran-claim-capturing-american-spies/1793490001/

17: THE MONROE DOCTRINE REVISITED

1. https://cronkitenews.azpbs.org/2016/03/19/19044/
2. https://www.breitbart.com/national-security/2019/02/08/u-s-admiral-maduro-distrusts-venezuelans-so-much-he-uses-only-cuban-bodyguards/
3. https://www.nbcnews.com/news/world/russia-sends-2-nuclear-capable-bombers-venezuela-n946246
4. https://www.militarytimes.com/flashpoints/2019/03/25/pompeo-says-russian-troops-in-venezuela-increases-tensions/
5. https://ijr.com/bernie-sanders-fails-call-maduro-dictator-venezuela/
6. https://bigthink.com/strange-maps/which-countries-support-maduro-guaido
7. https://www.reuters.com/article/us-usa-cuba/in-major-shift-trump-to-allow-lawsuits-against-foreign-firms-in-cuba-idUSKCN1RS1VY
8. My interview with Luis Videgaray took place in January 2019. All quotes from him in this chapter come from that interview.
9. https://www.vox.com/policy-and-politics/2018/10/2/17925424/trump-mexico-trade-deal-nafta-workers-labor
10. https://www.reuters.com/article/us-trade-nafta-kushner-insight/how-trumps-son-in-law-helped-salvage-the-north-american-trade-zone-idUSKCN1MC04M
11. https://www.washingtonagnetwork.com/2018/12/03/leaders-sign-usmca-in-argentina/
12. See also, https://thenationalsentinel.com/2018/12/28/trump-may-cancel-nafta-outright-to-force-dems-hands-on-trade/
13. https://www.nytimes.com/2018/11/26/world/americas/honduras-brother-drug-charges.html
14. https://www.washingtontimes.com/news/2019/jul/4/joe-biden-opposed-helping-refugees-from-south-viet/
15. https://www.sfchronicle.com/nation/article/America-s-long-history-of-shunning-refugees-6639536.php
16. https://www.washingtonpost.com/news/the-fix/wp/2016/12/01/donald-trump-will-be-president-thanks-to-80000-people-in-three-states/

17. https://www.nbcnews.com/politics/immigration/record-number-undocumented-immigrants-flooded-southern-border-may-n1014186
18. https://time.com/3649511/george-hw-bush-quote-read-my-lips/
19. http://news.bbc.co.uk/2/hi/17301.stm
20. https://www.nytimes.com/2003/01/28/politics/state-of-the-union-address.html
21. https://www.washingtonexaminer.com/news/healthcare-for-illegal-immigrants-all-10-democrats-raise-their-hand

18: NO COLLUSION, NO OBSTRUCTION

1. https://slate.com/human-interest/2014/11/sol-wachtler-the-judge-who-coined-indict-a-ham-sandwich-was-himself-indicted.html
2. https://www.oxfordeagle.com/2018/05/09/show-me-the-man-and-ill-show-you-the-crime/
3. https://www.realclearpolitics.com/video/2017/06/06/lawrence_odonnell_trump_made_decision_to_destroy_his_presidency_by_not_blocking_comey_testimony.html
4. https://www.cnn.com/videos/tv/2017/07/30/rs-douglas-brinkley-trump-is-unfit-for-command.cnn
5. Fox News, May 2017.
6. https://www.cnn.com/2017/06/07/politics/norman-eisen-james-comey-richard-nixon-tapes-cnntv/index.html
7. CNN, August 2017.
8. MNSBC, August 2017.
9. Harriet Agerholm, *UK Independent*, February 17, 2017.
10. Stephanie Lindquist, *Chicago Tribune*, July 19, 2018.
11. James Comey, *A Higher Loyalty: Truth, Lies, and Leadership* (New York: Flatiron Books, 2018).
12. Comey, *Higher Loyalty*, 203.
13. Comey, *Higher Loyalty*, 210.
14. Comey, *Higher Loyalt*, 234.
15. https://www.washingtonpost.com/world/national-security/head-of-pentagon-intelligence-agency-forced-out-officials-say/2014/04/30/ec15a366-d09d-11e3-9e25-188ebe1fa93b_story.html
16. James Kitfield, "How Mike Flynn Became America's Angriest General," *Politico*, October 16, 2016.
17. https://www.npr.org/2015/04/15/399853577/former-fbi-agent-speaks-out-i-was-not-protected. Carrie Johnson and Evie Stone, *All Things Considered*, National Public Radio, April 15, 2015.
18. Greg Jarrett, *The Russia Hoax* (New York: Broadside Books 2018).
19. Comey, *Higher Loyalty*.
20. https://althouse.blogspot.com/2018/06/just-went-to-southern-virginia-walmart.html
21. Jarrett, *Russia Hoax*.
22. Comey, *Higher Loyalty*.
23. Jarrett, *Russia Hoax*.
24. Comey, *Higher Loyalty*.
25. https://news.yahoo.com/trump-time-will-tell-happens-sessions-201937363.html
26. Garrett Graff, "Robert Mueller Chooses His Investigatory Dream Team," *Wired*, June 14, 2017.
27. Michelle Mark, "Meet the All-Star Team of Lawyers Robert Mueller Has Working on Trump-Russia Investigation," *Business Insider*, May 17, 2018
28. Mark, "All-Star Team."
29. Sidney Brown, *Licensed to Lie* (Dallas: Brown Books Publishing Group, 2014).
30. https://www.businessinsider.com/who-is-andrew-weissman-mueller-trump-clinton-russia-investigation-fbi-2017-12
31. Glenn Greenwald, "Beyond Buzzfeed: The 10 Worst, Most Embarrassing US Media Failures on the Trump=Russia Story," *The Intercept*, January 20, 2019, https://theintercept.com/2019/01/20/beyond-buzzfeed-the-10-worst-most-embarrassing-u-s-media-failures-on-the-trumprussia-story.

32. Greenwald, "Beyond Buzzfeed."
33. Greenwald, "Beyond Buzzfeed."
34. Greenwald, "Beyond Buzzfeed."
35. Greenwald, "Beyond Buzzfeed."
36. Greenwald, "Beyond Buzzfeed."
37. https://boingboing.net/2018/12/10/robert-mueller-devotional-cand.html
38. https://www.bizpacreview.com/2018/12/02/snl-chicks-sing-twisted-all-i-want-for-christmas-is-mueller-or-a-coup-yet-were-going-to-ban-baby-its-cold-outside-698841
39. https://www.politifact.com/truth-o-meter/article/2019/mar/25/what-democrats-said-about-trump-collusion-mueller-/
40. http://edition.cnn.com/TRANSCRIPTS/1901/10/nday.06.html
41. http://www.msnbc.com/transcripts/all-in/2018-10-17
42. https://www.youtube.com/watch?v=QxRPwhdb5z0&t=5102
43. https://www.newsweek.com/donald-trump-jr-will-be-indicted-mueller-former-prosecutor-says-and-will-help-1315865
44. https://thehill.com/hilltv/rising/436750-davis-says-evidence-shows-trump-jr-could-be-indicted
45. https://www.washingtontimes.com/news/2019/feb/9/donald-trump-jr-expects-to-be-indicted-claims-repo/
46. https://www.washingtontimes.com/news/2019/feb/9/donald-trump-jr-expects-to-be-indicted-claims-repo/
47. https://www.washingtontimes.com/news/2019/feb/9/donald-trump-jr-expects-to-be-indicted-claims-repo/
48. https://www.washingtonpost.com/news/post-nation/wp/2018/05/31/muellers-investigation-cost-16-7-million-in-just-under-a-year-new-documents-show/
49. Executive summary, *Report on the Investigation into Russian Interference in the 2016 Presidential Election*, US Department of Justice, Washington, DC, March 2019.
50. https://www.nytimes.com/2019/03/24/us/politics/trump-robert-mueller.html
51. https://www.newsbusters.org/blogs/nb/curtis-houck/2019/03/22/kaboom-cnn-admits-no-further-mueller-indictments-huge-victory
52. "Read Attorney General William Barr's Summary of the Mueller Report," *New York Times Interactive*, March 24, 2019
53. C-Span 2, "Road to the White House," June 18, 2019

19: GOD AND THE SUPREME COURT

1. https://www.theguardian.com/us-news/2019/mar/10/trump-legacy-conservative-judges-district-courts
2. https://www.elitedaily.com/p/trumps-federal-court-judge-appointments-are-reshaping-the-us-judicial-system-in-a-big-way-15557091
3. https://www.elitedaily.com/p/trumps-federal-court-judge-appointments-are-reshaping-the-us-judicial-system-in-a-big-way-15557091
4. https://www.latimes.com/archives/la-xpm-2009-may-04-na-souter4-story.html
5. https://www.nationalreview.com/2018/09/brett-kavanaugh-nomination-stop-stalling-and-vote/
6. https://www.nbcnews.com/politics/justice-department/new-questions-raised-about-avenatti-claims-regarding-kavanaugh-n924596
7. https://www.nbcnews.com/politics/justice-department/new-questions-raised-about-avenatti-claims-regarding-kavanaugh-n924596
8. https://dailycaller.com/2019/03/25/michael-avenatti-indicted/
9. https://dailycaller.com/2019/03/25/michael-avenatti-indicted/
10. https://www.pewresearch.org/fact-tank/2016/11/09/how-the-faithful-voted-a-preliminary-2016-analysis/
11. https://www.imdb.com/title/tt1727387/

12. https://www.youtube.com/watch?v=NGGACRwYDo8

13. https://www.washingtonpost.com/posteverything/wp/2016/11/22/why-did-obama-win-more-white-evangelical-votes-than-clinton-he-asked-for-them/

14. Unless otherwise indicated all quotes attributed to Paula White in this chapter come from conversations, emails, and interviews with the author conducted in 2019.

15. https://www.washingtonpost.com/archive/local/1993/12/26/the-rev-norman-vincent-peale-positive-thinking-author-dies/9a5be738-2e33-4c8c-b046-b0280cad421a/

16. Sayne Lee and Phillip Luke Sinitiere, *Holy Mavericks: Evangelical Innovators and the Spiritual Marketplace* (New York: NYU Press, 2009), 110.

17. https://pagesix.com/2010/03/06/kid-rocks-offering-to-pastor/

18. Quotations attributed to Donald Trump in this chapter were made to the author by Paula White.

19. https://www.businessinsider.com/trump-on-god-i-dont-like-to-have-to-ask-for-forgiveness-2016-1

20. This story was told to the author by Cary Summers, the president of the Museum of the Bible.

21. https://www.charismanews.com/politics/55309-scalia-s-advice-on-who-should-replace-him-on-the-supreme-court-bench

22. Robert Knight, "Giving Trump's Accomplishments Their Due," *Washington Times*, May 6, 2019, https://www.washingtontimes.com/news/2018/may/6/giving-trumps-accomplishments-their-due/

23. https://www.washingtonpost.com/news/acts-of-faith/wp/2017/02/01/thrilled-with-trumps-supreme-court-pick-heres-what-evangelicals-want-next/

24. https://www.dailymail.co.uk/news/article-4183276/Preacher-branded-heretic-takes-place-Trump-s-side.html

20: Tiffany's Tale

1. Unless otherwise indicated, all quotes from Tiffany Trump in this chapter come from an interview with the author in 2019.

2. https://www.instyle.com/news/tiffany-trump-reelection-2020

3. https://www.bustle.com/p/tiffany-trumps-quotes-about-her-dad-speak-volumes-about-their-relationship-8687971

4. I told this story in *All the Presidents' Children* (New York: Atria Books, 2003).

5. https://time.com/4530197/college-free-speech-zone/

6. Unless otherwise indicated, all quotations from Donald Trump Jr. in this chapter are from interviews conducted by the author in 2019.

7. https://time.com/4645541/donald-trump-white-house-oval-office/

8. https://www.washingtontimes.com/news/2019/may/27/ian-bremmer-time-magazine-columnist-defends-fake-d/

9. https://www.washingtontimes.com/news/2019/may/27/ian-bremmer-time-magazine-columnist-defends-fake-d/

10. https://twitchy.com/jacobb-38/2019/05/26/deleted-journalist-ian-bremmer-gets-royally-spanked-after-posting-a-fake-trump-quote-to-teach-everyone-a-lesson/

11. Doug Wead, *All the Presidents' Children*, (New York: Atria Books, 2003), 105–123 and 287–288.

12. https://www.nytimes.com/2007/05/08/washington/08queen.html

13. https://www.standard.co.uk/news/uk/donald-trump-to-visit-uk-next-year-but-not-on-a-fullblown-state-visit-and-he-will-not-stay-with-the-a3655846.html

14. https://www.elitedaily.com/p/why-did-queen-elizabeth-meet-donald-trump-alone-two-royals-reportedly-refused-to-attend-9768125

15. From interview with Brad Parscale, 2019.

16. https://www.nbcnews.com/politics/white-house/donald-trump-arrives-britain-state-visit-n1013041

21: MELANIA'S REVENGE

1. https://www.foxnews.com/entertainment/melania-trump-haters-attacked-first-lady-throughout-2018-from-mocking-accent-to-slamming-christmas-decor

2. https://www.cheatsheet.com/entertainment/how-many-languages-does-melania-trump-speak.html/

3. Descriptions of Slovenia come from interviews conducted by the author during multiple travels to the country. For purposes of this book, the author recently followed up with Skype calls and emails to sources. My translator was Olga Kovalova.

4. https://abc7.com/he-would-be-a-great-leader-melania-trump-said-of-then-boyfriend-in-1999-interview/4472103/

5. This came out of a discussion with two White House sources who wished to remain anonymous. In general, sources were very respectful of the first lady and reluctant to provide the author with information about her.

6. http://elanguageworld.com/perks-of-being-multilingual/

7. https://abc7.com/he-would-be-a-great-leader-melania-trump-said-of-then-boyfriend-in-1999-interview/4472103/

8. https://www.cnn.com/2018/03/20/politics/melania-trump-cyberbulling/index.html

9. https://abcnews.go.com/US/great-leader-melania-trump-boyfriend-donald-trump-1999/story?id=58465095

10. https://abcnews.go.com/US/great-leader-melania-trump-boyfriend-donald-trump-1999/story?id=58465095

11. https://abcnews.go.com/US/great-leader-melania-trump-boyfriend-donald-trump-1999/story?id=58465095

12. https://abcnews.go.com/US/great-leader-melania-trump-boyfriend-donald-trump-1999/story?id=58465095

13. Unless otherwise indicated, all quotes from Donald Trump Jr. in this chapter are taken from interviews conducted throughout 2019.

14. Unless otherwise indicated, all quotes from Lara Trump in this chapter are taken from interviews conducted throughout 2019.

15. https://www.cnn.com/2018/12/15/opinions/melania-trumps-spokeswoman-speaks-out-grisham/index.html

16. https://www.cnn.com/2018/12/15/opinions/melania-trumps-spokeswoman-speaks-out-grisham/index.html

17. https://www.nytimes.com/2018/10/07/world/africa/melania-trump-africa-trip.html

18. https://www.nytimes.com/2018/10/07/world/africa/melania-trump-africa-trip.html

19. Unless otherwise indicated, all quotes from Lara Trump come from interviews and email follow-up questions conducted in 2019.

20. https://abcnews.go.com/US/great-leader-melania-trump-boyfriend-donald-trump-1999/story?id=58465095

21. https://www.nytimes.com/2018/10/03/us/melania-trump-africa-trip.html

22. https://www.cnn.com/2018/09/26/politics/melania-trump-africa/index.html

23. https://www.nytimes.com/2018/10/03/us/melania-trump-africa-trip.html

24. https://www.nytimes.com/2018/10/03/us/melania-trump-africa-trip.html

25. https://www.nytimes.com/2018/10/07/world/africa/melania-trump-africa-trip.html

26. https://www.c-span.org/video/?460495-1/lady-melania-trump-marks-be-best-year-anniversary

27. https://www.c-span.org/video/?460495-1/lady-melania-trump-marks-be-best-year-anniversary

28. https://www.msn.com/en-us/video/t/eric-bolling-declares-melania-trump-is-the-most-important-and-accomplished-first-lady-in-american-history/vp-AAB28xS

29. https://www.msn.com/en-us/video/t/eric-bolling-declares-melania-trump-is-the-most-important-and-accomplished-first-lady-in-american-history/vp-AAB28xS

30. https://www.foxnews.com/entertainment/melania-trump-haters-attacked-first-lady-throughout-2018-from-mocking-accent-to-slamming-christmas-decor
31. https://www.foxnews.com/entertainment/melania-trump-haters-attacked-first-lady-throughout-2018-from-mocking-accent-to-slamming-christmas-decor
32. https://milnenews.com/2018/06/06/cnns-brian-stelter-called-out-for-lying-proving-once-again-hes-fake-news/
33. https://www.foxnews.com/entertainment/the-view-star-joy-behars-anti-trump-statements-of-2018
34. https://www.express.co.uk/news/world/1156597/michelle-obama-news-first-lady-state-dinner-melania-trump-white-house-latest
35. https://www.washingtonexaminer.com/news/michelle-obama-melania-trump-never-reached-out-to-me-for-advice
36. https://www.washingtonpost.com/opinions/laura-bush-separating-children-from-their-parents-at-the-border-breaks-my-heart/2018/06/17/f2df517a-7287-11e8-9780-b1dd6a09b549_story.html?utm_term=.a9c6cf9700f4
37. http://archive.boston.com/news/world/middleeast/articles/2009/04/24/official_report_other_data_show_more_than_110600_iraqi_deaths/
38. https://www.usatoday.com/story/life/2018/12/04/laura-bush-touched-melania-trumps-invitation-white-house/2208982002/
39. The author had three separate conversations with the president from 2016 to 2019. This took place in 2019 and was voice recorded.
40. From conversations with George W. Bush, 1988.
41. https://www.cnn.com/2018/10/11/politics/melania-trump-be-best-initiative-bullying/index.html

22: YOU CAN CALL HIM GREAT

1. Interview with Eric Trump, 2019.
2. https://www.achievement.org/achiever/jimmy-carter/
3. This conversation took place in 2019 at the White House.
4. https://news.gallup.com/poll/116500/presidential-approval-ratings-george-bush.aspx
5. https://www.huffpost.com/entry/bernie-sanders-is-not-a-socialist_b_8047266
6. https://news.gallup.com/poll/116500/presidential-approval-ratings-george-bush.aspx
7. https://quoteinvestigator.com/2016/07/05/fable/
8. https://fns-prod.azureedge.net/sites/default/files/resource-files/34SNAPmonthly-9.pdf
9. https://www.foxnews.com/opinion/tommy-hick-president-trump-legacy
10. https://www.forbes.com/sites/chuckdevore/2019/02/01/manufacturers-added-6-times-more-jobs-under-trump-than-under-obamas-last-2-years/
11. https://www.dailysignal.com/2019/06/17/how-trumps-tax-cuts-are-helping-the-middle-class/
12. https://www.businessinsider.com/trump-tax-law-paycheck-calculator-every-income-level-2018-3
13. https://www.forbes.com/sites/teresaghilarducci/2019/04/09/five-good-reasons-it-doesnt-feel-like-the-trump-tax-cut-benefited-you/#6792681c13e0
14. https://www.apnews.com/51fdeebd6f5340af874cdac8e223fed7
15. https://www.nytimes.com/2018/12/10/style/2019-financial-crisis.html
16. https://thehill.com/blogs/in-the-know/in-the-know/456942-bill-maher-roots-for-recession-so-that-trump-loses-in-2020
17. https://www.forbes.com/sites/lawrencelight/2018/07/31/4-financial-savants-warn-about-the-great-crash-of-2020/#4e168b356197
18. http://www.huppi.com/kangaroo/L-carterreagan.htm
19. https://www.cbsnews.com/news/john-mccains-100-years-in-iraq/
20. https://www.washingtonpost.com/news/politics/wp/2018/03/20/15-years-after-it-began-the-death-toll-from-the-iraq-war-is-still-murky/

21. https://suntzudo.weebly.com/sun-tzu-ten-principles-of.html
22. Interview with Jared Kushner, 2019.
23. https://www.history.com/news/alexander-hamilton-maria-reynolds-pamphlet-affair
24. https://www.breitbart.com/tech/2018/03/19/flashback-maxine-waters-confirms-obama-has-database-with-information-on-every-individual/
25. https://www.breitbart.com/tech/2018/03/19/flashback-maxine-waters-confirms-obama-has-database-with-information-on-every-individual/
26. Interview with chief of staff, Mick Mulvaney July 9, 2019.
27. https://www.cnbc.com/2018/09/27/president-trump-cites-chinas-respect-for-his-very-very-large-brain.html
28. https://www.theatlantic.com/magazine/archive/2013/06/abraham-lincoln-is-an-idiot/309304/
29. https://www.bbc.com/news/world-us-canada-41573846
30. https://www.townandcountrymag.com/society/politics/a9923248/john-f-kennedy-student-life-at-choate-rosemary-hall/
31. https://www.theatlantic.com/daily-dish/archive/2009/09/how-stupid-is-jimmy-carter/196430/
32. Interview with Jimmy and Rosalynn Carter, 1981.
33. https://slate.com/news-and-politics/2004/06/the-stupidity-of-ronald-reagan.html
34. http://www.cnn.com/2008/SHOWBIZ/TV/11/03/chevy.chase.snl/index.html
35. https://www.dividedstates.com/list-of-obama-gaffes-blunders-mistakes-and-stupidities/
36. https://time.com/15556/barack-obama-aretha-franklin-respect/
37. https://shorensteincenter.org/news-coverage-donald-trumps-first-100-days
38. https://www.goodreads.com/quotes/tag/right-and-wrong
39. https://www.washingtonpost.com/news/post-politics/wp/2017/01/20/the-campaign-to-impeach-president-trump-has-begun/
40. Doug Wead, *All the Presidents' Children* (New York: Atria, 2003), 345.
41. https://www.politico.com/news/2019/09/26/nancy-pelosi-impeachment-trump-002118
42. https://www.youtube.com/watch?v=v9wv9ms7KwM
43. https://www.theguardian.com/books/2018/oct/07/doris-kearns-goodwin-leadership-in-turbulent-times-trump
44. https://www.cnn.com/2019/05/28/politics/allan-lichtman-donald-trump-2020/index.html
45. https://www.vanityfair.com/hollywood/2016/10/ken-burns-donald-trump
46. https://www.huffpost.com/entry/ken-burns-donald-trump_n_575daa58e4b0ced23ca85aa4
47. https://www.newsbusters.org/blogs/nb/brad-wilmouth/2018/06/26/schmidt-invokes-hitler-trump-faction-trying-impose-cruelty
48. https://www.washingtonexaminer.com/news/msnbcs-nicolle-wallace-claims-trump-is-talking-about-exterminating-latinos
49. https://www.realclearpolitics.com/video/2018/03/22/nbcs_michael_beschloss_like_xi_putin_and_stalin_trump_may_be_president_for_life.html
50. My interviews and conversations with President Trump took place from 2016 to 2019.
51. https://www.theguardian.com/us-news/video/2015/jun/16/donald-trump-us-president-republicans-video
52. https://www.washingtonexaminer.com/trump-says-he-has-a-secret-plan-to-beat-the-islamic-state
53. Interview with Jared Kushner, 2019.

ACKNOWLEDGMENTS

1. This happened during an interview with the president in January of 2019. This conversation was edited for the reader's convenience. It can be heard in its entirety in the audio version of this book.

INDEX

ABOUT THE AUTHOR

DOUG WEAD is a *New York Times* best-selling author who has written more than thirty books. He has served as an adviser to two American presidents, co-authored a book with one of them, and served on the White House senior staff. He lives outside of Washington, DC, with his wife, Myriam.